PEOPLES OF THE WORLD SERIES

THE PEOPLE OF ASIA

PEOPLES OF THE WORLD SERIES

Editor: Sonia Cole

THE PEOPLE OF ASIA

Gordon T. Bowles
Professor Emeritus of Anthropology
Syracuse University, New York

Weidenfeld and Nicolson
London

First published in Great Britain by
Weidenfeld and Nicolson
11 St John's Hill, London SW11

ISBN 0 297 77360 7

Printed in Great Britain by
Willmer Brothers Limited, Birkenhead

Contents

Maps

FIGURE

Tables

Acknowledgements

The listing of all individuals who offered advice or provided materials during the preparation of the text would be prohibitive, but mention must be made of those to whom a special word of appreciation is due. Foremost are the specialists who reviewed and corrected sections of the manuscript: Joseph Fletcher of Harvard University for Inner Asia, and my Syracuse University colleagues, Agehananda Bharati and Susan Wadley, for south Asia. Those who generously loaned books, pamphlets or unpublished data include Carleton Coon, Henry Field, William Howells, Owen Lattimore and Robert White. To all of these, my special thanks. I am indebted, also, to Professor P. K. Hitti for permission to quote from his book, *The Arabs*, and to George Allen and Unwin Limited for permission to quote from *The Vedic Age* by R. C. Majumdar and A. D. Pusalker. Professor Omoto has given me permission to copy his charts relating to the Ainu. I have also taken the liberty of referring to and modifying tabular data which are provided with text references, but I trust my other Asian, European and American colleagues will be long suffering with any errors they may discover. I have borrowed much from them through years of consultation and cooperative endeavour.

Anthropologists who travel to far corners of the earth are probably more beholden to their spouses than are those in less venturesome disciplines. This is particularly true in the present instance and the fact that my wife was formally accorded the status of recorder during a two-year expedition to north India and the Himalayas on behalf of Harvard University underscores this observation. My debt to her is enormous not only as a co-worker in the field but above all for her editing and typing assistance throughout the preparation of this book. The debt extends also to our two daughters, Anne Pipal and Barbara Swann, both of whom aided significantly in coping with the computer, and to Mary Hyde who provided professional guidance in programming. I am especially grateful, also, for the patience of the series editor, Sonia Cole, whose pencil has been applied so gently, thoughtfully and constructively.

Finally, and warranting special note, this volume is the fulfillment of an obligation to the Guggenheim Foundation from which I received a fellowship at the outbreak of World War II. The original award was for an analysis of Hawaiian skeletal materials which were excavated and preserved under my supervision on behalf of the Bishop Museum of Honolulu. The sudden events of Pearl Harbor cut short this task, but in 1947 I was permitted to alter the topic to the subject of this text. Subsequently, however, the task received only intermittent attention until 1970 when I was invited to contribute to the series of which this book forms a part.

My own field data incorporated in the sections on biological assessment were gathered on the West China–East Tibet border when I was a Harvard–Yenching Fellow (1930–2) and the remainder while a Research Associate of Peabody Museum of Harvard University (1935–7). Professors Earnest A. Hooton, Roland B. Dixon and Alfred M. Tozzer were primarily responsible for shaping my academic career, but all textual errors are my own responsibility.

Introduction

All societies have traditions about how they and the rest of mankind came into being. The question of origins and the problem of classification have been among man's most persistent obsessions, and invariably the explanations have been self-centred. Existence is generally attributed to the acts of supernatural beings or to mystical forces; but, as horizons expand, separation from the rest of the world becomes less distinct, and in the more complex societies the discovery and exploration of natural causes have largely replaced the call upon spiritual forces for the explanation of many of life's mysteries. There are no longer any distant lands inhabited by giants or half-human creatures, and the mystery, if any, is not why people are so different but why they are so much alike.

Until a few decades ago it was assumed that there once existed primary races – described in terms of fixed morphological traits such as skin colour, hair form and head shape – and that secondary races were formed through hybridizations. Darwin initiated the process of replacing typological thinking with the concept of populations [238] and in the *Descent of Man* (1874) he devoted several chapters to refuting the notion that races were separate species. Had he possessed our present knowledge of genetics, his arguments would have been even more forceful. We now know that, however different 'races' might appear, the chemicals and control mechanisms of heredity are surprisingly similar among all human beings – and indeed among primates as a whole. It is estimated that only a few significant mutations would be required to evolve a new species. *Homo sapiens* has practically the same basic gene structure as *Homo erectus,* and perhaps more than eighty to ninety per cent in common with the gorilla and chimpanzee. Differences between the most diverse modern populations amount to probably no more than one or two per cent.

Human populations are highly polymorphic: they possess a wide genetic potential which increases variation through chance mutations or new genetic combinations in each generation, allowing in turn a greater production range of new proteins. If advantageous, they are likely to be retained; if deleterious they are likely to disappear or remain 'hidden' as recessives. Completely stabilized breeding isolates – or 'Mendelian populations' – are exceedingly rare, but undoubtedly close approximations have existed. Today the most likely candidates are the Bushmen of the Kalahari, the Pygmies of the Ituri Forest of Zaire and surviving pockets of forest-dwellers in New Guinea, Malaya, the Philippines and south India.

Changes in the biostructure of a population can be interpreted then as alterations in frequencies or percentages of specific genes. Furthermore, as some traits are more adaptive than others, adaptation becomes a relative matter, but no trait can be considered wholly non-adaptive. The secret of man's adaptive capacity lies mainly in his cultural achievements, his social environment: the sets of interaction networks, value systems, economies and behaviour patterns – the hallmarks by which societies are distinguished. The conscious responses of individuals are invariably culturally conditioned, and the manner in which these responses relate to mating patterns determines the group's common biological heritage.

The usual criteria for determining a zoological taxon apply to man as a species but are not strictly applicable in determining his subspecies or minor varieties. For thousands of years he has been artificially creating new gene pools; his diet range far exceeds the usual definition of 'omnivorous'; and, thanks to his technical achievements, he has learned to survive in every conceivable environment. The Eskimo was able to adapt culturally because he possessed the skills necessary for adjustment to arctic conditions. The external environment, in turn, subjected him to new adaptive pressures which automatically called into play processes of natural selection affecting the internal environment and ultimately the gene pool of the population. In the case of man, therefore, adaption is cultural as well as biological, and the two are always interacting.

New methods of comparison and classification have been devised and, while morphological traits remain important, the concept of population has largely superseded that of race and the latter term should be used only as an abstraction. Large divisions of mankind are designated by the regions they occupy – west or east Asian – and local populations defined as the biological equivalents of culturally determined ethnic groups – Arabs, Afghans or Armenians – or as social groups within a society such as caste, religious or kin isolates.

In some societies in which the group concept of patrilineal descent is strong – as was the case among the early Arabs – marriage across ethnic barriers (exogamy) was not only permissible but even desirable so long as this meant the propagation of Islam. This was certainly true of urban Arab communities in west and central Asia during the period of the expansion of the Arab caliphate of the seventh to ninth centuries. Such communities were far less dependent on kin ties for socio-economic cohesion than were the camel-breeding, pastoral-nomadic Bedouin, among whom endogamy was the rule.

Mate selection rules were altered to meet the requirements of social structure. During the first millennium BC both China and India were expanding southward and adding to their populations through the assimilation of minorities. Both societies were patrilineal and patrinymic, but as they began to stabilize, marriages outside the larger group were gradually discouraged. Rules were devised to prevent marriages between close relatives; and because the social structures and kinship systems differed, mate selection rules followed different paths.

It can thus be seen that rules of endogamy (in-group marriage) and exogamy (out-group marriage) are socially conditioned and are not to be confused with inbreeding and outbreeding which have specific biological meaning: endogamous marriages might produce outbreeding and, conversely, exogamous marriages could result in inbreeding. Comparative studies of populations must necessarily take into consideration not only their known histories and traditions, but – equally important – the social regulations by which the societies are maintained.

The contents of this study are divided into six parts. The first includes Asian ideas concerning classification and the continent's geographical, ecological and palaeontological background; the next four discuss respectively the histories of the people of the western, southern, eastern and northern quadrants of Asia from the end of the Ice Age to the dawn of written records, and histories of past empires, including their responsibility for linguistic and religious conversions, movements and migrations. The final part analyzes and summarizes the biological data for the four quadrants.

In the collection and analysis of these data three major problems were encountered. The first was the unevenness in quality and quantity: biological studies have become so complex, demanding the teamwork of so many specialists, that adequate coverage is exceedingly difficult to secure. By contrast, studies of material and social culture of relatively small societies can be undertaken by a single competent anthropologist. Thousands of studies are available, but they relate to such a variety of biological categories that the results often serve only as a general guide rather than a true comparison. The continuing IBP (International Biological Programmes) beginning in 1964 [406] have done much to co-ordinate national studies of potential anthropological significance, but it will be many years before they will provide adequate universal coverage.

A second problem relates to methodology. Obviously, specimens of extinct and early forms of man can be studied only through their skeletal remains. Apart from dating, research of phyletic significance is generally limited to comparative bone morphology, and remains are usually so fragmentary that it is impossible to reconstruct organisms as wholes. Restorations depend largely on size and shape comparisons or on bold conjecture.

The number of individuals represented in collections of fossils presumed to belong to a given species or variety are now becoming sufficiently large to permit some population studies and speculation concerning more definitive taxonomic relationships. At the *Homo erectus* level, for example, there are several substantial Asian collections. The European and African assemblages are smaller, but it is as necessary to apply the concept of racial differentiation to *Homo erectus* as to *Homo sapiens* [397a, p. 6]. Possibly within a few decades the collections can be used as acceptable population samples. Already certain biological computer programming techniques have been applied to the analysis of such features as cranial capacities, arcs and angles and the structural–functional mechanics of balance, locomotion and manual skills.

The third major problem relates to the identification of populations. Fortunately, Asian societies – even some of the larger ones – have been stabilized regionally for sufficiently long periods of time to permit assessment of their historic migrations and mate selection processes. Usually it is only in the highly industrialized regions and urban concentrations that traditionally controlled mate-selection patterns have tended to break down and to lessen opportunities for separate biological assessment.

As new fields of study are initiated, the task of selecting the most relevant data becomes ever more difficult. Each new approach adds another facet to the ever-expanding inquiry into man's past. Some prove significant, others are quickly outdated. This is as it should be, and the following chapters will have served their purpose if they call attention to the restraints and uncertainties of human groups not merely as biological populations but as social entities, whose collective behaviour is constantly subject to the binding force of ethnic identity – fancied or real – and to the political winds of the moment. Hopefully such awareness will assist the reader towards a better understanding of a powerfully resurgent Asia in an era of rapid transition.

PART I

ASIAN HOMELAND AND ORIGINS

I

Traditional Concepts of Racial Classification

From the beginning of written records people have indicated their awareness of characteristics differentiating them from their neighbours, but in the three main regions of early Asian civilization – Mesopotamia, the Indus Valley and the Yellow River basin – the tendency was to emphasize inner psychic differences rather than external physical appearances, and it seems to have been a universally accepted fact that the two could not be separated. Psychic differences were assumed to be innate and collective behaviour therefore predictable. People were to be classified from the inside out, as it were, and such signals as physical appearance, language and even dress, though of secondary importance, were regarded as reliable indicators of innate inner differences.

The analysis of the people of Asia in this study has been limited to man's non-psychic biological phenomena and especially to traits considered to be significant indicators of large groups rather than to localized differences. In discussing early classifications, however, the very nature of the available data sometimes makes it necessary to refer to non-biological phenomena.

The manner in which biological differences were indicated in the three ancient regions of civilization followed closely their preferred media of expression. In Sumeria and early Egypt these took the form of painting and sculpture. Skin colour, lip contours, hair form and body proportions distinguished social classes as well as races. In the later Mesopotamian civilizations of Akkadia, Babylonia and neighbouring Persia, human representations stressed head shape, hair form, beard type and mid-facial diagnostics, especially the nose and eyes, a reflection probably of increased contact with peoples of the north – those referred to typologically as Armenoid.

Among the Semites the earliest distinctions were in written accounts which referred to nations not races. In the Old Testament, an important source of ethnographic information, racial definitions – apart from references to dark-skinned Ethiopians – are exceedingly rare. Accounts of the creation are highly anthropocentric but the separation of man into races appears as rather an afterthought. As recorded in *Genesis* 8, Noah had three forebearer sons: Ham of the Hamites, Shem of the Semites and Japhet of the Japhetic wanderers. No one bothered much about their appearances. In western Asia no helpful descriptions appear until the time of the Greeks, when the empire of Alexander had reached the Indus.

In the Indus Valley civilization traces of racial distinctions are detectable in the figurines and sculptures at Mohenjodaro but their message is not clear [228]. Even in the Rigvedic accounts of the Aryans, biological references are limited to the dark skins and flat noses of their enemy, the Dasyus. Later orthodox Vedic–Hindu tradition was absorbed with biological analogy, as seen in the social structure, and not with distinctive morphological traits. Ancient Aryan society was characterized as having four stratified *varna* or class divisions based on the analogy of the four dismembered sections of the sacrificially offered body of primordial man at the time of creation. The Brahmins – priests, scholars and poets – who emanated from the mouth were equated with the head; the Kshatriyas or Rajanyas – nobles and warriors – emerged from the arms and were construed as the torso; the Vaisyas – farmers, traders and artisans – came from the thighs and were therefore the legs; and the Sudras – serfs and slaves – were the feet. Under the feet were the dark-skinned outcastes.

The four *varnas* correspond to the four *pistras* or classes of ancient Iran [18] and to the general four-fold division characteristic of other early Indo–European societies. The word *varna* means colour and is often assumed to refer to racial differences, but is never so defined. According to one version, primordial man (Purusha), from whose body the four classes issued, was no less a being than the creator Brahma himself [167], and it was more likely the canons of art that dictated the colour to be used in depicting his body segments [377].

In any case, while the caste–class system probably had a racially oriented beginning, the highly colourful *varna* tradition was metaphysically symbolic and not directly concerned with biological details. As in the case of western Asia, the first useful descriptions of peoples are from Greek sources, starting with accounts of the various tribes encountered by Alexander during his conquest of the north-western corner of the Indian subcontinent. Although these accounts too are largely concerned with tribes, geographical locations, fighting qualities and military equipment, there are occasional references to skin, hair and eye colour and to facial morphology. They tend to confirm studies based on skeletal materials of the period and of populations that still exist in the area.

Chinese written sources are mainly descriptions of neighbouring barbarian tribes. The major problem has been not lack of data but the peculiarities of written Chinese which often make identifications difficult. Ideographs used arbitrarily for their sound values rather than meanings may be quite deceptive since sound values have a way of changing over time. Furthermore, the basic phonological peculiarities of Chinese leave much to be desired in approximating sound renditions of alien names. It is only when cross-references from sources using phonetic scripts provide clues that mistaken identities can be avoided.

The first descriptions that can definitely be associated with a markedly alien population date from the sacking of the Chou capital by western barbarians about 771 BC. They are described as having red hair, green (or blue) eyes and white faces. It has generally been assumed that they were either Indo-European or early Turkic invaders [240].

We are indebted to Hippocrates and Herodotus for the first descriptions of the Indo–European-speaking Scythians and Sarmatians – early inhabitants of central Asia. The Tocharians were among the earliest of that linguistic group to penetrate Sinkiang and possibly China proper, but they have been identified as belonging to the centum or western group [288], to which most of the languages of Europe belong, and not to the satem – that of the Iranian and north Indian languages. Nowhere in Asia was an attempt made at systematization in the biological realm comparable with that of Aristotle and even in the western world nothing more extensive was attempted until the Renaissance.

The first genuine zoological taxonomy of man was probably that of Bernier, who in 1688 proposed a division into four groups based on skin colour: European White, African Black, Asiatic Yellow and Lapp. In the mid-eighteenth century Linnaeus [218] added hair and eye colour and, by dropping the Lapps and adding the Red Man, gave us our four-fold division of primary races which has doggedly held sway in popular thinking even to this day. The Yellow division was described as having brown eyes, black hair and a sallow complexion.

Cuvier [74], the late eighteenth- and early nineteenth-century protagonist of catastrophism, suggested the novel idea that, since the gorilla had black skin colour, he might be the progenitor of the Negro race; the chimpanzee, with lighter pigmentation, might be ancestral to Europeans; and the orangutan, with brownish pigmentation and living in insular Asia, could be the progenitor of the Yellow race. He may have had in mind that this Asian ape shared with the majority of the Yellow race the distinctive feature of the inner epicanthic or so-called mongoloid eyefold.

The first relatively modern classification, but one that in the light of more recent scientific thinking carries the stamp of medieval reasoning, was that of Blumenbach [30], a senior contemporary of Cuvier. To the original four primary races he added Malay as a fifth. To him we owe the rather inappropriate terms Caucasic, Mongolic and Ethiopic. Fortunately, the last of these was soon dropped but Negroid as a substitute is scarcely more satisfactory as it has frequently been applied to the deeply pigmented populations of parts of Asia and Oceania, creating the impression without adequate biological proof that they share a close common ancestry with African Negroids. Ripley [313], commenting on the term 'Caucasian' in his *Races of Europe*, calls it an absurdity, noting that if blue eyes and fair hair are implied by the term neither of these characteristics of an 'ideal blonde type' is to be found within hundreds of miles of the Caucasus mountains. In Blumenbach's view, the Caucasian was the most primitive (original) and closest to perfection, and from this primal population the Ethiopian 'digressed' into Africa and the Mongolian 'digressed' into Asia. Blumenbach proposed his designations at a time when scholarly attention was being focused on Armenia just south of the Caucasus and its pivotal peak, Mount Ararat. The search was on for Noah's Ark, and possibly this had something to do with his selection of that area as the centre of man's dispersals. Since then earlier versions of the Deluge, antedating the biblical account by over a thousand years, have been recovered from various ancient Near Eastern sites, notably from Uruk in Sumeria cited in the epic of Gilgamesh [117]. There seem to be various centres of dispersal [315].

The term 'Mongoloid' is not so far-fetched but the most intense manifestation of Mongoloid traits, as Blumenbach admits, is to be found among the Tungus and not the Mongols. He selected 'Mongoloid' because it was familiar to Europeans. It is an unhappy coincidence that 'Mongoloid' is not infrequently confused with mongoloid idiocy, known clinically as Downe's syndrome, a condition associated often with the age of the mother but attributable usually to a chromosomal aberration. Gene linkage manifestation of the inner epicanthic fold is apparently incidental and has nothing directly to do with idiocy. One of the most unfortunate books ever written on the subject of race was Crookshank's *The Mongol in Our Midst* [72] which purported to demonstrate that mongoloid idiocy was directly attributable to hybridization between Europeans and 'Asiatics' since paleolithic times and atavism to the Mongoloid stage.

In spite of the introduction of some rather inappropriate terms, Blumenbach [31] did revive the term 'anthropology', which had first been used by Aristotle, and he added skull shape to his scheme of classification, the first major introduction of a skeletally based characteristic. Although his taxonomic categories were limited he did emphasize the continuity of human variation – the impossibility of separating man into clear-cut racial compartments – and the importance of environmental influences.

The sixty-four-year period between the publication of Blumenbach's major discourses on man (1795) and the appearance of Darwin's *Origin of Species* (1859) must have been exciting times, to judge by the debates that centred around the concept of environmental influences. Apart from Blumenbach and Cuvier, the names of Buffon, Leclerc, Maupertius, Kant, Lamarck, Monet, Wells and Wallace loom large during that period. Each had his own theory, but all except Wallace remained faithful to the concept of special and separate creation and conceived of variation as being limited to the specific or genetic range. It is clear from the debates [135] that, apart from Darwin, only Wallace [390] had caught a glimpse of the grand sweep of organic evolution and the meaning of natural selection. In some respects his vision even antedated and influenced that of Darwin with whom he was in correspondence while abroad studying the fauna of insular southeast Asia [391].

It is interesting that Darwin in his *Origin of Species* [78] scarcely touched upon man even as a species. Only later, in *Descent of Man* [79], did he concentrate specifically on man's origins and races, but even in this treatise he failed to dwell systematically on the causes of variation. His concern was more with man's behaviour as a social and sexual being, a rather odd limitation in view of the many pages he devoted to the general subject of raciation among other species. Unquestionably, the biblical concept of special creation had a great deal to do with delaying an earlier expansion into man's study of himself. It was not until a full century later that the study of man's origins and variations had approached a level comparable with that attained by Darwin in his classification of the fauna of the Galapagos Islands.

In the century between 1870 and 1969 no less than twenty-five attempts were made in the field of human taxonomy and doubtless others will be made in the future*. Each author reflects some new perspective not previously incorporated or for some reason avoided; all possess the common feature of attempting to classify the varieties of a complex species using typological systems which could never be applied to more than segments of natural populations.

Of the various typological classifications, it would be difficult to select any one as being more accurate or scientific than another. Apart from these highly artificial and rigid classifications, some students have advocated use of the concept of localized or 'geographical races' [124]. The geographical race has the advantage of not generalizing initially on physical traits, but it fails to take into consideration the cultural distinctions by which localized ethnic groups can be distinguished within a given area. The geographical race also assumes a higher degree of panmixia (non-selective mating) and a greater dependence on topographical barriers as deterrents to migration than can be supported by

* For further summarization, see Buxton [46].

historic documentation. In defence of the concept, however, two important features should be mentioned. The general rules governing population are applicable, and it is probably the only sensible division to employ in areas where genetically construed assortative matings bear little relationship to culturally determined patterns of mate selection. Highly industrialized and urban-oriented societies would be cases in point. In these respects the peoples of Asia are generally less panmictic than those of Europe except possibly in the urban concentrations.

Speculative inquiry concerning man's origins was relatively uninhibited by religious dogma in southern and eastern Asia in comparison with western Asia and Europe during the Middle Ages. In the west man was conceived as static; in the east he was generally capable of great transformations and was closely related to all other forms of life.

The blocking of scientific inquiry into man's natural origins was largely a result of European ecclesiastical thinking, and we owe a very sizeable debt of gratitude to the eclectic philosophers of the Orient in providing much of the stimulus that eventually culminated in the Darwinian theory of organic evolution – especially the concept of natural selection – as the main factor in the process of change.

As Needham [258] points out, by the seventeenth century Europeans were making efforts to synthesize the conflicting ideas of theological vitalism and mechanical materialism, but eventually there came a time in the development of modern concepts of natural science when it became necessary to add a more organic philosophy. This came with Darwin, Planck and Einstein among others; but the way was paved by a line of philosophers working backwards from Whitehead to Engels to Hegel and ultimately to Leibnitz, who probably more than any other was influenced by Chinese philosophers. In particular, it was during his study of Confucius Sinarum Philosophus in the year 1685–6 that Leibnitz, while defining his concept of the monad, drew upon the ideas of the Taoist, Chuang Tze, and such neo-Confucianists as Chou Tun-I and Chu Hsi. In later chapters it will be seen how the ideas of these Chinese philosophers affected mate selection patterns of different ethnic populations in east Asia and influenced their genotypic structures. In a very real sense what people believe affects the way they think and act, and these in turn, through social selection, exert tremendous impact on what they become both biologically and culturally.

Christian theology stressed the omnipotence of God's role; the older Jewish ideas were more concerned with Yahweh's great deeds in helping man than His role in cosmogony. Yahweh meant simply Being, or Existence, and implied no beginning or end. In the course of time, Existence did become anthropomorphized and Jehovah did bring organisms into being, but it was the process of breathing life into inorganic matter that was all-important rather than the idea of special and separate creation – and to this extent the concept comes close to some early Indian ideas. Only in the later accounts of the creation as recorded reputedly by Moses in the Old Testament was the culminating act of God's creative effort emphasized. Later this became a powerful theme, especially as Christianity began to cope with pagan polytheism, and the concept of God's monotheistic omnipotence, an idea apparently unique to those who accepted the biblical interpretation, made God the focal point not only to their religion but of their entire system of values. Eastward, in other Asian traditions, ideas were concerned with change rather than fixity, with the fundamental kinship of all creatures rather than their discrete and separate identity.

In the earliest versions of the Rigvedas, the various deistic beings perform their respective roles paralleling those of the polytheistic pantheons of the other Indo–European traditions. Brahma is the agent creator as are Zeus and Jupiter, but the later Hindu tradition conceived of all living creatures as the products of a primal cosmic union between Heaven and Earth, an idea not unlike that to be found in the non-Semitic, non-Indo–European tradition of Sumeria. In the Vedic version, after acquiring their respective forms, the various creatures passed through specified states of existence, died and were reborn into other states in a never-ending series of karma rebirths within a millennially grand cycle of time, a cycle to be repeated in numbered but finite sequences. With the development of the heretical ideas of Jainism and refined Brahmanic Monism in the middle of the first millennium before Christ, newer ideas concerning the cycle of rebirth emerge, ideas recognizably tangential to the concept of organic evolution.

While differing in many of the respective overt religious manifestations of their philosophical beliefs, both the Jains and the Monists conceived of an initial universe of matter. According to the Monists, the Absolute is neither existence nor non-existence and the primordial matter of the universe is water, from which the other elements evolve. Kama (desire), a kind of consciousness, united the existent with the non-existent and this supreme united reality, Purusha, was both the begetter and the begotten. From this point on orthodox Vedism takes over and the deity agents perform their various roles.

Jainism goes even further. In the beginning, the Universe was in a state of chaos: matter was in the form of minute particles of energized life-monads or *jivas*. Each life-monad started with the necessary atoms of ether, air, fire, water and earth and, in combination with other life-monads, which were collectively expressed as different living organisms, they separately and collectively passed through a series of 84,000 graded rebirths. These became transformed progressively in collective expression as organisms through the varied existing forms of geological, botanical and zoological entities until ultimately they emerged as human beings. At each progressive stage each life-monad automatically attracted or added to itself the necessary faculties of sense, intellect and feeling to fulfil its new life destiny as it passed through the sequence of transmigrations.

While there is no coherent concept of progressive phyletic radiation in these philosophical notions, there does exist the idea of change through a continuous cycle of metabolic transformations of food within the living body into varied life forms and simultaneously the transformations of impulses, feelings and actions. After death and decomposition the further recombinations of decomposed organic substances turn again into food for the next cycle in some other form of living organism. This seems to be the nearest Indian approach to an evolutionary thesis, but Indian philosophies are concerned more with the nature of organisms than with their behaviour. The opposite is the case with the Chinese.

Within the range of early ideas expressed in the great debate between the Taoist and Confucian schools, the former approaches most nearly the Indian rationalizations. Among Taoists, spirit essence pervades all matter in all of its varied and particularized organic as well as inorganic forms. Within this universe of matter and spirit essence purposeful idealized behaviour expressed in sympathetic responsive action leads towards harmony in the natural world – a collective balancing of the limitless spirit essences of all beings in the universe. The concepts of transformation of matter and spirit essence are present, but each individual organism and object is unique. There is no idea of rebirth and, while there is nothing that could be termed theistic intervention, there was an initial union of the natural spirit essences of Heaven and Earth which resulted in the emergences of all lesser forms of natural beings. If not subverted or deflected to tangential goals, the object of all beings would normally lead towards the attainment of harmonious coexistence. This is the Tao, 'The Way'.

The apposite ideas of the Confucian school also acknowledged the difference between matter and spirit essence, but maintain that all organisms (objects) have rules of behaviour assigned to them in accordance with their respective roles. Harmony in nature depends upon right action and the observance of rules.

The characteristic behaviour patterns of the two schools have been described as passive–intuitive response on the one hand and fixed or predetermined action on the other, but there are numerous gradations and heretical digressions which blur the distinction between the two. A common feature in both points of view is the initial absence of theistic intervention. Heaven and Earth have spirit essences but are aspects of nature and in no sense are deities. The subsequent emergence of a theistic pantheon is traceable to later redactions and, while deities came to be increasingly powerful and took on duties assigned to them by the basic Heaven–Male and Earth–Female principles, the original Chinese philosophies were essentially humanistic and atheistic.

The most pertinent aspect of Chinese cosmogony as it relates to organic evolution appears to be the notion of progressive growth and improvement. Matter is always changing and spirit essence changes with it. In the beginning, crude creatures were shaped out of the original gaseous vapours, and only gradually did they assume their respective permanent forms. Not only were the original human beings naked and ignorant of all of the domestic arts, but their appearance was crude if not bestial and, knowing nothing about proper social behaviour, like most animals they were promiscuous. Culture heroes designated as 'sovereigns' under the spirit of Heaven taught them the various arts which converted these proto-humans into domesticated social beings.

It is easy to see that with such philosophies in both India and China there were no strong religious scruples against the acceptance of the modern theory of organic evolution. There was no idea of an all-pervading, omniscient, omnipotent deity by whose spontaneous acts the universe and all beings therein were divinely and separately created, an idea that appears to be limited to the traditions of the monotheistically oriented later Jews.

Elsewhere in east Asia ideas concerning human origins seem to fall into two categories: those that attribute man's creation to divine action, and those that trace progenitors back to some kind of union between spirit deities and animals. Japan is an example of the former and Korea of the latter. According to the Japanese origin myth, which some scholars have tried without much success to relate to Polynesian sources, a brother–sister deity couple descended from the lower heavens and brought forth not only human beings but a host of other creatures and inanimate beings including the celestial bodies. The Korean account is in keeping with the stronger linguistic affiliation of the Korean language to the Altaic group: Tan-Gun, the Korean progenitor, sprang from the union of a spirit tiger and a she-bear.

Following a similar pattern, other northern and central Asian creation myths bear little direct relationship to the complex philosophical rationalizations of ancient India and China but are excellent examples of the trickster–transformer traditions that characterize so much of the folklore, magic and religion of the north. According to Tibetan legend the Tibetan people are the descendants of a monkey and a she-devil incarnation of the deity Chen-re-zi ('the Compassionate One') – the Indian Buddhist saviour Avalokiteshvara, the Chinese Kwan-Yin or Goddess of Mercy. Details of the union are as bizarre as the circumstances of the Compassionate One's incarnation but scarcely more so than the Mongol account of their ancestry.

The secret history of the Mongols traces the ancestry of the Great Khan and of his people to the union between Börte Chino, the 'blue-grey wolf' and Ho'ai'maral, the 'fawn-coloured doe'. Details of this union, which took place on or near Mount Burkhan Khaldun, near the source of the Onon River, fail to clarify whether the couple should be considered as theriomorphic spirit deities or anthropomorphic spirit animals. Nothing could be more fanciful, but the concept of close identity between man and beast stands in striking contrast to the divinely inspired anthropocentric ideas of Judeo–Christian theology.

It is interesting that, while many original ideas suggestive of organic evolution seem to have been inspired in southern and eastern Asia, and ideas about life-monads and matter–soul entities in India anticipated the Aristotelian concept of entelechies by many centuries, little attention was paid to the varieties of man and their classification. In most instances, man's origins were related solely to the people of the tradition concerned. In the case of the Rigveda it was the Aryans; in Chinese philosophy it was the people of Han, the dwellers in the Middle Kingdom. Only in the Near East and, by extension, Egypt, is there some equivocation and an early recognition of the necessity to note at least the difference between the darker-skinned peoples of Africa and the lighter-skinned peoples of Eurasia. It may have been for this reason that ideas of variety and classification originated in the circum-Mediterranean area.

2

Asia's Ecological Regions

The classical Greeks were aware of lands and peoples beyond the Persian empire, but Asia to them meant the coastal fringe of the Troad, Lycia and Phrygia across the Hellespont, the bridge to further Greece. Their ideas concerning Asia's eastern limits were conflicting, and even Herodotus was vague about the derivation of the name. Some historians have suggested that Asia might have been the territorial name of a local pre-Indo-European deity [151] just as Europa, the wife of Zeus, was identified originally with what is today a corner of southern Europe, the land where she was first wooed and from which she was later abducted and carried off to Crete. Others derive the two names from ancient Assyrian or Hebrew, Asia signifying the rising sun and Europe the setting sun [151].

During early Roman days Asia was expanded into a province with fixed boundaries, but following the breakup of the Roman Empire the term assumed again some of its previous vagueness and generalized connotations. First it was applied to all of the Pontic lands south of the Euxine Sea, then to the entire eastern half of the Orient and finally to the lands beyond. By late Byzantine times Asia Minor had been clearly differentiated from Asia Major and Asia as a whole had acquired broader regional significance to include even the lands of the Hunnic tribes and the Celestial Empire of Ch'in. Beyond Asia stretched vast expanses of ocean out to the edges of the earth, and beyond that lay black oblivion.

The use of Asia in its present continental meaning was a development of the post-Magellan age of exploration, when ideas concerning the world assumed their present global dimensions, but during the previous millennium the distinction between Europe and Asia in human terms was dictated largely by the fluctuating movements of peoples and the fates of empires, rather than by the logic of geography.

Asia rests squarely in the centre of the earth's major continental blocks and serves to interconnect all of them. On the north-western side of the continent's triangular-shaped perimeter it merges with Europe along the crest of the low-lying Urals, but prior to navigation only three major routes existed between the two continents: the Volga basin, the Transcaucasian land corridors and the Bosphorus bridge to Thrace. Sinai and the narrow strait of Bab-el-Mandeb at Aden have served as connecting points with Africa, and in the north-east and south-east corners, where short stretches of open sea exist today, land bridges periodically joined Asia to the New World of the Americas and permitted access to Australia and the now-submerged extensions of the continent.

Since early Holocene (post-glacial) times, some twelve thousand years ago, Europe and Asia have formed a single land mass. Before that time glacial ice sheets combined with fog-enshrouded bogland and inland seas had periodically all but separated the two continents just east of the Urals. During such periods, which coincided with critical stages of human development, contact routes were confined to Anatolia.

In a highly controversial book, Griffiths Taylor [375] once referred to the positional relationship of Eurasia's outlying continents as 'tripeninsular' (Map 1).

The structural peculiarities of the continents themselves were of vital importance in creating different environments, in channelling man's movements and in stimulating trade and cultural innovation – structural peculiarities which trace back to the very earliest period in the shaping of the earth's outer crust.

Here and there across the face of the Asian continent stand gaunt reminders of a geological age in the primeval past when the present land surfaces were still in their formative stages: balding, round granitic rock surfaces and schist formations, tired segments of the earth's original lithosphere which emerge irregularly and in apparently unrelated patches in the middle of Siberia, along the coast of China, Korea, India and Arabia. Some

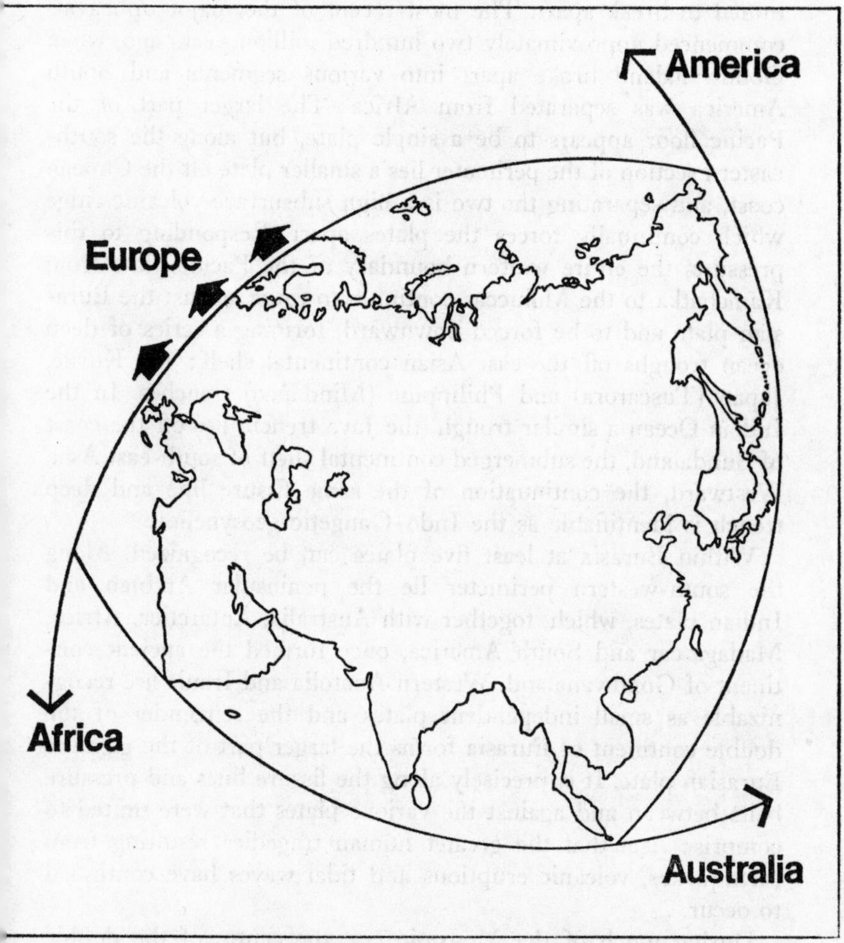

Map 1 Eurasia: the centre of a tripeninsular world

are worn smooth through glacial wear; others are badly cracked and scarred through heat, wind and water action. Like icebergs whose tips alone float above the ocean surface, these exposed granitic blocks are actually parts of gigantic shields or plates, whose bulks lie largely hidden under mantles of eroded outwash with only the higher parts exposed [372].

Such plates are of varying sizes, and many have been irretrievably lost or 'melted' back into the interior mass. Others have con-

B

tinued to break apart. The most recent of the major upheavals commenced approximately two hundred million years ago, when Gondwanaland broke apart into various segments and South America was separated from Africa. The larger part of the Pacific floor appears to be a single plate, but along the south-eastern section of the perimeter lies a smaller plate off the Chilean coast, and separating the two is a high subsurface volcanic ridge which continually forces the plates apart. Responding to this pressure, the entire western boundary of the Pacific plate from Kamchatka to the Moluccas continues to press against the Eurasian plate and to be forced downward, forming a series of deep ocean troughs off the east Asian continental shelf: the Kurile, Japan (Tuscarora) and Philippine (Mindanao) trenches. In the Indian Ocean a similar trough, the Java trench, lies off the coast of Sundaland, the submerged continental shelf of south-east Asia. Westward, the continuation of the same fissure line and deep trench is identifiable as the Indo–Gangetic geosyncline.

Within Eurasia at least five plates can be recognized. Along the south-western perimeter lie the peninsular Arabian and Indian plates, which, together with Australia, Antarctica, Africa, Madagascar and South America, once formed the ancient continent of Gondwanaland. Western Anatolia and Irania are recognizable as small independent plates and the remainder of the double continent of Eurasia forms the larger part of the gigantic Eurasian plate. It is precisely along the fissure lines and pressure belts between and against the various plates that were united to comprise Asia that the greatet human tragedies resulting from earthquakes, volcanic eruptions and tidal waves have continued to occur.

During much of the Mesozoic era, the centre of the double continent was submerged under a large inland sea known as Tethys. In the course of time the entire Tethys area was filled by accumulated debris eroded in the wake of the formation of mountain systems which followed a number of separate fissure lines. The mountain-building process started in the north along the Lake Baikal Rift Valley and successively moved south-westward to climax in the formation of the Taurus and Himalayan ranges. These last were the most important from the human point of view and took place in three stages.

The first stage occurred during the early Tertiary, probably in the mid-Oligocene, some thirty million years ago, when parts of the Taurus and central Himalayan ranges emerged. Checked by the weight of the first Himalayan upthrust, the 'snouts' of the Arabian and Indian plates were tilted sharply downward to form deep geosynclinic troughs. As the facing mountain folds crumbled and weathered, the eroded debris slowly filled the valley troughs, and in time the fertile plains of the twin rivers of Mesopotamia (Tigris and Euphrates) and those of north India (Indus and Ganges) were formed. At first the latter were apparently a single river known as the Siwalik, with two major branches. The eastern, which followed the course of the present Brahmaputra, instead of emptying into the Bay of Bengal skirted the Himalayas westward along the course of the Ganges and joined the present Indus to flow into the Bay of Karachi. The second upthrust took place during the Miocene and the third commenced as late as the Pliocene, only some eight to ten million years ago, a movement that is still progressing at the rate of a few metres per century. It was during this last upthrust that the Ganges section of the Siwalik River reversed its course to flow eastward and join the Brahmaputra in Bengal.

While these events were taking place in successive convulsions along the major quake-ridden Taurus–Himalayan faultline, a similar phenomenon was taking place offshore with the formation of a series of volcano-dotted archipelagos stretching in a festoon of arcs from Indonesia and the Philippines in the south to Japan and Kamchatka in the north, a part of the sensitive Pacific perimeter sometimes referred to as the ocean's 'rim of fire'.

Asia is so vast that only superlatives can do it justice. The land surface alone totals over sixteen million square miles or nearly four times that of Europe – more than the New World continents combined or the collective remainder of the earth's habitable regions: Africa, Oceania and adjacent island chains. Within this huge area of roughly a third of the earth's land surface live over two-thirds of its inhabitants and a greater variety of mankind than exists on any other continent. The distance from Asia's northernmost tip to its southernmost equatorial outpost is over five thousand miles, and nearly six thousand miles separate Aden in the west from Cape Anadyr in the east. Its ecological zones range from the cold arctic tundra, taiga forests and steppelands of the north to the hot, humid, tropical monsoon forests of the south.

Apart from size, Asia's most distinctive surface feature is unquestionably the broad intermediate plateau belt which stretches across most of the mid-section of the continent from Anatolia to Manchuria. Great rivers flow from the perimeters of this plateau belt, but the heart – the high central Tibetan massif – is largely an area of internal drainage containing some of the world's most rugged terrain and a series of its most arid deserts. It is the height, aridity and silent desolation of much of the Tibetan section of this plateau zone that makes the entire zone so unique. The central regions of all other continents are either relatively flat and open or marked by isolated ranges which can be circumvented or crossed with comparative ease. But the Tibetan plateau, which lies squarely in the middle of the continent, has been such a deterrent to free migrational movements that it is probably no exaggeration to place it on a par with the Sahara as one of the earth's two greatest land barriers (Map 2).

The ninetieth degree longitude bisects Asia into two roughly equal halves and, on the Tibetan plateau, falls within a degree of Lhasa, 'dwelling place of the gods'. It serves as a convenient line by which the regions penetrated by the early Indo–European speakers in their migrations eastward during the second millennium BC can be separated from those occupied by the early east Asian and Siberian populations. Today it more or less separates the Finno–Ugric and Samoyed populations from the Tungusic in Siberia and, in the south, the south Asian populations from those of south-east Asia.

A second significant feature of the Tibetan plateau, and not unrelated to the first, is also orographic. The western end terminates in a mountain complex sometimes referred to as the Pamir Knot, or Pivot [221], or more poetically as the 'roof of the world'. Like the arms of a giant octopus, five separate series of mountain ranges radiate out from this pivotal mountain complex, stretching across the continent in so many directions almost to the sea. Towards the north-east a spectacular arm is formed by a series of seven massive ranges of varying height and size, lying obliquely parallel to each other along the Lake Baikal rift: Sayan, Tannu Ola, Altai, Tarbagatai, Ala Tau, T'ien Shan and Alai. Alternating with these ranges is a series of seven passageway corridors –

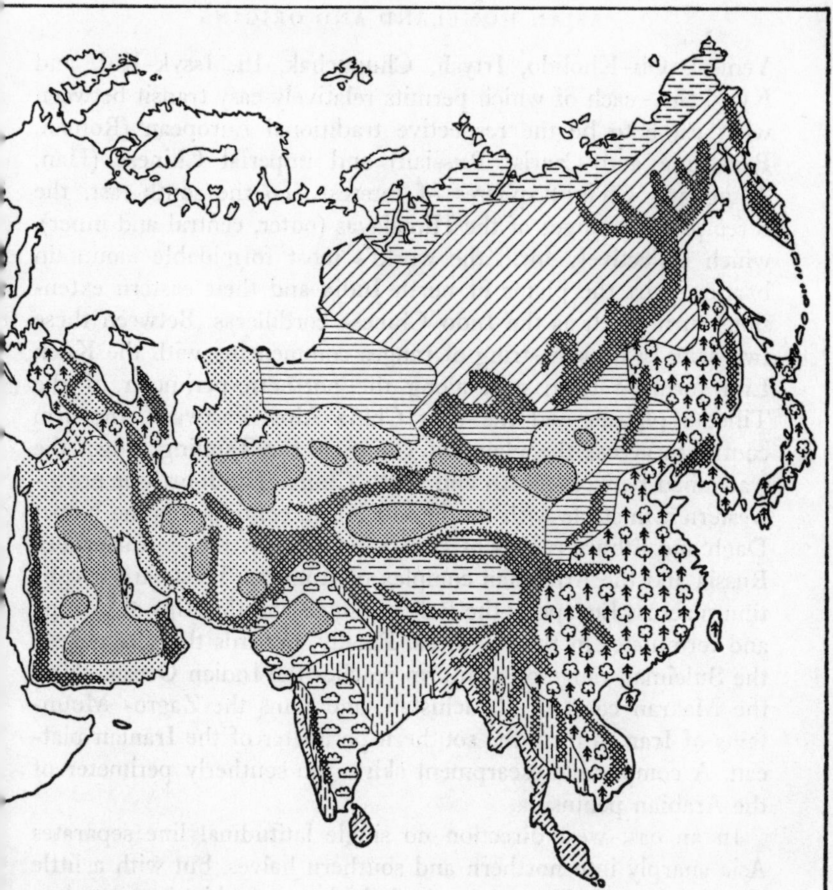

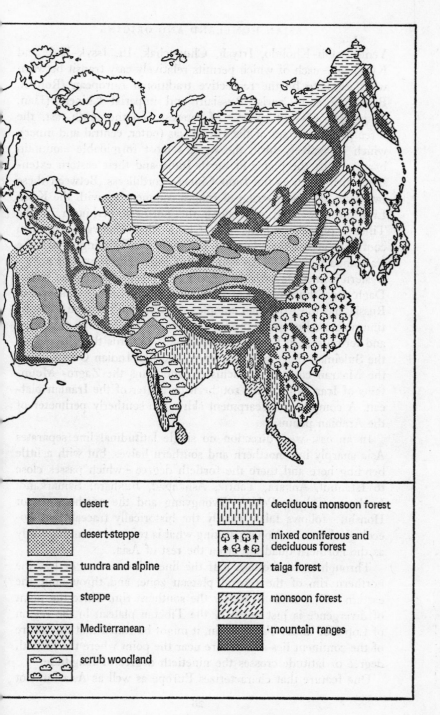

Map 2 Asia's ecological regions

Yenisei, Ob–Khobdo, Irtysh, Chuguchak, Ili, Issyk–Kul, and Kyzyl Su – each of which permits relatively easy transit between what came to be the respective traditional European (Roman, Byzantine and Czarist Russian) and imperial Chinese (Han, T'ang and Ch'ing) spheres of interest. To the south-east, the three parallel ranges of the Himalayas (outer, central and inner), which collectively form the world's most formidable mountain barrier, skirt the plains of north India and their eastern extensions turn south as the Indo–Chinese cordilleras. Between these two arms, a broken string of ranges commencing with the Kuen Lun forms a third arm along the northern perimeter of the Tibetan plateau and the west China Alps. Eastward, the arm continues across the plains of China as the Tsinling range, the watershed between north and south China. The fourth or north-western arm starts with the Hindu Kush, continues as the Kopet Dagh and Elburz ranges of Iran, the Caucasus range of southern Russia and the Armenian complex of Anatolia. Westward it continues across Europe as the Balkan ranges and the Alps of Europe and terminates in the Pyrenees. Finally, towards the south-west, the Suleiman range or fifth arm reaches the Indian Ocean, skirts the Makran coast of Baluchistan, and joins the Zagros Mountains of Iran to form the southern perimeter of the Iranian plateau. A comparable escarpment skirts the southerly perimeter of the Arabian peninsula.

In an east–west direction no single latitudinal line separates Asia sharply into northern and southern halves, but with a little bending here and there the fortieth degree – which passes close to Istanbul, Ankara, Tabriz, Ashkabad, Bukhara, Samarkand, Kashgar, Kalgan, Peking, Pyongyang and the northern tip of Honshu – follows fairly closely the historically traceable ethno-ecological demarcation separating what is referred to in this study as the northern quadrant from the rest of Asia.

Throughout its western half the line follows more or less the northern rim of the central plateau zone, and throughout the eastern half it tends to follow the southern rim. Since the point of divergence is just north of the Tibetan plateau in the region of Lop Nor in the Tarim basin, it might be stated that the centre of the continent lies somewhere near the point where the fortieth degree of latitude crosses the ninetieth degree of longitude.

One feature that characterizes Europe as well as Asia but not the other continents is the large number of peninsulas. Europe itself is often considered the largest of Asia's peninsulas, but nine others form most of the remaining outer zone: Anatolia, Arabia, India, Malaya, Indo-China, China, Korea, Kamchatka and Anadyr. These projecting land masses have been singularly effective either as cul-de-sacs, preserving pocketed enclaves of ancient populations, or as land bridges leading to other continents, and sometimes as both.

If one were able to obtain a complete panoramic view of Asia from outer space on a clear day – a highly improbable phenomenon – one would probably note first the huge peninsulas of the west and south: Anatolia, relatively green; Arabia and India, mottled reddish-brown with patches of green; Malaya and Indo-China, dark green. Across the middle of the continent would be seen the broad, reddish-brown central plateau and desert belt, spotted here and there with patches of white, and to the north the mixed light and dark green expanses of Siberia.

As expected, the climatic and biotic maps bear a logical relationship. Where temperature extremes are great, rainfall is light and consequently the flora tends towards xerophytic scrub and grasslands with appropriate fauna. Where rainfall is heavier, the vegetation ranges from temperate to tropical, with corresponding changes in animal life.

On the basis of land formations and related climatic and biotic zones, Asia falls naturally into four major ethno-ecological regions or quadrants, all of which impinge upon the centrally located Tibetan plateau. In many ways this plateau stands alone, but its ecological and biological ties are strongest with the north. The cultural ties of its inhabitants are divided between the east and the north, although in matters religious the Tibetans have always been closest to the south. The term 'central Asia' in the conventional sense refers to Soviet Central Asia, exclusive of Kazakhstan but including Afghanistan north of the Hindu Kush and Sinkiang south of the T'ien Shan – a decided misnomer from the point of view of geographical location. From this viewpoint Tibet should be referred to as part of central Asia, but for reasons explained above it is assigned here to the northern quadrant. If a flight of fantasy is permissible, on the map the land surfaces of Tibet and Sinkiang are shaped and interlocked like the classic 'yin' and 'yang' symbols. Carrying the symbolism further, Sinkiang throughout history has been a corridor for the passage of enlightenment both eastward and westward, whereas the Tibetan plateau has appeared as a dark and forbidding land, a fitting reminder of its historic role and prohibiting stance.

To a remarkable degree, the cultural and biological groupings of the peoples of the four quadrants correspond with the geographical limits of their respective ecological regions (see Map 2). The northern quadrant is by far the largest. It includes all of the territories north of the great mountain barrier, or approximately half of the continent. Since late Miocene times this entire expanse of desert, steppe, forestland and tundra has been the range of grazing and foraging animals. The southern limits have varied with time and climate but have included all of the animals of the major pastoral nomadic societies and most of the now-extinct big game animals. It has provided the economic base for most of the major nomadic empires – Scythian, Sarmatian, Hunnic, Turkic and Mongol and, through diffusion of the domesticated camel from central Asia westward, the Arab. Agriculture has been important but peripheral and supportive, and only in very recent historic times the primary source of power or mobility.

Western Asia since the dawn of history has been the crossroads of mankind, a part of the world that might prove to be a segment of the larger region where biologically recent man originated. It was here that man may have first begun the domestication of plants and animals, and here the earliest permanent settlements have been distinguished. The western quadrant is the core area of the wild ancestors of most of the upland cereals and grasses – barley, wheat, oats and rye. Some three-quarters of the world's important domesticated plants and animals are of Asian origin, and most of them survive today in wild form in or near their original centres of dispersal. The neolithic revolution was not only technological, economic and social, but demographic and hence genetic, and the latter aspects of this revolution have been fully as important as the cultural. Whether or not the south-east Asian horticultural area proves to be older remains to be seen.

The southern quadrant well deserves its title, 'the Indian subcontinent'. Separated from the rest of the land mass by a high mountain perimeter, the diamond-shaped region was first a tropical east–west bridge for early man and, from neolithic times onward, both recipient and donor of significant cultural stimuli. In

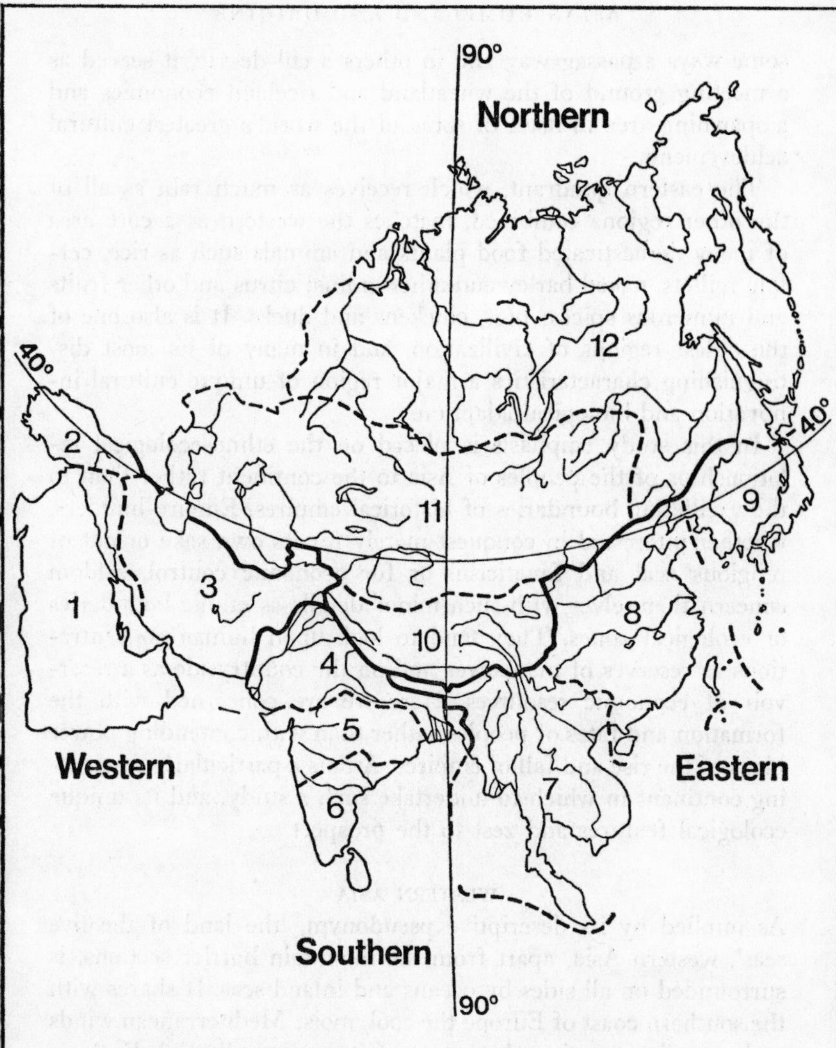

1 Arabia and Greater Syria
2 Anatolia and the Armenian Highlands
3 Irania, the Hindu Kush and the Pamirs
4 The Indo-Gangetic Plains and Foothills
5 Western India, the Central Plateau and Orissa
6 The Dravidian South
7 Greater South-east Asia
8 China
9 Korea and Japan
10 The Tibetan Plateau and Borderlands
11 Central Asia, Sinkiang & Mongolia
12 Siberia, Manchuria and Hokkaido

Map 3 **Asia's human quadrants**

some ways a passageway and in others a cul-de-sac, it served as a meeting ground of the wheatland and riceland economies and a spawning area in itself of some of the world's greatest cultural achievements.

The eastern quadrant, which receives as much rain as all of the other regions combined, matches the western as a core area of many domesticated food plants and animals such as rice, certain millets, naked barley and other grains; citrus and other fruits and numerous spices; pigs, chickens and ducks. It is also one of the oldest regions of civilization, and in many of its most distinguishing characteristics a major region of unique cultural innovation and biological adaption.

In this study emphasis is placed on the ethno-ecological relationships of the peoples of Asia to the continent rather than to the vacillating boundaries of historical empires. Empire-builders, whether interested in conquest merely for its own sake or out of religious zeal and fanaticism or for economic control, seldom concern themselves with such minor details as ethnic boundaries or ecological zones. They tend to look upon human concentrations as reserves of manpower and on the countryside as a reservoir of economic resources. Here we are concerned with the formation and fates of peoples rather than with contending power blocs or the rise and fall of empires. Asia is a particularly fascinating continent in which to undertake such a study, and its unique ecological features add zest to the prospect.

WESTERN ASIA

As implied by its descriptive pseudonym, 'the land of the five seas', western Asia, apart from the mountain barrier sections, is surrounded on all sides by oceans and inland seas. It shares with the southern coast of Europe the cool, moist Mediterranean winds and coastal vegetation along part of its western littoral. Ecologically, the region divides into three rather distinct subregions: greater Arabia, Anatolia and Irania. By reason of location, greater Arabia, the hot southern subregion half, has been linked as much to Africa as to Asia. Conversely, the peoples of the relatively cool northern plateaus of Anatolia and Irania have maintained as close historic ties with Europe and Central Asia as with greater Arabia. In political terms, western Asia includes all of the peninsular Arab states, the Sinai peninsula of Egypt, the present-day states of Jordan, Israel, Lebanon, Syria, Iraq, Turkey, most of Iran and Afghanistan and the mountainous regions of Pakistan, including Baluchistan and the North-west Frontier Province down to the plains of the Indus.

Greater Arabia, sometimes referred to as 'Semitic Asia' [221, p. 324], is used here to include the greater Syrian portion of the Fertile Crescent as well as the Arabian peninsula. From the coastal escarpments along the Red Sea and the Indian Ocean, which reach altitudes of six to eight thousand feet in the Yemen plateau and over ten thousand in several sectors, the Arabian plate slopes gently downward in a north-easterly direction towards the Persian Gulf. Northward and eastward from Yemen the escarpments drop to four or five thousand feet and even lower in the Hejaz and Oman respectively. Because of this orographic configuration, attributable to the downward tilting of the Arabian tectonic plate, the occasional westerly rains are cut off from reaching inland. The narrow coastline is humid; the hills are forested; and the *wadis* of the mountain perimeter are tilled and sharply differentiated from those of the hot arid interior. Inland, the northern half of the peninsula forms a dry desert steppe grazing zone marked by three clusters of partly agricultural oasis settlements: the Jebel Shammar, the Qasim and the Nejd. The southern half is largely a vast desert more than six hundred miles broad – the Rub 'al Khali, 'Abode of Emptiness'.

Northward, the grazing grounds extend to include all of the Syrian desert and most of the Jazira, the interfluvial zone between the mountainous and forested Mediterranean section of the Fertile Crescent and the twin river alluvial plains of Mesopotamia. The contrast between the two is striking. The upper courses of the Euphrates, which receive permanent tributaries only from the Anatolian plateau, have been of vital significance to Syria by providing a steppe hinterland and sustenance to caravan routes north-eastward to the Armenian highlands and eastward to Kurdistan and the twin lake regions of Van and Urmia. The middle and lower courses form, as it were, a major tributary of the Tigris, which receives numerous other tributaries from the eastern Kurdish and Zagros highlands.

The two arms of the Crescent are sharply contrasted. The western arm divides into north and south Levant and Palestine. North Levant includes the coastal agricultural strip, Latakia, the hinterland forested Ansariye range and, further inland, the fertile valley of the Orontes flowing northward from Homs to Antioch. To the east lie the plains of Aleppo, and to the south the Jebel Shamaria. In southern Levant the high Lebanon range occupies most of the coastal terrain, while inland the anti-Lebanon hills and the high plateau of Damascus flank the fertile Bekaa Valley. Fifty miles to the south the Jebel Druz marks the border with Jordan. The broad coastal plain of Palestine in the south catches the cool, humid Mediterranean breezes, but the low hills of Judea are hot and dry. Beyond them the Jordan Valley drops steadily downward to the barren saline wastes of the Dead Sea at 2600 feet below sea level, the lowest and one of the hottest land-locked regions in the world. The eastern arm of the Fertile Crescent, or Mesopotamia, includes the grasslands of the north-west, the irrigable fertile plains of the centre and the swampy lowlands of the south.

Anatolia is by far the greenest of the subregions. Forests cover the mountain slopes of the Taurus range, the Kurdish Alps and the relatively low coastal escarpment that encircles the interior plateau. The western section facing the Aegean Sea is mountainous and well forested, the source of the Meander (Menderes) which lives up to its name as it crosses the coastal plain to reach the sea near the site of ancient Troy. The central or Anatolian plateau section, formed by one of the old lithosphere plates, ranges from four to six thousand feet in altitude and receives an annual rainfall of only fifteen inches. Steppe grazing lands, alternating with scattered areas of internal drainage and brackish lakes, cover much of the surface and in the centre the Halys cuts a deep channel across the flats as it curves northward towards the Black Sea. Along the southern border the Taurus range separates the plateau from Syria and has given it a degree of isolation, encouraging the development of a separate identity. Eastward the Armenian section centres round the plateau basin of Lake Van at the foot of Mount Ararat and the encircling Armenian highlands, the source of both the Tigris and Euphrates Rivers. Rainfall ranges up to forty inches but tillable areas are relatively limited. Along the narrow Pontic or Black Sea coast precipitation is even higher, but along the broader Aegean and Mediterranean shores and in the Adena or Cilician Plain north of the Levant it drops to less than thirty inches, an amount barely sufficient to meet the requirements of productive tillage, orchards and vineyards.

The Iranian plateau contains almost as great ecological extremes as Anatolia. The northern section, Azerbaijan, centering round Lake Urmia, is linked to the Armenian highlands and the Kurdish Alps. Encircling the main plateau is a series of mountain ranges comparable with those of Anatolia but higher. Eastward some of the Hindu Kush peaks in Afghanistan reach altitudes of more than 25,000 feet, and the most populous parts of the interior are at 4000 and 5000 feet. The greatest extremes are between the Mazanderan coast along the southern fringe of the Caspian Sea, with its dense, almost tropical, rain forest, and the virtually rainless expanse of the Khorasan Desert, an uninhabited and largely saline-encrusted region of internal drainage in the heart of the eastern half of Iran. The upper hills range in vegetation from scrub to dense forestation. Otherwise, most of the land is bare except where man has been able to expand the green oases by carrying water out to the remoter regions through an elaborate system of underground *kanat* (*qanat* or *karez*) tunnels and a network of surface irrigation ditches. Along the eastern frontier in Afghanistan, the high ranges of the Hindu Kush and adjacent sections of the Suleiman range hold the winter snows long enough to provide ample water to most of the upland valleys and alluvial fans of the Pathan hills during the late spring thaws. Cutting across the plateau from north to south, the low-lying hills of east Khorasan bisect the plateau and separate the enclosed saline basins of the Dasht-i-Kavir and Dasht-i-Lut from the fertile plains of the Helmand River and Zabulistan (Seistan) – the fabled land of Sohrab and Rustum – the Sakistan of ancient times. Southward lie the hot arid slopes of the Makran coast of southern Iran and Baluchistan, the Gedrosia of Persian antiquity.

SOUTHERN ASIA

Southern Asia is far more compact, and the subregions are less sharply differentiated than those of western Asia, but the extremes may be as great if not greater. Politically it includes the Indus Valley regions of Pakistan up to the foothills of the Suleiman range, all of India, Bangladesh and Sri Lanka (Ceylon), but excludes the Tibeto–Burman areas of the Himalayas above the *pahari* regions, Assam and the plateau sections of Kashmir. By eliminating these areas, the diamond-shaped subcontinent of greater India can be divided fairly simply into the northern alluvial plains of the Indus and Ganges Rivers and the plateau including the Deccan and Sri Lanka in the south.

Except for the forest and meadowland regions of Kashmir and the adjacent Dhaula Dhar range and *pahari* foothills, the Indus Valley is exceedingly arid and hot and depends almost wholly on irrigated agriculture along a relatively narrow zone beyond the river, with scattered upland grazing grounds for sheep and goats. The eastern margin tapers off into the great Thar Desert which, except for a few marginal oases, remains uninhabited.

East of the low-lying Doab watershed, the Ganges basin receives the full effect of the summer monsoons. Agriculture is limited chiefly to both irrigated and non-irrigated rice. The climate is hot and dry in the early spring but water is plentiful during the growing season. Along the foothills from Nepal to Assam are stretches of dense subtropical *terai* forest. Malarial for the most part and uninhabited in limited stretches, it still harbours wild buffalo, tigers and leopards. At one time it extended westward to the now-dry glacial moraines of the Jammu foothills, where attempts at afforestation have been hampered by overgrazing and irrigation schemes which have lowered the water table in places by as much as seventy-five feet. In the extreme eastern section below the junction with the Brahmaputra, the hot plains and delta fan of the lower Ganges are constantly threatened by floods and tidal waves which periodically take their toll in the millions.

South of the Vindhya range, the northern half of the peninsular subregion includes the basins of the Narbada and Tapti Rivers of central India, and southward from heights of 4000 to 5000 feet along the eastern wall of the western Ghats the Mahanadi crosses the peninsula and breaks through the eastern Ghats at sea level. From north-east to south-west, thorny scrub gives way to dry deciduous woodlands in the central highlands and wet deciduous forests (*sal*) in the hills of southern Bihar and Orissa. A dividing line follows the somewhat artificially imposed linguistic and political border separating the Indo–Aryan-speaking north from the Dravidian-speaking south. The subregion includes the Deccan plateau, the flanking tropical monsoon coast of Malabar on the west; the Coromandel coast on the east; the basin of the Kistna and the Godavari delta north to the Orissa border. Continuing south, Sri Lanka has a hot humid coastal perimeter and a less moist high central plateau. Off the Malabar coast, the scattered islet reefs of the Laccadives and Maldives form two series of low-lying dune-rimmed lagoons.

EASTERN ASIA

The east Asian region is more clearly demarcated than any of the other regions except for the sections extending from Assam westward into the valleys of the central Himalayan ranges. A glance at the map (Map 2) will show that Bhutan, Sikkim, most of Nepal and parts of the adjacent mountainous regions of Uttar Pradesh and Himachal Pradesh comprise this intermontane extension. Except for the descendants of the ruling Rajput 'princes', who created a string of petty states along the entire Himalayan frontier of India during the early centuries of the Christian era, the intermontane valley populations have closer linguistic and other ethnic as well as biological ties with the Tibeto–Burman-speaking peoples of eastern Asia and Tibet than with the plains and *pahari* populations of India.

The demarcation line runs from approximately the coastal border between Bangladesh and Burma northward along the western rim of the Lushai hills and includes most of the hilly regions of Assam and the western intermontane extension. From the northern borders of Assam and Burma the line follows the ethnic frontier of west China to Kansu – the limits of Chinese colonization and former imperial garrison outposts. Eastward the line follows rather more arbitrarily the Great Wall of China in a north-easterly direction across the Ordos region and other parts of Inner Mongolia and along the Chang Pai range north of the Yalu River to the Pacific just north of Vladivostok.

Assam today is a part of India, but prior to 1822 it was an independent state under the Ahom (Shan) kings and derived its name from that dynasty. In 1822 it was annexed to Burma and, after the first Burma war of 1826, it was annexed to India. Geographically, Assam falls within the greater Indo–Chinese region, and ethnically, except for the valley bottoms of the Brahmaputra and its tributaries which have been populated largely from Bengal, the populations have been intrusive from the east and are culturally and biologically related to the inhabitants of Burma and the rest of south-east Asia and south-west China. After annexation to India, an 'inner line' was drawn between the lands of the hill tribes and the districts inhabited by plains dwellers – a line that delineates fairly faithfully this ethnic frontier, as does the 'inner line' along the NEFA (Northeast Frontier Administration) zone north and east of the Brahmaputra.

The south-eastern subregion falls within the tropical monsoon forest belt but rainfall and other climatic factors range widely from the area of greatest rainfall in the world – the Cherrapunji district in Assam, with over 400 inches per annum – to the centre of the dry belt in Burma, which receives less than ten inches and is characterized by a xerophytic flora and desert fauna. Each of the eight states (Assam, Burma, Thailand, Malaya, Cambodia, Laos, Vietnam and parts of south China) has one or more large river valleys with corresponding 'core areas', a perimeter of mountains and at least one plateau and, in most instances, sections of dense and fairly inaccessible tropical forests. In Assam, the Brahmaputra and its tributaries form the central valley; the eastern Himalayas outline the northern perimeter; the Garo, Khasi, Jaintia and Sinteng hills constitute the first row of southern hills and the Patkai, Naga, Chin, Lushai and Tippera ranges the second row. Manipur, the seat of the former classical state of that name, rests strategically in a broad plateau plain between the Naga and Chin hills.

The central heart of Burma – the basins of the Irrawaddy and its main tributary, the Chindwin – is surrounded on the north-west by the south Assam ranges and the Arakan Yomas and on the north-east by the upper sections of the Indo–Chinese cordilleras and the Kachin hills. Along the southern half of the eastern border to the Thai frontier it is flanked by the Shan plateau and the Karen hills. The gorge of the Salween River, which cuts across the Shan States, is so deep and steep-walled that it is almost totally uninhabited except in its lowest courses.

In Thailand, the Menam (Menam Chao Phra) starts in the northern highlands; its lower valley basin is flanked on the west by the south Karen and Tenasserim hills and on the east by part of the Laotian plateau and the upper basin of the Se Mun, which flows into the Mekong. To the south-east the saucer-shaped country of Cambodia is surrounded by a ring of low hills and small plateaus which encircle the lower Mekong basin and its tributary, which drains into the centrally located Tonle Sap. Finally, Vietnam has a narrow coastal strip and a broad interior plateau and mountainous zone with two main rivers: the Red, which flows past Hanoi in the north and, in the south, the Mekong and its delta complex with the population centre in Saigon. The peninsular part of Malaya, although attached to the continent by the isthmus of Kraa, is more like an island, with a high mountain plateau and dense forest interior surrounded by a coastal settlement perimeter.

North of Indo–China, the provinces of Yunnan, Kwangsi, Kweichow and parts of Kwantung, though politically part of China, are sparsely inhabited. Numerically the Chinese are in the majority and occupy most of the riceland, but they are concentrated in less than twenty per cent of the territory. The remaining eighty per cent is occupied by 'tribal' populations whose mainly hilly tracts have been designated by the People's Republic of China as autonomous regions.

The rest of 'China proper' includes all of the remaining eighteen provinces except on the western perimeter where it follows the ethnic boundaries of the Tibetan borderlands. Most of Manchuria and Inner Mongolia are excluded. The three main river basins of China are separated from each other by mountain ranges so as to form ecologically three separate areas. In the south the West River – which joins the Pearl at Canton and flows into the South China Sea – falls within the tropical monsoon belt and receives over 100 inches of rain annually. In central China, the huge Yangtze basin supports two-thirds of China's population, averages some 60 inches of rainfall and produces a mixed crop of rice, wheat, sorghum, millet and vegetables. Extensive lake regions, swampland, scattered forests and the vast agricultural 'Red' basin of Szechuan differentiate it from the north and the south. Northward, the Yellow River (Huang Ho) cuts through the loess lands of the west and bends sharply southward from the arid Ordos to the Tsinling range, which deflects it eastward to the former flood plains of Hopeh and Honan, the rich alluvial farmlands of the north. The region is too dry to support extensive rice cultivation and the crops are largely limited to wheat, sorghum, millet, mustard, rape and a variety of vegetables and fruits. Historically, the Yellow River has been most unpredictable. At intervals of approximately a century it has shifted course to flow alternately north and south of the Shantung peninsula, leaving untold thousands homeless or dead in the wake of each successive flood. In 1938 it was artificially diverted southward by the Nationalist forces in an effort to halt the Japanese drive towards Nankin, but in 1947 it was returned to its former northern channel and stabilized by an elaborate system of dams, dikes and levees.

Korea and Japan are a part of eastern Asia, but ethnically they might be classed as marginal. Structurally, both the Korean and Japanese languages are related to the Manchu–Tungusic branch of the Altaic group, to which most of the languages of northern Asia belong, and many of their basic social values, especially in religious and magical beliefs and practices, have northern affinities. The massive Sino–Korean and Sino–Japanese cultural assimilation overlay, the introduction of such southern crops as rice, taro, silk and tea and the use of the water buffalo in the south place the two countries within the Chinese and Indo–Chinese sphere. The Ainu in northern Japan and the marginal Amur tribes in northern Korea are referred ethnically to Siberia.

Ecologically, Korea stands in sharp contrast to Japan. Much of the old granitic plate along the eastern perimeter is visible in the central and southern sections where the forests have meagre purchase. The plate itself tilts downward from the high east coast escarpment of the Diamond Mountains toward the Yellow Sea, so that most of the major rivers flow westward to the coastal fringe and the richest ricelands of the peninsula. Most of the heavy forests and ore deposits are in the mountainous northern half.

By contrast, the four main islands of Japan and the northern and southern island chain extensions lie along the volcanic faultline stretching from the East Indies to Kamchatka. Structurally the islands are mainly volcanic and combine upthrust sections of igneous rock with sedimentary formations. The central mountainous spines of the main and offshore islands contain thirteen live or semi-active volcanoes, and scattered along their slopes are more than three thousand economically significant hot springs. So mountainous are the main islands that less than twenty-five per cent of the surfaces can be tilled, and so indented are the coastlines that they total more than seven times what they would be if the land surfaces were to be compressed into a circle. Along the Japan sea coast of northern Honshu the heavy snows from Siberia are deposited in drifts twenty to thirty feet in depth, whereas elsewhere in the north winter precipitation is relatively light. The southern prefectures lie within the monsoon and typhoon belt of the south seas so that semi-tropical conditions prevail except for restricted arid regions of Kyushu where only cactus and other xerophytic plants can survive.

NORTHERN ASIA (INNER ASIA, SIBERIA AND HOKKAIDO)

Region names are often confusing when compass directions are used in the context of a Europe-centred world. This is especially true of Central Asia, so named doubtless because it occupied the mid-section of the land route between China and Byzantium. To add to the confusion, the term 'Inner Asia' conventionally includes Manchuria and the Turco–Mongolian steppe in addition to Central Asia and Tibet. In this study northern Asia includes almost all of Inner Asia, Siberia and Hokkaido.

The importance of Tibet as an east–west and north–south barrier has already been referred to. The Indus, Ganges, Brahmaputra, Salween, Mekong, Yangtze and Yellow Rivers all originate on the plateau, but because the valley walls that cut through the encircling ranges are so steep and in places so tortuous, they cannot be used as passageways except in isolated sections. Tibet covers an area of roughly a million square miles or nearly a third the area of Europe, and the perimeter is so formidable that the lowest crossing point between the passes north of Kabul in the central Hindu Kush and the Burma road in Yunnan – a distance of over two thousand miles – is just under 13,000 feet. To complete a transit in any direction requires crossing at least one 16,000-foot pass.

In this high plateau region evidence of the ancient Himalayan upthrusts is most apparent. The northern two-thirds slopes gently southward from 16,000 feet along the foothills of the Kuen Lun range to 13,000 just north of the inner Himalayan ranges (Alin Kangri and Tangla). Two-thirds of this Chang Tang (north plain) section, like the Takla Makan Desert of Sinkiang, is a land of internal drainage dotted with extensive patches of salt flats and brackish lake beds – encrusted remnants of the ancient Tethys floor. The mountain chains alternate between folds of igneous crust, extrusions of volcanic lava and sedimentary sea bed formations. Veins of gold, silver, copper and ferrous ores alternate with beds of marine fossils and volcanic pumice. Such grasses as can survive are so siliceous that they cut the intestines of domestic herds, and there is no potable water except during the late spring thaw.

North of the Tibetan plateau the vast expanses of Turkestan and Mongolia, between the Caspian Sea and the Khingan Mountains of Manchuria, form the second subregion. It may be divided into a desert oasis and caravan route southern zone and a grassland–steppe corridor northern zone, each some five hundred miles wide. Ecologically these two zones differ substantially, but ethnically they are not so easily distinguished. The first stretches from the fabled oasis bazaar cities of Merv, Samarkand and Bukhara in Turkmenistan and Uzbekistan to the outer rim of the Gobi Desert and the Great Wall in the east. The fluvially supported oases depend almost wholly on the melt-snows from the central plateau massif and its outer ranges. Northward the steppe zone, which stretches from the Volga to the Kerulen tributary of the Amur, is the homeland of all the great Inner Asian nomad–pastoral empires of the past. Except in the west along the courses of the Ural and Volga Rivers, the steppe zone follows the watershed and includes the broad upper valleys and meadowlands of the great basin systems of the Ob, Yenisei, Lena and Amur Rivers. The populations of the western or Turkish and eastern or Mongol halves of each of the two zones have been relatively stable for the past few hundred years, but this has been due mainly to the steady eastward expansion of Russia from the time of Peter the Great, and the increasing strength of China during the early period of the Manchu dynasty.

Siberia is by far the largest subregion and the most sparsely inhabited. The taiga birch and conifer forest zone covers most of the southern two-thirds, and the remaining third forms a tundra belt rimming the arctic seas. Apart from recently intrusive European industrial and agricultural pursuits, the entire economy is one of reindeer herding and scattered tillage. An exception is the fairly extensive grassland cattle-raising Yakutsk basin of the mid-Lena. From west to east the river basins are occupied by major divisions of Uralic, Altaic and Palaeo–Asiatic-speaking populations whose economies and migrations are extremely complex.

3

Early Man in Asia

Until the past few decades it had generally been assumed that Asia was man's original homeland, and such a notion may still prove correct. Recently, however, the pendulum of palaeontological evidence has swung in favour of Africa, and the swing is most impressive.

During the past fifty years, hundreds of skeletal remains and isolated teeth of hominoid apes and more progressive man-like hominids have been recovered from the eastern half of the continent between the delta region of the Nile and the ore-laden ranges of the veldland. By far the largest number have come from localized terraces and valley walls of the canyon-like Great Rift Valley of the lake country and the southern part of the Ethiopian highlands, but the oldest are from the Fayum, some sixty miles south-west of Cairo. This former brackish lake bed has a most unusual history dating back to the Oligocene, which lasted from roughly thirty-eight million to thirty million years ago. During most of this epoch Africa was isolated from the other continents, and the flora and fauna were developing their own specializations.

Early in the Miocene epoch, when the world landscape was dramatically altered, Arabia was slowly elevated to connect Africa again with Eurasia. Where soil and rainfall permitted, tropical parklands alternating with forests provided an almost continuous favourable migratory range across the entire southern half of the Old World as far east as Java and China.

As the Miocene progressed, the plateau barrier across Asia continued to rise and to separate the continent into two major climatic zones. Shielded by this barrier, the northern half remained cool and, in sections, subtemperate. A gradual drying-up process created conditions that favoured the expansion of grasses and scrub parklands and the proliferation of grazing animals. But, while the northern zone encouraged the migration of ungulates, it inhibited that of the more tropically adapted fauna. The southern zone on the other hand favoured hominoid migrations, and new ape forms began to appear which were to have a bearing on man's ancestry.

These new forms included a group known collectively as the dryopithecines, apes of the Dryas flora (oak complex) environment, which shared with man a number of dental characteristics and which had partial bipedal locomotion. An even more progressive genus, *Ramapithecus*, also expanded from Africa into Europe and Asia; morphologically it is nearest to man of all the Miocene-Pliocene primates and has recently been recognized as a hominid, or at least a quasi-hominid [154]. Named for Rama, one of the avatars of Vishnu and symbol of purity, *Ramapithecus* was first discovered in India and subsequently in China; it may even have reached Europe [348], but the oldest specimens of about fourteen million years ago come from East Africa [347, 197].

Skirting the southern border of the central Himalayan range in a crescentic sweep from Kashmir to Bengal lies a disconnected chain of low-lying foothills known geographically as the Siwalik front [357] which rises rather sharply from the plains of north India to heights varying from 9,000 feet in the west to 1,000 feet at the extreme eastern end, where the river Tista reaches the lowlands of Bengal. As part of this complex, the rich fossil-bearing beds north of Delhi have been the most productive. These beds were laid down between early and mid-Miocene times about twenty to fifteen million years ago when the entire Himalayan mountain complex was very much lower than it is today and the outer perimeter, the region now occupied by the Siwaliks, was still an unraised part of the great Indo–Gangetic plain. The climate was generally tropical, but large areas were covered with interspersed forests, savanna parklands and swampy waterholes, an area rich in game, waterfowl and wild fruits in season, an ideal environment for the larger pongids. These included the genera *Dryopithecus* and *Ramapithecus* as well as a third genus, *Gigantopithecus* whose range extended eastward into China. The preserved fossils were probably swamp victims caught along the margins of waterholes and subsequently submerged under sandy alluvial silts and gravels. That the submontane *terai* or forest zone was less a dense, malarial jungle and more a parkland during the Miocene is attested by plant fossils, presumptive evidence that seasonal rains swept further inland before reaching their levels of major precipitation.

Towards the end of the Miocene, these beds were caught up in the final mountain-building process and buckled upward by a suballuvial thrust which folded the fossil-laden layers until they eventually cracked open along their longitudinal axes to reveal their entrapped contents. Presumably, therefore, if the mantle of accumulated silts now covering the Indo–Gangetic plain were to be removed to tap these underlying Miocene deposits, which stretch from the Siwaliks to the Vindhya escarpment, the results might prove revolutionary. On the basis of clues provided along some of the Miocene and Pliocene terraces of the Narbada, Tapti and Godavari basins, these should prove equally significant and are far more accessible. It seems likely that they will become the next target for intensive prospecting.

North India, in fact, provided an ideal environment for the dryopithecines and for *Ramapithecus*, which appears to have been derived from one of the dryopithecine radiations. The finds include parts of lower and upper jaws and teeth from the Nagri or middle formations of the Miocene beds. Discovered by Pilgrim in 1910, most of the later specimens were collected by Lewis [213] in 1932.

One of the most convincing reasons advanced for an African genesis has been the recovery of hundreds of specimens of *Australopithecus*, the 'southern ape', first from South Africa and then spectacularly from East Africa. According to potassium-argon dating techniques, the African australopithecines existed during the late Pliocene and early Pleistocene from about four or five million years ago until after one million years ago. Outside Africa, there was ample room within a favourable environment for movement around the Indian Ocean arc to Malaysia and northward to Europe. With increasing adaptibility to bipedal locomotion, it is difficult to explain why such man-like creatures should apparently have remained so confined. Particularly in the face of the earlier distribution of dryopithecines, the absence of australopithecines outside Africa is puzzling. One possible exception consists of the remains of a hominid named *Meganthropus* from Java.

Apart from the Siwaliks, a second area in Asia of major importance in the story of human origins is the region of insular south-east Asia. Considered frequently as part of Australasia and hence linked with Oceania, this whole area – including Sumatra, Java, Borneo and Palawan and the inter-island spaces and coastal perimeters of the mainland – was eustatically raised to form an extension of continental Asia during Miocene and most of Pliocene times. The deep sea break between this region, known as the Sunda shelf or Sundaland, and the island area further east falls just east of Bali and Borneo and bisects the Philippines along a floral–faunal demarcation line named appropriately after its naturalist discoverer, A. R. Wallace [390, 391]. Because of its strategic position, Sundaland was crucial to the peopling of the Pacific and the later hominid finds are therefore considered elsewhere.

The most productive region of Sundaland for early hominids has been the eastern half of Java and specifically three locations within that region: Sangiran, Trinil and Kedung Brubus. It was from the early Pleistocene Djetis beds in the first of these localities that the *Meganthropus* remains – two large morphologically similar jaws and scattered teeth – were recovered by von Koenigswald during two separate seasons, 1941 and 1952 [186]. Resemblances with the australopithecines and the contemporary *Homo habilis* of East Africa have been noted in such features as the mandibular contours and the molar cusp patterns, but in absolute size both the lower jaws and the molars fall within the lower range of the later *Homo erectus* group [397]. Some palaeontologists classify *Meganthropus* as a robust australopithecine, others as a variant of *Homo erectus*; still others assign it the status of a separate genus [349]. The dating remains a problem. The matrix from which the finds were extracted has been dated within the range 0.75 to 1.9 million years ago.

Recent discoveries of *Homo erectus* specimens from Northern Kenya and Ethiopia promise to add a wholly new perspective to the question of the antiquity of man [66]. Until recently the trend had been to view the australopithecines as the direct antecedents of the genus *Homo*. The dating of these finds at more than 1.5

million years shows clearly, however, that the two hominids were contemporaneous. In Asia, discoveries from the Djetis beds in the Sangiran area other than *Meganthropus* consist of the remains of at least two early *Homo erectus* specimens, the oldest yet found in Asia and equivalent in age to that of several progressive australopithecines and *Homo habilis* from Africa. In addition, there is a series of more progressively advanced forms of *Homo erectus*, including the so-called 'Java Man' from the overlying Trinil beds of the mid-Pleistocene and dated at close to half a million years ago.

The third major area is south China. *Gigantopithecus* was first discovered and identified by von Koenigswald [185] from teeth purchased from a Hong Kong drug store in the early thirties. He guessed correctly that their place of origin was south China. Numerous additional teeth and parts of three mandibles have since been recovered *in situ* from Kwangsi Province [49, 283]. Various dryopithecine teeth and fragmentary bones have come from south-western Yunnan and the southern provinces and a ramapithecine was recovered from a coalfield in Kueiyuan district, Yunnan [402]. Chinese scientists also claim a new genus, *Hemanthropus*, from Kwangsi, but its taxonomic status remains unclear [289]. Perhaps it is an australopithecine as suggested by Simons [346].

A curious feature about our current knowledge of early man is that we seem to know more about his earlier stages than we do about the phase transitional to the level of *Homo erectus*. Once this level is reached, the entire scene is changed. The *erectus* group ranged far and wide, extending on the northern front from Algeria, Spain, France, Germany and possibly Hungary, eastward as far as north China and, in the south, from south Africa following the Indian Ocean arc to Java. Interestingly, most of the discoveries have been geographically marginal, whereas those of the australopithecines were largely localized in East and South Africa. Furthermore, whereas the definitely identified remains of the australopithecines seem to be limited to Africa, the largest collections of the *erectus* group are still from two widely separated regions in Asia: Sundaland (Indonesia) and China.

The dramatic story of the Dutch anatomist Eugene Dubois, who forsook a comfortable career in his homeland to devote the better part of his adult life to the role of a medical officer in the

East Indies Colonial Service so that he could hunt for the 'missing link', is too well known to require detailed repetition. Almost miraculously, it would seem, he did discover a fossil creature fitting the description suggested by the famous German naturalist Ernst Haeckel, the originator of the law of biogenesis. Dubois went to the East Indies because he knew that fossil-bearing Pleistocene beds had been located on the major islands. He found what he went for, and the success of this brilliant discovery near the village of Trinil on the upper level of the Solo River in east-central Java is appropriately memorialized today by a stone plinth on the east bank of the river bearing simply the initials P.E. (*Pithecanthropus erectus*), mute tribute to his predictive genius. Some irreverent quip has suggested that this might stand for the statistical term 'probable error' but, if so, he must have had in mind Dubois' final attitude towards his own great discovery and not that of the initially unimpressed but later converted scientific world.

This discovery opened up the whole field of scientific inquiry into man's biological genesis and simultaneously a veritable Pandora's box of conflicting views concerning the true nature of Dubois' finds. Briefly, the most important items in his booty consisted of a remarkably low-vaulted, beetle-browed and thick-walled calvarium or skull cap, a jaw fragment, a few teeth and a complete but somewhat pathologically distorted femur and pieces of other femora. The skull cap (calotte), generally referred to as 'Java Man', has a cranial capacity of approximately 950 cubic centimetres, barely below the minimum range of modern man. While these startling discoveries date from 1891–2, it was not until a series of further discoveries were made by von Koenigswald [350] and his associates between 1931 and 1939 and subsequent discoveries had been reported by Jacob [169, 170] and Sartono [329] that the full scope of the earlier discoveries could be assessed.

Altogether, the greater portions of eight skulls, together with a number of additional teeth and assorted minor fragments of mandibles and other bones attributable to *Homo erectus javanensis* ('*Pithecanthropus*') have been recovered. Collectively the specimens are remarkably similar and the reports on the African finds suggest little morphological change over the span of a million years [46a]. There remain, however, two additional specimens from the same region in Java but from a different time level. One of these is the skull of an adult originally labelled P–IV, and the other a portion of an infant skull (*H.e. modjokertensis*) whose adult morphology is necessarily hypothetical. Two things about P–IV are rather remarkable: one is the extraordinarily heavy and thick skull walls, and the other the lowness of the cranial vault. The two specimens came from cemented gravels overlying fresh water clays of the Poetjang formation of the same deposit in which the meganthropine remains were found – the basal Pleistocene Djetis faunal beds below those of the Trinil bed formation. Even so, their age falls far short of the age level dating of the East African specimens.

The story of the discovery of 'Peking Man' is almost as dramatic as that of 'Java Man'. For some years after the turn of the century it had been noted by scientific sleuths in Peking that the 'dragon bones' being ground up to become part of the pharmacopoeia of Chinese drug stores were in reality the mineralized bones and teeth of long extinct fauna. Some of these teeth looked remarkably human. Acting on a hunch that bird dog tactics might pay off, a Swedish expedition studying the palaeontology of the Gobi Desert during the early twenties traced the main hunting grounds for these 'dragon bones' to fossil-bearing breccia deposits in limestone fissures near the village of Choukoutien in the low-lying Western Hills some thirty-five miles southwest of Peking. In 1923 Zdansky, one of the palaeontologists, reported a human tooth recovered from collections made during the 1921 expedition. On the basis of this one find, Davidson Black, a Canadian anatomist at the Peking Union Medical College, working in concert with the Geological Survey of China, ventured to create a new genus which he named *Sinanthropus pekinensis* (now known as *Homo erectus pekinensis*).

Following this discovery, excavations were begun in 1927 by the Cenozoic Laboratory of the Academia Sinica and have been carried on intermittently since then, in spite of political upheavals and changes in personnel and organization. The first skull cap was discovered in 1929 by Pei [46a, p. 212] and during the intervening decades six other crania, a number of mandible sections, and a few scattered post-cranial skeletal fragments and teeth of at least sixty individuals have been recovered. After the untimely death of Dr Black, and up to the occupation of north China by the Japanese in 1939, analysis of the Peking materials had been entrusted to the capable hands of Franz Weidenreich [396] and his Chinese associates. Unhappily, during the period of wartime confusion all of the original specimens were lost, but excellent casts survive. Recently a virtually complete new specimen has been discovered in the same fissure complex [411] and other finds have been recovered from the neighbouring province [49, pp. 39–77].

The most important of the latter finds include a mandible of a type more archaic than that of Peking Man, recovered in 1963 from a rock shelter site near the village of Chenchiawo in Lan-t'ien district, Shensi Province [403], and in the following year a fairly complete skull of the same general type but geologically much older, from the neighbouring site of Gongwangling (Kungwangling) in the same district [404].

Until more is known about the meganthropines, they may be regarded as tangential since they were morphologically aberrant though contemporaneous with the P–IV and *modjokertensis* pithecanthropines. Even so, eastern Asia alone has produced at least four identifiable evolutionary gradations from an equal number of time phases in the development of the *Homo erectus* group: *H.e. modjokertensis* (P–IV), Java Man (*H.e. javanensis*, Lantien (Lantian) Man and Peking Man. Unfortunately, data on the P–IV-*modjokertensis* specimens are inadequate for comparative purposes, but Table 1 gives some idea of the general range in sizes and shapes of the respective crania compared to the other groupings.

Table 1. *Geological age and cranial capacities of Asian varieties of* Homo erectus

	Lantien Man Lantien, Shensi (Kungwangling)	Java Man Trinil	Peking Man Choukoutien
Gelogical age (BP)	700–400,000	550–350,000	450–300,000
Cranial capacity (cc)	778	775–975	914–1225
Cranial length (mm)	189	177–199	186–199
Cranial breadth (mm)	149	130–156	137–143
Auricular height (mm)	87	89–102	115

Unlike the australopithecine remains, which include parts of the pelvis, long bones and most of the foot bones, pitifully few fragments of the post-cranial skeleton of *Homo erectus* have been recovered. Reconstruction depends on a single whole femur and parts of other femora and on hand bones and other specimens from East Africa. These remains suggest bipedal walking and running stance only slightly less upright than that of modern man and a full grasping ability. *Erectus* level man had very large and projecting brow-ridges – a veritable shelf (supra-orbital torus) – very thick bones of the cranial vault, a short face, a broad nose, an edge-to-edge bite, no forward projection of the chin, some mid-facial prognathism and large molars. The third molar or wisdom tooth is generally smaller than the other two and is absent in one instance, suggesting that a trend towards elimination had already begun, although modern man has not yet generally attained this goal. Significantly, the medial incisors are 'shovel-shaped', as are those of most east Asian populations today. Forward-projecting malars or cheekbones follow the same trend. The occurrence of these and other characteristics of Peking Man suggested to Weidenreich that possibly there was a genetic continuity between man of the mid-Pleistocene period and the so-called racial Mongoloids of today, an idea reserved for later discussion.

As in the case of *Australopithecus*, the skeletal remains of *erectus* level man in Asia are so localized that it becomes necessary to depend upon his cultural achievements to determine the full range of his presumed habitat. Whoever may have been responsible for shaping the Oldowan pebble-chopping tools of East Africa, Peking Man was undoubtedly the fashioner of rather crude and roughly comparable chopping tools associated with his remains. They were made mainly of granite from a nearby outcrop and greenstone pebbles from a local stream bed. The majority were core implements, rather large, and somewhat circular in shape with high backs and portions of the smooth pebble surface untouched. Less frequently, flake tools with retouched edges were produced but they had no special overall shape. Quantities of broken bone indicate the removal of marrow, and the fact that the basilar portions of the human skulls were invariably broken away is taken as evidence of cannibalism. Any idea, however, that cannibalism could have had more than ritual or gourmet significance is utterly fanciful. Man would soon have eaten himself out of existence had he depended to any extent upon human meat for survival. Peking Man's main food supply consisted of elephant, rhinoceros, horse, buffalo, water buffalo, camel, wild boar, sheep, antelope, deer and at least hackberry and doubtless other fruits, as well as tubers in season.

The relative crudeness of the artefacts and the apparent lack of interest in bone as a raw material for tool-making suggests the likelihood that Peking Man's level of industrial achievement remained more or less at an advanced Oldowan pebble industry level. His most unique accomplishment was the controlled use of fire. Charred animal bones prove that fire was intentionally used, but not necessarily that it was produced. This seems to be the earliest proven use of fire, although recent discoveries in Europe raise the question of priority.

Comparable tool assemblages were also found associated with Lantien Man at Chenchiawo. Typologically most of the tools from both sites were sufficiently similar to the chopper tools of the Sohan (Soan) industry in the Punjab, the Anyathian in Burma and the Koṭa Tampan in Malaya to suggest that in all three areas men of the *erectus* stage were responsible for their manufacture. Despite the widespread occurrence of the chopping tool industry throughout much of Asia south of the central plateau, it is rather striking that no artefacts of any kind have been recovered in definite association with Java Man. It is generally assumed that this is due to failure of discovery rather than to Java Man's limited capabilities, just as it is assumed also that, in time, the skeletal remains of *Homo erectus* will be discovered on the Indian subcontinent.

While Asia seems thus to have been stagnating industrially at the chopping tool level, Africa was making the first spectacular advances in the manufacture of bifacial handaxes, which subsequently spread rapidly north to Europe by way of Gibraltar and to Asia by way of Egypt, reaching those continents by the end of the lower Pleistocene. Acheulian handaxes have been found in greater Syria, Arabia [34] and Central Asia [67] as extensions of the rich finds at Satani Dar in Armenia, the coastal sites on the eastern shores of the Black Sea and the south-west Asian area, and throughout most of India as far east as Bengal and south to Madras. Recent discoveries of artefacts closely resembling the bifacial handaxes of Africa have also been reported from China [34, pp. 83–97], but nowhere in Asia have they been found in direct association with skeletal remains. It is possible, as Bordes

[34, pp. 81 and 136] suggests, that Java Man was responsible for the Pajitanian handaxe-like chopping tools from the appropriate time level in Java.

If the makers of the early handaxes were of the *erectus* type, then presumably two entirely different industrial techniques were employed in different parts of the world by men at a comparable stage of biological evolution. By the early part of the third interglacial (*c.* 200,000–100,000 BC), which ushered in the Middle Acheulian type of handaxe, the final major biological transformation had commenced. Already the 'early' transitional forms leading to modern man had appeared, as attested by various skulls from Europe and North Africa. Towards the latter part of the period advanced handaxes, similar to those of Europe, had made their appearance in India, but there are no associated skeletal remains, and no complete artefact assemblages to indicate whether the Indian handaxes were the result of diffusion or local innovation. In the temperate zone climatic change stimulated innovation, but in tropical regions such stimulus was generally lacking.

A new tool-making method, which started between 100,000 and 70,000 years ago at the beginning of the fourth glaciation, was completely different from previous techniques. The flakes were detached from a core with a single blow, which meant that the core had first to be prepared with a striking platform. Handaxes continued in use in the west but were gradually diminished in size and numbers, and possibly therefore in usefulness. They tend to disappear progressively in an easterly direction and were apparently absent in most of Asia. The new flake tools are associated with early *Homo sapiens* remains and the oldest have been found only in North Africa, Europe and the adjacent parts of western Asia.

The climatic changes of the last glaciation undoubtedly exerted new environmental pressures, altering man's habitat through changes in the biota and stimulating enforced migrations into new environmental niches. There were changes in man's feeding habits, tools and types of shelter. On the biological side, the late third interglacial saw the emergence of taxonomically 'intermediate' forms of modern man collectively known as neanderthaloid, who were followed early in the fourth glaciation by 'Neanderthal Man'. Unfortunately, the earliest discoveries in western Europe of a somewhat aberrant or extreme variety often referred to as 'classic', which exhibited a number of so-called 'primitive' but in the zoological sense 'specialized' traits. Most of the subsequent finds from central, southern and eastern Europe and adjacent regions of Asia were never in as extreme form as in France and Germany. This chance sequence of events was responsible for distorting and confusing our knowledge of man's biological history during the latter part of the Ice Age.

All neanderthaloids, 'classic' and otherwise, have now been elevated as a subspecies of modern man, *Homo sapiens neanderthalensis*. Similarly other regionally separated but contemporary populations such as *Homo sapiens soloensis* from Java are treated as subspecies [154]. Such a classification, however, assumes a greater degree of genetic and geographical discontinuity than would appear justifiable. It would suggest also that the term 'subspecies' might be equated with 'races' – a somewhat dubious procedure.

Genetically different populations must have evolved separately from earlier forms, and subsequent populations in respective areas have probably retained a number of structurally distinguishable characteristics. The array of neanderthaloid and 'recent' characteristics was variable and unpredictable, and transitional forms never followed the same progressive lines in any two regions or populations. Some authorities have suggested that man may have passed from the neanderthaloid to the 'recent' stage at different times in different places. It is probably more correct to say that the particular gene pools of localized populations varied from region to region and that, in some populations, certain neanderthaloid trait complexes were retained because of their possible adaptive value, whereas in others they were altered.

The geneticist might add that the transition from one species or subspecies to another is a matter of degree, and only a limited number of significant mutations may be needed to effect the change. So today all populations preserve in their gene pools various traits which modern man has been eliminating because of differences in survival value; regionally, through the same processes of natural selection, other traits have been retained or added. It is possible therefore to speak only of progressive trends of change in varying tempos and with different selective values.

Morphological traits, however, can prove very deceptive. Edge-to-edge bite, for example, is common among Tibetans, but it is not necessarily the retention of a neanderthaloid trait: more likely it is due to a selective adaptation to diet. It is often impossible to distinguish between new mutations or recombinations and retained archaic features, particularly since similar mutations can occur repeatedly.

Another important consideration is the recognition of the human continuum from one geographical region to another, or what Weiner refers to as the 'spectrum theory'. Even so, it is evident that biologically distinguishable populations do exist and have existed, and Asia is a particularly good continent in which to observe the manifestation of the theory. This is not so merely because of its position, humanly speaking, in the centre of the world, but because of its major geographical configurations which bear such close relationship to the four-fold regionalization of man around the high central plateau of Tibet and the Pamirs.

In Asia the largest concentration of neanderthaloid finds is from Palestine. These include one skeleton from Tabun Cave and nine adults and a child from Skhul Cave, both in the Mount Carmel area of Israel; some thirteen individuals from Jebel Kafzeh (Qafza); a complete skeleton from Amud Cave near the sea of Galilee; a skull from Zuttiya Cave; one adult and six children from Shukba Cave, and a child from Ksar Akil. Six adults have also been recovered from Shanidar Cave in northern Iraq, and some crania with neanderthaloid traits from Hotu Cave near the Caspian Sea in Iran. The most northerly remains are those of a boy from Teshik-Tash in Uzbekistan.

A tremendous gap still exists in our knowledge of man in south and east Asia during the transitional period from early modern to the recent *sapiens* stage, suggesting either that neanderthaloids were late in reaching these areas, or that their remains are yet to be discovered. Part of a skull cap found in a limestone cave near Mapa village in Kwantung Province, south China, has neanderthaloid characteristics but its date is uncertain. It is sufficiently similar to a cluster of individuals known as Solo Man of east Java and Niah Man of Sarawak, Borneo, to rationalize that it may be from about the same period of 35,000–40,000 BC. The Solo and Mapa remains share a number of the same transitional characters exhibited by such west Asian neanderthaloids as those of Shanidar, Mount Carmel and Teshik-Tash, but there seems to be some reluctance to call their eastern contemporaries

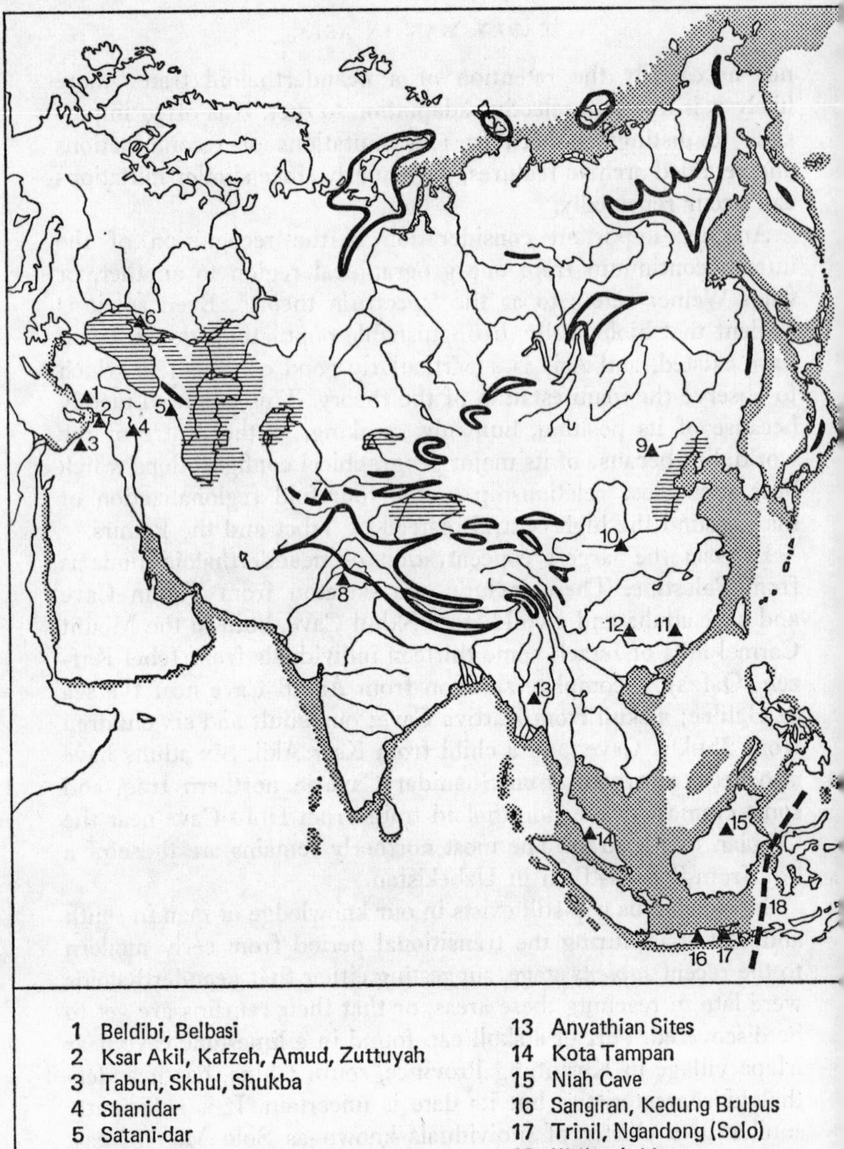

Map 4 **Palaeolithic sites and Asia's land surfaces during the Fourth Glacial Period**

neanderthaloid. This is due in part, if not largely, to the fact that the east Asian artefacts are not typically mousteroid. Also, the European and central Asian finds reveal a concern for the after-life, whereas no such tendency is apparent in the east Asian remains.

All of the greater Syrian, Anatolian and central Asian finds show evidence of intentional interment; they were true burials. The legs were usually flexed, arms folded, and associated objects imply a concern for the welfare of the departed. All ten skeletons at the terrace site of Mugharet-es-Skhul on Mount Carmel were arranged in this manner and one was clasping the jaws of a wild boar. At Shanidar one individual appears to have been crushed by a rock fall, but another was intentionally buried and his grave pit strewn with flowers. The Uzbekistan burial was surrounded by a semicircle of inverted goat skulls with horns attached.

Even before the end of the Ice Age man had acquired the technological means to push his habitable zones to virtually their present limits, and with few exceptions these limits must have been reached by Holocene times, about 10,000 BC. The exceptions would include the higher mountain valleys, the remote interiors of tropical forests and deserts and the most isolated islands. Account must be taken of the changes in response to isostatic and eustatic fluctuations as the glaciated areas receded and the expanding ocean obliterated shorelines and converted coastal ranges into islands and peninsulas.

At the height of the last glaciation, about 23,000 BC, the continental outlines and archipelagos of Eurasia differed markedly from those of today (see Map 4). Sundaland (Indonesia) was a peninsular extension of continental south-east Asia. Both Hainan and Taiwan were attached to China, and the Japanese islands and the northern half of the Ryukyus formed a southern extension of Sakhalin, all but converting the Japan Sea into a brackish lake. It is still a moot point whether the strait of Tsu was raised as an isthmus corridor to cut off the Japan Sea in much the same way that the Baltic was isolated to form Lake Ancylus. Further north, the coastal areas around the Sea of Okhotsk and Kamchatka were vastly expanded and a wide land bridge connected Asia to North America.

As indicated in Table 2 the total land surface may have been increased by as much as one-third around the perimeter of the continent. Inland, vast areas were covered by ice sheets, glaciers and extensions of inland seas. The most important change, therefore, was an expansion of the tropical regions by as much as thirty per cent in southern Asia and over one hundred per cent in the east. In all probability the peoples north of the central plateau who had penetrated into the Yenisei and Lena basins late in the third interglacial were either isolated or withdrew into Turkestan, if not further south, while those south of the plateau probably increased in numbers and expanded along the Siberian coast to Alaska.

Table 2. *Estimated land surface additions and losses at the height of the Fourth (Würm) Glacial Period* (*c.* 30,000 BC)

	Land surface area today (in thousand square miles)	Approximate increase at height of glaciation	Approximate loss due to ice sheets, inland seas and marine transgressions	Gain or Loss
Western Asia	2,500	16%	3%	+13%
Southern Asia	1,600	25%	2%	+23%
Eastern Asia	2,800	105%	2%	+103%
Northern Asia	8,000	15%	35%*	−10%
Total Asia	16,000 †	30%	20%	+10%

* Includes ice-free areas presumed to have been uninhabitable.
† Excludes Sundaland (insular south-east Asia and continental sea floor).

The savannas across much of Arabia and the present desert-steppe zone of northern Asia eventually lost most of their plant cover and became arid as they are today. In the north, big game lost their grazing lands and many became extinct, as did the mastodons, mammoths and other large mammals that were trapped on the Japanese insular chain. Others were isolated, as was the fate of the tigers which still survive on Borneo, Sumatra, Bali and in Korea, and the almost extinct orangutans on Borneo.

The present continental limits of Asia were stabilized at about the commencement of the Holocene, which antedates the development of neolithic communities by about two thousand years. Before considering this transition, the major cultural and biological developments up till then may be summarized.

In western Asia, throughout the early Stone Age (Palaeolithic) the industries reflect the European and African cultural spheres and seem to be quite distinct from those of eastern Asia. Similarly, on the biological side, finds of neanderthaloid man of the mid-Pleistocene are closer to those of Europe than are the skeletal finds of equivalent date in eastern Asia.

Southern Asia seems to be a cultural meeting ground between western and eastern Asia. As we should expect, the western and southern sections are allied more closely to western Asia, while the artefacts of parts of northern and eastern India have similarities with eastern Asia. Eastern Asia was distinctively different both culturally and biologically, except for some possible typological similarities with eastern Europe.

Northern Asia seems to have been uninhabited in the Lower Palaeolithic, except possibly easternmost Siberia, on the evidence of chopping tools and big flake artefacts of the Choukoutien variety near Vladivostok [261]. By the middle Palaeolithic northern Asia seems to combine European cultural and biological heritages in the west (Inner Asia and western Siberia) with expansions northward from China; in the east, the region of overlap falls in central Siberia and Mongolia. The central plateau of Tibet seems to have been uninhabited until late in the Neolithic. With the exception of inner Asia and Siberia as far as Lake Baikal, where the middle Palaeolithic assemblages can be linked with eastern Europe, the Asian sequences tend to develop quite independently and to reflect their local traditions.

By the beginning of historic times each of the four major regions, and varyingly the different subregions, had developed not only the foundations of their respective civilizations but also their biologically distinctive populations.

In closing this survey of what might be called 'the case for early man in Asia', it might be added that if a century ago Africa earned the title of the Dark Continent – the abode of mysterious naked savages – Asia today probably deserves the same label, but for different reasons. It is certainly as mysterious and tantalizing so far as scientific exploration is concerned. It is only a matter of time however before what appear now as dim and uncertain outlines of man's genesis will come into sharper focus. Only then shall we be able to judge accurately the role of Asia in the dawning pageant of history.

PART II

THE WESTERN QUADRANT

The Ancient Orient:
Traditions and the Verdict of History

4

Europe or Asia? A Matter of Definitions

Ever since the dawn of history a kind of reverse tug-of-war, one of pushing rather than pulling, has existed between the accultural and colonizational pressures of European conquests eastward into Asia, and of Asian incursions westward into Europe. Neither has remained permanently in the ascendancy and both have left their indelible biological and cultural heritages in the wake of the directional shifts, each of which has lasted for approximately a thousand years. Periodically both have been challenged by third forces expanding from the middle ground, the region held in turn by the Persian, Arab and Ottoman empires and referred to rather incongruously as the Middle East.

It would be impossible to separate the biological from the cultural impacts. In some periods the biological may have been more extensive or lasting; more often the wholesale religious, linguistic, aesthetic and other cultural conversions have been more pervasive and permanent.

Apart from the past few decades, which have seen the dramatic shrinkage of former vast colonial empires and the transfer of authority to scores of newly emerging nations, the pages of recent history covering the past half millennium have been concerned mainly with the building up of these empires and the rivalries between power blocs. By the end of the last century European power was paramount throughout the world and seemed likely to remain so. The empires of the east had had their day. The Ottoman Porte was finally contained, the Mughal empire dismembered and Manchu China had all but fallen apart. The white man's burden had become a reality.

During the thousand years from the final collapse of Rome and the commencement of the Hunnic invasions in the fifth century until the last phase of Ottoman expansion into the Balkans towards the end of the fifteenth century, Europe had been the constant victim of Asian conquests and colonization. For at least a millennium before that the trend was reversed. Europe went through a period of expansion: first during the hellenization of the known Orient at the expense of the Achaemenid Persians and later during the period of Roman conquests eastward temporarily as far as the Indus.

Before this the barbarian 'hordes' – a deliberate misuse of the term – of Europe were receiving the foundations of their civilizations from the ancient lands of the Near East and Egypt. By 500 BC the incursions of Indo-European-speaking peoples from the black earth regions of the Ukraine and the steppelands south of the Urals had all but ceased; but from as early as 1500 BC, roughly the commencement of the Iron Age, for some thousand years they had been the driving force throughout the entire Near East and Irania, penetrating into the Balkans and on to the plateau highlands of Anatolia and Persia and southward to the peninsulas that lay beyond. This was the formative period of both Persia and Greece, the organizational period of India and the first major period of barbarian penetration of China.

Had Rome been more concerned with the recovery of the former Greek territories and less with the conquest of Egypt and western Europe, and had it not been for the successive conquests of the various nomad empires of Asia from the fifth to the fifteenth centuries, most if not all of the earlier Hellenic world and Byzantium might conceivably have remained within the religious, political and linguistic orbit of Europe. Had this been so, the cultural line dividing the peoples of Eurasia into two continents might well have followed the eastern borders of Irania and Turania rather than the eastern borders of present-day Greece and Russia.

The underlying biological rationale for such a conjecture has a certain validity which requires exploration. It would be only one of many instances in which 'cultural transformations' obscure biological heritage. In Anatolia, for example, Turkish is now the primary language of the vast majority of the population, though the ancestry of an estimated eighty per cent of the population was probably Indo–European-speaking – Greek, Armenian and Kurdish – before the consolidation of Turkish power in Anatolia beginning under the Seljuks in the eighth century. The previous incursions of Indo–European speakers and subsequent language conversions of the conquered populations also obscured the presence of still earlier non-Indo–European speakers, about whom very little documentation survives.

The same might be said of Turkmenia until the powerful presence of the Indo–European-speaking Sarmatian and Scythic populations was gradually eclipsed by the incursions of Turkic speakers from the east. Old Iranian (Aryan) speakers – Tat and Talyesh – still inhabit parts of south-west Turkmenia and the Caucasus, and the newer Persian Tajiks occupy a corner of Chinese Turkestan. The genetic heritage is apparent in the mixed populations not only of Turkestan but even of China proper, which was penetrated by Indo–European speakers in the latter part of the second millennium BC. Were the expansions into Turkmenia in the late prehistoric period only from west to east, or had there already been movements periodically back and forth across the steppelands? Part of the answer can be derived from recorded history, part from the artefact assemblages and human remains of prehistoric populations, but always the environmental circumstances, both artificial (cultural) and natural, were powerful forces, as either deterrents or stimulants.

Each of the major and many of the minor regions of Asia have characteristically different patterns of population distribution and stability in their relationships to the land and to each other. Most are settled and layered in hierarchical social strata with varying degrees of controlled intermarriage between the strata. Others are still nomadic and tribally organized into exogamous lineages and remain isolated and aloof from miscegenation with neighbouring populations.

Asia's western quadrant not only is the most central in global perspective but has probably witnessed more cross-migrations, mixtures and mass conversions than any other part of the continent. While the intensities of the shifting eddies and currents of human movement, gene flow and political control have varied in time and space, probably no period has witnessed greater changes than the fifteen hundred years from the start of the Christian era to the beginning of the Age of Exploration.

5

The Earliest Human Settlements

The epiglacial phase from about 10,000 to 8000 BC following the end of the Pleistocene more or less coincided with the transitional Mesolithic cultural dispersals, which lasted far longer in most of northern and eastern Asia than in western Asia and Europe. Hunting and gathering remained the major sources of food, but as the bigger game continued to disappear – presumably owing to climatic changes and shrinkage in vegetation cover – new techniques had to be devised for the capture of smaller game. Man turned to the rivers and coasts: to spearing, trapping and harpooning of fish and marine mammals, and to the gathering of crustaceans and molluscs; to the making of nets and the snaring of land birds and waterfowl. In places, simple pottery and other cooking devices tremendously increased the exploitation of plant products. Hunting of smaller game meant the manufacture of smaller points, arrowheads, microlithic blades and the use of obsidian.

The Mesolithic was a preparatory stage, during which man depended mainly on the hitherto largely unexploited resources of nature. With the Neolithic came the ability to produce and store food, notably cereals such as emmer wheat, rye, barley and sesamum, and to domesticate animals such as sheep, goats, cattle and pigs. Reed [312] suggests that domestication of the dog began when it served as a source of meat, and that its continued use as a food both in Asia and aboriginal America bears out this idea. Its assistance in hunting and herding would have come later, after man learnt to corral livestock [147].

The order of domestication of various plants and animals

probably varied from region to region and was determined by the species available and the relative abundance of wild food resources during the stage of incipient agriculture [241].

The ability to control the production and storage of life's essentials encouraged the growth of larger permanent settlements, and these in turn led to technical innovation, the division of labour, the formation of social classes and ultimately the superimposition of administrative controls. Biologically, such developments meant an increase in the demographic dimensions of a limited number of populations (gene pools) – those possessing the knowledge of food production – at the expense of others who retained the earlier type of natural economy and who could not expand numerically beyond the limits set by nature.

As urban centres developed they attracted traders, artisans and labourers from ever-increasing distances, a process accentuated during the age of metals with the emergence and expansion of empires and the commencement of the historic period about 3000 BC. For a millennium or more after the start of this first 'population explosion' western and Inner Asia remained the most favoured quarters because they were the homeland regions of so many of the ancestral wild forms of the most important cultivated plants and animals. By the end of this period, the Nile Valley and the adjacent Abyssinian highlands had developed a comparable neolithic nexus and similar developments can be traced in the Indus Valley, the Yellow River basin and in at least one if not two river basins of south-east Asia, not to mention that of the Danube in Europe.

Among the oldest known proto-neolithic (about 8000 to 6500 BC) open settlement sites are those of Tell-es-Sultan, near ancient Jericho in the Jordan Valley, Zawi-Chemi and nearby Shanidar in Iraq Kurdistan, and Ali Kosh in Khuzistan. The earliest levels at the first two sites are termed Natufian because they are characterized by the same general artefact and bone assemblages as were found at an earlier cave site in Wadi-el-Natuf on the seaward slope of Mt Carmel. The people who camped seasonally in rock shelters and at the mouths of caves and in the first open settlement sites could not have numbered more than two hundred individuals. At least a dozen similar sites of slightly later date have been located in the same general area as well as a number of others discovered more recently at Belbasi,

Beldibi rock shelter and Öküzlü'In in southern Anatolia [241, pp. 9–30]. When studies of these assemblages have been completed they may even surpass the Palestinian sites in antiquity. Altogether some thirty cave and open camp sites have been discovered from this early proto-Neolithic period, and their regional limits are likely to expand.

Iran is not as well known prehistorically as Syria or Iraq but at least three early sites have been excavated containing artefacts ranging in date from the middle Palaeolithic to current occupancy in one case by families of dervishes. The vast flat saline-encrusted sandstone heart of the central plateau, which was covered by a brackish lake until neolithic times, will probably yield only scattered surface artefacts, but the opposite is true of the surrounding rim of Jurassic limestone foothills. These outer slopes, including those of the Zagros and Elburz ranges, extend in a fifty- to hundred-mile-wide band around the plateau from the 1500-foot contour level to the watershed and, in sections at least, are literally 'peppered with caves' [68]. From among this plethora of caves and rock shelters four were selected for excavation: Tam Tama near Lake Urmia; Bisitun near Kermanshah in Khuzistan; and Belt and Hotu Caves in Mazanderan overlooking the Caspian Sea.

Hotu Cave has been referred to in connection with its mousteroid artefacts and neanderthaloid skeletal remains. At this level, man's food consisted mainly of cold and temperate climate ungulates – gazelles, wild sheep, goats and oxen, deer, elephants, horses and pigs. The recently excavated site of Djebel Cave suggests the possibility that it was in this region of Mazanderan and neighbouring southern Turkestan that the first domestication of animals took place.

While proto-neolithic settlers advanced to food production, the remaining mesolithic hunters sought out the most favoured alluvial fans and river valleys. Some were along the rivers flowing into the central plateau lake or where the lake shores were sufficiently sweet to support marsh grasses and waterfowl. Much of the surrounding terrain also provided grazing for domestic flocks and wild game. At least one neolithic site, Sialk, has been located east of the Zagros Mountains and not too far from the ancient lake shore.

The full Neolithic, which began in different communities between the seventh and sixth millennia BC, was not characterized by a uniform step-by-step technological sequence from one type of artefact to another, or in types of ceramic ware – some cultures were aceramic – or even in house types and settlement patterns; rather, it was an adjustment of the genius and whim of separate small communities to the ecological resources and advantages of local environments. The classic notion that the Neolithic implied universally the presence of specified domesticated plants and animals, pottery, polished stone tools and stereotyped settlement patterns is quite erroneous; nor were the biological consequences to man uniformly the same.

Permanent settlements of substantial size with populations ranging from a few hundred to two or three thousand began to develop at such sites as Çatal Huyuk and Haliçar in the south-central plateau along the slopes of the Taurus Mountains of southern Anatolia and in the arc of the Fertile Crescent, and trade objects began to move in ever-increasing quantity throughout the area. In Iraq the best known sites are Karim Shahir and Jarmo, and in Palestine the most extensive is Jericho. On the Iranian plateau the mound site of Sialk near Kashan was occupied periodically from Neolithic to recent times. During the earliest period the inhabitants dwelt in lean-to shelters. Later they built houses of poured mud walls (pisé or adobe) and finally of sun-dried brick. The pottery changed from black to black-on-red painted ware similar to some of the wares of Elam and Turkestan. At the same level, spindle whorls proved the use of textiles, probably of wool from domesticated flocks. In the final phases metal was in use. The dead of the painted ware period were smeared with red ochre and buried in a flexed position under the houses; many wore shell ornaments from the Persian Gulf.

Among the later neolithic sites are Susa in the Elamitic foothills north of the modern Ahwaz, Tepe Hissar near Damghan, and Tepe Giyan near Nihavend. All were occupied well into the historic period and the inhabitants must have played important roles during the periods of pillage, invasion and conquest that plagued the city-states of Mesopotamia from Sumerian times onward. An important feature of the Zagros terrain is the rather forbidding 9000-foot Pusht-i-Kuh ('Mountains of Snow') range which extends for some 250 miles from the bend of the Diyala River north-east of Baghdad to the southward bend of the

Karkheh near Susa. It was this barrier more than any other that limited effective access in strength between Mesopotamia and Irania to two regions: the valleys and mountain passes near the Diyala and Zab Rivers in the north – the present Iraq Kurdistan – and the valleys and mountain passes near the Karkheh and Karun Rivers in the ancient land of Elam (Susiana), the now rich agricultural province of Khuzistan east of Basra.

As early mercantilism developed it became an important factor in knitting together the social fabric of local communities into village units and regional societies. By Neolithic times a small trade-connected cluster of such village units had become recognizable in northern Syria and southern Anatolia, each village with a number of common as well as distinctive cultural features – material, religious and aesthetic – and probably speaking dialect variants of a common language or group of languages. A similar cluster with different cultural characteristics developed in the Kurdish and Zagros foothills of the Iranian highlands, and a third cluster was formed along the Levantine coast in Palestine and Syria. At a somewhat later time a fourth cluster seems to have developed in the foothills along the Red Sea escarpment of Arabia, revealing language affiliations with yet another complex crystalized in the adjacent highland foothills of Ethiopia.

It may prove impossible to determine how many clusters there were and which of them is the oldest. With the exception of the Arabian escarpment, about which so little is known, each cluster of artefact assemblages seems to have certain features which appear to antedate the same or comparable traits in each of the other clusters. At best, it seems likely that priority will be established not by village clusters or even on the basis of separate village communities, but by traits. What appears to be old in one micro-society appears late in another, and so on, in a kind of mixture of shared diffusion and discrete innovation. Each community appears as a distinctive mosaic and attempts at grouping suffer from the same difficulties as plague biologists and linguists who concern themselves respectively with 'races', 'families' and 'stocks'. At best, one can speak only of the characteristics of specific sites or regions, always bearing in mind the possibility of stimulus as opposed to direct diffusion and of innovation (discovery or invention) either more or less simultaneously or at different times. Consistent patterns of development appear to be exceedingly rare until the emergence of effective political controls, which generally imposed different degrees of conformity at different levels of administration.

South of the Fertile Crescent, climatic changes during the early Holocene transformed the Arabian peninsula much as they did other parts of the Near East. In the earlier periods Arabia was mainly savanna-covered and provided forage for large game animals and their parasitic palaeolithic hunting populations. As amelioration of the climate continued and the tundra and forest belt in the northern parts of the continent receded, the peninsula became increasingly dessicated and reached its present level of aridity by about the commencement of the Neolithic. In the northern fringe, hunting persisted but on a limited scale and, as the Neolithic progressed in the desert–steppe, domesticated animals were introduced: first sheep and goats (*c.* 6000 BC) from the surrounding highland foothills, then cattle and pigs (*c.* 3000 BC). The camel came from Turkmenia into Assyria about 3000 BC and spread to the Jazira and on southward around the margins of the true desert. Soon after the onager or Iranian donkey was added to the list; the horse, which later became famous in Arabia, was not introduced until the second millennium BC. With these changes, which drastically reduced the grazing lands, there developed simultaneously a symbiosis between hunter and nomad pastoralist, and also a special kind of interdependence between the nomad pastoralists and the sedentary populations of which they were adapted extensions.

The cultural transformations that occurred between the tenth and fifth millennia BC were tremendous throughout the Near East, and on the basis of subsequent developments it can probably be assumed that concern for the supernatural and the after-life had kept pace with material progress, though very little has been recovered in the way of intentional burials. Skeletal remains from the Mesolithic are exceedingly rare and it is doubtful if 'two distinct races' can be distinguished, as stated by Mellaart [241, p. 14]. The two races referred to are termed 'graceful proto-Mediterranean' and 'somewhat sturdier Eurafrican'. While the use of such terms is questionable, the remains do indicate a wide phenotypic range, however inadequate they may be for statistical analysis.

By Neolithic times a few common burial grounds are identifiable and by the historic period special treatment of the dead, especially of the élite, was a common practice. 'Royal' or princely tombs, many of which contained the skeletons of scores of attendants and slaves, can be traced back at least five thousand years. It is noteworthy that all of the human remains, both proto-historic and historic, fall skeletally well within the general range of today's populations in the same general areas.

For this last reason the idea has been advanced that since Neolithic times most of the currently identifiable 'aboriginal' and older minority populations have either remained in their present marginal refuge areas – such as mountain valleys, jungle forests and insular outposts – or form the genetic substrata of the majority populations occupying the fertile alluvial valleys. These usually comprise the technologically superior farming, manufacturing and trading communities whose numerical expansions are attributable largely to their productive capacity, efficiency in commercial enterprises, exploitation of marine resources or in the attractions they provided to aliens. The latter may be minimal or extreme at any level: elites from conquest or commerce; middle-class traders and merchants; craftsmen; or labourers at the subsistence level. Changes in gene pools occur constantly and from at least four causes: equilibrial responses to adaptive pressures, frequency alterations owing to gene flow and miscegenation, mutations, and chance factors attributable to drift – all affecting gene structure.

6

Greater Syria and Arabia: the Semitic Sphere

ANCIENT SYRIA

The earliest periods of lowland cultivation (alluvial tillage) are known as Hassuna-Samarran (*c.* 5500–5000 BC) and Halafian (*c.* 5000–4500 BC) after their type sites of Hassuna and Samarra on the middle Tigris and Halaf on a tributary of the middle Euphrates. They differed from the earlier foothill valley sites by the addition of copper ornaments and mixed copper-alloy tools, which classifies them as chalcolithic, but during the next two periods – Ubaid and Uruk–Gawra – which lasted somewhat over a thousand years, the transition to true farming was both rapid and spectacular. Unlike the foothill sites, which were abandoned as communities moved down to the plains, the lowland settlements were established in permanent favourable spots above the flood level. They grew in successive layers into what are known today as *tepe* or settlement mounds, which frequently reached such heights that recovery of the earliest levels is exceedingly difficult. Roughly, 4500 BC can be taken as the beginning of irrigated wheat fields and date palm groves surrounding the settlements. The following Jemdet–Nasr period (*c.* 3100–2900 BC) witnessed the first development of urban life and the close of the preliterate period.

Much has been written concerning the expansion of populations during the Neolithic, but the potential for truly rapid expansion was not achieved until after the shift to the plains. Even so, such sites as Uruk (Erech, the modern Warka) probably did not exceed three thousand inhabitants and preliterate Jemdet–Nasr was not much larger, although its emergence marks the beginning of urban communities with relatively complex religio-political institutions and social stratification.

The first people to be identified historically were the Sumerians who occupied the lower reaches of the twin river basin. Their settlements began about 3000 BC and by 2800 BC, which was well into the Bronze Age, at least thirteen independent city-states had been established including Ur, Eridu, Kish, Umma, Lagash, Isin and Larsa. The populations have been estimated to range from about ten thousand for the smallest to thirty thousand for Lagash [315, p. 112]. Thus far no one has been able positively to identify the Sumerians linguistically, and the skeletal remains are too limited and poorly preserved to be of much help in comparative studies. They probably would fall within the range of many of the neolithic collections from the Middle East and the Indus Valley [69].

Although languages are notoriously untrustworthy as indicators of biological heritage, they often reveal much better than fragmentary bits of bone the interskeining of relationships at any given time and within a given region between communities and nations. This is particularly true of an area such as western Asia, which is so rich both in caches of well preserved clay tablets and in the number and antiquity of known written languages.

Sumerian, an agglutinative language, is the oldest known written language to have been deciphered [191]. While its closest affiliations remain uncertain, structural and vocabulary similarities have been noted with Elamitic, an ancient language of the Zagros foothills; with the Caucasian complex sometimes referred to as Japhetic; with ancient Altaic which by a stretch of the term might be called proto-Turkic [190]; and with the cluster of early languages of Anatolia often referred to as Asianic but more recently identified as Caucasian. The ties, in any event, seem to be with the languages of the northern and eastern highlands rather than with ancient Semitic, and on this basis a movement of highland peoples, possibly from the region of the Caspian Sea on the plains, is postulated [22].

Futher east, the recently excavated site of Tepe Yahya, about sixty miles inland from Bandar Abbas at the strait of Hormuz on the Persian Gulf [199], merits attention. From the evidence of cuneiform tablets, the city was contemporary with Sumerian civilization and has been described as 'proto-Elamitic'. It appears to have been a trading post between the Mesopotamian and Indus Valley civilizations, the first of its kind to have been discovered in Irania, west of Baluchistan, although water route stops are known to have existed near Jask and Bahrein.

Wherever the Sumerians came from, their sophisticated city-states served as models for their successors. Even before Sumerian times, probably as early as the beginning of the fourth millennium, proto-Semites had begun to settle in the middle Mesopotamian region north of Sumer and opposite the Zagros. They came both from the south, along the Arabian coast of the Persian Gulf, and from the western part of the Fertile Crescent, the latter migration emerging as the Akkadians after the name of their city state Agade. By the end of the third millennium they had absorbed and finally conquered Sumer under the leadership of Sargon I after the Sumerians had become merely an elite priestly aristocracy ruling over a largely Semitic farming population into which they were ultimately assimilated. An interesting note concerning the farming communities was their practice of maintaining communal inter-settlement groves and grazing grounds known as *edin* or *eden* – inspiration possibly for the fabled biblical Garden of Eden [315, p. 111]. Half a century later the new Semitic empire of Akkadia was invaded by the Guti from Gudea in the Commagene region of Iraqi Kurdistan, but the Guti formed only an élite veneer who held control for less than a century.

A third dynasty was briefly revived at Ur but was so weakened by continuing Elamite encroachments from the adjacent Zagros foothills that it fell easy prey to a new influx of Semites from Syria – the Amorites. Like their predecessors, the Amorites were probably also mixed with migrants from the Anatolian plateau and they too settled along the desert margin rivers, but in the region just north of Akkadia. The first Amoritic cities were Ashur or Assur and later Babylon, whose most famous ruler and lawgiver was Hammurabi. The name Amu or Amor was originally the designation of a region in northern Syria, but during the eighteenth century the Amoritic empire assumed the name of Assyria after the first capital Ashur. At its height Assyria incorporated most of the cities to the south as well as the west Semitic lands of Canaan and Phoenicia and the plateau region of Urartu to the north. Southward, Assyria maintained a rather tenuous and intermittent hold on the Nile delta but, though its power fluctuated, it survived for nearly a millennium.

During the Assyrian period the states of Media north of the Zagros, Persis to the south and Urartu were consolidated and by the end of the second millennium BC Assyria was being increasingly challenged by their growing strength. As defensive measures the Assyrians launched campaigns against them and adopted the policy of replacing captured prisoners with Semites from Syria. This wholesale transplanting of vanquished populations has been expressed as 'a veritable shuffling of peoples' [126] and if figures can be trusted, as many as 65,000 Median prisoners were settled in the foothills and as many plains-dwellers were sent to the plateau. Similar resettlements were conducted in the south and in Urartu, and when Samaria was conquered in the eighth century BC, 30,000 Israelites were exiled to Media. In spite of these efforts, the pressures continued from all sides, and, while the Assyrian empire at its height reached from the Caspian Sea to Egypt, it was unable to stop the plague of minor incursions from Irania. Assyria's final defeat, however, was at the hands of a revived southern Mesopotamia in 612 BC, under the Chaldean kings of Babylon. These had temporarily aligned themselves with the Medes but later gained control of the entire Fertile Crescent area and held it for nearly a century. The identity of the Chaldeans is not clear. The name appears to be a corruption of Khaldu, an ancient Semitic tribe which originated in the coastal southlands along the Persian Gulf, and is probably not to be confused with the Khaldu of Cappadocia in Anatolia.

The next people to emerge in the unfolding Semitic drama were the Aramaeans, whose homeland, like that of the Amorites, was along the 'saddle' of Syria and in southern Cappadocia above the bend of the Crescent. They had acquired the camel and probably some genetic admixture from the Aral basin. They first appear on the horizon about 1000 BC as 'uncouth Bedouin' nomads [315, pp. 227–8]. Their way of life, like that of their successors, was more commercial – if that is the word – than imperial.

The Aramaeans were not fated to develop an empire. They expanded rather slowly in their Syrian homeland where they established a number of cities identifiable in history by names incorporating the prefix *bitu* or 'house' (cf. Beth-le-hem and

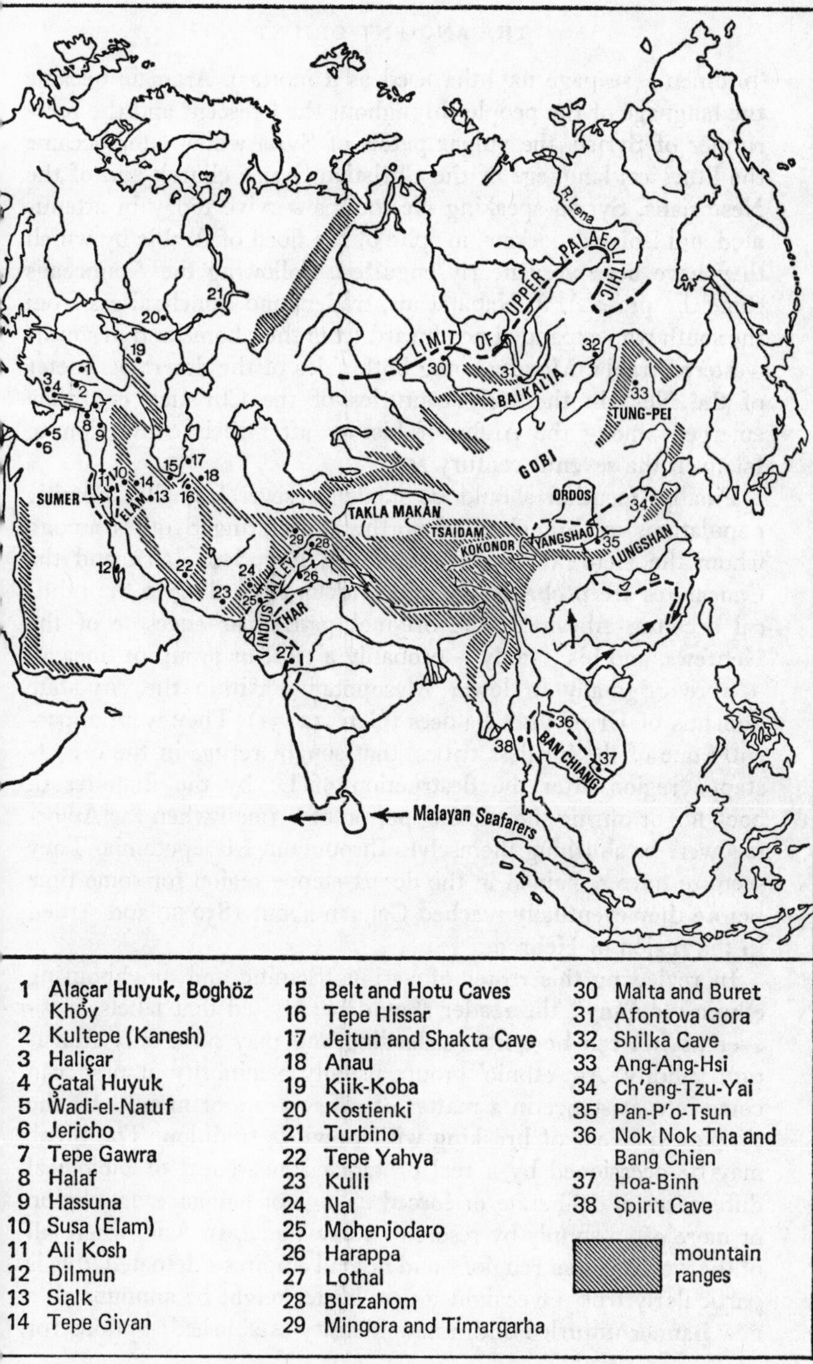

Map 5 Early settlements and focal areas of Asia's major populations (3000–1500 BC)

'bitumen' – seepage naphtha used as a mortar). Aramaic became the language of the people throughout the Crescent and the forerunner of Syriac, the vulgar patois of Syria which later became the liturgical language of the Christian Syriac church and of the Nestorians. Syrian-speaking Nestorians survive today in attenuated and isolated pockets, in spite of the flood of Arabic by which they have been very nearly engulfed. Following the Aramaeans came the proto-Arab Nabataeans, traders and camel-raisers from the south who expanded northward from their homeland in southwestern Arabia. Moving along both sides of the desert perimeter of the Nejd in the early centuries of the Christian era, they emerged among the Arabs of history after their conversion to Islam in the seventh century AD.

Finally, mention should be made of several smaller Semitic populations or 'branches' of northward-drifting Semites among whom the Hebrews (Semitic Habiru), Egyptian *Apiru* and the Canaanites are probably the best known. According to the biblical account, Abraham, the original patrilinear ancestor of the Hebrews, and his 'family' – probably a tribe or group of lineages – were originally in lower Mesopotamia within the city-state domains of Ur of the Chaldees (Gen. 12:31). They were apparently one of the 'restless tribes' that sought refuge in the desert-steppe region after the destruction of Ur by the Elamites in 2006 BC, or during the ensuing period of turmoil when the Amorites were establishing themselves throughout Mesopotamia. They seem to have remained in the desert-steppe region for some time before they eventually reached Canaan about 1850 BC and settled in the region of Hebron.

In reviewing this roster of various Semitic and neighbouring ethnic groupings, the reader should be advised that labels, however useful, can be quite misleading and may have only transitory validity. An 'ethnic' group, usually a minority at first, can come into existence in a matter of a few years or months by the simple expedient of breaking with previous tradition. The break may be occasioned by a real or fancied awareness of biological differences, a deliberate or forced change of language or religion or more often simply by resort to a new name. In Asia, where all of the world's great religions and nomad empires originated, this is particularly true. Overnight a new leader might be announced, a new banner unfurled and a new identity established; options for such developments are enhanced where populations are mobile and fanaticism easily intensified. Ethnic identity is not to be confused simply with the modern trend towards political independence; patriotism as an overriding virtue seems to have been a peculiarly European invention. The ancient and most significant value attached to loyalty has always been more characteristic of parts of the world where it has been given to a specific religious leader, liege lord or lineage rather than to a country or to humanity. In this sense, Asia has possibly had more than its share of extreme loyalties.

The numerically greatest nomadic as well as settled populations have been Asian, and until the development of the maritime empires of medieval and modern Europe the greatest empires were also Asian. The problems therefore of determining ethnic identities and continuities over the past five thousand years – roughly the span of history – become well nigh insuperable. Of the hundreds if not thousands of names of peoples that have flashed across the pages of history, probably less than half can be positively identified by anything more than names; and even though language, religion or material culture may be positively determined, such labels generally fail to identify biological ancestry or heritage. Even genealogies, more often than not fictive in their beginnings, have become notorious bulwarks of religiously oriented fanaticism rather than indicators of true kin networks – especially when the fates of leaders, nations and empires are at stake.

Methods of burial or other forms of disposal are also crucial to any biological study of ancient peoples, but many tend to destroy rather than preserve – cremation, exposure to vultures, wolves and the elements, and especially watery burials. With rare exceptions such as mummification or freezing, the only biologically useful remains are skeletal. Various art forms may offer clues to ancestral identity but few such portrayals can be fully trusted. Often it is only the élite whose identities are thus preserved or survive through burial and the masses, whether 'civilized' or 'barbarian', pass unmentioned into the lost pages of the past. Skeletal remains are best preserved in arid regions where dessication is quick and burial in sandy soil easy. The relative thinness of the population also makes the conservation of space less necessary. Throughout western Asia, burial has been mostly by ordinary inhumation in cemeteries protected from predation; but, by the same token, fear of disturbing the dead has frequently prevented the remains from being studied, even those from pre-Islamic times.

By the beginning of the second millennium, Egypt had lost much of the political and military cohesion that had characterized the Old Empire and was unprepared to resist the pressures of barbarian invaders from Palestine who infiltrated the delta region during the late eighteenth century BC. There is some uncertainty about the identity of the Palestinians – the Greek rendering of the biblical Philistines – although based on the depicted facial features, clothing, weaponry and associated artistic motifs they appear to have been mainly migrants from Minoan Crete (Keftiu). Following the Palestinians, the later invaders are known in history as the Hyksos but their identity remains uncertain. They may have been 'Canaanites' who had acquired the use of the war chariot from Phoenicia, which was at that time being subjected to incursions by chariot-using Indo–European Hittitic and Semitic–Aramaic invaders from the north and probably by maritime marauders along the coast.

During the period of confusion arising from the Palestinian–Canaanitic invasion and infiltration of lower Egypt, some of the Hebrews took advantage of the situation and migrated to Egypt partly to escape the Assyrian invasion from the east but mainly as a relief from local famines in Canaan. The 'escape' later from Egypt under the leadership of Moses took place about the middle of the sixteenth century BC, after the Egyptians had managed to drive the intruding Hyksos from the delta.

GREATER SYRIA IN MEDIEVAL AND MODERN TIMES

Sur, or Suri, was originally a small district in the upper Euphratic steppeland, but 'Syria' was used in Graeco–Roman times to include what came to be known as the Levantine coast and the valley of the Orontes. During the Ottoman period it was limited specifically to the adjacent district of Sham in the steppe-desert highlands of the Hamad (Hamath) with its capital at Damascus, one of the original strongholds of the Amorites. The name has been applied loosely since then to different segments of the Fertile Crescent and to the entire region between Turkey and the Nejd in Arabia. Syria has never had any natural geographical limits except possibly in the north, and did not emerge as an independent nation until very recent times. Prior to its nominal conquest by Egypt in the middle of the second millennium BC, when the Hyksos were driven from the Nile delta, it was a land divided among rival city-states. From ancient Egyptian times to the end of the First World War, Syria was a province of an alien empire or the administrative seat of alien rulers. Possibly a more ethnically correct name for the present state of Syria would be Aram, the land of the Aramaic people, the Arabic Esh Sham.

The Babylonian conquest of Syria and Palestine was largely political and military, but after the destruction of Jerusalem in 586 BC many Jews moved south into Egypt and colonies of defeated Assyrians from Mesopotamia moved westward into Syria, some migrating as far south as Samaria, the ancient kingdom of the northern Hebrews. Most of the newcomers accepted the schizmatic faith of the northern Jews, but northern Judaism had already begun to incorporate the worship of a number of Syrian and Assyrian gods into its religious practices and it was this heretical trend that led to the final break between the Samaritans of the north and the Jews of Judea, the land between the Dead Sea and the Mediterranean. Even greater changes occurred after the death of Alexander and the breakup of the Macedonian empire into three rival kingdoms: the homelands and Phrygia under the Antigonids; Syria, Armenia and Babylonia and parts of Irania under the Seleucids; and Egypt and Palestine under the Ptolemies. It was during the Seleucid–Ptolemic period (*c.* 323–50 BC) that hellenization of the whole of western Asia reached its peak. The language of most of greater Syria had previously become Aramaic except among some of the Hebrews, but during the three-hundred-year period under the Seleucids and Ptolemies Greek became the everyday language even of the elite Syrians and many of the Hebrews. Greek temples to Dionysus were built around the Crescent and even the strongholds of Judaism were invaded. Many Hebrews forsook their religion and the very fate of their spoken language was at stake. Thus by a quirk of fate, while a number of upper-class Jews were turning to Syrian Hellenism, Aramaic peasants were being converted to Judaism.

In the second century BC, after the power of the Ptolemies over Palestine had weakened, Syrian forces moved southward and sought to destroy the nationalistic spirit that continued to characterize the heart of Judaism. About this time also the first serious inroads were being made into the settled regions of the north by southern Arabs and Bedouin from the Nejd. As a last hellenizing effort on the part of the Seleucids, Jerusalem was seized and the Temple converted to the worship of Zeus Olympius, but even this effort proved abortive. By the end of the second century, a Jewish rebellion under Judas Maccabeus not only recovered Jerusalem but turned the tide in favour of Judaism. Eventually, however, the opposing power of the Hellenic Jews was too strong for the Maccabeans and they in turn were defeated by their own co-religionists and scorned as apostates. This was only one of the many internal dissensions among the Jews, who never regained the unity they had enjoyed under David and Solomon. With the ultimate demise of the Seleucids and the succession of Rome to power, the schisms among the Jews were merely compounded. Many turned to Rome for assistance; others joined forces with the weakened Ptolemies and some even served in the Egyptian army. Still others went into exile in Arabia and Abyssinia.

In the time of Christ, the Pharisees – successors to the Hasideans – a reorganized remnant of the Maccabean rebels, and the Sadducees – whose identity stemmed from the denial of immortality and the existence of angels – were only two of the many powerful contending factions, most of which were opposed to the hellenized Herod. It was not until the final destruction of the Temple in AD 70 that the spirit of the Jews seemed finally to have been broken and a new era commenced for that strife-torn people. The dispersal (Diaspora) that had started under Assyrian rule in 721 BC was increased during the period of Babylonian oppression and greatly accelerated with the destruction of the Temple. Most of the new exiles settled in the circum-Mediterranean area, especially in Egypt, though the process of exiling lasted for centuries. In Himyaritic times (*c.* AD 400) many went to the Yemen, and still others moved northward into Asia Minor. They expanded numerically through intermarriage and conversion and many moved on into the Balkans and throughout Europe, with concentrations in the central and eastern states. This northern migration, named after the Ashkenaz district of northern Anatolia, although much 'diluted' through miscegenation, accounts for over ninety per cent of today's total Jewish population. The Sephardic Jews, who account for most of the remainder, were originally Judeans who had migrated gradually along both sides of the Mediterranean to Spain from which they were expelled in 1492.

Throughout the centuries since its period of vassalage to Rome, Palestine has continued to remain a land of strife and contention. At the partition of the Roman empire in AD 395 it became nominally Christian and, in addition to attracting pilgrims from throughout Christendom, became also the lost Holy Land of many Jews. The defeat of Byzantium in AD 636 marked the turning point not only of eastern Christendom but also of the newly emerging religious empire of Islam. Christian monasteries and churches were destroyed and communicants were massacred or converted to the new religion. Immigrant Arabs began to settle and, as rivalries over succession to the caliphate intensified, a series of schismatic rebellions followed. One of the most serious was that of the white banner Omayyads (Umayyads) who moved the seat of government from Mecca to Damascus only to be followed by the black banner Abbasids who transferred it to Baghdad. In AD 936 Egypt broke away under the Fatimids and fifty years later Fatimid Egypt was ruled for a time by a mad monarch whose fanatical followers hailed him as an incarnate deity. The story of his career makes a fascinating page in history, but more permanent was the creation of a new cult which survives today among the Druzes in the Hauran and in their mountain refuge on the border between Syria and Jordan.

One of the darkest periods in Palestinian history and of Christendom was that of the Crusades, nine in all, between 1096 and 1272. Little remains of these abortive efforts to recapture the holy places except the ruins of a few castles and the memory of the thousands who perished, including most of the fifty thousand or so children who died of diseases or were drowned at sea during the course of the notorious Children's Crusade. Subsequently, Palestine and Syria were subjected to successive invasions from the east, first by the Kurds, whose best known leader, Saladin, was responsible for the defeat of the Third Crusade; then by the turkicized Mongol Tamerlane (Timur), followed by the Egyptians under the Mamelukes and lastly by the Ottoman Turks.

During the four hundred years under Turkish rule Arabic, the language of 'The Book', spread rapidly in its displacement of Aramaic, and wherever Turkish officials were not essential they were generally replaced by Arabs. Only in the northern Levant around Alexandretta, Aleppo and Antioch were Turkish settlements of any size established. A secondary effect of Turkish domination was the movement southward of displaced Muslims from the Balkans and Caucasia who had earlier sought refuge in Anatolia from czarist oppression but had subsequently been relocated in greater Syria.

With the defeat of Turkey after the First World War and the establishment of the British and French mandates, most of the Turks returned to Turkey; Syrians and Palestinians assumed more prominence in public affairs; and the pressure of Christians and Jews was lessened. Many of the latter who had earlier fled their homeland began returning from their various exiles, and, when partition finally came to Palestine after the Second World War, another era began for the children of Israel. The paramount purpose of the zionist cause was to fulfil the millennial dream of recovering the lost homeland. The dream was based almost wholly on religious nationalism and not on economic or extra-ethnic considerations. Israel received an influx of Arabic-speaking Sephardic Jews from countries in north Africa and the Middle East and simultaneously contingents of refugee Europeans, but there was no expectation that Israel would emerge as a military-economic threat to the Arab world.

In the biological realm it seems likely that in time a measure of genetic stability will be achieved in Israel, but for the present the tendency to maintain a variety of separate, culturally conditioned, self-perpetuating immigrant populations is strong. It will continue to remain so as long as emotional and economic ties with previous lands of sojourn are maintained at their present levels. Probably no state has concerned itself more with the genetic and related bio-medical consequences of immigration and miscegenation than has Israel. The fear of latent disease vectors, of undesirable genetic strains, and ultimately of overpopulation are of paramount concern [131]. Nor is the cultural mosaic considered any less significant. A modernized Hebrew–Jewish common culture does appear to be emerging, but its ultimate distinguishing characteristics will unquestionably stamp it as remarkably alienated from ancient Palestinian traditions and from the surviving native population. Israel is assuming more the appearance of an amalgamated and transplanted European nation than that of an Asian state. For these reasons the recent immigrants, mainly Ashkenazic communities, have been omitted from the present study which is concerned primarily with the older native Palestinian populations, both Jewish and Gentile, including the religiously isolated Samaritan colony at Nablus (Shechem) and samples of old Jewish mercantile colonies in neighbouring countries. Omitted also are the small colonies of Afro-Asian Jews – Yemenite, Hashemite, Ethiopian and Indian – whose relationships as immigrants in their new homeland are more like those of alien minorities than segments of a majority population.

North of Palestine, modern Syria and Lebanon have continued to be arabized but the cleavage between the true Arab Bedouin and the sedentary arabized Syrians (Aramaeans) is more marked than in Palestine, where the greatest differences can be noted between the settled Arabs of the urban and oasis centres and the Bedouin of the desert–steppelands.

In Lebanon there is a marked contrast in environments and inhabitants between the narrow coastal shoreline with its commercial port cities – the ancient Phoenicia – and the limestone ranges of the interior, whose chalk-white colour gave the country its name (cf. semitic *laban* – 'white'). The inhabitants of the urban centres are thoroughly cosmopolitan and mainly orthodox – Muslim, Christian, Jewish or Armenian – but the mountains have provided refuge for a number of esoteric sects. In the anti-Lebanon range are the Arabic-speaking Shiite Metwali (Mitwali), probably Aramaeans, but claiming Persian descent. The Moranites, a schismatic Christian sect living mainly in the northern mountains, were originally Monophysites or Gnostics, and in spite of their conversion to the Roman Church between the eighth and twelfth centuries, traces of their earlier Monophysitic and Gnostic beliefs still set them apart as a separate community. Other Christians, mainly in Syria, include colonies of Greek Orthodox, Greek Catholics, Syrian Orthodox, Syrian Catholics, Armenian Chaldeans, Jacobites and, more recently, various Protestant denominations. In Syria, in addition to the Druzes, two other secretive Shiite communities deserve mention – the Ismailis at Homs and around Antioch, and the Alawiya in the Levant.

Both stem from the Fatimites who trace the caliphate through Muhammad's daughter Fatima and her husband Ali, rather than through his nephew Omar. The Ismaili, otherwise known as Assassins, trace the caliph ('successor') through Ismail, the great-great-grandson of Ali's second son Hosain; the Alawiya follow another closely related line.

The Levant – from the French *lever* ('to rise', viz. the Orient) – is applied rather loosely to the entire Anatolian–Syrian coastal strip between Lebanon and Hatay (Antioch) – the ancient Laodicea, the 'Liche' of the Crusades. Under French mandate it was named the territory of the Alaouites, the northernmost concentration of the Alawiya known locally also as Nosairi, Nusairiyeh, Ansharie or Ansariye, who number nearly half a million and form two-thirds of the total population. The remainder are mostly Syrian, Armenian, Turkish and European merchants engaged in the tobacco trade and general commerce.

Most of the villagers of the fertile lands adjoining the Hamath in Syria, such as those of Hafar, Mharde, Hijane and the intermontane Bekaa Valley of Lebanon – the site of the Roman district seat and the temple of Baal-bek – are arabized Aramaean Muslims intermixed with a few Christian communities. The larger urban centres of Damascus, Aleppo, Homs and Hama, though perhaps eighty per cent Muslim, maintain segregated quarters for Christians, Jews and other minority sects.

In northern Syria and Iraq the steppe region of the 'saddle' – the Sur of the ancient Semites and the Zor of Ottoman times – has served as the grazing ground for flocks and the spawning ground for nomad pastoralists ever since Neolithic times. Doubtless the same time depth applies to the major steppe–desert and Euphrates trade routes which connect the Syrian urban centres with such Iraqi–Mesopotamian cities as Mosul, Baghdad, Hilla (Babylon), Kish and Basra.

Today Bedouin Arabs occupy most of the grazing grounds, which extend across the Iraq border into Turkey. Only in the riverine settlements and trade routes oases, including the renowned Palmyra and Zenobia, are arabized Syrians – the mixed descendants of Amorites, Akkadians, Assyrians and Aramaeans – in the majority. Undoubtedly, these descendants of the early northern Semites have mixed with the Armenians of Anatolia just as their forbears intermarried with the proto-Armenian Khaldu or Khaldis, the 'Chaldeans' of Xenophon's account.

Eastward in Iraq the pressures of the immigrant Arabs, both Bedouin and 'settled', have been even more marked than in Syria but only since the beginning of Islamic times. In the earlier periods, the contest for land and trade was largely between remnant colonies of Ottomans, reminders of the period of the sultanate, and proto-Arab Nabataeans with their trading headquarters at Petra, together with their northern Semite predecessors.

In modern Iraq – the ancient land of Nimrod which corresponds roughly to the limits of biblical Babylonia – the majority population considers itself a homogeneous nation although its genetic structure is probably less stable than that of Syria–Palestine, in spite of the patchwork of religious communities in the latter area. During early historic times, the greatest migrations into Iraq were by northern Semites from Syria into Mesopotamia, with varying degrees of admixture from the Anatolian foothill populations – Hurri, Hatti and Hittite. Today it is these northern Semites and later settled Bedouin from Arabia who comprise the larger part of the Iraqi nation. The pressures from the Iranian plateau, apart from the earliest Sumerian intrusion, were largely secondary: Gutean, Elamitic and Kassite. During the succeeding Achaemenid period there was great destruction of cities and movement of the native Semitic peoples back into Syria and Palestine, but if historical accounts can be trusted the garrisoned armies of Xerxes and Darius were largely withdrawn after their defeat by the Macedonians. The same cannot be said of the Graeco–Roman period. Alexander settled a hundred or more Greek–Macedonian communities in greater Syria, Irania, Turkmenia and the Indus Valley and at least a score of major cities still bear his name. According to Herodotus, ten thousand colonists were brought from the homelands and Phrygia, and more thousands are recorded in other sources. A great many of these later returned under Parthian pressure, but enough of the genetic and cultural heritage remained to provide an element of romance to the historic traditions of the entire regional span from Alexandretta to Kandahar. Real or fancied evidences of blondism are frequently referred to, though blue eyes and blondism are not characteristic of the majority of Greeks and Macedonians. More often, references are to the Apollo-like aquiline noses and facial features, which are by no means limited to the Grecian homelands (cf. [47]).

The Indo–European-speaking Kurds, whose origin may be a mixture of Guti, Kassites and later intrusive early Iranians, form today one of the most powerful and vocal minorities in Iraq, but their nationalistic aspirations have failed to reach a level of unity with their kinsfolk in neighbouring lands. Of the five to six million or more Kurds, roughly eighty-five per cent are divided equally between Turkey and Iraq. The remainder are divided between Iran and the Trans-Caucasus states of the Soviet Union. Their high point in history was their emergence as the Ruwendian (Ayyubite) empire during the period of the Crusades. Scattered throughout the Kurdish foothills are communities of Assyrians (Aisors), Nestorians – who claim descent from the Assyrians of ancient fame – and colonies of Armenians and Turkmeni.

Iraq harbours also a number of other minor esoteric sects such as the Mandaeans and Yezidis. The former, known also as Sabians or Nasoreans, survive as scattered colonies in the Khuzistan foothills and in the marshlands of the south. They are probably of Amoritic origin but profess a religion derived in part from Manichaeism and Greek Gnosticism, recognizable through acquired Aramaic scriptures as a fusion of Judaism, Nestorian Christianity and the ancient Babylonian worship of Marduk.

Related somewhat distantly to the Mandaeans are the Yezidi, whose name derives either from the second Omayyad Caliph Yezid (AD 720–4) or from Yezd, the Iranian centre of Zoroastrian worship (cf. Persian Yazdan – God) in central Iran. They are actually Kurds who had at one time been converted to orthodox Sunni Islam but had never given up many of their earlier tenets. About the fourteenth century they came to be distinguished for their respect for Satan (Persian Sha'tan), the 'Peacock of Angels' [4]. They were never actually 'devil-worshippers' though often referred to as such, a tradition deriving from their emphasis on Light and Darkness, reverence for the sun and fire worship. The Yezidi are largely mountaineers with irrigation agriculture and varying degrees of transhumance or sedentary pastoralism. Under constant oppression by Turks and orthodox Sunni Kurds alike, many splinter groups had shifted in search of political and economic security, a pattern of life that tended to keep down the population, intensify endogamy and increase the atmosphere of distrust that they shared mutually with their neighbours. In 1840 the total population was estimated at about 200,000 – of whom roughly one-third lived in Anatolia and the remainder in Mesopotamia, chiefly in the mountains northwest of Mosul – though outpost settlements existed as far removed as Tashkent. Today they number approximately a million.

The possibility of conflicting tenets and sectarian schisms had already begun in Muhammad's lifetime when as many as sixty-three sects were recognized. The Prophet considered this inevitable and a necessary prelude to ultimate amalgamation into a single worldwide body. He had not, however, anticipated the problem of succession and the major schism between the followers of Fatima, his only surviving daughter – the Shiites – and the orthodox Sunni who supported Uthman of the powerful Umayya (Omayya) families of Mecca. It was the latter who seized the caliphate on the death of Ali and commenced the worldwide empire. A major feature of the Omayyads was the recognition of four classes: the Amsar aristocracy or Arab Muslims; the Mawali, converts from other religions; the Dhimmi, adherents of the two previously revealed religions, Judaism and Christianity; and slaves – distinctions that have always been more characteristic of the Sunni than of the Shiites.

ARABIA

The peninsula of Arabia was probably the ancient Semitic homeland, but the whole of greater Syria and Arabia ought probably to be referred to as greater Arabia and defined as the region occupied primarily by peoples considering themselves Arabs, no matter how questionable their claims may be. The saying, 'people are what they think they are' is probably nowhere better illustrated than in the so-called Arab countries. Obviously such a definition puts a premium on the peoples' assessment of themselves and leaves open the question as to what is being referred to: language, religion or biological kinship? Until the expansion of Islam from the late seventh to ninth centuries, Arabs were largely confined to the central and southern half of the peninsula; it was never anticipated that what began as a religious effort to convert the then Arab world to Islam would expand into a world-wide Jihad, a holy war of global dimensions.

The northward movement took place in the early centuries of the Christian era. The initial basis of Islam seems to have been the polytheistic religion of the proto-Arabic Nabataeans which centred round the worship of the chief deity Allah and the Black Stone of the Ka'aba.

One of the enigmas of the story of Islam is that the Prophet Muhammad (Mahomet) was himself city-born, a scion of the Quraish tribe living in the oasis urban centre of Mecca; yet to him the way of the Bedouin, the nomad pastoralist, represented the more perfect life, one that was closest to the Will of Allah and unsullied by the sins of the city. Islam may be regarded as a fusion of the borrowed Jewish idea of monotheism, by which Allah was elevated to the position of a universal, omniscient and omnipotent deity, the mystical aura surrounding the Ka'aba, the sanctity of the scriptural recitations and rules of conduct revealed to the Prophet Muhammad, and a script derived largely from Aramaic Syriac.

In spite of the belief and the claim of the Bedouin themselves to greater antiquity and purity, probably the settled Semitic population of the Yemen–Asir highlands was the older and gave rise to the later expansions northward around the perimeters of the great Arabian and Syrian deserts. Final penetration of the desert areas probably took place from the north southwards.

The term 'Arab' today is frequently applied rather indiscriminately to all orthodox Muslims of whatever sect who are speakers of Arabic as a mother tongue, regardless of other cultural characteristics or places of residence. In this sense, the religious–linguistic aspects of ethnic identity supersede political considerations or biological kinship. The word 'Arab' is unquestionably Semitic but of uncertain origin. Following earlier usage, 'Arab' is equated in this study with populations tracing kinship to the inhabitants of the peninsula before the spread of Islam in the seventh century, whether in Arabia or elsewhere, and not to peoples who for other reasons – such as speaking Arabic or reciting the Koran – might be identified as Arabs.

In view of the many common physical traits shared by the coastal Arabs with the older populations of Somalia and Ethiopia – such as facial features, pigmentation and hair form – as well as fundamental similarities between the Semitic and Hamitic languages, many authors assume that the two populations may have shared a large measure of common genetic heritage. But whether this older substratum can be said to have originated in greater Arabia or in north-east Africa remains an open question. A commonly accepted interpretation is that the inhabitants of both areas started with a similar genetic and cultural heritage at some time late in the epipalaeolithic period. Proto-Semitic hunting populations were already recognizably present throughout the peninsula and the Fertile Crescent regions by as early as 5000 BC, but had been vastly altered on the Asian side of the Red Sea by an early population expansion from the north in protoneolithic times. During the next two or three millennia substantial settlements developed in all of the fertile west coastal and submontane valleys of the Yemen (Arabia Felix), as well as some regions of the Nejd or desert hinterland adjacent to the Hejaz. It seems likely, therefore, that the classic two-fold division of the Arabs into northern and southern halves might well have originated sometime in the early part of the third millenium BC, which is probably about the time when the Bedouin – the present-day central and north Arab population – is first identifiable. The basis for such a suggestion rests on the fact that the Bedouin have always been dependent on the domesticated camel for survival. A wild species of Camelidae was present in Pleistocene times but it was never domesticated locally, and there is no evidence that the domesticated camel had reached as far south as the northern part of Arabia or even the Syrian desert much before that time.

The seat of camel domestication was apparently in Turkestan, and it must have been taken over either by some hunting population of the Syrian desert or by intrusive settled Arabs who moved into the Nejd from the Hejaz and Yemen. Thus ethno-zoological evidence supports the Bedouin tradition of a northern origin possibly somewhere in the Jazira, the inter-riverine steppe zone north of Baghdad between the Tigris and Euphrates. (For a general discussion of Arabs see N. A. Faris, *The Arab Heritage* [108].)

The term 'Bedouin' (sometimes written as 'Bedawin') means literally 'outdoor people' (*bedu-in* or *ahl-bedu*), although they speak of themselves as the 'people of the tent' (*ahl el beit*) as distinct from the *ahl hadar* or 'settled people' [104]. Above all they are camel-raisers, and because of the rather fastidiously regulated adjustment of the camel to a desert and semi-desert environment, the Bedouin are more sharply differentiated from the settled Arabs than is usually the case when a distinction can be made between the nomadic and sedentary segments of a large ethnic population. The term 'nomadic' as applied to the Bedouin is somewhat equivocal since it includes some permanent desert oases settlements of tent-dwellers. The term 'desert tent-dweller' would be a more realistic characterization.

The Bedouin are probably more dependent on the camel for their economic necessities than are any of the peoples of present-day Turkestan – a dependence well illustrated by the following quotation:

> It [the camel] is the nomad's nourisher, his vehicle of transportation and his medium of exchange. The dowry of the bride, the price of blood, the profit of gambling, the wealth of a sheikh – all are computed in terms of camels. It is the Bedouin's constant companion, his alter ego, his foster parent. He drinks its milk instead of water, which he spares for the cattle; he feasts on its flesh, he covers himself with its skin; he makes his tent of its hair; its dung he uses as fuel and its urine as a hair tonic and medicine. To him the camel is more than 'the ship of the desert'; it is the special gift of Allah. [149]

Camels were just as essential to the welfare of the Bedouin as the Bedouin were to the trans-desert trade of the settled Arabs. Without the camel, commerce between lands dependent on desert caravan transportation would be severely restricted. The Bedouin monopolized the transport with their 'ships of the desert', but ironically today it is the settled Arabs who are threatening the traditional way of life of the Bedouin by their use of mechanized transport.

Until the age of modern weaponry, neither the power of the Turkish Sultans nor that of the settled Arab sheikdoms could curb Bedouin independence. Not only were their political structures well organized, but use of their terrain was controlled by exacting toll and demanding tribute from desert-marginal settlements. These measures elevated the Bedouin tribes to a level superior in political prestige, at least to the settled dwellers who were generally looked upon with disdain.

Throughout the course of Arab history the Bedouin have always been viewed with mixed sentiments. While being admired for courage, hardiness and skill, they have been criticized for their uncouth manners, their lack of cleanliness, the shallowness of their Islamic pretensions – all of which are reflections of a basic conservatism and independence.

Additional evidence of the relatively late development of camel-dependent nomadism is the dependence of the Bedouin in varying degrees upon the assistance of semi-symbiotic and servile hunting populations who act as herders and guides to waterholes and forage grounds. The status relationships of the so-called 'vassal tribes' to their 'noble' Bedouin overlords is not consistent, nor do the 'vassal tribes' trace their origins to a common ancestry as do the Bedouin. They are believed to be surviving remnants of hunting populations already present in the desert–steppe regions prior to the development of nomad pastoralism.

The most numerous of the 'vassal tribes' of Syria and the Nejd are probably the Solluba (Sulluba, Slyeb, Sulaba, Soliba) of whom twenty-three 'subtribes' can be listed, but the extent of interrelationships between the 'subtribes' and the Bedouin varies regionally, and intermarriages sometimes occur in spite of prohibitions. They are known locally as Rwala Sulluba or Howeitat Sulluba, depending on the 'overlord' tribe to which they are attached.

Other so-called 'vassal tribes' are the Hteym (Hiteym, Hutaym, Heteym), whose distribution extends into Mesopotamia and Egypt, and the Shararat, some of whom remain independent hunters. Quite unrelated are the travelling tinkers or Sani of the south, whose services are sold or bartered, and the agricultural and cattle-breeding Zatut and Shahara, who live in beehive-shaped huts and caves on the south-east coast and are described as 'gipsy-like castes' [279]. Finally, there are coastal and insular fishing populations, such as the Bautahara of the Kuria Muria Islands, the Bilhof, Afar, Jeneba, and Insakht along the Indian Ocean and Red Sea coasts, and the slaves of the south.

Slavery has existed since biblical times, and while accurate figures are not available, the negroid and mixed negroid slave population has been estimated as high as half a million [281]. Slaves were usually retained by the urban élite and generally freed after seven years upon acceptance of Islam. Freed slaves usually intermarried and it was possible for such persons or their children to become sheiks or even emirs.

In contrast with the desert-living Bedouin who have captured the imagination of Europeans are the inhabitants of the farming and fishing settlements and the commercial centres, most of which are located either on the sea coast or in the foothill slopes and adjacent plateau highlands and upper valleys. Land transport is by donkey rather than camel, and offshore coastal shipping by means of the famed dhows – possibly traceable to south-east Asian craft.

Thousands of inscriptions and hundreds of monuments, some dating back to the Bronze Age, have indicated the existence of at least four kingdoms in southern Arabia: Sabaean, Minaean, Hadramautian and Katabanian. The earliest levels indicate trade with Sumeria and later with Indus Valley cities and Egypt. Saba is presumed by some to be the biblical Sheba, but there is little to identify these kingdoms except lists of kings. The languages were all early proto-Semitic and, in syntax, close to classical Arabic. By cross-reference, the oldest cities date from at least 1500 BC and many inscriptions of the sixth century refer to the Achaemenid conquests. Trade in frankincense, gum arabic and spices northward to Syria and Mesopotamia was already extensive in biblical times, and *gaza* (cf. gauze) was one of their favourite staples [108, p. 32]. Like so many misnomers, gauze appears to have come originally from India, the home of cottons and probably silks. Gaza was the Phoenician transfer port for overland caravans.

Arab historians distinguish between what are termed true Arabs (Arab al-Ariba) – the descendants of Shem, son of Noah through Yaarub, son of Qahtan (Kahtan or Kaftan), the present-day Yemeni – and the Adnan (Arab al-Musta'riba), the 'naturalized Arabs' [281, p.2], descendants of Abraham through Ishmael. They distinguish further between these two and the marginal mixed tribes of biblical days – the Amaleks of the Hejaz and south Jordan, the Midianites and Hadramis and such older tribes as the Moabites and Edomites south of the Dead Sea, as well as those to the north: Israelites, Ammonites and Aramaeans, with whom they recognize distant relationship.

Most of the Adnan are Bedouin, who comprise several divisions of which the Modher and Rabia-el-Faras, including the Anaze, are among the largest [339]. Though not denying descent through Ishmael, they make rather a fetish of their more immediate ancestry as part of the Ma'add tribe.

The Rwala (Ruwalla) or Djelass [45] form one of four sub-divisions of the northern Anaze (Anazeh, Aneza) division of the Adnan branch. They now occupy most of the desert–steppe lands of north-west Syria but originally migrated from the Nejd to their present habitat in the seventeenth century. In the north-east are the Shammar (Jarba), a branch of the Nejd Shammar Bedouin, who also moved north-westward in the seventeenth century and, after displacing the Muwali (Mawali), were in turn forced eastward in the nineteenth century by the Rwala. The Muwali, who are described as bedouinized Aramaeans, were forced into the less favourable grazing lands north of Aleppo. Other tribes related to the Shammar are the Howeitat (Huwetat), Sherarat and Beni Sakhr in the southern sections of Jordan.

The Bedouin of Sinai (Towara, Ayaida, Tiyaha and others) and the Terabin of the Negev should also be counted among the Adnan tribes, but all are varyingly mixed with migrants from Egypt and the peninsula. The little colony of Jebeliyeh in the vicinity of St Catherine's Monastery, though thoroughly 'bedouinized', are reputedly the descendants of Bosnian and Wallachian serfs donated to the monastery in the sixth century AD by Justinian [115].

The worldwide legacy of Islam owes a great debt to the Bedouin nomads. The most powerful military wings of the Arab empire were unquestionably the camelry and cavalry of the Bedouin, without whose fanatical zeal the green and white banner of Islam would never have been carried as it was from Mauretania in the west to China and the borders of Mongolia in the east.

The Arabs actually drove the Chinese out of Turkmenia in the eighth century but were finally stopped by the rebel usurper An Lu-shan after his seizure of the celestial throne. Taking advantage of the Arab defeat, the T'ang successor regained his throne in 763, with the aid of Uighur and Arab mercenaries, to whom in gratitude he offered land in Kansu province. Tradition has it that many Arabs took advantage of the offer, but the percentage of settlers is not stated. Undeniably this was the start of the Muslim community in China, which totals roughly two per cent of the nation's population today. The Tungan maintain their integrity within the People's Republic of China as the only autonomous administrative area where the language is Chinese but the people have a recognizably mixed biological ancestry and the territorial limits are determined on religious (Islamic) grounds.

Mention should be made also of the tremendous expansion of Arab trade eastward to India, the East Indies and the seaports of southern China. China's debt to these Arab traders was enormous, but the debt was mutual. Most of China's overseas trade with India and Africa was through Arab traders until after the T'ang dynasty, but the Arabs acquired the principle of the compass and other inventions which were until then unique to the Chinese [258, vol. II, p. 361].

7

The Plateaulands from Anatolia to the Pamirs

ANATOLIA

The plateau corridor of Anatolia (Turkish Anadolu) has served as a migration and trade corridor since palaeolithic times but the ties of the inhabitants, both genetic and cultural, have been closer to Irania, Turkmenia and the lands to the north than to Syria. The western third, roughly identifiable with Lydia and Phrygia, became a part of the Helladic lands which looked for trade and other cultural ties to Crete and the Peloponnesus rather than eastward to the central heart of the plateau. The latter was intersected by a number of north–south passageways, and eastward the Armenian highlands section was oriented towards the Caucasus foothills, the Caspian Sea and the river courses flowing southward toward Mesopotamia.

By the late Chalcolithic and early Bronze Age, about 3000 BC, each of these three sections was recognizably divided into several minor provinces, but the divisions were more cultural than biological. The largest urban centres were in the centre – Alaçar Hüyük and Kanesh (Kultepe) on the upper Halys in Cappadocia. To the latter was attached by 2200 BC a colony of Assyrian traders which became in time the focal point for the dissemination of writing. Shortly after, bands of marauding Indo–European speakers commenced their incursions from the north.

The earliest of these movements which were to plague the peninsula for centuries was across the Bosphorus from the lower Danube basin to south-western Anatolia by a people speaking a language known as Luvian. Skeletal evidence reveals no distinctive differences between the older populations and the intruders.

A more or less contemporary migration identified as Palaic (Palan) moved eastward along the Pontic coast into Paphlagonia and a third, Hittitic, followed the same course around the Black Sea but penetrated to the central basin. As the population increased a centre was established at Hattusus (Boghaz Köy) on the Halys, and later another centre was created in eastern Anatolia near Lake Van.

The origin of the Indo-European-speaking peoples has not been fully determined, but it is believed that the early neolithic populations of the lower Danube and the Black Earth region of the Dnieper and Don Rivers of southern Ukrania are identifiable as among the earliest of that group. This is not to say that they were a single people speaking a hypothetical common proto-Indo-European language, but rather that the local populations spoke languages belonging to a common group with similar syntax and cognate vocabularies.

In all there were at least three major and numerous minor series of incursions from the north around the Black and Aralo-Caspian Seas or across the Caucasus. The first major series was that of the Luvians, Palans and Hittites (Neshians). The second was during the twentieth century BC when the Iranians migrated and pillaged south as Thraco-Phrygians into Anatolia, Mesopotamia and Iran and as Aryans into India. There was also a thrust eastward into Sinkiang. The third series – that of the Cimmerians, Scyths and Sarmatians – took place between the seventh and first centuries.

The movement of Indo-Europeans southward into Anatolia was mainly a slow proliferation with occasional pillaging. By 2500 BC the horse had been domesticated, either in the steppelands of southern Russia or in Turkestan, but its use was limited to traction. Not until two or three centuries later did it become a riding animal. The Indo-European incursions and the ultimate conquest of the whole of western Asia is attributable largely to the use of the chariot in the first stage and to the saddle in the second. The development of what Childe [61, pp. 195–7] termed a pastoral aristocracy, and the ability to organize a powerful striking force, marked a new phase in world history. Indo-European languages were carried not only throughout western Asia but deep into the southern and eastern parts of the continent and even into the northern fringe of Africa.

The inhabitants of Anatolia whom the Indo–Europeans encountered were mostly peasant farmers concentrated in the tilled river valleys. The uplands were hunting grounds and the meadows and steppes were inadequately exploited. It was these latter that attracted the northern herders, who gradually pre-empted them and created an interconnected network of kin-related communities.

In the west, the cities of the Troad fell victim to the maritime powers of the Aegean and the horse-riders of the hinterland but in the centre the indigenous peasant farmers, known as the Hatti, came to live on a more or less symbiotic basis with the chariot-riding elite, whom historians refer to as Hittites – a term more properly applied to the entire population and not merely to the ruling class. Other peoples known as the Hurri and Khaldu (Halde) infiltrated more as traders than farmers from the Armenian highlands into central Anatolia and the northern Jazira about 1800 BC.

All of the earlier populations – Hatti, Hurri and Khaldu – spoke related languages classified as Asianic, but may prove to belong to the Caucasian group. Although there may still be confusion about the language of the élite, it has been identified as Indo–European and should probably be referred to as Neshian or Kaneshian, after its earlier capital Nesh or Kanesh (Kültepe), rather than as Hittitic [220, p. 54.]

By the time the Hittites developed an empire they had become assimilated into the local Hatti population, and the ruins of the later capital Hattusus (Böghaz Köy) reveal identifiably distinctive artistic and religious characteristics such as the pointed metal helmets and garments reminiscent of the steppelands and architectural styles similar to those of Syria.

During the periods of Assyrian and Achaemenid rule, colonies of settlers moved up from the plains and plateau-dwellers moved to the lowlands, but western Anatolia, especially along the sea coast, was the scene of fresh Indo–European incursions. This second series began about 2000 BC: first the Mitanni who entered from Iran; then the Illyrians, who crossed from Thrace into the western section; and finally the early Aeolic, Doric and Ionic movements into the Helladic peninsula and around the Aegean. In Greece the invaders subjugated and assimilated the earlier

Pelasgians who were probably related linguistically to the Asianic speakers of Asia Minor.

The third major series of incursions commenced in the seventh century BC with the Cimmerians, whose name is preserved in Crimea. They moved from their Black Earth homeland into Anatolia by way of the Caucasus and were soon followed by Scythic invasions into the Armenian highlands and Irania.

Somewhat later the Graeco-Roman period was one of extensive hellenization. Colonies of Greeks, Macedonians and hellenized Persians were settled inland on the plateau and along the Pontic coast and Greek trading stations were established at crucial Black Sea ports. Lycians and Lydians were added to the Indo-European speakers in the west – the former spoken by colonists from Crete and the latter cognate with Phrygian. In the third century after Christ several thousand Gauls, first enemies of Rome, then mercenaries, settled in Anatolia as Galatians and gave their name to the region known today as Galicia.

No fixed date can be given for the entry of the first Turkic immigrants into Anatolia, but it is known that during the fourth century a number of nomads were brought as slaves from Turkestan to the eastern and central regions. Later wandering nomadic Seljuks in search of new grazing grounds crossed northern Iran around the Caspian Sea and began moving into the higher and more favourable grounds further west. It has been assumed that by the fifth century the nomadic herding practices of the steppelands were well established throughout the peninsula and had largely replaced the scattered pastoral activities of the farming villagers. At first the Turkic tribes served as mercenary cavalry in the Roman defences against Parthian encroachments. Later they assisted the Arabs, and in the eighth century became powerful enough to take over the central plateau and consolidate their hold over the entire western region. For the next few centuries they expanded eastward across Irania and southward into Syria, and by the ninth century, when Arab momentum had started to slacken, the Seljuks were looked upon as successors to Roman rule and their empire referred to as Rum, a name previously applied to Rome.

Seljuk expansion was shortlived, however, and the Rumian power was unable to stem the tide of Mongol pressure that was sweeping across the Eurasian steppelands. By the thirteenth century the Seljuk domains were fragmented by the invading Mongols, and the Ottomans were as yet merely bands of nomad raiders with no thought of consolidation. One day, so the story goes, a band of four hundred members of the Osmanli tribe of Oghuz Turks chanced upon a battle scene between the Seljuks and the Mongols. Joining the losing side more in sport than in recognition of distant kinship, they helped to bring about the Mongol defeat. Though the story may be apocryphal, the Mongol defeat marked the beginning of Osmanli–Ottoman infiltration and the eventual conquest of vast domains which reached to the heart of Europe in the fourteenth and fifteenth centuries.

As in other parts of the Sultan's domains, Turkish became the official language and conversion to Islam was encouraged. The major concern of the sultanate was to preserve law and order. Colonies of settlers were moved about wholesale to break up potential centres of rebellion and to maintain at least an uneasy peace. In 1828 100,000 Armenians in Transcaucasian Armenia came under Russian control. Many fled to Turkey and were later forcibly moved to the western districts, where they suffered oppression and massacre at the hands of the displaced Kurds and Turks. Even so, the Armenians preferred the sultanate to czarist rule in spite of Russia's pose as the protector of Echmiadzin, the holy city of the Armenian Christians.

Since the defeat of the sultanate and the post-First World War modernization of the nation, the more violent schemes of turkicization have disappeared and a more orderly policy initiated. Many thousands of Armenians have returned to Soviet Armenia; Anatolian Greeks have been exchanged for Macedonian Turks; and the Turkish district of Alexandretta has been incorporated into the nation. The Turkish aspect of the nation has become the pervading policy and the transfer of the seat of government from Istanbul to Ankara has fixed the identity of Turkey as an Asian nation.

For various reasons the Turkish-speaking majority appear to have achieved greater genetic stability than the Arabic speakers of greater Arabia. Proof is in the lower variances in both polygenic and monogenic traits, but in spite of this gradual approximation to a balanced genetic state, several minorities remain unabsorbed and resistant to assimilation. Of these the largest is the Kurdish community, totalling over ten per cent of the population. Minor religious sects include the Yezidi – referred to under Iraq – and the mixed Turkmen–Kurd Qizilbash (Kizilbash – 'red hats'), followers of Mazdaism whose scattered colonies extend into Iran, Afghanistan and Turkmenia. Once they were thought to be Christians because they drank wine, practised baptism and communion and allowed their women to go unveiled. Their reputed nocturnal orgies and licentious feasts are doubtless exaggerated, but they remain secretive about their religious beliefs.

From the Caucasus have come colonies of Caucasian-speaking Circassians (Cherkess or Andijhe), Georgians, Lazes, Mingrelians and Abkhaz, and Mongol–Turkic-speaking Nogai and Mongol Kalmuks. There are also colonies of early czarist refugee converts to Islam – Albanians, Pomaks and Bulgars from the Balkans; Turkish-speaking Azeri (Azerbaijani), Avshars (Afshars) and Turkmen from the east; and, scattered throughout the central plateau, numerous pastoral nomadic Yuruks (Yoruks), descendants probably of the old nomadic immigrants. Pockets of Arabs and Syrians dot the adjacent Jazira and every large city has its concentration of Jewish merchants and traders. Finally, beyond the Asian frontier in Europe, the inhabitants of Thrace are largely Turkish-speaking, as well as about one-fifth of the population of Cyprus.

IRAN

Iran was previously known as Persia, but some four millennia ago it would have been more appropriately applied to the steppe country of central Eurasia – the original homeland of the Iranians. History explains how this came about, but the wonder is that the nation has endured so tenaciously and preserved its Persian character in the face of the many threats to its integrity, changes in dynasties and environmental problems.

Like greater Arabia, Iran has a gigantic desert interior and a mountainous perimeter. The most extensive cultivated regions are around the outer slopes, while the inner perimeter is encircled by a string of disconnected oases. But here comparisons cease. Arabia is largely sealed off from the threat of invasion by land, but Iran has been invaded time and again from three directions. The more densely inhabited regions are so separated, and have such varied environments and ethnic ties, that unification has been a constant challenge.

During late neolithic and early Sumerian times – about 3000 BC – the hill peoples of Elamitic Susa in the Zagros foothills and at Sialk and Giyan on the plateau were making a distinctive black on red painted ware decorated with animal-style motifs. Similar wares have been found at Damghan near Teheran, at Anau and Jeitun in Turkmenia and near Kashgar in the Tarim basin. Identity of the early painted-ware-makers is not clear, but in Elam there is evidence of assimilation of Sumero–Akkadian civilization. A proto-Elamitic script was developed and later replaced by the Akkadian cuneiform and language, but even the development of a well organized city-state was not enough to compete successfully with Sumeria. The latter conquered the plateau as far north as Sialk, but the occupation was short-lived. Meanwhile the peoples producing the painted ware were being subjected to pressures from the north. Stratigraphically, the painted ware shows gradual intermixture with a characteristic black and grey-black ware associated with a central European 'Nordic' style battleaxe. At Sialk the displacement was abrupt, with a layer of ash between the two pottery levels. Ghirshman [126] postulates that the grey-black ware-makers infiltrated from the north, slowly at first and then, having become established, moved rapidly southward down the western margin of the plateau. If his interpretation is correct, the ash layer at Sialk would represent the destruction of Elam's northern outpost by Sumeria, and the appearance of the black and grey-black ware the conquest of the plateau by the Indo–Europeans. It is presumed that the latter intermixed with the painted-pottery-makers to produce the four known peoples of the plateau: the Guti and Lullubi in the north and the Kassites and Elamites of the centre and south. All four developed related languages [126, p. 50] but were at different levels of civilization. The northerners remained at a less complex level than the Kassites and Elamites, who were more directly and forcefully brought within the greater sphere first of Sumeria and later of Akkadia.

The Kassites in the central Zagros, the modern Luristan, were sometimes called Kassi or Kas-pi – a name related possibly to a former home on the Caspian Sea or to their monopoly of the tin trade from that area. They rose rapidly to power and temporarily held an extensive empire in the lowlands. During Assyrian times, the fusion of the earlier pre-Indo–European-speaking 'Elamitic' semi-nomadic and sedentary population and the conquering Indo–European-speaking elite was still not completed when new developments took place in the Aralo–Caspian basin.

The Iranian Mitanni, who initiated the second series of Indo–European invasions, settled on the lands of the Khaldu. Following them, the Mada infiltrated the lands of the Guti and Lullubi. Fusions took place again, resulting in the respective empires of the Mitanni and the Medes. Further south, the intermixtures of the new invaders with the Kassitic-Elamitic populations became identified as the Parsa (Pers, the modern Fars) Iranians, whose first dynastic rulers were the Achaemenids. More or less contemporary with these incursions southward were comparable thrusts by the same people eastward across the Irtysh steppelands and through the Baikal faultline corridors into Sinkiang, Zungharia, the Altai complex and Baikalia.

Following the pattern of the earlier mixed populations, the Parsa Iranians passed through a period of assimilation of the higher civilizations of the border kingdoms. As Ghirshman [126, p. 121] suggests, the Achaemenid rulers 'from the beginning ... showed the originality of their creative spirit which could adopt a foreign idea and yet reshape it along the lines of their own genius'. They held the advantage in numbers and commanded a remarkably powerful and novel force of mounted archers. After establishing a seat of government at Parsagade, Aramaic was adopted as the primary language of the court and scribes were recruited from the plains. Because of its size and the variety of vassal states, the Achaemenid empire has frequently been called the first truly world empire. At its height it stretched from the Aralo-Caspian basin to Egypt and from Asia Minor to the borders of India. The Assyrian empire though great had remained almost wholly Semitic, and its rulers seemed to secure the imperial limits with a garrisoned perimeter, but that of the Achaemenids was imposed by necessity, not choice. In this sense it was limitless.

Cyrus was the first of the Achaemenids to expand control over neighbouring states. After conquering the Medes he shifted his capital to Ecbatana ('place of assembly'), the former seat of the defeated Median empire – the present Hamadan. While these events had been taking place in the west, other Iranians were moving from the basin of the Oxus south-eastward across and around the lower ranges of the Hindu Kush and descending to the valley of the Indus as the Aryans. Their entry into the lowlands began just before the middle of the second millennium BC.

After Mesopotamia, Syria and Egypt had been conquered and the Parsa capital moved to Pasagarde near Susa, Darius, successor to Cyrus, turned his attention to the northern and eastern borderlands which posed a constant threat from the rear. But even before the western frontiers could be consolidated, the desert–steppe zone of the northlands became the scene of further nomadic ferment.

The third series of Indo–European incursions, often referred to as Scytho–Sakian, began about 700 BC and continued until the turn of the Christian era. While the Cimmerians were moving around the Black Sea into Anatolia, the Scyths moved southward into Iran. Somewhat later the Saka from the valleys of the Altai mountain complex and the Tarim basin started their infiltrations around the Kopet Dagh and the Paropamisus range.

By some time between the seventh and fifth centuries, four major settlement concentrations of Scytho–Sakians had developed within the northern border of Irania: Sogdians in the two oasis areas of Samarkand and Bukhara on the Kashka and Zaravshan Rivers in what is now Uzbekistan and in the Ferghana Valley of Kirghizia; Chorasmians (Kwarezmians) in the oasis settlement complex area around Khiva in the lower Amu Darya (Oxus) in western Uzbekistan; and Bactrians in northern and central Afghanistan, centering around Balkh.

From the earliest days of the Achaemenids, efforts had been made to bring these regions more closely under imperial control, but their relative isolation militated against easy incorporation. The only practical approaches were through the Caspian corridor between the Elburz range and the Khorasan Desert or around the southern perimeter through Gedrosia and Arachosia. It was in Bactria that Cyrus met his death, and later it was the Karakum Desert regions of Sogdia and Chorasmia that checked the momentum of Alexander's conquests. This was also the region that was plagued by insurrections during the later Seleucid period. To the south the Khorasan Desert has always separated the western and eastern Iranians throughout history.

The pages of Iranian history during the Scytho–Sakian incursions are filled with the names of petty rulers, dynasties and city-states which rose and fell in disconnected sequence. Even with the aid of coins and sculpture, the history of this region remains only partially understood. Most of these kaleidoscopic changes were relatively meaningless so far as changing the genetic structure was concerned. They were usually related to shifting allegiances and the fates of petty rulers rather than to the movements of peoples. Two lists of some twelve or thirteen 'nations' survive from the Achaemenid period – one compiled by Darius, the other by Herodotus. They are in essential agreement but their determination appears to have been based on political rather than ethnic considerations. With the exception of the Medes and Persians in the west and the Hyrcaneans and Parthians in the north, all of the listed peoples and petty kingdoms were beyond easy access from Parsa (Persis) and were constantly asserting their independence. Three of them – Bactria, Sogdiana and Parthia, backed by reservoirs of mounted nomadic, desert–steppe horsemen – became powerful enough to require constant attention.

After defeating the Persians and seizing Susa and Persepolis, Alexander abandoned his own Macedonian throne and chose to rule from the plateau as emperor of Persia and 'King of Kings'. The move initiated a series of upsetting events which bore unforeseen consequences throughout the ancient world.

Having stabilized the western frontiers as far as the Nile, Alexander next turned his attention eastward, but as soon as he had managed to conquer one region another broke out in rebellion. In spite of stationing his best troops at key points, building a line of fortifications along the desert margin and marrying Roxana – the daughter of the Viceroy of Bactria – it required two years to pacify the region. Only then was he able to launch a partially successful campaign against India. Shortly after, fatigued with years of campaigning, his troops threatened to mutiny and he was forced to return to Pasagarde. It was his experience in east Iran, apparently, that made him realize how difficult the governing of that part of his empire would be. As a gesture of conciliation he initiated a policy of equal favouritism and a hoped-for union of Iran and Greece. At a mass celebration he is said to have married ten thousand of his Greek–Macedonian troops to Iranian girls, and he sent thirty thousand of his men to settle in Bactria.

During Alexander's lifetime the plan of unification was apparently successful among the Iranians but not among the Macedonians, who felt that the conquerors should rule the conquered. It was largely this disaffection that caused the break up of empire immediately after Alexander's death.

Under the Seleucids, in spite of rivalries that tore the empire apart, the policy of joint sharing of offices was continued, but to ensure adequate European representation substantial numbers of settlers and militia were brought eastward from the overpopulated regions of the Balkans. New centres were created, including Seleucia, and a military road was built between Bactria and the capital. In spite of these efforts Bactria again revolted and this time became an independent state, but with a decidedly Greek majority. Shortly after, Parthia followed suit but remained largely Iranian.

The origin of the Parthians is traced to the Parni or Aparni, a Scytho–Sakian nomad tribe identified as part of the Daha. Their main occupation had been pillaging along the by-paths leading to the Siberian gold fields and the caravan routes connecting Syria with the oasis settlements of Sogdiana and Media. Following these major revolts a spate of minor rebellions ensued, and in the general turmoil many Greek and Macedonian settlers returned to western Iran or to their native homelands. Only Bactria was strong enough to retain its Greek traditions and Graeco–Macedonian settlers and develop eventually a new Graeco–Bactrian tradition of its own. Although Seleucid power declined, hellenization continued. Even in regions under Parthian control, Greek replaced Aramaic as the language of the élite and the court in all of the urban centres.

By 250 BC the Parthians under the Arsacids had developed into a powerful force which gradually gained control of the northern two-thirds of Iran. Eventually even Bactria lost its nominal independence and the centre of control shifted from Persis in the south-west to Parthia in the north-east – a shift that profoundly influenced the development of Persian civilization.

The north was the homeland of Iran's two greatest spiritual leaders: Mani, the founder of Manichaeism, a blend of Christianity and Persian Magism; and Zoroaster, the reformer of Mazdaism, the earlier native Iranian religion. Zoroaster grew up during the spread of Gandharan Buddhism northward in the third century BC. His teachings reflect many Buddhist tenets but stress universal control by the principles of Good and Evil and the duality of all nature – the good spirit Ahuramazda and the evil spirit Ahriman. The struggle would continue between these two forces until good would eventually triumph, but this would only be realized as human action became better and evil acts were finally suppressed. Such a philosophy is reminiscent of the contemporary concept of the dual nature of the universe in both India and China. The Zoroastrian cult banned the use of intoxicants and *haoma* (*soma*), probably the old Persian name for hashish. Fires were kindled daily on open altars, and since earth, fire and water were sacred and should not be contaminated, the dead were exposed to scavengers and the elements on specially built platforms, the dessicated bones being periodically gathered up and placed in rock-cut ossuaries. Later there was a gradual shift to burial in sarcophagi and ultimately to collective inhumation. A large Parthian necropolis has recently been discovered near Susa that promises to yield valuable data in the biological realm.

Of biological interest also was the trend toward close inbreeding – the encouragement of brother–sister and even of mother–son unions, if Strabo can be credited. Such practices were common also among the Magi, who centred in Media [278, p. 22]. Later, during the period of fanatical Muslim oppression, many Zoroastrians fled to India where today, as the Parsi (Persian) community of nearly six million, they continue their forms of religious worship and occupy an important niche in the larger Indian society. In Iran, a small but devout community continues the ancient religion at Yezd, the city of God.

Before Zoroaster had become active in the north, Buddhist missionaries had already carried their religion into Bactria, and the philosophical ferment that had swept both India and Iran by the fifth century was echoed by developments in the Tarim basin and China.

The spread of Manichaeism and Zoroastrianism should not be taken as implying that either of these religions was that of the Parthians, who had their own religion but were tolerant of other faiths. They especially encouraged Judaism and permitted the establishment of a small vassal Jewish state on the Persian Gulf. They also developed a form of syncretic worship of Ahuramazda, Mithra and Anahita, but the cult of Anahita – the Syrian form of Athene – seems to have been predominant. The Parthians' tolerant attitude was extended also to the arts and sciences. A form of heavy mail armour was developed for the cavalry and camelry, and irrigation was extended in the oasis areas. Ambassadors were exchanged with China and trade flourished between the two countries. Later this grew into the famous silk trade which characterized the period of Roman domination. Finally, one of the greatest contributions of the Parthians was the development of the Pahlavi script from Aramaic. The ascription is contained in the national poet Firdousi's famous epic, *Shahnama*, 'Book of Kings'. There were actually two forms of Pahlavi (late middle Persian Pehlevi): Pahlavik in Parthia, in which most Manichaean literature was written; and Parsik, or standard Persian, spoken in the south-west. The latter had four dialects: Khotani, Chorasmian, Sogdian and the language of the Kushans. Old Persian, the language of the Avestas, was derived from Scythic and referred to by the Persians as Saka.

In China it is quite likely that the central state of Chou and its feudatory vassal states had been in touch with the various Indo–European-speaking tribes of the Tarim basin for centuries. There is a tradition that even as early as the fifth century BC the Taoist sage Lao Tse made a pilgrimage to central Asia in search of wisdom. While his sojourn has not been substantiated, it seems highly improbable that the period of the great philosophies in India, Greece and China would have been contemporary wholly on the basis of chance.

The period 129–125 BC was a convulsive one for the entire world. The chain of events started with the final defeat of the Seleucid armies of Antiochus by the Parthians under Mithradates. After their defeat the Seleucids retired to Mesopotamia, marking the end of Graeco–Roman efforts to control the plateau. For the Parthians, however, trouble was around the corner.

Inspired by the successes of their skirmishes in Sogdiana and under pressure from the east, the Saka, who were joined by the Tochari (Chinese, Yüechih) from the Tarim basin in Sinkiang, began their incursions into Bactria. The Yüechih–Tochari are described sometimes as Turkish, but their leaders spoke a west

Indo–European language and the followers may have been a Celtic–Turkish mixture. They were hard pressed by the Turkic Hsiung-nu nomads of western Mongolia, who had been pillaging the frontier towns of China and the silk route caravans between China and the Roman world. It was largely this pressure from the rear that drove the Yüechih–Tocharians deeper into Sogdiana and Bactria.

And so, with the successful conquest of the entire eastern half of the Iranian plateau by Sakian invaders and their Yüechih–Tocharian allies, the permanent separation of the two halves was finally completed. Periodically, Iran was to regain control of parts of the east, which continued to intensify its separate identity and which was to become in time the nation of Afghanistan. The period of Sakian–Tocharian incursion and conquest is referred to as Kushan, but this is merely a dynastic name and relates more to Afghanistan than to Iran. In the long run the conquest's primary importance was in strengthening the trade route linking China with India by way of the east Iranian highlands.

In Iran the Parthians periodically made efforts to regain power but were eventually defeated by a re-emergent Persis under the Sassanids after the seat of government had been shifted to Persepolis near Pasagarde, the early Achaemenid capital. With this change the Parsa, now altered in their religious beliefs by the missionizing zeal of the Zoroastrians, brought the nation a step further toward religious if not political unification.

During the period of Roman occupation of Asia Minor and Syria, only feeble efforts had been made to prevent Parthian encroachments into Mesopotamia, but the Roman generals were well coached in Parthian tactics of temporary withdrawal into the northern desert–steppe. Parthian mobility, however, proved to be no match for the even more mobile nomadic warriors of the distant northern steppes, who now emerged as the Scytho–Sarmatians and the Alani. The former eventually became assimilated into the Iranians of the north, but the Alani moved into the central Caucasus. Some crossed the central defiles into Armenia and began marauding into central Anatolia and Iran and across the entire Fertile Crescent. Though eventually those who had crossed the Caucasus southward were absorbed into the general population, the nucleus that remained north of the mountains retained their separate identity and survive today as the Ossetes, an island of Indo-European speakers surrounded by speakers of Caucasian languages.

In the succeeding centuries under Arab domination there were no substantial changes in the gene pool of the nation apart from the addition of a number of communities of both settled and nomadic Arabs. This period was far more important in the cultural than the biological field. The Persians made various abortive attempts to recover their kingdom between the defeat of the Sassanian Mazdakite king of Persia in AD 632, when the Parsis fled to India, and the brief revival of Persian power under the Samanids in AD 900, but the most important development was the succession of a Persian to the Abbasid throne. By a chance alliance, a Persian had become ruler over the entire Arab empire, but when the emperor died the empire was divided; thereafter the Arabs lost effective control of Iran. Under the caliphate of Harun al-Rashid, however, most of Persia was converted to Shiite Islam.

During the period of Arab control of Turkestan many converts had been made to Islam, and Turkish converts were enslaved or employed as mercenaries, a practice that later significantly affected the history of the entire Middle East and Europe. During the Samanid period (AD 900–1229) only the southern half of Iran was under Persian domination. The remainder was taken over first by the Turkic Ghaznavid dynasty of Afghanistan and later by the Seljuk Turks.

The impact of Mongol and Timurid conquests was of more consequence to Afghanistan and India than to Iran except for the immigration of the 'Black Sheep' and 'White Sheep' Turkmen and colonies of Uzbeks. The career of Timur (Tamerlane) was short-lived (1395–1405) but the Turkmen dynasty lasted until 1499, when a new Persian dynasty, the Safavid, recovered the throne. Under the Safavids there was a revival of the earlier Persian culture combined with much of the artistic tradition and genius of the Semitic world and new elements introduced from Turkestan.

The Safavids had brought a sense of unity to Iran but they were unable to prevent further encroachments by Turkmen and Afghans. Several minor dynasties followed, the last being that of the Turkish Qajars in this century. Only after the abdication of the last of the Qajars and the election to the throne of Reza Khan did Iran finally gain a sense of true national cohesion.

Today over three-quarters of the inhabitants of Iran speak modern Persian as their primary language, and the concept of Iranian nationality is strong. In spite of this, nearly half of the surface area is inhabited by peoples formerly or still speaking Turkic, Semitic or non-Persian Indo-European languages. In the Turkish group are the Azeri of Azerbaijan, part of the classical Urartu around Lake Urmia and the lower Araks River in Transcaucasia. Others include some of the transhumant Bakhtiari and the Qashqai of the Zagros highlands, several nomadic tribal confederations in the south and recent immigrant Turkmen, Uzbeks and Karakalpaks and the older Turkic Qajar tribe of dynastic fame near the Azeri in the north. Arabs are concentrated along the Iraq frontier in southern Fars and in the Khorasan desert.

Of the old and middle Persian speakers the most historically significant are the Gilani and Mazanderani hill peoples facing the Caspian Sea, the Talyshes in Soviet Azerbaijan and the Galeshi in the Zagros. Most of the Bakhtiari now speak Persian, though many are bilingual and continue to use Turkic or Arabic. Their claim to Mongol ancestry seems to have little historical validity. In addition are scattered Indo-European-speaking peoples including colonies of Armenians in the north, Kurds on the Iraq and Turkish frontiers, Lurs of the northern Zagros and the Baluchis in Makran. Colonies of Persian and Tajik-speaking Aimaq Jamshedi, Firuzkuhi, Taimeni and Taimuri and a few Afghan Tajik colonies are scattered throughout eastern Khorasan and along the Afghan frontier.

The complexity of the peoples of Iran stems as much from the variety of religious faiths and types of economy as from differences in language and other ethnic considerations. Most Farsi (Persian) Iranians are either Shiite or Sufists but there are still some Manichaeists, Nestorian Christians and old Zoroastrians and a small colony of Mazdaists at Yezd. Along the borders of Iraq are Semitic Aisor (Assyrian) Ismaili, Yezidi Kurds and Armenian Chaldaeans, not to mention scattered colonies of urban Jews. Small cults centring round the worship of Marduk, Monophytism and Gnosticism survive, in syncretism with tenets of other faiths. There is also a clear distinction between the nomadic tribes and the settled populations – the cultivators of the irrigated lowlands, hill slopes and oases, and the urban concentrations. The transhumant nomads, who winter in the foothill lowlands and migrate to the upper valleys in the spring and summer, are almost exclusively Turkic or Iranian or mixtures of the two.

The Arabs and other Semitic nomads on the other hand are more likely to graze their flocks and herds in the lowlands and around the desert perimeter. All are organized into confederations of tribes, subtribes and lineages whose allegiances and alliances are of varying degrees of brittleness. A splinter subtribe, decimated by disease or warfare, may take refuge within the framework of an alien confederation but preserve its former identity. Local feuds may result in the constant realignment of tribes within a confederacy or the shifting of grazing grounds. Within the nomadic Khamseh confederacy, for example, the Basseri [17] are Persian speakers, but one hundred years ago when the confederacy was formed two of the tribes were Turkic speaking – the Baharlu and the Aynarlu. Now the latter has become sedentary. In its place, another small Turkic-speaking tribe has become dependent on the Basseri, and just east of the latter are 'various Arab tribes, some Arab-speaking and some Persian of the same dialect as the Basseri'. The example is only one of many similar instances illustrating the intricacies of a highly complex greater society.

AFGHANISTAN, TAJIKISTAN AND THE MIDDLE INDUS

Modern Afghanistan reflects little of the grandeur of two centuries ago when the empire of Ahmed Shah Durrani extended throughout eastern Persia and the valley of the Indus. Even more vast were the lands ruled by Babur, the mixed Turkic–Mongol–Afghan founder of the Mughal empire. But political boundaries are often deceptive and tell little about ethnic complexities.

Within many Muslim countries tribal alliances and acceptance of Islam remain far more significant than centralized power or the shifting lines of military control. Vassalage remains as a reflection of relative strengths of internal political units, and no part of Asia reflects this better than Afghanistan.

In many respects the ecological factors are exactly the reverse of the Iranian. The heart of the nation, instead of being a desert, is formed of a series of high mountain ranges with areas of dense forestation; the arid regions and areas of internal drainage lie beyond or are peripheral to the cultivated foothills. The central mountains of the Hindu Kush, moreover, are much higher and more massive than any of the Iranian ranges. They contain glaciers that hold the heavy winter snows longer and temper the climate generally. Great rivers flow in all directions out to the foothills. Surface ditches provide irrigation as they do in parts of the Kurdish foothills and *qanats* are seldom necessary. The land serves both as a gigantic barrier facing the steppes of Inner Asia and as a refuge area for a tremendous variety of populations. Only one major pass connects the steppe plains of the south with the Merv Desert and the basin of the lower Oxus. Another major route circles the western Parapomisus range and a third crosses the high spur connecting the Hindu Kush with the Pamirs.

The nation's current territorial boundaries are quite arbitrary. In the north the Oxus (Amu Darya) may be a convenient geographical and military boundary, but Uzbek, Turkmen and other Turkic populations comprise the majority on both banks; and southward, Turkic villages extend far into the Hindu Kush foothills. On the western border the scene is a veritable mosaic. Interspersed Iranian- and Persian-speaking Afghan settlements line the river valleys on the Afghan side of the frontier while, on the Iranian side, scattered Afghan Pashto and Tajik communities extend westward to the Khorasan desert. To the south the border bisects the lands of the Baluchi, who pay scant attention to its political significance. On the east the frontier is marked by a string of fortifications and outposts known as the Durand Line. The 'line', which was negotiated between the British and the Emir's representatives at the conclusion of the Afghan wars in 1893, cuts through the lands of several Pathan tribes; it was designed as a trucial frontier splitting the buffer lands of the Pathans into two confronting military zones. The Pathans, however, are actually Afghan hillsmen, and ever since the formation of Pakistan in 1947 the Afghan government has refused to recognize the terms of the old agreement. A realignment based on ethnic grounds would inevitably move the frontier eastward in many sections – in some places as far as the Indus.

Finally, the Wakhan Valley corridor was recognized nearly a century ago as a buffer zone designed to separate the southern border of czarist Russia from the northern outposts of British India. Wakhis, however, live on both the Soviet and Afghan banks of the Wakhan River and across the southern range in neighbouring Pakistan. Further south the Kafiri and various settled Afghan tribes straddle the Afghan–Pakistan frontier.

Afghans, who comprise roughly half the population of political Afghanistan, form a nation whose member tribes recognize a common eponymous ancestor and share a common language but are divided into two distinct groups: the mainly plains-dwelling Afghani and the hill-dwelling Pathans. While Iranian Pashto is the primary language of both Afghans and Pathans, the border between standard Pashto in the south-west and the Pakhtu dialects in the north-east cuts irregularly across both Afghan and Pathan tribal lands in an east-west direction just south of the Peshawar plain. Several other linguistically related but otherwise ethnically distinct minority populations are interspersed in various parts of the country. Persian is also an official language of the country and the primary or secondary language of a fair percentage of the total population. The western Afghans have absorbed much of Persian culture but the eastern Afghans in the Indus Valley reflect many of the life habits of greater India, an identity intensified during the Mughal period.

According to Persian chronicles of the Mughal court, Afghana – the original ancestor of all Afghans and Pathans – was the grandson of the biblical Saul. After the release of the Israelites from Babylonian captivity, part of the Beni Israel – identified as the descendants of Afghana – resettled in Ghor (Hazarajat) in Afghanistan and others settled near Mecca. Centuries later a descendant of the Mecca colony became the famous Khalid bin Walid, companion of the Prophet and the greatest of the early Arab conquerors. Hearing of Khalid's conquests, the Afghans of Ghor sent a certain Qais to learn about the new faith. Qais was converted to Islam and became the founder of the Afghan nation. Thus it is that lineages bear such names as Moses, Isaac, Solomon, Jacob, Joseph and Esau; and among personal names David, Jesus, Joseph, Mary and Martha are not uncommon. Knitted together by threads of tradition and coffee-shop gossip, genealogies play a powerful role in intensifying a sense of unity. During the Babylonian captivity many Jews were transferred to Media, and in late Parthian times several colonies were settled in east Irania. It is just possible, therefore, that a fusion of some patrilineages might justify in part the Afghan tradition.

The persianized western Afghan Durrani–Tarin (Abdali) tribe, who claim distant relationship with the royal Barakzai line through common descent from Sharbun, the eldest son of Qais (alias Abdurrashid), consider themselves superior to all other Afghans or Pathans. They occupy most of the irrigated lands and total more than half the nation's twelve million inhabitants – more than twice that of any minority. Most are native Pashto speakers but many are bilingual. Of the non-Durrani, some are agriculturalists, others have either retained or returned to nomadic economies such as the Spin ('White') or Tor ('Black') Tarin on the borders of Baluchistan.

Most of the eastern Afghan tribes in Pakistan consider themselves descendants of Kharshbun, the second son of Qais. They include among others the Daudzai and Mohmandi of the Ghorian Khel, all of the Yusufzai Khels, the Tarklanri of Bajaur and the Shinwari of the Khyber.

Because of their numerical superiority, and their hold on official positions both governmental and military, Durrani Afghans are heavily represented in all urban centres, border posts and military installations, but among those not connected with government services the regional economies of the Afghan majority differ widely. Possibly the most striking are the Pashto-speaking Hazaras of the Hazarajat – nomadic herders living in black, goat-hair (vellum) tents. They raise no crops but trade with the settled Hazaras for bread-meal and other essentials. In the north most of the settled Afghans are Pashto speakers, except for the nomad pastoral and caravan trading Ghilzai. The relationship of the Ghilzai to the Afghans has not been resolved: they speak Pashto or Persian, but have traditions of origin from the old Turkish Khalak tribe of the Oghuz confederacy. Some winter along the Oxus; others prefer the foothills of the lower Indus and cross the Bolan Pass through Baluchi country during their annual passages between the plains and the plateau.

Both Iran and Afghanistan remain strongly patrilineal, tribe- and kin-oriented in their political institutions, but this has not prevented either intertribal or interethnic mixtures, practices that were encouraged during the period of zealous islamization. Efforts have been made to identify historic ethnic or tribal names with existing populations, but even when identities can be established, as in the case of the Saka with Sekistan (Seistan), the connections are usually localized and seldom verifiable except through questionable genealogies.

The term 'Afghan' has been in use from as early as the ninth century and its first historical usage was in the Persian chronicles of AD 1030, but accounts of its origin seem scarcely more probable than the ancestry of Mahmud of Ghazni. Tradition claims him as an Afghan but he is known to have been a Turkish slave in the Samanid court who escaped to the land of Ghor in western Afghanistan. After marshalling support and establishing his seat of rule at Ghazni, he brought Indian rule over Afghanistan and southern Persia to an end and successfully invaded enemy territory as far as Benares. His invasion marks the beginning of the Muslim era which lasted until 1857. Very possibly the Khilji dynasty of the thirteenth century can be associated with the Ghilzai, and there is no question that the Lodi dynasty (1450–1526) was Afghan–Pathan. A combined Ghilzai–Afghan force even conquered the Safavid Persian empire and held it briefly in the early eighteenth century.

Under Persian guidance intertribal rivalries were brought under control and Afghanistan in its own right became a political power. Under Ahmad Shah the Afghans conquered much of northern India, defeated the Mahrattas at the battle of Panipat in 1761 and, after turning on their former masters – the Persians – extended their empire to the shores of the Caspian. During the reign of Timur – not to be confused with the Turkish–Mongol Timur (Tamerlane) – the capital was moved from Kandahar to Kabul to control internal insurrections more effectively. Earlier during one of these insurrections a scion of the Barakzai lineage had seized the Durrani throne and deposed the former Saddozai ruler.

The Afghans have been in the lower valleys of the Hindu Kush and Suleiman ranges for at least a thousand years. Before that they were probably limited to the Suleiman range, and the Pathans probably preserve, without many changes, the older ancestral socio-political institutions.

The most 'displaced' language population is undoubtedly that of the Brahui of northern Baluchistan and southern Afghanistan. Their language, although Dravidian, has incorporated numerous Iranian and Turkish loan words; but biologically the Brahui are not significantly different from the surrounding Iranian-speaking populations. Their presence on the plateau in relative proximity to the Indus Valley has stimulated controversy among Indian scholars [332] concerning the original homeland of the Dravidians (see Chapter 14).

Within the complex of the Hindu Kush range and its extensions into the Pamirs, the most isolated and presumably the most ancient peoples are the Burushaski–Yeshkun speakers of Hunza and Yasin in the northernmost part of greater India. The languages are probably related to the Caucasian group, and Grierson [136] believed that they were spoken over a much wider area southward in the Indus Valley at the time of the Aryan invasions about 1500 BC; and that, while the Indo-Aryan invaders were pressing eastward from the lower Kabul Valley and on to the plains of the Indus, they were also moving northward into Kohistan, where their old Iranian language was converted by degrees through borrowings from Burushaski into those forming today the larger Dardic group: Dardic, Khowari and Kafiri.

The east Iranian languages include the Dardic group: Shina or Shinwari spoken in Gilgit, Chilas, Astor, Dras and the Dardic colonies in Baltistan; and Kashmiri and its dialects in the Vale of Kashmir, Riasi and Kishtwar. The dialects of Kohistani are spoken between the Pathan *mirates* of Dir, Swat and Buner on the Panjkora and adjacent tributaries of the Indus and the Burushaski-speaking regions north of Gilgit. Most distinctive are Bashkarik, Torwali and Maiyon, which are spoken in the upper valleys of the Panjkora and adjacent minor tributaries of the Indus.

The problem of the Kafiri is more complex. The term Kafiri ('Non-Believer') relates to their pre-Muslim religion, which centred round the worship of a magical black stone and numerous spirit deities inhabiting the Lutukh Valley [314]. The Siaposh ('Black-Skin') Kafiri (Kati, Ashkuni, Paruni and Waigeli) live in side valleys of the Alingar, a tributary of the Kunar in Afghan Kafiristan. In the Chitral Valley of Pakistan the Kalash Kafirs speak a Kafiri-related language but have been relatively isolated from the Afghan Kafiri for several centuries [332, p. 109].

While the peoples speaking these languages were in process of consolidating their positions in the Kunar and Indus basins, other old Iranian speakers were penetrating the Pamirs from the north through Badhakshan into the Wakhan Valley and across the Kush range into Chitral. The languages of Badakshan belong to the Ghalcha group (Ishkashimi, Zebaki, Wakhi and Sarikoli – the last in Soviet Tajikistan).

Related to the Ghalcha group is the new Persian Tajik, the primary language of Tajikistan, the largest minority group in Afghanistan. Intermediate between the Ghalcha group and Tajik – which was modified both in structure and vocabulary by Turkic and Mongol – are three dialects spoken in isolated valleys of southern Tajikistan: Yagnobi, Pashai and Yadgali. In Afghanistan many who claim to be Tajiks speak Pashto or Persian as their primary language but they remain Tajiks in their material culture and social structure.

Scarcely less complex are the Hazaras, the second largest minority. The name means simply 'a thousand' in Persian and was used as a military term by Mongols and Turks. Used loosely of a company, brigade or division, it is apparently cognate with Hungarian *huszar*, originally meaning 'freebooter'. In western Europe this took two forms: the light cavalry hussars and, at sea, the pirating corsairs. In greater India Hazara appears commonly as a place name, and ethnically it is applied to the inhabitants of Hazarajat in west Punjab and Swat.

When 'Hazara' is used without qualification in Afghanistan it is taken to mean the inhabitants of the central mountainous region. These Hazaras are reputedly the mixed descendants of invading Turkic and Mongol armies, but it is difficult to substantiate this claim. Schurmann [332, p. 75] suggests that they are probably either mountain Tajiks who have mixed with later immigrant Mongols or the reverse, basing this opinion on the fact that they are completely sedentary and, like the mountain Tajiks, have no tents.

Even more confusing is the identity of the fourth largest ethnic population – the Aimaqs. In old Turkish the word means a tribal unit [332, p. 49], but it was used by the Mongols to designate a mixed tribal group and their territory. It is so used by the Kazakhs today, but the Afghans usually refer collectively to the four tribal divisions – Jamshedi, Taimuri, Firuz-Kuhi and Taimanni (Taimeni) – as the Chahar or Khor (four) Aimaqs. They omit from this list the Hazara–Aimaqs whom they class as Hazaras. The Aimaqs, however, consider the Hazara–Aimaqs as Aimaqs and the Taimuri as a distinct tribal group. All live in common *yurt*-type shelters.

Far more easily identified are the recent immigrant populations which preserve their alien languages and other ethnic attributes. Among these are the Turkic-speaking Turkmeni, Afshars, Uzbeks, Kazakhs, Kirghiz, Karakalpaks and Qizilbash along the northern frontier. In the cities are Jewish traders and in the west small colonies of Arab nomads.

Finally, there are old resident Persian communities dating to the time of Nadir Shah Pasha and two small communities of Mongols. The Mongol or Mogholi colonies [332, pp. 26 and 38] are said to date from the Chaghadai (Chagatai) Mongol invasions of the thirteenth century. Their secret records tend to confirm this claim, although they number now only a few hundred and of these only the most elderly have retained their native language [166].

Recent efforts by Pathans towards unification and independence seem as unlikely to succeed as the comparable struggle of the Kurds in the west. Intertribal rivalries and acculturational exposure to differing civilizations have created rifts which time alone cannot mend. Pathans separate rather sharply into three distinct tribal groups: a strongly Indian-influenced group in the central Indus basin north of the Khyber, who are more closely allied to the plateau Afghans than to the hill tribes south of the pass; the hill tribes between the Khyber and the Suleiman range; and finally the southern Pathans of the Suleiman sector.

Authorities differ in their listing of the small eastern tribes of the central Indus north of the Kabul River. Some give the number as eight; others as high as fifteen. The largest is unquestionably the Yusufzai – 'sons of Joseph' – whose principal tribal chiefs are the Wali of Swat and the Mir of Dir. Other major tribes are the Tarklanri and Mohmandi, whose lands fall on both sides of the Afghan–Pakistan frontier, and the Shinwari, who are mainly in Afghanistan [21].

Today the five *khels* or subclans of the Pashto-speaking Yusufzai number over 130,000 and comprise more than ninety per cent of the state of Dir and over fifteen per cent of the state of Swat. They and the three Mandan *khels* jointly form the Mundai clan of the Khakai section of the Kand tribe; the remainder of the Khakai never left the plateau.

The invasion of the Swat Valley by the Yusufzai is well documented and presents an example of what must have happened many times over along the north-western frontier of India. In the eighteenth century they received by lot a section of the plateau grasslands south of Kabul next to the territory of the Tarin Ghilzai. Pushed gradually eastward by their more powerful Tarin neighbours, they received aid from the Mohmandi who were concentrated mainly on the plateau above the Khyber Pass considerably west of their present location. Joining their Mohmand allies and several other Kand clans, they plundered the caravan routes between Kabul and the plains. Annoyed by these incidents, the Afghans eventually drove the Yusufzai out of their eyries along the Khyber and down into the Peshawar Valley, where they became overlords over a subservient population. A century later, having recovered from their earlier defeats, they once again took the offensive. This time, joining with the Ghorakhel, they moved northward against the Dilas in the lower Swat Valley. Eventually they forced the defeated Dilas over the eastern watershed passes into the Hazara district and pushed up the Swat Valley, burning and pillaging as they went. The oppressed Swati were eventually forced into their present home in the upper tributaries just south of the Chilas bend of the Indus.

Following frontier tradition the conquered lands were assigned by lot to the various Yusufzai clans. Enemy survivors remained as slaves and menials. In succeeding generations some were freed and incorporated as full clan members; many of the women had already been concubined or freed as legal wives. Others remained under conditions of perpetual bondage. Later, Gujari herdsmen were permitted pasturage rights to portions of the upper valleys, paying rental in kind. Hindu merchants, shopkeepers, artisans and craftsmen were attracted into the area by trading prospects; *mullahs* and other professors of the Muslim faith moved in as missionaries; and not far behind came specialists in Muslim art and architecture.

Between the Khyber and the Suleimans, the Rohilla ('hillsmen') are considered to be the only true Pathans. All others should more properly be called Afghans except the Ghilzai, the 'third strain' within the Afghan perimeter. Listed among the Rohilla are the Afridi (probably the Aporytae of the Greeks) who actually straddle the Khyber, the Orakzai, Bangash, Khatak, Thuri,

Waziri, Bannuchi, Mahsud, Darwesh and the questionable Utman (Uthman) *khel* north of the Kabul river. Of these, Ibbetson [160] claims Qureshi Arab origins for both the Bangash and Khatak. In so far as biological data can be trusted, such origins appear at least reasonable. The Arab scribes' tradition of using the ruse of an unknown parentage was a customary method of indicating mixed ancestry, and as Robertson Smith [314a] points out, throughout the Arab–Muslim world Qais is a 'dummy name' for an eponymous ancestor designed to meet the needs of the genealogist.

Collectively all of the tribes of the Karlanri group are reputed to be the descendants of a southern *khel* Kakar woman and an unknown father. According to Caroe [47, pp. 21–4] the Karlanri *khels*, forming the core of the most warlike and colourfully romantic of the famed north-west frontier tribesmen, are the oldest of all the Pathans in point of residence in their present homeland. He suggests that the Paktues of Herodotus were very likely Pathans and that Kaspaturos was the Peshawar of today.

The southern *khels*, those in the Suleiman sector, include among others the Shirani, Mandi, Kakari, Musa and Tarin. In a more questionable status are the so-called Ghalji (Ghilzai) on the Indus: Marwati, Bhitanni, Gandapuri, Lohani and Mian. It is from these settled Ghalji that the Khilji–Lodi dynasties of the Mughal empire were derived. To the south of the Pathans, the Baluchi tribes occupy all of Baluchistan except for the pocket of Dravidian-speaking Brahui.

PART III

THE SOUTHERN QUADRANT

The Human Pageantry of Greater India

8
Pre-Harappans, Harappans and Aryans

Southern Asia is by far the most socially complex and densely populated of the four major regions, and in many respects the least known. The lateness of recorded history, the tremendous range in religious ideas and practices, the variety of languages and scripts and the contrasting types of environments and economies have been largely responsible. In spite of these complexities, the biological range is not as great as might be expected.

In a land of such contrasts it is not strange that one of its great scholars should have written: 'In statecraft her rulers were cunning and unscrupulous. Famine, flood, and plague visited her from time to time and killed millions of her people. Inequality of birth was given religious sanction and the lot of the humble was generally hard . . . Yet our overall impression is that in no other part of the ancient world were the relations of man to man, and of man and the state, so fair and humane' [18, pp. 8–9].

Western scholars are less charitable in their estimates of Indian civilization [299], but this may be due to their preoccupation with the astonishing developments in the philosophical and religious spheres. Their interest has centred also on the unique manner in which Indian society became fragmented through the proliferation of caste and the exaggerated extremes that came to prevail between the palaces of the princes and the pallets of the paupers; between the reincarnated dead and the living dead; between splendour and squalor; and between mathematical exactness and the vagueness whch so often seems to prevail in quarters unexpected.

New things may be added but they seem never to destroy or

replace what preceded them. A person may become a Muslim or a Christian but he continues to be aware of the niche he previously occupied within the fabric of Indian society and the limitations he faces in his new role. Social, political and economic institutions are all conditioned to greater or lesser degree by religious sanctions, and total society seems to be a mosaic of an infinite number of interrelated subsocieties, each with its own set of rules, degrees of permissiveness and sense of cohesive solidarity.

In spite of the schisms that have torn the subcontinent apart in recent decades, and the antithetical tenets of Islam and Hinduism, nothing has destroyed the awareness of a common Hindu heritage, summarized by Rawlinson [299] as an almost universal belief in the authority of the Vedas and the sacredness of the cow, the worship of the great gods Shiva and Vishnu in their innumerable aspects, and the institution of caste. Possibly this pattern of social accommodation represents also the continuity of which Indian scholars are aware and which led one of them to comment: 'The icons discovered at Mohenjodaro are those of gods and goddesses who are still worshipped in India, and Hindus from Himalaya to Cape Comorin repeat even today the Vedic hymns which were uttered on the banks of the Indus nearly four thousand years ago' [228, p. 38].

In comparison with other ancient civilizations, however, the antiquity of significant datable sources remains relatively shallow. Historical documentation is mainly epic and legendary, or was until Roman times. For earlier periods dependence on archaeological data is imperative. The Palaeolithic has been referred to in Chapter 3. No pre-sapient hominid remains have yet been found, but thousands of artefacts from hundreds of sites point to probable contact and migration either westward or eastward or both during all major periods. Microliths reminiscent of the Mesolithic of Syria and Anatolia have been found in more than thirty sites, but their concentration in the western half seems to imply introduction from that direction. The dating is uncertain [288, pp. 36–7], but man was living in scattered hunting and gathering communities on the alluvial plains and in the marshlands and open parklands of the major river valleys. The Deccan plateau was undoubtedly more densely forested and interspersed with stretches of savanna and rich in wild game and food plants.

Coastal and inland trade routes connected these mesolithic communities with comparable ones in Irania and with those of a radically different tradition in south-east Asia.

The densest sections of the coastal forests and plateau escarpment were apparently not penetrated until possibly as late as ten thousand years ago, and in pre-agricultural times the biological differences among the various populations were probably not as great as they are today. Ancestors of peoples now restricted to the denser forest regions very likely roamed the more open plains and hunted game in the foothills of the Himalayas. The lower Indus basin was far greener than it is today and, while man doubtless contributed to its dessication, the river also has played tricks on both flora and fauna. As with the Yellow River in China, the outlet has shifted from time to time and in its southernmost meanderings it flowed for a time into the Rann of Cutch [357, pp. 504–20].

There is no proof that agriculture was developed independently but the possibility cannot be ignored. Many of the millets, beans, peas and other legumes, radishes, cucumbers, jute, hemp, mango, tree cotton, peppers, eggplant, oil seeds and possibly Jacob's tears existed in wild form and may have been domesticated in the subcontinent.

So much more is known about the mesolithic, neolithic and chalcolithic periods of western Asia than of the southern or south-eastern peninsulas that it is easy to overlook the importance of these areas. India apparently derived much of its Neolithic as well as its metal-age civilization from two sources – one along the Makran coast and Baluchistan in the west, the other from south-east Asia by way of the Arakan coast and Assam [107]. Our knowledge of the first source is documented from numerous sites in the arid regions along the foothill rim of the Indus Valley; the second is still largely covered with dense vegetation and is only beginning to be understood.

Painted wares similar to those of Elam, Sialk and Giyan have been found in Seistan and Baluchistan and are presumed to have been transmitted, but there are so many 'culture areas' in the Kulli, Nal, Zhob, Lora and other valleys of the southern Suleiman complex that no direct connections with plains cultures are assignable. In the lowlands the situation is quite different. Until recently it had been thought that the Indus Valley or Harappan civilization sites were actually scattered mesolithic hunting and gathering communities transformed into more concentrated permanent neolithic and Copper–Bronze Age settlements. Recently the discovery of a number of wall-enclosed, complex urbanized, mound-based neolithic settlements in the now dried-up Sarasvati River bed in Rajasthan and others in Kathiawar and parts of southern Gujarat have changed this view. The technical levels achieved by the pre-Harappan communities were in no sense inferior to many of those in Baluchistan.

The distinctive features of the Harappan civilization have also become clearly defined. Unlike Mesopotamian sites, there is remarkable uniformity in the artefact assemblages at given time periods from the earlier Amri–Harappan, dated from 2300 BC [2] to the later Mohenjodaro period from about 2000 BC. There are no pyramidal or large temple structures as in Mesopotamia, and the methods of water supply and drainage are unusual; the hypocaust system which heated a grand central bath is unique. Other individual features include the ceramic techniques, the system of weights and measures, and the differentiation between the citadel and slave quarters. All point to the existence of considerable social stratification and an extraordinarily complex system of administrative controls. It is puzzling, however, that the script of some three hundred glyphs – presumably syllables – remains largely undeciphered. The glyphs seem to relate more to taxes, deeds and accounts than to events of historical significance. Recently, a partial decipherment has been claimed by a Finnish team [277] and, if substantiated, the language would be identifiable as 'proto-Dravidian'.

During the period of its greatest expansion the Indus Valley civilization extended throughout the entire river basin from the Himalayan foothills and the Doab or Ganges watershed to coastal Gujarat, with an estuarine dock at Lothal and an outpost at Thana near Bombay. Based on the discovery of Indus Valley seals in Mesopotamia, Sir Mortimer Wheeler [398] makes a very cogent case for the derivation of the Harappan civilization from the Mesopotamian (Sumero–Akkadian). He is more cautious than Rawlinson, who states categorically that 'the Indus Valley folk were an intrusive stock who shared a common ancestry with the Sumerians' [299, p. 17].

Such proposals seem scarcely justifiable on the basis of our present knowledge, but either a Sumerian or a Semitic origin is possible. Both are frequently suggested, but Dravidian and Mundari are more often mentioned by Indian scholars and the decipherment referred to would tend to support the former. They point to the Brahui, a pocket of Dravidian speakers in the Baluchi hills, and to various religious symbols on the seals and other artefacts which parallel many presumed survivals in south India, notably the worship of the lingam, the sacred bull and the tree of life. A Mundari origin presupposes that Mundari-speaking populations must once have occupied most of the subcontinent; and that they are identifiable as the Dasyus who were driven into their present quarters by a migration of Dravidian speakers from Irania before the development of the Harappan civilization.

Early neolithic and Bronze Age migrations into India have not been clearly defined and skeletal evidence from Baluchistan is far from satisfactory. There are numerous burial grounds but cremation was common in some regions; in others, disposal was partly by ordinary inhumation with the body extended or slightly flexed and partly by 'fractional' urn burials. In the latter method the corpse was exposed until decomposition was complete. Usually only the skull and a few long bones were preserved. Unfortunately the urns were painted and attracted the attention of amateur antiquarians who were not interested in the contents. The remains of fewer than fifty individuals have been recovered, but more promising cemeteries have been discovered and remain to be explored.

From the Indus Valley and neighbouring sites the picture is somewhat brighter. Recently Sen [338] undertook a critical review of the major skeletal studies prior to 1964. Over two hundred individuals from seventeen different sites in seven states and provinces were included, but only the skulls were numerically adequate for statistical analysis. With refreshing candour he dismissed appraisals based on racial typology and discarded all isolated and distorted specimens or those of questionable sex-age identification. He found that the Harappan series was within the range and variability limits of present-day populations of the northern Punjab, and that the smaller Mohenjodaro series followed the same pattern for the southern Punjab and Sind. Leaving aside the question of the ordered sequence of migrations and demographic fluctuations, there is no skeletal evidence to show that a biologically new 'element' could be held accountable for the development of the Indus Valley civilization. All efforts to prove the contrary have been based on far too scanty evidence to indicate more than a genetic range substantially greater than in the plateau region to the south.

Estimates of total population have varied widely, but the rationales for the differences – climate, food supply, diseases and technology – and their analyses vary significantly.

The Indus Valley civilization had spread from its southern bases northward to the Himalayan foothills by about 1800 BC, but the northernmost sites fall short of the more tortuous gorges of Kohistan ('land of snow peaks') and the vale of Kashmir. The latter region was doubtless known to the settled peoples of the plains, and scattered mesolithic artefacts have been found, but recent excavations in Kashmir point northward as the source of these early proto-urban settlers.

The artefacts from the Burzahom site just north of Srinagar – dated from 1850 to 1540 BC depending on horizon level – are strongly reminiscent of southern Siberia (Minusinsk), Transbaikalia, the Inner Asian perimeter and north China [8]. They include pit floor pole houses, textured pottery, rectangular knives, bone harpoons, ovoid or quadrangular polished stone celts and stone rings. Food consisted of deer and dog among the larger animals, and the occurrence of the polished celts suggests some agriculture. The dead were smeared with red ochre and buried in a flexed position. The earlier palaeolithic artefacts from Kashmir are more closely allied to those of north India, so it might be conjectured that the builders of Burzahom crossed the Hindu Kush by 2000 BC or thereabouts. It is doubtful if access could have been possible much before the late neolithic, or that the Tibetan plateau was penetrated from the west before that time.

For the rest of greater India – the Ganges basin, the Deccan and the peninsular and insular south – far less is known, but clearly nothing like the civilizational developments had taken place at comparable levels of antiquity. It was not until after the entry of the Aryans that urban civilization was extended into the middle Ganges area and parts of the Deccan. By the beginning of the first millennium, however, there appears to have been a sudden burst of energy throughout the entire Ganges basin and along the eastern or Coromandel coast as far south as Chingleput in Madras.

Various theories have been advanced to account for the abandonment of the Indus Valley cities, but there is no agreement on the precise causes, which were probably multiple. Climatic changes seem now to be largely discounted but, as in the case of China, dessication owing to overgrazing and forest denudation were undoubtedly contributing factors. Another may well have been the technological adjustment to the monsoon forest zone, which at that time extended throughout the Ganges basin and across the Doab. Archaeological evidence also supports the idea of gradual weakening and ultimate abandonment of major sites owing to the vagaries of the river and lowering of the water table [107]. More acceptable sites were apparently located in the Doab, Rajasthan and down the west coast and eastward; the ability to cope with the forest environment may also have been facilitated by contact with south-east Asia. Penetration seems certainly to have occurred westward from Assam before 2000 BC.

If Agrawal [2, pp. 202–3] is correct, the copper axes and other artefacts from numerous caches scattered throughout the Ganges basin, though unique both typologically and in alloy, approximate most nearly to many of the recently discovered specimens from Thailand and the dates are appropriate. The C^{14} datings of the latter range in the vicinity of 3000–2500 BC and those of the Doab about 2300 BC. He believes, however, that the task of clearing the virgin forest lands of the Ganges would have required the use of more than copper celts and stresses the importance of iron artefacts, which make their appearance about 1700 BC. Some of the extensive mound burial sites in north-east Thailand contain as many as several hundred urn burials, dated by the thermoluminescent dating technique to as early in some instances as 4630 BC. This raises questions which may not be easy to resolve. The occurrence of urn burials of such antiquity is itself important, but the associated bronze artefacts, especially socketed celts of high tin content cast in moulds, may prove revolutionary [107, p. 349].

The oldest known pottery appears to be from south-east Asia and Japan, so if there is confirmation that cast bronze of high quality were actually produced in the same area in the fifth millennium BC, present concepts would be drastically altered concerning the earliest centres of civilization. The necessary natural resources are present in abundance and in close proximity to each other in peninsular and insular south-east Asia, both high-quality clays for ceramics and tin and copper for bronzes, but evidence of steps in metalworking from the earliest stages to the use of mould casting will have to be demonstrated before the sceptics will be satisfied. This particular issue has caused heated arguments among specialists and speculations among amateurs. Whatever the outcome, it is likely that many revisions will have to be made in current concepts of man's accomplishments in the great river valleys of the ancient world.

Thus far nothing discovered in India can compare in time depth or clarity with early Chinese historical documents. It has been estimated [355] that the oldest of the Vedic sources are from the sixth century BC; the reconstruction of early Indian society has had to depend largely on interpolations based mainly on the Vedas, the Arthashastra and early western accounts dating from about the fifth century BC.

It is consistent with Indian prehistory generally that the artefact assemblages and sequence appear to be different from both western and eastern models and seem to combine elements from both, but in such modified forms and combinations that many appear as anachronisms. As Wheeler [398, p. 80] points out, the term 'Neolithic' makes little sense in India where, in a number of sites in the hillier regions of Orissa, Bengal and Assam, highly polished stone axes with pointed butts are found intermixed with lunate (moon-shaped) microlithic blades, copper or bronze beads and spear points. Elsewhere shouldered stone hoes or adzes occur in similar combinations and date from the beginning of the first millennium BC. Nothing comparable with these finds occurs in the Indus Valley or in western Asia, although the latter complex is found throughout south-east Asia and into China as far north as Canton.

Most authorities still favour the idea that, while many of the Indus Valley axes and adzes – notably the socketed axe – show the closest similarities with those of Iran, the Caucasus and the Kuban Valley and are not found in the Ganges basin, they may nevertheless be the original inspiration for the highly curvilinear style of some of the axes, and the specialized alloys may have been merely later Gangetic innovations. The fact remains, however, that the forms of some of the Gangetic axes and especially the adzes are very similar to the shouldered stone celts of Bengal, Assam and south-east Asia.

It might be argued that the stone adzes are copies of bronze prototypes, as can be demonstrated in various similar contexts, or that they themselves were the prototypes of the bronze artefacts. If the western bronzes prove in time to be earlier, then possibly the two views are not irreconcilable and, as Fairservis [107, p. 349] has phrased it; 'both were probably part of an indigenous development perhaps derived ultimately from a technological advance diffused from the west but then more definitely Indianized'. This may be just another instance of the frequently observed phenomenon in India of accepting a novel idea with alacrity and altering it in style or content so fundamentally that it becomes completely incorporated into the enduring greater Indian tradition and traces of its alien origin are all but obliterated.

The so-called Chalcolithic, Pre-Harappan and Harappan periods in the Indus Valley, Gujarat and western Maharashtra are generally contemporary with the so-called neolithic of the Deccan and eastern India. If Sankalia's summation [323] is correct, there were five contemporary culture phase areas:

(1) *Neolithic*, with only polished stone celts and pottery limited to hand-made jars in the east (Assam, Bihar, Bengal and parts of the adjacent Deccan);

(2) *Neolithic–chalcolithic*, with polished celts and blade tools and hand-made pottery in the west coast (Karnatak, Gujarat and Baluchistan);

(3) *Chalcolithic*, with stone blade and copper tools, wheel-made painted pottery and wattle and daub houses in central India (north Karnatak and Malwa);

(4) *Chalcolithic–bronze*, with stone blades, copper and bronze tools and wheel-made pottery in the north-west (Sind, Saurashtra and Punjab);

(5) *Chalcolithic–bronze*, with copper or bronze but no stone tools, wheel-made pottery and wattle and daub houses in the north (Uttar Pradesh and western Bihar).

Following the Bronze Age and, in fact, quite late – probably after the beginning of the last millennium before Christ – there appears suddenly in peninsular south India and parts of the

Deccan a megalithic complex of dolmens, cromlechs and menhirs associated with iron artefacts similar in many respects to that of the Mediterranean. Some scholars believe that this tradition might have been seaborne from the west; others, that it is related to the megalithic complex of south-east Asia and Japan. Whichever is correct, it survives today in attenuated form in the southernmost part of the peninsula [121].

To summarize, the above archaeological evidence suggests that, during the second millennium before Christ, settlements associated with copper and bronze tools and northern black polished ware spread very rapidly down the Ganges Valley eastward into Bengal. Within a matter of centuries the entire basin had been largely cleared of forests and was supporting a relatively dense population which, at least in its biological aspects, is probably reflected in the majority of the present-day inhabitants. Meanwhile, beginning about 1000 BC or even earlier, there was a spread of the south-east Asian culture complex and a possible minimal immigration via Assam and Burma into Bengal and central India. In the Indian subcontinent the chronological sequences of Eurafrica and western Asia are recognizable only to a very limited degree and cannot be relied upon to indicate movements of peoples. Culture stimulus or diffusion seems likely to have been of more importance than large-scale migration.

One of the most momentous events to stir the minds of European thinkers of the late eighteenth century was unquestionably the discovery of the structural and morphophonemic similarity between Sanskrit and classical Greek and Latin and, ultimately, of the cognatic relationships of the entire Indo-European group of languages. The initial discovery by Coeurdoux in 1767 and, independently, by Sir William Jones in 1786 revolutionized ideas about man's origins and past wanderings and gave rise to numerous new disciplines of scholarly research. This, in turn, led to the systematization of biblical archaeology and to speculations concerning the Ten Lost Tribes. The discovery in the classical realms of philology, linguistics and archaeology was probably fully as important in its day as were Darwin's demonstrations and speculations in the field of organic evolution nearly a century later. The discovery affected even the political arena as parliamentary debates in London began to echo the refrain of the obligation it imposed on the peoples of the British Isles to 'assist our distant Aryan cousins'.

Such studies, especially those relating to the structure of language, were not new to the Indian scene. The works of the great Indian grammarians, the oldest known to scholarship, were already familiar to the Arabs and knowledge of these had been passed on to Europe by Arab scholars at the height of the Muslim hold on Spain. By AD 1030, Albiruni had become aware also of the distinction between classical Sanskrit cultivated by the educated classes and the regional vernaculars; but according to Grierson [136, p. 1] it was an Indian-born Turk – Amir Khusrau – who in AD 1317 first listed the twelve most important languages of Hindi. In the heyday of Muslim Turkish expansion, Khusrau's bias in favour of Arabic over Persian is understandable, but he is more charitable in comparing it with Hindi. It is clear that he had a scholarly grasp of both the variety of languages and the greatness of Hindi.

In spite of the spate of scholarship – both Asian and European – that has concentrated on the problem of language origins and diversifications, many vital questions remain unanswered. Not until 1856 was it known that the Dravidian languages of the south were to be distinguished as a group from the Indo-Aryan languages of the north; and it was only in 1906 that the linkage between the Munda languages of central and eastern India and the Mon-Khmer languages of south-east Asia was finally determined.

Many problems remain to be solved, but the main outlines of the peopling of the subcontinent have become increasingly clear in the past few decades. It has been established that the Mundari languages are a part of the great Austro-Asian or Austronesian group, including not only the Mon-Khmer languages of the continent but also the Malayan group of Indonesia and Madagascar and the Micronesian and Polynesian groups of the Pacific. It is generally assumed that the Mundari languages were introduced by the shouldered celt or copper-bronze artificers but the relationship of Dravidian to the Indus Valley population is still a puzzle, and, as in the case of the Munda group, the application of the term Dravidian has added to the confusion.

It has sometimes been said that to begin the study of India with Old Indic, Vedic and Sanskritic is to do it the hard way unless one is already familiar with the Avestas, Old Slavonic and Lithuanian. However true this may be of languages, it is probably the easiest point of departure when one is studying the people. It is in the four Vedas (cognate with Old English 'wit') and in particular the Rigveda, that an insight can be gained into the socioeconomic, political and religious life of the ancient Aryans.

Some time during the early centuries of the second millennium is the date generally given for the beginning of the Aryan incursions into India by way of the north-western passes – probably between 1700 and 1600 BC. It is described as an invasion in the Rigveda, and the fact that the Indus Valley cities appear to have been destroyed through violence and fire is cited as proof, but there is nothing to indicate that the Aryans came in as a well organized army of conquest originating on the plateau. On the contrary, as noted by Rawlinson [299, p. 20], they probably entered 'as immigrant tribes, bringing with them their wives and families, their flocks and herds'. The epics recount their progressive movement eastward and their encounters with the Dasyus ('slaves'), who are described as 'dark-skinned, noseless [anasu], and short-statured', but whose phallic rituals were more abhorrent than their physical characteristics. The Aryans may have begun their marauding on the plains in small bands, just as the Pathan and Baluchi tribesmen were doing in the not too distant past and, from bases in the broader valleys which fingered up into the foothills, may have eventually launched attacks in force against the dwellers on the plains. If, therefore, the Vedic account can be relied upon, the final assaults could have been both sudden and overwhelming.

By careful analysis of the Vedas it has been possible to reconstruct something of the religion, economy and social institutions of the Arya or 'noble ones'. The religious rituals and symbolisms are very close to those of the ancient Iranians as described in the Avestan *gāthās*, and the pantheon to that of the Graeco-Romans. The names of many of the latter are cognate and their roles as deities similar. The Aryans possessed no temples or images but worshipped their spiritually anthropomorphized deities on open altars. The flesh of sacrificed cattle was eaten and beef otherwise was served on special occasions. The Aryans were sedentary pastoralists – raising sheep, goats, asses and horses in addition to cattle. Horses had been known along the Indus in Harappan times but, like asses and oxen, were used only for simple traction. The Aryans introduced the chariot; saddles were not used until several centuries later. The main crops were barley and wheat: from the former they made a distilled drink.

In social structure the Aryans distinguished between a hereditary priesthood and a class of warriors; artisans included goldsmiths, copper workers, bronze casters and carpenters. Poisoned arrows were used in warfare but they had neither cavalry nor elephants and there seems to have been no knowledge of iron. They were monogamous, did not practise child marriage and lived in half-timber construction houses.

Later Hindu civilization represents a fusion and refinement of the material culture and religious and social institutions of the Aryans with additions from Harappan and pre-Harappan sources. The caste system, however, was at a rudimentary stage though society was already stratified into four classes or *varna*. According to the Vedas, the primary method of disposal of the dead was by cremation, but archaeological evidence points to simple inhumation, the usual method on the Iranian plateau and in the Aralo–Caspian basin.

Within the past few years, through the efforts of an Italian expedition and the Pakistan Archaeological Survey [77], several proto-historic sites were excavated in the states of Swat and Dir in the North-west Frontier Agencies, an area forming part of the ancient Buddhist Gandhara. The culture complex, identified by cemetery contents as the Gandhara grave complex, was excavated by the Italians at Mingora in Swat and by the Pakistanis at Timargarha in Dir. Both revealed three separate occupation periods: Period I, extending from the sixteenth to thirteenth centuries BC; Period II, from the twelfth to tenth centuries; and Period III, from early in the sixth century to the Achaemenid invasion.

Burials of the Gandhara grave complex differ markedly from those of Harappa–Mohenjodaro and have been related to sites in northern Iran and Turkestan, notably Tepe Hissar. Furthermore, using the Penrose distance method of determining morphological similarity, Bernhard [23] concludes on the basis of twenty adult skulls of both sexes recovered from eighty-two Period I graves that the closest and most striking similarities are with Bronze and early Iron Age skulls of the Volga and Caucasus area 2500 BC–AD 500 and Tepe Hissar in Iran. He noted especially a lack of close similarities with skulls from Mohenjodaro and Harappa. On the basis of these analyses, Bernhard's conclusions agree with those of Dani, based on cultural comparisons, that the earliest graves (Period I) are those of the Aryan invaders.

9

Later Invaders and the Development of a Caste Society

The millennium from 1500 to 500 BC was characterized by expanding trade and the development of the Brahmi and Kharoshti scripts from Semitic Aramaic, the presumed precursor of most of the Indian alphabets, but there was little concern for recording events. This lack was balanced in part by the commitment to oral transmission, especially of the four Vedas, but the first reasonably reliable dates from Indian sources are those of the Maurya empire of Chandragupta in the fourth century BC. In spite of this, political complexity had attained the level of city-states along the Ganges as early as the seventh century BC. By the sixth, the first empires had already begun to form – Kosala in the upper section and Magadha–Maurya in Bihar. It was to the Maurya court that Megasthenes was sent as the Seleucid ambassador, and to him we owe a vivid picture of Indian society [299, p. 55]. From his accounts and others, including the Chinese pilgrim, Fa Hsien, the Maurya capital Pataliputra – near the present Patna – in the third century BC must have been about as cosmopolitan a city as could be found anywhere. This was a high period of Indian sea trade with the Persian Gulf ports of Mesopotamia and the Red Sea ports of Egypt. Overland trade was by caravan from Taxila to Balkh, from there down the Oxus to the Aral Sea and by a now extinct river connecting the Caspian with the Black Sea.

Even more spectacular than the reign of Chandragupta was that of his grandson Asoka. Within a few years the latter had extended his empire south to Mysore, east to the borders of Assam, north to Nepal and west to the Hindu Kush. Only the

Dravidian states of the far south remained unconquered – the kingdoms of the Cholas and Pallavas and the Isle of Lanka. In his latter days, filled with remorse following his merciless slaughter of innocents, Asoka was converted to Buddhism, but before he took his vows and retired to a monastery he dispatched missionaries to all corners of the known world, even to Greece and Egypt.

Faced with Brahmanist revolts, Asoka's immediate successors were unable to stem the tide of a return to orthodoxy, but as the gates were slowly closed on Buddhism in India the faithful followed Asoka's admonitions and carried their message abroad. In the south, Ceylon became the base for the conversion of south-east Asia, and through Gandhara and Sinkiang the scriptures were carried to China, Japan and Korea, and less directly to Tibet and Mongolia.

Few traces of the early Persian and Macedonian conquests survive, but as with most armies of occupation the biological impact was probably minimal. By the middle of the third century BC, the known historical world from Rome to China entered a convulsive period whose most lasting effects, both cultural and biological, were probably felt in India. In the west, the Seleucid empire was unable to prevent its own gradual dismemberment. Graeco–Bactria broke away and was shortly followed by Parthia. In the east, the hitherto separate feudatory states of the Chou dynasty were finally amalgamated into a single centralized empire of Ch'in (222–206 BC) and in India began the historic 'Age of Invasions' [18, p. 57].

While Parthian attention was still largely directed towards Persia and Mesopotamia, that of Bactria was concentrated on Gandhara, and the Punjab was brought under Graeco–Bactrian control. Several petty kingdoms were established, the largest having their seats of government at Kabul, Kandahar and Sialkot, but all were extinguished within a few decades by the growing strength of Parthia. In the meantime disturbances had recommenced in the desert–steppe zone to the north and part of the Parthian success over the Graeco–Bactrians may have been due to the movement of Saka Iranian nomads southward into Bactria about the middle of the second century BC.

The conquest by the Yüechih–Tochari first of Bactria and subsequently of the lands held by the Saka south of the Hindu

Kush was of direct concern to India. Chinese and Greek sources agree that after 128 BC the Saka, pressed from the north, began their incursions into the valley of the Indus. They had already carried their conquests throughout Gandhara and Sind eastward into the upper Ganges and all but two or three of the petty Graeco–Bactrian kingdoms had been conquered. In Indian histories the Saka are often referred to as Indo–Scythians. Their dynastic histories are moderately well known but there is considerable uncertainty concerning the succeeding dynasty of the Kushans.

The name Kushan is supposed to be derived from a subtribe of the Yüechih–Tochari but there is archaeological and historical evidence that the peoples of the Kushan empire spoke mainly Iranian. The people, at least, who were incorporated into the Kushan empire were already speakers of these languages and they preserved them for centuries after the empire's consolidation. Kanishka, the greatest of the Kushan rulers, began what is referred to in India as the Saka Era in AD 78 [18, p. 61].

The Kushan dynastic period covering the first two centuries of the Christian era saw the development of the 'Greater Vehicle' (Mahayana) school of Buddhism, the mixed Graeco–Bactrian, Gandharan and Indo–Scythian schools of art and the rapid spread of Buddhism into Sinkiang. In spite of their religious zeal, the Kushans were unable to stop the newly revived Sassanian–Persian empire from recapturing the eastern provinces of Irania and invading the Punjab, a conquest that carried minimal biological impact but was of considerable cultural significance. From AD 250, immediately after the Persian withdrawal, until the commencement of the Gupta empire in AD 335, the whole of the Punjab, Sind, Kathiawar and the upper Ganges had reverted to control by petty Sakian kingdoms and confederacies of semi-nomadic east Iranian tribes. New direct trade routes were established through Kashmir and across the high eastern Hindu Kush and Karakoram passes, and along the desert route to China through the Tarim basin.

The establishment of the Gupta empire marked the end of Iranian control but fresh incursions commenced in the north-west in the last half of the fifth century. The invaders are referred to as Huns or Hunas (Hunna), but their identity is still a matter of dispute. Some authors claim they were Iranian speakers, others that they were Turkic–Mongol. European historians of the time refer to the Hunna as White Huns or Hephthalites (Ephthalites). Whatever the leadership, the actual attacking force was probably a motley array of mercenaries and freebooters, both Turkic and Iranian. The speed with which the Hunna carried out their conquests and the sparseness of documentation make it seem likely that pillage rather than settlement was the motive and the biological impact was probably minimal.

The success of the Hunna depended on ready access to replacement mounts, adequate stabling and supplies for their cavalry. Their superiority depended on swiftness of attack and excellence of equipment, not on numbers. They consolidated their hold on western India from Gujarat to the Doab and established a line of kings whose exploits were recorded on memorial stelae; but their hold on the land lasted scarcely thirty years. Under their aegis, however, the older Saka–Tocharian élite, together with survivors of the earlier Graeco–Bactrian aristocracy, seem to have become the major element, identifiable later with the most senior Rajput lineages. This would appear at least to be a more rational interpretation of the impact of the Hunnic invasions than the far more colourful and highly embellished acounts of Rajput origin from the solar, lunar, fire and other deities as claimed today by the thirty-six leading clans.

The question of Rajput origins has long been a matter of dispute. Some would derive the 'sons of princes' from Indic–Aryan, Dravidian and Mundari tribal sources who were elevated to the fold of the Kshatriya. Others consider them to be descendants of the Hunnic or Saka–Tocharian élite. Biological evidence offers little support to either view, or possibly partial support to both. The explanation of tribal origins seems to lie not so much in detribalization as in the powerful hinduizing or brahminizing process which was under way at the time throughout north India.

The most powerful argument favouring local tribal origins is probably reflected in the histories of the local kingdoms of the Parihars, Pawars and Chandels (not to be confused with the Chandala or scavenger caste) who established kingdoms in Kanauj and inspired the building of so many of India's famous temples, including those at Khajuraho.

According to traditional Indian accounts [354] the Hunnic incursions were so overwhelming that they destroyed all memory of descent from the first and second 'swarms' – the Yüechih–Tocharians and Sakas and later the Kushans – during and following their defeat by the Sassanians. However overwhelming the Hunnic deluge, it was one of military conquest rather than of social and religious conversion. For warrior leaders to assume the titles and roles of rajas and Rajputs was an easy shift in the process, and the later emergence and growth of the subsequent Rajput empire was a natural consequence. Rajputs today form a substantial part of the population throughout all of the Hindu populations of north India and, as claimants to the mantle of the Kshatriya, are listed together with the Thakur and Chettri as belonging to the warrior *varna*. Their social position is enviable since they are neither weighed down by the exacting duties of the higher-ranking Brahmins nor subjected to as many inhibitions. Many are or were *zamindari* (landlords) or in the mercantile trades and, if agriculturalists, were and remain more often independent farmers than tenants. Many of the former rulers (maharajas and rajas) trace their Rajput ancestry back for more than a thousand years and in various parts of India the Rajputs served as proprietors of tax-free village estates. Manoeuvring to acquire recognition and classification as Rajputs became the goal of many an inferior splinter caste.

From the sixth century onward tremendous changes took place in the history of India, but apart from periodic Arab incursions of the ninth and tenth centuries these remained mainly in the cultural realm – dynastic changes, the breaking up and re-formation of empires, political conquests, religious conversions, the development of new art styles and the accentuation of urbanization processes. There were no large-scale incursions to alter drastically the larger gene pool of greater India as a whole. Such additions as did occur were largely confined to the Indus basin and the western littoral.

India was for a time reunited under the great Harsa (AD 606–48), and while his empire was not long-lasting the most persistent new development was the emergence of several Dravidian kingdoms in the Deccan and the southernmost part of the peninsula. The eighth and early ninth centuries witnessed the formation also of numerous Rajput kingdoms and principalities in central and northern India, but the most dramatic development was the beginning of the islamization of the west: the conquest of the

Indus Valley and parts of the south at the end of the ninth century, and the creation of the Ghaznavid empire by the Turkic Mahmud of Ghazni about the year 1000. To these must be added the subsequent expansion of the Mughals, who shifted the centre of control from the highlands of Afghanistan to the strategic watershed region of the Doab between the Punjab and the petty kingdoms of the Ganges. Although the inflow of new genetic materials may have been only moderate during the millennium following the Hunnic invasions, there were great internal demographic shifts, both migrational and differential, and the class–caste system became much more rigidly stratified and intensified. With the expansion of the holy Jihad to India there were also wholesale conversions, either to Islam by Hindus or to Hinduism by pagan tribes. Among the Rajputs, some were converted by the sword, others were forced to accept Muslim overlordship or fled to the comparative safety of the Pahari regions or the Deccan.

The next major invasion was by Ala-ud-din Khilji in 1294. After a whirlwind conquest of the north he turned his attention to the centre and south. He annexed Gujarat and most of the Deccan and broke the back of Dravidian resistance in the south. The effects of these campaigns were temporarily devastating but more materially destructive than genetically dislocating. The previous disruption of the earlier Rajput rulers had, if anything, the opposite effect. The Khilji period was more a brilliant and temporarily crippling military conquest as was that of Timur or Tamerlane in 1398. It was the brilliance of the latter's campaigns that has made him a legendary figure, rather than the permanence of his conquests. It remained for the Mughals, the sixth in the series of invaders, to achieve a measure of lasting impact. Their rule began with the invasion of the Punjab in 1525 and culminated in the establishment of permanent control under Akbar, roughly contemporary with the Elizabethan period in England.

Except for brief periods, greater India was never a major imperial power beyond the natural confines of the subcontinent. As with China the land was so vast that the sheer logistics of maintaining a united nation were often insuperable. Horse-riders from the north-west were a constant threat, and more often than not were successful in their conquests of the lowlands. Like the

Mongols and the Manchus, the Mughals forsook their upland homes to gain control of the densely populated river valleys: Akbar the Conqueror, like the great Khan, after consolidating his hold on the northern and central regions of his new domain, felt impelled to recapture the homeland from which his forebears had initiated their conquests. The expansions of the western and Inner Asian powers were motivated chiefly by a sense of imperial conquest, whereas those of India remained mainly in the philosophical and religious fields or were dependent in varying degrees on mercantilism and trade. Their impact, nevertheless, was global in dimension.

In other respects too, Indian civilization has tended to be unique. From earliest times the socioeconomic orientation of the subcontinent has been primarily towards cattle-raising, and kinship was never as important as it was in either western Asia or China. Kin groupings and genealogies had their place in the developmental stages, but they were not the primary basis on which society as a whole was organized or structured. Kin ties were and remain at the caste (*jat*) level and not at the larger community or national level. A caste, or subcaste, loosely considered to be endogamous, is divided internally into a number of exogamous units. The term for these units – 'clans' or 'sibs' – varies from region to region, but in the Hindi-speaking areas they are called *gotras*, literally 'cattle pens' or 'cattle herds', an appropriate reference to the sanctity of bovines.

Cosmic symbolism is manifested in class stratification through the functional behaviour and interrelationships of the respective classes. Ideally, the Brahmins guide and instruct the three subsidiary classes. They manifest their control and mediation through the performance of rites and rituals both sacerdotal and mundane. It does not matter that all Brahmins are not priests. What matters is that Brahmins should be engaged in ministerial activities directed towards ritualistic, instructional or healing ends. As noted by Prabhu [293] the great Bhishma himself propounded the theory that a Brahmin might take a wife from any *varna*. If she was a Brahmin or a Kshatriya, the sons would be Brahmins; if a Vaisya, they would be Vaisyas; and if a Sudra, they would be Sudras. This permissive hypergamy of the ancients is still variously observed but its greatest impact was in caste formation.

The *varna* were from the beginning merely classes, whereas the *jati* (castes) were occupational groupings or the products of cross-matings between classes. In cross-matings the ranges might be extreme, but were separable into natural and unnatural. The usual classical injunction was that a man should take a wife from the same or a lower social stratum. The children would be of the mother's stratum but separately identified. This was preferred and considered to be natural or *anuloma* [16]. If a man of one of the three higher levels took a woman from the fourth, a new intermediate level was created. By continuing this process over the centuries, the complexities were eventually created. The reverse or otherwise ritually unacceptable unions were referred to as unnatural or *pratiloma*.

The importance of such classical interpretations is largely symbolical. There is little relationship between caste and distinguishable biological differentiations. In a recently published analysis of the Brahmins of Gujarat, Malhotra [176] has demonstrated that the traditional account of the origin of the various Brahmin castes by a process of branching from a common source could not be biologically substantiated. He concludes that the class must have grown by the addition of migratory endogamous groups from the north and accretions from local sources.

Estimates as to the number of Indian castes vary from three to five thousand, depending on different regional methods of classification. Also, in some areas tribes are considered castes whereas in others they are excluded [174]. Even at the Brahmin level there is no consensus, and at no other level are gradations so zealously guarded as among the Brahmin élite [322].

Various terms have been employed to designate the processes of change within the ever-changing greater society of India (Hindustan). Of these, probably the most referred to are de-tribalization and sanskritization; both have specific rather than generalized significance. De-tribalization implies the breakup of internal tribal structure but carries with it no special model or reorganizational goal. A tribe may become a tribal caste by acquiring some or all of the basic caste essentials such as a *panchayat* (five-man council), the services of a rite-performing *purohit* (priest), a suitable genealogy and an identity with a sectarian temple. On the other hand it might elect to join a religious movement which places sectarian identity above tribal authority; or it may sufficiently submerge its tribal identity by assuming a new name, migrating to a new region, changing its occupation and perhaps learning a new language. Sanskritization is a rather deceptive term which implies the adoption of behavioural aspects of the classical caste system such as food and commensal habits, avoidance of pollution, ritual purification, observance of *pujas* (rites) and rules concerning mate selection rather than merely the assumption of such factors as occupational emphasis and the flaunting of names and claims. De-tribalization may include aspects of sanskritization, but this term is more often applicable to efforts towards changing caste status than to entry into the system. Hinduization is even more inclusive, referring as it does to the worship of Hindu deities, the acceptance of religious mythologies and artistic canons, patterns of social behaviour and material culture. Internally, hinduization has accounted for tremendous demographic changes; externally it has been extended to foreign lands with missionary zeal and its impact persists to this day in much of south-east Asia.

In spite of the sincere hopes and expectations of a few social reformers of post-independence India, the legislative assembly recognized from the beginning that caste could not be legislated out of existence, but measures have been taken toward achieving this goal. Among the most powerful have been (1) the non-recognition of traditional caste privilege as the basis for legal action; (2) the abolition of caste privilege as the basis for exclusion from public institutions; (3) the staged enforcement of compulsory education; (4) the initiation of universal franchise; (5) the guaranteeing of specified individual rights and privileges.

There is no doubt that progress has been made in all five areas of social reform but this does not necessarily mean the demise of the caste structure. In fact, as pointed out by Srinivas [358]: 'In Independent India, the provision of constitutional safeguards to the backward sections of the population, especially the scheduled castes and tribes, has given a new lease of life to caste'. He is doubtless referring to the specific re-designation of the previous 'depressed classes' and 'aboriginal tribes' as scheduled tribes and castes, and the encouragement given to these sectors of society to become better educated and more politically and legally minded, but the effect has been mixed. Understandably, the scheduled castes have not been above taking advantage of situations to improve their lot and there is no question that their loyalty to their own particular groups has been strengthened. The hitherto vertically structured and religiously sanctioned values are gradually assuming more horizontal orientation with strong political overtones and a trend towards amalgamation into larger collective groupings.

10

Cultural Pressures and their Demographic Impact

The political and military events of the past twenty-five years have created a sharp ideological and orientational cleavage between the Muslim communities of Pakistan and Bangladesh and the greater Hindu–Buddhist–Sikh–Jain–Lingayat–Parsi–Indian–Muslim–Christian and Animistic–tribal communities of the rest of the subcontinent. But the outwardly manifested differences have not erased and cannot erase the mutual awareness of a common cultural heritage or the self-perpetuation of a biological continuum on the part of all of the endogamous communities. It would now seem, however, that common language may yet prove to be a more powerful cohesive and divisive force than the network of interrelated socio-religious tenets. In addition to the adoption of Pashto and Urdu as the official languages in Pakistan, of Bengali in Bangladesh and of Hindi in India, there has been an internal realignment of state boundaries to conform more closely to the limits of local language areas. This has meant a simplification of communication at the local level but a sharpening of the differences at the national level – differences that divide the Indo-Aryan states of the north from the Dravidian states of the south. These moves seem to tend in the direction of linguistic and general cultural separatism, but it is the expectation of the legislature that, in the long run, the advantages of the plan will outweigh its present disadvantages.

The biological impact of the dislocation of some ten to fifteen million people at the time of partition was of tremendous moment to the families involved, but it has been negligible in comparison with total population increase, changes in caste–class differentials, the availability of food supplies and the control of endemic and epidemic diseases. Most of the areas of greatest human dislocation have been in the north and adjacent sections of the central plateau following the floods and famines of 1942–3, 1960 and 1970 in Bengal; the trans-border migrations of 1947–8 in Bengal and the Punjab at the time of partition, and again in 1972–3 during the emergence of the new state of Bangladesh. The south, on the other hand, has been the scene of greatest increase in tensions on the language issue, notably between the Indo–Aryan- and Dravidian-speaking populations.

In the northern and western regions there have been other problems, especially the political overtones of an increasing awareness of a common Pashto heritage on the part of the Pathans of Pakistan and Afghanistan, and to a lesser degree a similar trend among the Baluchis of Iran, Afghanistan and Pakistan. There remains also the continuing problem of potential famine and unrest resulting from the lowering of the water table in the largely melt-water and runoff-dependent irrigation of the relatively arid Indus basin in contrast with the largely monsoon-blessed regions of the Ganges. Finally, border tensions and surveillances persist on both sides of the India–Pakistan frontier, between Pakistan and Afghanistan in the Suleimans, along the cease-fire line in Kashmir and Baltistan, and along the entire zone of confrontation in the plateau portion of the Indus basin between India and the People's Republic of China.

In the east the tensions are of a somewhat different character but possibly are no less acute. Uncertainty prevails in the upper Indus between India and China and continues into the basin of the upper Ganges – the Tsangpo – especially along the North-East Frontier Administration (NEFA) sector, to which China has consistently laid claim. The creation of a specially administered Nagaland region in the Patkai and Naga hills, and changes in the Chin hills borderland zone between Assam and Burma, have somewhat eased tensions created by the Naga move towards independence, but many unresolved problems remain between Burma and India and between India and Bangladesh.

It is understandable, therefore, that dislocations have occurred in trade and in the traditional patterns of symbiotic dependences, both social and material, which have persisted for centuries. Scores of thousands of Tibetans have recently sought sanctuary in Nepal, Bhutan, the Pahari regions of the north and the uplands of Mysore. The wool, grain, borax and tea trade with Tibet has been curtailed in favour of China and the annual transhumant migrations limited largely to Ladakh. Religious pilgrimages to Mt Kailas and other sacred Himalayan peaks have been largely discontinued and pilgrimages of Hindus and Muslims across international borders generally curtailed. On the other hand, there has been a very significant increase in the number of conversions to Islam in Muslim lands, and to Sikhism and Buddhism, as well as de-tribalization in India. The wholesale conversion of nearly three million outcaste Mahars of Gujarat and Maharashtra to Buddhism under the leadership of Dr Ambedkar is an outstanding example.

Apart from conversions, so many new names have appeared in the decennial census listing of scheduled castes and tribes that direct comparisons with previous census listings have become all but impossible. In Pakistan ('Land of the Pure'), while the census is careful not to distinguish caste levels characteristic of earlier censuses under British administration, the proportions of individuals comprising the various former caste communities has probably not changed substantially from those listed in the 1931 census, in spite of increase in the number of converts. Before partition, the populations of the Punjab districts in Pakistan ranged from about sixty-five to ninety per cent Muslim and those of east Punjab in India were Hindu in approximately the same proportions. Now the proportions are well over ninety per cent respectively in the Muslim and Hindu parts of the Punjab – changes owing more to migration than to conversion.

The proportion of Sikhs has remained relatively constant, a reflection on their role since their founding in the sixteenth century and of their strategic location in the Doab watershed area between the basins of the Indus and the Ganges and the religious watershed between the predominantly Muslim and Hindu regions of the north. Guru Nanak, the founder of Sikhism and a member of the Khatri caste, was born in 1469 near the holy city of Amritsar. From his youth he had been familiar with problems of Hindu–Muslim coexistence and deeply sensed the need to bring about some form of reconciliation between the two religious communities. He conceived of a universal God superior to Allah or any of the Hindu deities or those of any other religion, but by selecting and syncretizing what he considered to be the best of Hinduism and Islam his new religion came to be so identified with India that it never achieved the level of a universal religion. Converts were mainly from the Jat, Arora and Rajbangsi castes, and the Sikh community never achieved complete dissociation from caste–class distinctions.

Unquestionably, the greater societies of India, Pakistan and Bangladesh will eventually move away from the internal restraints imposed by caste and class, however long this may take. In India this is certainly the intent of the law and, in Muslim countries, is inherent in the teachings of the Koran.

The subject of Eurasians falls largely outside the scope of this volume, but it may be pertinent to clarify the distinction between Eurasians generally and Anglo–Indians, a term which applies to all permanent British residents of Greater India – both mixed and unmixed. Most are retired civil servants, military personnel, merchants and professionals or their descendants who have continued to maintain family ties with the subcontinent. Population estimates of Eurasians vary from a half to two million and would include those of mixed Portuguese and French ancestry. The former are concentrated mainly in Bengal, Goa and the Konkan coast; the latter in Tamilnadu, Madras city and the enclave of Pondichery.

11

Frontier Tribesmen and Plains Dwellers of Pakistan

The ethno-linguistic line separating the Iranic-speaking 'hill tribes' from the Indo–Aryan (sanskritic) speakers of the lowlands corresponds roughly to the geographical border between the plains and the lowest fringes of the plateau escarpment. The primary direction of gene flow has been from west to east (highland to lowland), but periodically in the past there may have been an opposite trend which stopped with the establishment of the Durand line (see Chapter 7). In Afghanistan and Baluchistan permanent colonies of plains Gujari, Jati (not to be confused with *jat* 'caste') and 'Hindus' (regardless of caste) are scattered in and near urban centres, some possibly dating from Kushan, others from Gupta times. The line referred to is not, therefore, exact, and biologically a higher degree of endogamy exists among the hill tribes than among the peoples of the plains. Internal differences in social structure among the peoples of the plateau and the variety of centuries-old symbiosis between the border tribes and the peoples of the plains are more distinctive than language differences, and provide a number of clues to the processes of miscegenation and migration that must have taken place in the past.

When Islam reached the Indus basin more than a millennium ago it was carried first by Arabs along the coast and later along inland routes by a mixed array of Turks and Iranians. In Pakistan today the entire frontier is characterized by tribal populations of two radically different types. One is based on agnatic kinship, which recognizes an eponymous male ancestor and is subdivided into filial lines of descent; the other is stratified on the basis of ranked subordination and structured toward military ends.

Probably no tribe belongs strictly to one or the other extreme, but in general the northern Pathans are more definitely kin-organized and sedentary, while the Baluchis, Brahuis and border Pathans of the south are structured more along military lines and are mixed sedentary, nomadic and migratory. There appears to be high correlation between terrain, natural resources, migration routes and internal social structure [282].

According to Ibbetson [160, p. 17], one of the most important institutions relating to the process of tribal formation among Baluchis, and less so among the southern Pathans, was the *hamsayah*. Under its provisions, a disaffected splinter group might shift tribal allegiance and claim protection from a related or neighbouring group – a 'substitution of land for blood' as the basis of tribal unity. The descendants would be automatically incorporated into the new host tribal group, and records of such changes preserved in tribal lore.

The eastern plateau escarpment stretches for over 800 miles. Both geographically and ethnically, this crucial Kush–Suleiman frontier divides into three sectors: the southern or states sector of Baluchistan (Kharan, Kalat, Las Bela and Makran), ridged sharply by the Kirthar range; the intermediate or Suleiman sector, which fronts the Agency territories of Baluchistan; and the northern or Pathan–Kohistan sector (formerly the North-west Frontier Province and now the North-west Agencies Frontier) from the southern border of Waziristan to Gilgit. Each sector has one main trade route and two or more subsidiary east–west passages.

The heart of the southern sector is in many ways the most forbidding and isolating. The Kirthar range, a sheer limestone cliff barrier rising 700 feet above the desert plain, serves as the political border of Sind. A few minor passes cut across the main ridge but the major route follows the deep gorge of the Gaj River. The tangle of mountain terrain in the hinterland makes passage elsewhere difficult and limits the grazing grounds.

Behind the limestone façade lies Kalat ('Fortress') – the highland stronghold of the Brahui – a region easy to defend and one in which this Dravidian outlier has been largely isolated for possibly as long as four millennia. In neolithic times, as suggested by their location, the Kalat sites may have been connected with other sites along the Zhob and Lora Valleys and the Kej (cf. *kach*, Arabic 'lower') river sites along the Makran coast. For millennia these coastal havens have assisted the passage of seafarers following the trade route between Arabia and India. However, it was probably through the Gaj river route to the 'Lake of Fish' (Manchhar) near Amri that the first settlers moved from the plateau to the plains.

The Brahui, who straddle the Baluchi–Afghan border, are divided into three territorially defined sections, each section being subdivided into six to twelve subsections [235]. The majority practise nomadic and sedentary herding or oasis agriculture. Settled or migratory smiths, carpenters and other craftsmen – speaking Pashto, Sindhi or Jatki – serve the respective needs of the local communities. Most of the subsection names are recognizably Brahui Dravidian, but such names as Saka, Lari Luri, Jatak, Kurd, Gujar and Sunar are alien, and admixtures of such groups with Iranian and possibly Turkic peoples seems clear. The neighbouring district of Las Bela ('Forest of the Lassi') is the homeland not only of mixed Sindhi–Arab Lassi and Baluchi but of a score of small isolated and extremely mixed populations, ranging from Iranian Tajiks and Pathans to pockets of Turkic speakers from the north and remnants of older pre-Aryan peoples. The most complex are the coastal fishing communities. They carry genetic traces ranging from east African negroids and south coastal Arabs to the Laskars of Gujarat and the Malayali Dravidians of Malabar.

The northern half of the middle or Suleiman sector is inhabited by Ghilzai and nomadic plateau Pathans such as the Pani and Luni; in the southern half by Baluchis of the Rind confederacy – the Marri, Bugti, Dombki and Khetrani and several minor subtribes. The Baluchi, whom Dames [76] identifies with the Parthians, are relative newcomers in their present homeland, which extends from southern Iran to Sind, the range of the classical Gedrosia. The Makran Baluchi have a tradition of north Iranian origin and of residence in Seistan until about the year AD 1000. During the next half-millennium their migrations are traced in two directions: one southward into Makran and the other eastward and north of the Brahui into the lower Suleiman ranges and the adjacent plains of Sind. Today these are referred to as the western (Makran) and eastern (Suleiman) branches, separated by the island of Dravidian-speaking Brahui. The name Baluch or Biloch is thought by some to be derived from the Persian word for cockscomb, a reminder of their swagger and marauding propensities. As a result of their reputation the tribal names are mainly pejorative (cf. *rind* and *lund*, Persian for 'debauchee' and 'knave' respectively and *marri*, 'plague' in Sindhi). Holdich, [152] however, suggests that the ancient Boledi is derived from the Assyrian *Bola*, the Phoenician god Bael or Bel ('lord'), an indication of the high status of their leaders whose memory survives both in the name of the country and that of the Bolan Pass.

The Suleiman Baluchi speak an Iranian language structurally similar to Pashto but with numerous loan words from Arabic, Jatki (western Punjabi) and Sindhi. Makran Baluchi contains many more Arabic and Persian loan words, and some historians [152] claim Arab origins for both but especially the various Rind tribes. Such an assertion lacks supporting historical and archaeological evidence but accords with their own traditions of Qureshi Arab descent. The founding ancestor is presumed to have settled in Aleppo before expulsion by the Omayyad Caliph in the latter part of the seventh century. In all likelihood they are the result of a hybridization of Parthians, Scythians and Arabs with probable Brahui admixture.

Continuity is strong between the Makran Baluchi of Iran and Pakistan but the ethnic complexity of the latter is most extraordinary and has probably been so for thousands of years. The large block of western Baluchistan (300 square miles) has a sparse population of tent-dwellers except where the north–south routes from Seistan cross the east–west routes from Iran. The scattered settlements and nomadic communities reveal a variety of ethnic sources and at least three levels of social stratification. There is usually a dominant élite class, frequently differing in language and sometimes religious affiliation from a highly mixed subservient class, and a symbiotically attached nomadic 'band', again often with distinctly different traditions of origin.

In the Suleiman sector the migration routes and passes are more numerous and the grazing lands of the plateau and plains more extensive and closely interconnected than along the lower Sind border. Wholesale migrations of Brahui, Ghilzai and other

Powindah (probably from the Persian *powal*, 'to graze') tribes take place annually between the winter grazing lands along the lower Indus and the summer pastures on the plateau. Furthermore, the nomadic populations of southern Iran are continuous and interconnected with those of Makran and Las Bela in Baluchistan and those of western Sind. In the northern or Pathan sector, on the other hand, annual migrations are generally confined to local transhumant movements between the sedentary winter settlements in the lower reaches of the large river valleys and the higher upland pastures of the same or adjacent valleys. For these reasons trade and migration are more likely to be interdependent and synchronized in the south: the Ghilzai, Brahui and some Baluchi nomads carry far more of the annual trade between the plateau and the plains than the Pathans to the north, who are almost wholly sedentary agriculturalists with the added factor of high valley transhumance. Trade through the northern passes is carried on mostly by professional Pathan caravanners linked to urban settlements, and their movements between fixed caravanserai are often through alien tribal territories bringing them under constant surveillance.

In the Khyber portion of the northern sector the former pass was cut into the southern wall of the Kabul River gorge at a height of more than 1000 feet above the river. Sheer cliffs rose above for several hundred feet. A new route follows the river more closely. When Alexander penetrated the Punjab in the fourth century BC the route was more dangerous and followed a northerly passage from the Kuner Valley through Mohmand country into the lower Swat Valley. Apart from the direct Kabul–Kuner and Khyber routes, there are two important but less traversed routes: one across the Dorah-An Pass (11,500 feet) to the north through Kafiristan, the other from the northern tip of the Chitral Valley over the Baroghil Pass (12,460 feet) into Wakhan, the 'goose-neck' of Afghanistan. South of the Khyber subsidiary passages include the Kurram Valley route from Kohat to Kabul, the Tochi Valley route in Waziristan between Bannu and Ghazni and the southern or Gomal pass route.

Contrasting with the hill tribes of the Iranian plateau border, the western plains-dwelling Punjabi and Sindhi – the majority population of Pakistan – merge imperceptibly into the inhabitants of the eastern Punjab. The major distinguishing features relate to dress and diet, emphasizing the religious cleavages which today more than ever distinguish the three major religious communities – Muslim, Sikh and Hindu. Throughout the entire Sindhi–Punjabi-speaking area the largest single socially distinctive group was classified as Jati in earlier censuses. Whether Muslim, Sikh or Hindu, the Jats account for roughly twenty-five per cent of the population, nearly three times that of the Rajputs. Formerly the Rajputs, Jats, Gujars, Arain, Khatri, Meo (Muslim Rajputs) and a few smaller splinter groups were classified as tribal castes regardless of religion, social status, occupation or legitimacy of lineage claims.

During the period of Mughal supremacy there was much shifting of religious ties, especially among the Jat cultivators and herdsmen. *Jat* in Punjabi means a grazer or herdsman but, as noted by Ibbetson, changing the Punjabi soft *t* to a hard *t* in Jatki in Muslim areas changed its meaning to cultivator. The term *jat*, in other words, is not confined to any particular religious community, language, occupation or even class–caste.

The Gujars (Persian *gurjara*, 'herders') claim to have entered India at the time of the Hunnic invasions. Most of them moved south from Sind where they established a kingdom in a region preserving their name in its modified Indo–Aryan form, Gujarat. The Muslim and Hindu Gujars are scattered throughout Pakistan and north India and are varyingly mixed with other populations of the plains. They predominate in the Punjab where they are generally indistinguishable physically from most of the other Kshatriya castes and clean Sudras. Most of the plains Gujars have turned to farming, but in the hills they continue to raise cattle or serve as herders. The Ahirs (Sanskrit *abhira* or 'milkers') are more frequently associated with their traditional occupation than the Gujars: they may be of the same origin but with an Indian rather than Iranian designation and their caste level is higher in the north than in the south.

Apart from castes of tribal origin there are numerous relatively endogamous groups, some claiming western Muslim origins – Arab, Iranian or Pathan – and others identifiable as converts. They include the Sayad or Pir (priests), Qasab (butchers), Sheikh (traders), Arora and Awan (ranging from farmers and craftsmen to domestics), Julaha (weavers), Mochi (leatherworkers), Musalli (sweepers) and Faqirs and Mirasi, who are variously engaged in fortune-telling, begging and minstrelsy. At the bottom of the scale, a Chuhra menial who refuses to remove nightsoil can become a Musalli.

Finally there are scattered migratory bands of semi-nomads in Gujarat, Sind, the Punjab, Rajasthan and neighbouring districts of the upper Ganges who speak languages classified as Gipsy. Most of the world's five million or so gipsies live in Europe or in lands brought under European colonial control. European gipsies generally claim Arab descent in spite of the nickname associating them with Egypt. Some trace their ancestry to the biblical Jews, and the fact that their Diaspora parallelled that of the children of Israel is cited as corroborative evidence. The German anthropologist Wagenseil was so convinced of their Jewish origin that they were officially classed with the Jews, and as a result, over 400,000 or nearly ten per cent of the total gipsy population met their fate in the gas chambers of Nazi Germany [65].

There is no doubt about the antiquity of the gipsies and the fact that most of them engage in some kind of metalworking (smelting, smithing, casting) and the raising of cattle and horses lends credence to the notion that, in part at least, they may be the traditional descendants of travelling tinkers and traders dating back to the Bronze Age. The most plausible theory of their origins appeared in 1793 in a Viennese gazette reporting that Bohemian gipsy word lists could be traced to Malabar coast languages of India [65, pp. 35–9]. Since then other gipsies have been identified with the Luri of Baluchistan and Sind; still others with the Dom of Agra and Oudh (Uttar Pradesh) and the Lohar or Lohara, whose migrations carry them across the entire Deccan to the west coast. Of the six 'true gipsy dialects' listed in the Linguistic Survey of India [136, p. 186], all have Dravidian bases and the total number of speakers in 1921 was approximately 10,000.

12

Northern Hindustan and the Lower Ganges Basin

Political India today is overwhelmingly Hindu – roughly seventy-six per cent – and Hindustan might seem appropriate as the name of the country. But for a secular state the name seems to place undue emphasis on religion, even though it does have the advantage of bridging the gap between the Indo–Aryan north and the predominantly Dravidian south. The irony is that the Indus, from which *Hind* is derived, is now in a Muslim state. However, the religious homeland of the Hindus and the sacred centres of pilgrimage lie in the Hindi-speaking regions of the north – the basins of the Jumna and Ganges Rivers, the snow peaks of the Himalayas ('Eternal Snows') and – holiest of all – the pyramid-shaped abode of the gods, Mt Kailas. The north is also the home of the Mahabharata and Ramayana epics and Ganges water is still used in the rites of upper-caste Hindus from Mt Kailas to Cape Comorin and from the Sarasvat River in the west to the Brahmaputra ('Son of Brahma') in the east. The seat of government is here, and at least the headwaters and main courses of the 'five rivers' (*Panj-ab*) – Jhelum, Chenab, Ravi, Beas and Sutlej of the Punjab, the main eastern tributaries of the Indus – remain within the borders of India.

Throughout India's history Kashmir has played a unique and colourful role. For the past 150 years it has been classed as a Rajput state under a maharaja whose domains were expanded by the supporting armies of the Dogra Mian Rajputs of Jammu. The inhabitants include Shinwari, Dardic and Kohistani tribes in the west, the anomalous Burushaski-speaking peoples of Yasin and Hunza to the north and the Tibetan-speaking peoples of

Baltistan and Ladakh on the plateau. Today the peripheral western and northern areas and most of Baltistan, overwhelmingly Muslim in faith, fall within the Pakistan-occupied zone. Ladakh, though ethnically Tibetan, remains a part of India as do the primarily Sikh–Hindu parts of Jammu and the Sikh–Hindu-dominated Vale of Kashmir, but the society of the latter region has no direct parallel.

The Kashmiri language is classed as Shinwar–Dardic and is closer to the Iranian-grouped Kohistani and Pashto than to Indo-Aryan Jatki or Punjabi. The majority of the inhabitants are Muslim but the élite Kashmir Pandits ('learned ones') who control the economy and occupationally fill the roles of many of the clean castes of the plains are nominally Sikhs and Brahmins and more properly identified as Dogri from the Jammu foothills. The ruling caste is Kshatriya Rajput, and most of the cultivators, artisans and menials, including the sweepers, are Muslim.

In the predominantly Hindu communities of eastern Punjab, as in the rest of north India, the Brahmins are mostly Sarsut or Saraswat, whose internal hierarchy is related to their client castes who serve only Brahmins. Except in Bengal, the Brahmins of India, who average regionally between three and five per cent of the population, are divided into five 'southern' or *dakshinat* groups and five 'northern' or *utrahak*. The latter derive their respective identities from the Punjab, Kanauj, United Provinces, Orissa and Bihar territories lying north of the Vindhyas. In addition, a number of minor 'brotherhoods' are confined mainly to priestly and other professional groups such as physicians, lawyers, teachers and engineers, or have taken to farming. The prevailing sense of caste–class hierarchy is far more pervasive than that of religious affiliation or community of interest. The opposite may be said of Pakistan, and it is probably mainly for this reason that the latter is constituted as a religious state, whereas India adheres strictly to past traditions of secular administrative controls. The case of Bangladesh seems to be intermediate. It is constitutionally secular but in population overwhelmingly Muslim.

Among the Kshatriya or second class, the main difference between the endogamous groups designated as 'tribal castes' (Jats, Rajputs, Gujars and Khatri and, in Uttar Pradesh, Thakur and Chettri) is that they assume specific status-role relationships as castes within the *jajmani–kamin* ('patron–client') social structure. The Gujars, although not a caste, are often accorded caste treatment, especially in the Punjab and Himachal Pradesh.

In a typical northern Hindu village community under a *panchayat* of elders all four classes (*varna*) are usually represented and there may be as many as thirty castes. The village itself is often divided into several sections (*patti*), each with its own house lots, tilled fields, common pasturage and wastelands, and owned entirely or in part by a Thakur or Rajput landlord (*zamindar*). Separate parts might be owned by individuals of different castes but rarely by members of the lower castes. This joint ownership system of land tenancy is prevalent in the north but not in Bengal, Sind or the south, and is presumed to have been introduced from the Iranian uplands [12].

Usually the headman (*lambardar, mukiya* or *pradhan*) of each *patti* is the senior member of the major landholding lineage and the lands are held in perpetuity by the separate branch lines. Depending on economic circumstances, a number of Kshatriya families or lines will receive the priestly and instructional ministrations of one or more Brahmins from the same or a neighbouring village and the services of members of various Vaisya and Sudra castes and of outcastes in a complex patron–client network.

Below the 'twice-born', who comprise the three upper classes, are the Sudra – a term now in general disuse but for which no suitable alternative has been suggested. A division is often made between the 'clean' Sudra, who include most of the artisans and craftsmen, cultivators and herdsmen, and the 'unclean' Sudra such as the *dhobi* (washermen), blacksmiths, potters, leatherworkers and cobblers. Outside the pale completely are more than seventy 'scheduled castes' (outcastes) including sweepers, strolling minstrels, mendicants and 'criminals' (including the *thugia,* a name which has crept into the English language as 'thug').

PAHARI HILL DISTRICTS

The northern perimeter of the subcontinent, which stretches from Kashmir to Assam, is more sharply defined both culturally and biologically than either the western or the eastern, a consequence of ecological factors. Along the western and central sections of the Himalayas from Nanga Parbat at the great bend of the Indus to Kanchenjunga – the meeting point of the Ganges and Brahmaputra basins and the border peak between Nepal and Sikkim – a broad intermontane zone separates the central from the outer or subsidiary ranges. The numerous valley sections, which range in altitude from 5000 to 9000 feet, and the scattered plateaus ranging from 12,000 to 16,000 feet contrast with the average foothill plains altitude of about 1500 feet. These areas serve as home territories for a wide variety of relatively isolated populations whose identities with their respective valleys range in time depth and political independence, correlating rather closely with the degree of isolation and size of habitable territory. In the western Himalayas, from Kashmir to the Nepal border, access to the larger inner valleys is less difficult than to the valleys of the central or Nepal sector. Furthermore, the *terai* or forest belt along the foothills is more open. These advantages have attracted more plains populations on to the hill slopes and into the valleys, which have been utilized as refuge areas for countless centuries. Remnants of earlier pre-Indo–Aryan peoples persist, but they have been clearly at a competitive disadvantage and in most sections have been assimilated or their identities generally obscured. The local populations have become differentiated as Pahari or 'hill people' and their respective territories as Pahari states and districts.

In the more spacious valleys of the Nepal sector distances between the central and outer ranges average roughly a hundred miles. The drainages of the three main rivers (Karnali, Trisuli and Arun) have cut such deep and inaccessible gorges through the outer or Mahabharat range that they cannot be used as thoroughfares. The only feasible routes are across passes of 5000 to 7000 feet. Nepal, in fact, is hemmed in by high mountain walls, which have helped to preserve its integrity as an independent nation. Though classed as a Hindu–Rajput state, its dynastic origins date traditionally from the Licchavi dynasty of the third century AD. Apart from the intrusive and dominant Indo–Aryan Nepali-speaking castes, the underlying populations are biologically and linguistically allied to the Tibeto–Burman peoples of the high plateau and Assam and fall logically within the eastern and north Asian quadrants.

In the Pahari regions, and to a lesser extent among the Nepali, the classic four-fold, caste–class gradations generally parallel those of the plains, but the role behaviour, occupational limitations and mate selection proscriptions, as well as the patron–client relationships, are less clearly defined or rigidly adhered to. Among western hill Brahmins, for example, farming is the rule and few are qualified to serve as priests or teachers. The services of qualified caste members must be sought from the plains. On the other hand, smiths, leatherworkers, carpenters and masons are so important that they are socially acceptable at higher levels. Intercaste marriages are also common: the son of a Rajput and a low-caste woman may become a Rathi and the offspring of a Brahmin and a Kaneti may claim Rajput status.

Each of the three Pahari regions – western, central and eastern – also has its own specific forms of superimposed Thakur–Rajput administrative controls, its own variety of Hindu subsects and minor syncretic cults, which combine in various ways the tenets and practices of Hinduism, Buddhism, Lamaism, the ancient Tibetan Bön religion and local animistic beliefs. Economies and symbiotic networks also differ from region to region. For example, the Gaddi of Chamba State in Himachal Pradesh – traditional herders, whose name is derived from the word for throne, a reflection probably of their homeland near Shiva's snowy abode – have a peculiar form of double transhumance. They winter their flocks on the plains; as soon as spring thaws permit they plant their fields of barley and pulse in Brahmaur; and when the high passes open in late July they take their flocks to the high pastures in Ladakh, returning by harvest time to Brahmaur. The usual form of transhumance which characterizes such Pahari peoples as the Kishtwari of Kashmir, the Pangwali, Churahi and Chameali of Chamba, the Garhwali and various Bhotia of Kumaon and Almora is or was related to trans-border trade: the pack animals carry grain and other merchandise to Ladakh and Tibet in early summer and return with borax, salt, wool and hides in mid-autumn.

The Pahari and Tibeto–Burman-speaking Bhotia groups remain among the least intensively studied peoples of India both biologically and culturally. In the higher valleys of Chamba and Lahul, the Manchati and Lahuli speak languages classed as pronominalized Tibeto–Burman, related to those spoken by the Johari of the Milam and adjacent valleys of Almora near the Nepal border. Linguists have related their dialects also to Mundari, which they resemble syntactically, but the similarities have never been fully clarified [136, 36].

Among other characteristics of the hill populations are the regional persistence of polyandry and the levirate, both of which were traditionally common in various parts of Tibet and are associated with rules of inheritance. The tradition also lingers concerning the ancient socially élite class known in classical times as the Khas or Khasa. Today a people known as Khasa live in one of the enclosed foothill or *dun* valleys of Jaunsar–Bawar in the Pahari regions of Uttar Pradesh, and the root name Khas or Kasa is not uncommon in other parts of the foothills as far west as Kashmir.

In the classical mythology of the Vishnu Purana, Khasa was the wife of Kashyapa and the mother of the Yakshas and Rakshasas [228, pp. 267–318]. In the Mahabharata they are referred to as living in the Punjab, and efforts to identify them with specific tribal or other endogamous groups have ranged from the craftsmen who built Asoka's temples in the north to the Todas of the Nilghiri hills in the south. Some have claimed that they are in fact the Kha or Khas element in the martial Gur-Khas of Nepal.

Even more of a problem is an explanation for the presence of a number of caste-endogamous groups of intermediate, low-caste and outcaste grades with no known name equivalents on the plains. Among the former may be listed the agricultural Kanets and Girths of Kulu, the Rathi of Kangra district, the Koltas of Jaunsar–Bawar and a number of valley peoples in the upper tributaries of the Sutlej, Ravi and Jumna rivers. Among the scheduled castes are the Shlipkar (Silapkar) of Almora, who occupy the position of the Dom or scavengers of the lower Pahari regions and the plains. Scattered also in the lower slopes are the bamboo-weaving Rehr, and in the high Himalayas the strolling Hesi minstrels. Other scheduled castes such as the Koli, Dagi and Chanal are found as far east as Sikkim. Finally, there are the Tharu of the Nepal *terai* and the *Jangliwala* ('Jungle People') of Almora. These are listed as Pahari-speaking tribes but appear to be surviving remnants of pre-Aryan inhabitants of the plains.

In central and eastern Nepal, apart from the Brahmins and the ruling Rajupt family and various other Nepali-speaking caste communities of obvious plains origin, many of the Tibeto–Burman-speaking populations have become hinduized over the course of centuries and reflect today the caste structure of the plains. This is especially true of the Kshatriya, Thakur and Chettri castes among the partially hybridized Tibeto–Burman-speaking Newari and the Magar, Gurung, Rai and Limbu Gurkhas, who are often bilingual.

One thing, however, is very clear: while hybridization has occurred and will continue to occur, it has not obliterated the differences – either biological or cultural – between the Tibetans and other Tibeto–Burman-speaking peoples of the plateau and higher valleys and the Pahari and other Indo–Aryan-speaking peoples of the foothills and plains.

EASTERN INDIA AND BANGLADESH

The eastern border is geographically irregular but not difficult to define. Migrations of Indo–Aryan speakers from Bengal began their infiltration of the lower stretches of the Brahmaputra as early as two thousand years ago and were past the gates at Gauhati and in the Sylhet basin by the tenth century. Now they considerably outnumber the older Tibeto–Burman and Mon–Khmer-speaking peoples. Using AD 1500 as the demarcation date line, the western border of the former Ahom kingdom would be a reasonable boundary line for greater India. With the omission of Sylhet and the lower sections of the main Brahmaputra Valley, this corresponds to the present eastern boundary of Bangladesh which borders the Garo, Khasi, Lushai and Mizo hills of Assam.

The greater Bengal area is crucially located at the confluence of the two most sacred rivers, the Ganges and the Brahmaputra. It is a fertile region and the most densely populated; it has frequently been harrassed by flood, famine and epidemics, and for centuries has been a centre of political turbulence. The success of Islam in the most densely populated sections reflects its past history. The majority of the converts were from the middle, lower and outcaste groups; and, while the rifts on religious issues were more severe in Bengal than in the Punjab at the time of partition, the declaration of independence from Pakistan has demonstrated the powerful ties of common language and other aspects of a unique cultural heritage of the Bengali.

Bihar occupies rather an unusual position. It is the most

densely populated state in India and the seat of the most sacred cities of both Hinduism and Buddhism, but in many ways it remains a border state. More than half of the people speak Hindi. There is no major or standard language that can be called Bihari but rather a group of languages and dialects often referred to by that name which exhibit varying degrees of similarity to Hindi on the one hand and to Bengali on the other. The caste–class structure is also intermediate, and within its borders are several districts with majority tribal populations. The peoples of Orissa, especially the Uriya in the northern half, may also be considered within the greater Bengal area because there appear to be no endogamous groups strictly limited territorially to the state; the pattern is the same as that of Bengal with minor differences.

In Bengal the range of occupations and roles among various levels or strata is well illustrated by the Brahmins. Among those claiming such status – roughly six per cent of the population in the Hindu sections – the gradations are extreme. The Rarhi occupy by common consent the highest rank. They are occupationally limited to priestly services and most of them conform to this requirement. Next in order are the various Vaidik Brahmins who are largely limited to the priestly, teaching or related professions, while below them in the scale are the Pirali, Byasokta, Agradani, Acharji, Barna and Bhat.

The range of activities is particularly great because of the hundreds of thousands of pilgrims attracted annually to the numerous temple complexes along the Ganges. They conduct funeral rites, tell fortunes, read palms, recite epics and serve as water dispensers, or they may fall from grace and serve the interests of all but the most inferior castes. The term Brahmin thus represents a vertical spectrum running the gamut from the very highest levels to those barely above the level of outcastes. Some clients may even refuse to eat food in the houses of their Brahmin patrons. Deference to what might be called priestly and related services and the general avoidance of manual labour alone distinguish this widely disparate class.

Included in the second or Kshatriya class are the intrusive Rajputs, who have no traditional ties with the region but assume second-class status solely through their claimed descent from the Rajputs of the former warring kingdoms. Comprising considerably less than one per cent of the population, their social ranking is disputed by such local Bengal castes as the Baidya physicians and the Kayasth scribes. But the claim of the latter to Kshatriya status was disputed by the Baidya and denied by the High Court of Calcutta, who classed them as Sudra because of their treatment of the dead.

In a somewhat ambiguous position are the so-called functional castes collectively known as the Navaskha, who occupy third-class ranking as clean Sudras. Comprised of confectioners, perfume and betel vendors, oil pressers, gardeners, potters and barbers, they hold their rank largely because Brahmins accept water from them and grant them priestly services.

In fourth position are the Mahisya, Chasi Kaibarta or Koivarta, who are mainly cultivators, and the traditionally herding Goala who claim the right to inclusion among the Navasakha because of the role of many of them as domestics to the higher castes and the tradition of their legendary descent from a cross between Kshatriya and Vaisya ancestors. In addition to these is a mixed group, including the Pod cultivators and the Sadgops (traditional fishermen). They bear no special relationship to each other and are classed collectively in fifth position for a variety of reasons. More than fifty names appear in the list of scheduled castes.

The Muslim communities, though distinguished occupationally as Mullas, Sayyids, Sheiks, etc., following much the same pattern as in the Punjab, are otherwise regionally classified. Mate-selection patterns follow occupational lines by custom rather than proscription, the exception being for the sweeper categories, which overlap with those of the Hindu population of west Bengal.

13

Western India and the Central Plateau

In ancient times the high country south of the great river basins of the north was inhabited by demons and giants, the enemies of the gods, the avatars of Vishnu and the heroes who fought their way southward. In reality these malevolent beings are presumed to be the ancestors of the present Dravidian and Mundari tribes who still occupy large parts of the hilly districts. Since these early days the major thoroughfares, river basins and plateau regions of central India and the Deccan and the coastal strips of the peninsula have been largely pre-empted by Indo–Aryan speakers of the north. They now form the predominant populations of all but the four southernmost Dravidian states.

Central India, the northern part of the central plateau, bears again its classical name Madhya Pradesh ('Midlands'). Together with Rajasthan it forms a triangle divided into three sections – an apex region known as Bundelkhand; a western Malwa plateau and north–south causeway section joining the Chambal tributary drainage of the Jumna in Uttar Pradesh with the Mahi and Sabarmati River basins in Gujarat; and the hillier 'tribal' districts of the east. The base of the triangle is formed by the valley of the east–west-flowing Narbada and the flanking Satpura range, which together mark the dividing line between the northern and southern halves of the subcontinent.

South of the Satpura range, the Deccan plateau divides into northern Indo–Aryan-dominated and southern Dravidian halves. For convenience, therefore, greater India may be arbitrarily divided into three sections: the Indo–Gangetic plains; the plateau and adjacent sections of the midlands together with the primarily Indo–Aryan-speaking portions of the Deccan; and the Dravidian-speaking southern half of the Deccan including the extreme peninsular south. This trifold division separates the north Karnatak or Sanskritic populations of Maharashtra from the Dravidian populations of south Karnatak but does not vitally affect the unity of the Deccan. Modern states boundaries separate the non-tribal populations but are virtually meaningless so far as the tribal populations are concerned. Dravidian-speaking Gonds and Bhils are found as far north as Rajasthan, Uttar Pradesh and Bihar, and Telegu and Kannada-speaking tribes migrate freely into the northern or Indo–Aryan Marathi and Oriya regions of the Deccan. Similarly, Mundari-speaking Korku are found in western Maharashtra. For this reason the non-Hindu or partly hinduized tribes that have not been incorporated into the greater society merit separate consideration.

Subbarao [363] refers to the densely populated peripheral areas as 'areas of attraction' which recruit hill tribes from the 'isolated forest areas of the central plateau'. These migrants settle in the plains after undergoing various de-tribalizing and sanskritizing processes in the north and hinduizing in the south. They occupy the lowest levels in the social hierarchy, performing menial tasks as outcastes or at best rising to the level of cultivators. In an earlier exchange, pioneers and adventurers entered the central plateau from the north as missionaries (Brahmin, Buddhist and Jain); as conquering heroes (Maurya, Saka, Gujar, Rajput or Muslim); and from the south as Dravidian rulers; otherwise they appeared as merchants intent on exploitation and trade. Finally there have been migratory groups: hunters, herders, fishermen, dacoits, minstrels and mendicants whose services or propensities carried them either on to the plateau or down to the plains and coasts.

An exceedingly important fact of geography is the presence of the Thar Desert. Since early Holocene times, when climatic conditions were changing and hunting populations could no longer be sustained, this desert has been a gigantic barrier interposed between the Indus basin and the lower slopes of the Aravalli hills of the Deccan. The total area is roughly 100,000 square miles of which the western half, with a north–south length of roughly 400 miles and a breadth of over 100 miles, is almost wholly uninhabitable. The remainder supports no more than a score of oasis settlements and provides limited grazing for flocks and scrub for camels. The barrier has limited passage eastward from the Indus basin to two corridors – the Doab watershed route to the Jumna–Ganges basin, and the Sind route across the desert and marshlands of the Cutch, southern Rajasthan and Baroda. The historical consequence has been to force migration along the west coast southward and penetration of Rajasthan from the north.

The third major route southward was from Bengal along the Orissa coast, the ancient kingdom of Kalinga. So important are these areas of concentration – the Punjabi–Hindi north, the Bihari–Bengali east and the Gujarati–Marathi west – that samples are generally drawn from their centres for differential comparative analysis. As examples of the Dravidian south, various samples from both the east and west coasts are usually added to those of the Deccan to form a fourth area.

Gujarat is bordered inland by the Panch Mahals ('Five Ranges'), the homeland of the forest hill tribes. Between the tribes and the plains-dwelling Ujli Varan ('Bright Coloured'), the Koli substratum occupies a somewhat undefined position as one of the tribes and also as a part of coastal society.

The 'bright coloured ones' range from Brahmins through Kshatriya, Vaisya and Sudra. Of the two Brahmin castes, Audich signifies 'northerner' and is presumed to indicate origin; Nagar is thought to be from Naga, the serpent, and mythology connects them with their present habitat.

The Kshatriya include the Brahmana, Kshatri, Bhatia and Bhadela. The Lohanna (Luhanna or Luvana), who claim Kshatriya status but are not entitled to wear the sacred thread, were driven south from Multan through Sind during the Muslim invasions. Although forming a distinctive non-Hindu group, the Parsis (Farsi) – who fled their homeland Persia in the seventh century – are generally classed on a status level with the Kshatriya. Many have entered professions appropriate to this rank. Below the Kshatriya, but powerful in spite of their 'cultivator' label, are the Kunbi or Kanbi (Kunabi).

Kunbi townsmen are mostly traders and the countrymen mostly cultivators. The highest ranking are Pattidars ('shareholders'), while the majority are Banias who rank with other Vaishya castes such as the Khoja. Parallelling the Hindu Vaishya are the Muslim Sunni Bora, Miana, Memom and, among the Jains, the Oswal and Bannia. Various artisan groups such as the Kathi parallel those of the north, but the most numerous by far are the outcastes and, in particular, the Bambi and Bhangi, Balmiki, Valmiki and Dhed or Vankar. All recruit freely from each other or from tribal populations and outcastes or from the caste and Muslim groups.

In Maharashtra the impact of separatist consciousness has been growing within the past few decades and is well illustrated by the largest single group or (super) caste, the Maratha. It has been increasing in the decennial census returns at the expense of other groups, principally the Kunbi who are contiguous with the Gujarat Kunbi along the Konkan or coastal strip.

The Marathas are landowning cultivators claiming descent from the élite of the Marathi kingdom of the eighteenth century. The mixture represented by the original élite can only be assumed, but it undoubtedly included a variety of Vaisya and clean Sudra, including the Kunbi. The number of Marathas increased during the thirty-year period 1901–31 from 1,384,000 to 4,285,000, or more than three times the increases registered in any of the other groups, and now totals nearly half of the total population of the state. Such rapid growth in the subdivisions, both social and regional, is reflected in the high standard deviations in the extensive biometric study conducted by Dr Irawati Karve of the Research Institute at Poona [173].

The Brahmins are designated by classical ordination or region of origin or residence as Sarasvat, Amraoti, Barsi, Chitpavan, Nasik, Deshastha, Karada and Yajurvedi. The wide range in biological data indicates that Brahmins have been recruited from a large number of sources – a structural feature of west coast regional society.

Apart from the Konkan coastal strip which includes the city of Bombay, three other regions are recognized, each with its distinctive caste–class structure and peculiarities relating to migrational sources, intermarriage regulations and occupational differences. The first is Des or Desa in the Deccan, immediately adjacent to the Konkan coastal strip. The second is Khandesh, between the Satpura and Balaghat ranges, the upper valleys of the Tapti and Purna rivers; and the third or Nagpur region is the easternmost part of the state, including the former state of Bastar.

So distinct are the four regions that there are substantial differences in language. Even Konkani and Khandeshi are sometimes classed as separate languages although more generally as dialects of Marathi, the principal language of Desa. The language in the Nagpur region is mainly Marathi but the tribes speak a variety of Dravidian and Mundari languages.

Following Karve's classification in the Konkan, the Kayastha Prabhu, Pathare, Prabhu, Pathare Kshatriya, Khatri and Vaisya Vani may be listed with the Brahmins as professional groups. The intermediate or artisan and service castes include the Sonar (goldsmiths), Kasar (coppersmiths), Shimpi (tailors), Teli (oil pressers), Khosti (weavers), Bhajvsar (dyers), Nhavi (barbers), Parit (washermen), Burud (basket-weavers) and Gurav (temple musicians). In a separate category as intermediates are the agriculturalists, the market gardeners and labourers (Halbi, Koli and Agari). Among the untouchables are the Mang, Mahar and Chambhar (Chamar).

Between the caste populations and the 'primitive tribes' are the Sonkoli and Dhivar fishermen and the 'pastoral and semi-nomadic' Dhangar and Hatkar shepherds, the Gowari (cattle herders) and the Vanjari traders and pack animal drivers.

14

The Dravidian South, Sri Lanka and the Hill Tribes

Apart from the obvious difference in language, probably the greatest cultural contrasts between the greater societies of the north and south lie in the field of religion and the basic structure of the social hierarchy. The south has preserved and added to the heretical sects which lost their struggle in the north during the turbulent centuries just before the beginning of the Christian era and were forced southward in search of refuge. Among these were Jainism, which was unable to meet the challenge of the growing power of Buddhism, and later Buddhism itself, which was oppressed by a resurgence of Brahmin orthodoxy and found haven in the hill states of the north and the Dravidian states of the south – Sri Lanka (Ceylon) and the alien shores of south-east Asia.

According to tradition, Jainism was founded by Maha-vira ('Great Hero') sometime in the sixth century BC in the heart of the Ganges basin. His teachings stressed asceticism, the cosmic unity of all forms of life and the transmigration and transmutation of souls. Such beliefs naturally imposed strict vegetarianism and the observance of the prohibition against the taking of life. These philosophical concepts had long been tenets of Brahmanism but disavowal of the authority of the Vedas was the basis of the heresy. Today Jainism's adherents are in greatest strength in the Deccan, Gujarat and the Malabar coast. The once dominant Digambara ('Sky-Clad', or 'Naked') sect is all but extinct, but the adherents of the prevailing Svetambara ('White-Robed') sect still boast of the period during the twelfth century when their kings ruled in Gujarat and Kathiawar. Their sacred Mt Abu in Rajasthan remains a vital centre of pilgrimage.

Another heretical sect was the Lingayats. Developed as an offshoot of Shaivism, it emphasized reverence for the lingam (cf. English 'long' and Latin 'lingua'), the sacred phallus and symbol of Shiva. A host of syncretic cults has also appeared in the south, especially among the tribal populations, many of which combine either Vishnu or Siva with local Dravidian and Mundari deities and other supernatural beings, both tribal and non-tribal. Some emphasize the tiger and serpent gods, the gods and goddesses of cattle, crops and diseases; the deities of fertility and fecundity; and a variety of ghosts, demons and other malevolent spirits. With rare exceptions, religious adherence cuts across socially determined groupings. Castes are divided among Vaishnavites, Shaivites and Lingayats, and even among the Jains caste levels are distinguishable. It may never be possible to reconstruct the manner in which the various sects were established, but it is certain that Brahmins – and to these one might well add the priest–missionaries of the heretical sects, Buddhism and Jainism – carried their religious teachings with effective zeal throughout the south and created an ecclesiastical élite. But the full four-class *varna* system of the north was never imposed on the south.

There is far more social mobility in the south than in the north, especially at the lower caste levels. In the north conversion to Islam and, more recently, to Christianity has provided the easiest means of individual and group mobility. In the south mobility is usually achieved by migration or change of occupation or wholesale transformation. The example of mass conversion to Buddhism of some three million west coast harijan outcaste Mahar (Meher) has been cited, but success in this case was probably due to acceptance of the older and more conservative Hinayana form of Buddhism which is closer to orthodox Brahminism than reformed Mahayana, in spite of the latter's disavowal of caste–class distinctions.

In the north, the ploy of advancing genealogies to achieve higher rank is likely to depend upon the 'discovery' that a high-caste male ancestor was ostracized for marrying too far down in the social scale. In the south, even the humblest of the Sudra learn to recite a newly acquired tradition of descent from the union of a deity with a demon in the guise of a damsel, or from a high-caste couple who lost caste through elopement or suffered ostracism in pursuit of a noble cause.

The emphasis on appositional forces strengthened by dependence on mythology is strong in the south where Vaishaism and Shaivism remain in balance and represent the two main orthodox sects. In the north, where prominence is given to Krishna – the dominant avatar of Vishnu – Shaivism has been reduced to relative obscurity. In the south the *bhakti* or devotional movement and *mochsa* burning seem to be much stronger. The motion picture industry has discovered a lucrative market for 'devotionals' and 'mythologicals' which stress the Puranas [351] and the lives of saints. In the north it is the dramatic scenes from the Ramayana and Mahabharata tales that are commercially more profitable.

Possibly an even more important factor in north–south differences is the absence of the Kshatriya, especially the Rajputs, as a class–caste and the 'joint village' or common holding of land by superior tenures, mainly Rajput *zamindari*. In the south tenure is by the *raiyatwari* or separate ownership principle [12, p. 19]. In the latter form, permanent generational servitude implicit in the jajmani–kamin system is replaced by a freer relationship among the castes. Multiple-caste villages are common but residence is optional, and single-caste villages of Brahmins, Bannias or even Sudras are not uncommon and in some regions are the rule. In short, the *raiyatwari* village is conceived as Dravidian while the joint type is thought to have been introduced after the establishment of Rajput controls and to have been designed to assure Kshatriya domination. Villages came to be bestowed as rewards for exploits and services by Rajput rulers during the period of their expansion in the eighth and ninth centuries and revitalized by Akbar under Mughal rule. In Bengal the system was initiated under British administration.

A further distinction in the south is the functional caste division into 'right-hand' and 'left-hand' groupings. There seems to be no consistency in these groupings which are determined through local custom and tradition. The so-called non-functional castes are usually positionally neutral between the two.

Tradition ascribes the division to a dispute between artisans and farmers. Today the occupations are so distributed that they bear little resemblance to such a dichotomy, and in many regions different castes with the same occupation are found in both factions. Hocart [150] suggests that this moiety-like division represents the survival of a system antedating the four-fold *varna* classification which spread from the north southward in two directions across the peninsula and converged in the southernmost highlands. Its prevalence in the south and absence in the north is consistent with this view. It still takes various forms in Burma, Thailand and Cambodia but is rapidly disappearing in India.

In the religious field the spiritual climate of the south not only encourages stricter adherence to the older concepts of pollution and purification but also favours the development of new movements. In such an atmosphere the antithetical positions of orthodoxy and heterodoxy have little meaning. Salvation is sought within the framework of ancient ideas peculiar to Hinduism and ancient Dravidian theology. In fact, similarity with much of the symbolism of Harappan and pre-Harappan artefacts has been advanced as challenging evidence of the Indus Valley origins of the ancient Dravidians.

While the Indus Valley civilization failed to penetrate the Deccan, it may have been the inspiration for the neolithic Deccan Cattle Complex dating from about 2000 BC which continued relatively unchanged for about 1200 years. Several excavated sites show that cattle were stockaded, the dung being ritually burned to produce ash layer cumulations [5]. Fairservis [107, pp. 328–31] notes similarities between the herding practices of Harappa and contemporary sites in Iran from whence they were taken by nomad 'ash-mound' herders into the Indus Valley and later to the stockaded sites of the Deccan from about 2000 BC. Presumably it was these herders who moved south through Gujarat and on to the Deccan plateau from the Konkan coastal belt of Gujarat and Maharashtra. Later there was another southward movement when the expanding Harappan copper–bronze users provided the initial impetus for the development of a Dravidian ruling class.

The term Dravidian was originally used of a 'race', but such a population has never been defined biologically or even culturally except as the name of a language group, and its use as such is likely to continue. It is now assumed that the aristocracy originally identifiable as Dravidian was ultimately assimilated into the larger servile aboriginal population, which has often been referred to as pre-Dravidian, Veddoid or proto-Australoid, and that the previous language affinities are unknown. Such a proposal leaves open the question as to whether or not they might have been Mundari speakers.

Students of social structure have often noted the prominence given to females in the south and to the numerous peculiarities in mate selection patterns. In particular there was the unique form of polyandrous hypergamy, or liaison, among the clean Sudra caste of Nayars in Kerala. The women used to accept one or more lovers from among the Nambudri Brahmins in addition to their own Nayar husbands. The children were Nayars and in their matrilineal society belonged to their mother's lineage. Inheritance also was in the female line. Polyandry and hypergamy are, or at least were, met with in other parts of the south, but polyandry existed also in the Pahari regions and Tibet, and matrilineal descent is still the rule among the Tibeto–Burman Garos and the Mon–Khmer Khasi of Assam.

Kerala is unusual in many other respects. It has an old colony of Syrian Christians whose recently authenticated history [26] has been traced to St Thomas of Ethiopia and not to the St Thomas of the time of Christ, as tradition claims. The colony, whose fortunes have ebbed and flowed since its founding in the thirteenth century, is divided among Jacobites, Chaldaeans and Syrians – a reminder of the rifts still current in western Asia. There are also two small Jewish communities in Malabar. One, known as the 'Black Jews', claims to have been in Cochin since Roman times; the other has documentary evidence of residence since the tenth century.

Probably the preservation of these sects, and small pockets of Arabs and other mercantile trading groups, has been assisted by the narrowness of the coast and the sharp differentiation between coast and forest-clad hill country of Travancore, Cochin and Coorg – the homelands of numerous so-called primitive tribes.

The Malayali or 'cultivators' form the largest caste and there is little distinction between the scheduled caste groups and the hill tribes.

To the north in Karnatak (Mysore), where the state language is Kannada (Kanarese), the caste–class and tribal relationships are more complex. The variety of tribes and the large number of migrant castes is probably attributable to the extensive area of forested hills and the open valleys of the southern Deccan.

Among the Brahmins both the five northern and five southern castes are represented. Locally the latter are regionally identified as the Jurjaras of Maharashtra, the Telingas of Andhra, the Dravida of Madras, the Karnata of Karntak and the largest of the Brahmin castes, the Shaivite Aradhya. Among the Kshatriya until recently the highest position was that of the maharajas of Mysore – the Arasu.

Indicative of 'caste confusion' is the range of occupations and activities of the Handi Jogi caste, the Pandi Jogulu of Andhra, who are classed both as migrants and as living in settled communities. They have their own gods and goddesses and criminal groups, raise pigs and garden crops, hunt, tend cattle, act as bards, conjurers and herbalists, and frequently prostitute their women or serve as wandering labourers.

Occupying the lowest position of all agriculturalists are the Bakkaru (Baggaru) or Bagga Holeya. They are divided into several exogamous matrilineal clans or *balis*, worship both Vishnu and Shiva but are not allowed to enter village temples or even to live with other castes. Barbers and even washermen will not serve them and their presence is defiling to Brahmins. Many Holeya have become adherents of the reformed Adi Karnatak movement but are still shunned although engaged as labourers. In earlier literature they were often referred to as slaves; their lot was certainly permanent bondage.

Andhra, the land of the Telugus, has been a border zone between the north and the south. At one time the Andhras developed kingdoms whose domains extended across much of southern and central India and into the Ganges basin. Caste structure is intermediate between that of west Bengal and the Dravidian state of Madras.

The social organization and structure of the Tamils of Madras or Tamilnadu, 'land of the Tamils', is unique. Class stratification, dietary prohibitions and behavioural patterns relating to commensality and touchability persist – some in extreme form – but the social communities separate into three large groupings, occupational castes, cultivators and outcastes, each with its own social, economic and religious independence – temples, priestly orders and festivals – and each hostile to the others. Understandably this causes friction among the respective orders and between them and the Brahmins, whose authority is so openly flouted – a rift that is accentuated by Brahmin emphasis on Sanskrit.

The Paraiyan, known in English as the pariahs, form the largest of the old outcaste communities. They and the Pallans and Shanar or Nadars (toddy-tappers) are in constant feud with the larger castes of the next higher stratum, the group of four cultivators: the Vellalas, Maravans, Agamudaiyans and Kallans. In this grouped dichotomy it is said that 'a Kallan can become a Maravan by respectability', but no quarter is given to the Paraiyan who seem unable to change their spots.

Each caste has its extraordinary tale of origin. The Kallans claim to be descendant offspring of an illicit alliance between the god Indra and Ahalya, the wife of the sage Gautama [127]. The five major occupational castes known as the Panchalas claim Vishva Brahmin status which, needless to add, is challenged by the Brahmins. In a special category are the Kaikolans, the weavers, whose status is high because they provide the silk saris for the higher castes.

SRI LANKA (CEYLON)

Ceylon was known to the ancients as Sri Lanka. The Greeks and Romans called it Taprobane [104, 'Ceylon'], and the Arabs knew it as Seren-dip. 'Ceylon' is a corruption of the Portuguese Zeylan.

No other island in the Indian Ocean can equal the fabled exploits of Hanuman and the hero Rama who eventually defeated King Ravana, the ten-headed ruler of Lanka, and took over his kingdom. The certain history of Lanka begins with the Indo-Aryan conquest by an invading Sinhalese ('leonine') army from Malabar and Gujarat in 543 BC. Before that, all references are to the land of the Yakka demons of the Ramayana tales. Undoubtedly Ceylon had been a haven for many refugees, as it was to Mahinda, son of Asoka, who converted the inhabitants to Buddhism and left among the many monasteries and *dagoba* (pagoda) reliquaries the famous Temple of the Gautama's Tooth. From Lanka the *tripitaka* ('three baskets' or scriptures) were carried to Burma, Thailand, Cambodia and Java.

The peoples of Lanka reflect in their composition the course of the island's history. The Sinhalese are probably descendants mainly of Gujarati, but opinions differ concerning the Yakka. Some identify them with the Veddas; others think they were immigrant invaders from Bengal and Orissa. If so, such traces are no longer visible among the Tamils, who steadily increased until they now form nearly thirty per cent of the population. The Sinhalese account for nearly seventy per cent, and the Veddas – whom everyone concedes were the original inhabitants – are all but extinct. Probably no more than a handful of 'unmixed' aboriginals remain among the very mixed few hundred listed in the census. Alien to the three Indian populations is the small colony of Kaffirs of Puttalam (remnant of an African regiment) and Malays from the Straits Settlements. A few 'Arab' Moors and Eurasians, the latter a legacy reflecting the shifting fortunes of European powers, complete the roster. Tales are told of blue-eyed people near Jaffna, who are sometimes cited as sixteenth-century reminders of the Portuguese commander who, in his zeal to convert the natives, is reputed to have resorted to the biological expedient of putting the males to the sword and ordering his men to impregnate the females. Though doubtless apocryphal, since few Portuguese have blue eyes, there may be a grain of truth to the observation that 'the eyes of the natives get bluer as one nears a tea plantation'. Actually, all 'aliens', including the Moors, Malays and 'Burghers' (Eurasians), total less than two per cent.

Finally, off the Malabar coast the Maldive and Laccadive islanders are said to be mixtures of the original Malayali inhabitants with Arab intruders from around the rim of the Indian Ocean. The genetic instability of the population is far more distinctive than the linguistic ties which classify them with their Malabar coast neighbours.

TRIBAL POPULATIONS OF CENTRAL AND SOUTHERN INDIA

In 1959 the government of India recognized the special problems of the tribal communities by establishing a Scheduled Areas and Tribes Commission. The purpose was to protect their rights and encourage their economies. The Commission's report in the 1961 census lists 255 different tribes totalling nearly thirty million people or 6.8 per cent of the population. The line was drawn between populations already within the greater national social–economic sphere and those maintaining distinctive status regardless of economic interdependence, trade or the sale of services. The report also distinguishes between 'tribal communities' retaining hunting and gathering economies or practising shifting cultivation (*jhum*) from those with fixed fields. Of the former, 109 communities are listed totalling 2.6 million people, but owing to separate state classifications many are duplications. Thus both the Birhor and the Irula are listed in four states; and in Orissa the distinction is made between the Paidi and Hill Bhuiya; and in Mysore between the Kadu and Jenu Kuruba. A precise listing is impossible, and any kind of grouping on the basis of economy, language or social organization would be arbitrary and imprecise. There is the added factor of conversion to Hinduism or acceptance of a new religious movement or the tacit inclusion within the complex caste system. With the legal abolition of caste recognition there has been a shift towards language or state identity regardless of social implications.

While no two lists agree, more than 160 tribal groups are commonly given in the literature. This excludes several million classed among the scheduled castes. The tribal populations cluster into four hilly and generally forested areas separated by dense concentrations of caste–class peoples of the open valleys and watersheds.

In the Aravalli and Vindhya ranges of the west, between the Rajasthani speakers of Malwa and the Gujarati of the coast, live the Bhils. In the east, in the Chota Nagpur hills of western Bengal and northern Orissa and the adjacent hill districts of central India, are the various Mundari-speaking tribes and the Gondi-speaking Kui, Malto and Oraon. Between these two in central India and eastern Maharashtra are the central Gonds and Mundari Korku. Finally, in the Dravidian part of the Deccan and adjacent hills are concentrated the twenty or more Dravidian-speaking tribes.

Of the four tribal groupings, the western – which is dominated by the Bhils – and the central – where the Gonds are concentrated – are the most thoroughly hinduized. Both carry traditions of past Rajput dynasties and petty kingdoms. The Bhils of Rajasthan and Gujarat and the related Miana have often been identified as the Vedic Nishada who resisted the Aryan invaders, as did the later Bhils of the sixth and seventh centuries AD, when the Gangetic empires sought to control the Deccan.

The name 'Bhil' is derived probably from the Dravidian word for bow, their classical weapon. The language Bhili is Indo–Aryan, though mixed both in structure and vocabulary, but only about one-third of the Bhils speak Bhili. The remainder speak Hindi or Gujarati or the local Dravidian languages. In religion, too, they are mixed. Most Hindu Bhils stress the worship of Mahadev, one of the many names of Shiva, but they also have their own village, forest and water deities and local pantheons. They seldom call on Brahmins and there are no internal caste distinctions except among the lowland settled communities. Many claim Rajput status and there is evidence of Rajput infiltration before the Mughal conquests and of intermarriage with Rajput refugees. Bhils are generally slash-and-burn cultivators, cattle breeders or migrant labourers. Closely related to the Bhils are the Bhilala (Thakur), Bhumia, Rawat, Patel and Mukhri and several other minor groups.

The tribal Gonds are far more scattered and are identified by a variety of names. In the 1961 census they totalled slightly over three and a half million, whereas those returning Gondi, a Dravidian language, as their mother tongue numbered less than one and a half million. When Grierson undertook his classic study of the languages of the subcontinent in 1921 [136] Dravidian Gondi was spoken by roughly half the Gond population. Since then the number has dwindled proportionately by about fifteen per cent. Most of the remaining Gonds speak mixed Gondi and Hindi, referred to locally as Gondi–Chhattisgarhi, Gondi–Bagheli and Gondi–Oriya (Uriya), depending on the particular local Indo–Aryan language. Various other minor Gondi–Hindi dialects are spoken, and the migrant eastern Koya speak Dravidian Telegu. A few Gondi–Mundari speakers are completely de-tribalized and 'merged with Hindu populations'.

As explained by Fürer–Haimendorf [122], Gond is a generic term applied to many tribes appearing as the 'main population . . . in the very heart of India, described after them as Gondwana'. He questions 'whether there exists such an entity as a Gond people' and suggests that probably they are not 'off-shoots of a once homogeneous people' but attained a measure of cultural uniformity 'when they came under the sway of the same dominant linguistic influence'.

The name Gond was probably derived from Telegu *konda*

(highlands), a term applied to many other hill people, notably the Khonds who are classified as Mundari. The Gonds refer to themselves as Koi (Kui) or Koitur although they are known as Dhangi in Bengal, the local term for hillmen. As if this were not enough, it is possible that Dravidian Gondi was an acquired language and that originally they spoke a Mundari language such as Kolarian. Such an idea would fit into the broader theory of a former elite Dravidian ruling class moving in from the south or west. From them they acquired the cattle-breeding complex and the political machinery which welded them together into feudatory kingdoms.

There is historical proof that there were Gondi–Dravidian Rajput states which collapsed in the face of Maratha and Mughal onslaughts of the thirteenth to fifteenth centuries. Even so, Gond–Rajput origin of a number of Gond rajas was quite evident as late as 1947. Today the Raj Gonds survive as a reminder of their former grandeur although they number only a small percentage of those returning themselves as Gonds. The traditional Raj Gonds are not to be confused with the recent Raj Gond reformists and the various Gonds in scattered clusters, especially landholders, who have advanced claims to the title Raj Gond hoping thereby to raise their social status [122, p. 5].

Among the other 'tribal Gonds' of central India, whose range extends discontinuously from the Vindhya range southward to the gorges of the Godavari, are the Buffalo Horn (Dandami) Maria, Hill Maria, and Muria of Bastar in Madhya Pradesh, and in the same state the Dorla (Dorli), Dhurwa and Bhattra Gonds and the Parsi Gonds of Bastar. In addition, the Agaria, Ojha and Pardhan in central India are usually considered as Gonds [31]. It is said that worship of Burra Deo, the special deity of the Gonds, is their distinguishing characteristic, but the process of hinduization has gone so far that most Gondi now accept Bhagwan (Mahadeo) and various parts of the Hindu festival cycle, especially those connected with the goddess Kali. Many have also accepted the taboo against eating beef and buffalo meat but still eat goats, birds and fish, and a few still eat pigs, rats, snakes, bats and other wild animals. The social pressures toward hinduization seem to be determined more by intensity of contact with Hindu concentrations than by a sense of traditional ethnicity.

Of the eastern group, who are concentrated mainly in Chota Nagpur district of west Bengal and neighbouring districts of Orissa and Bihar, almost all are either Mundari-speaking or claim to have been so in the past. Two or three marginal groups speak Indo–Aryan or mixed languages in which traces of the Mon and even Tibeto–Burman languages of the lower Brahmaputra basin are recognizable.

The ethno-linguistic classification Munda and the derived term Mundari are deceptive. The name stems from the Sanskrit word for village headman – the local form of reference – and is unrelated to Austro–Asian sources. The terms Kol and Kolarian (languages), which are applied to both the Oraon and Munda, are preferable. They stem from the Mundari word *horo* – 'man' – hence Ho (Kho, Kol), one of the largest of the Munda 'tribes'. Lists of the Kolarian-speaking groups vary from ten to thirteen, depending on the basis of classification: language or total ethnic identity. Apart from the Ho, the main groups are the Santal, who presumably derive their name from their former place of residence – Saont, in Midnapur; the Oraon, the Kharia, the Khonds (of Orissa) and the Korwa.

The social structures, value systems and material culture differ markedly from group to group as do their languages. The main uniting feature is their physical characteristics, which associate them primarily with the Dravidian-speaking populations of the south and not with the Mon-speaking Khasi of Assam. A possible interpretation for this apparent discrepancy is discussed in the following chapter.

The fourth tribal grouping, sometimes referred to as the 'jungle tribes', is divided geographically into two scattered clusters in the Dravidian-speaking south: one, eliptical-shaped, stretches from the east corner of Karnatak (Mysore) to west central Andhra; the second is concentrated in the highland interior of Kerala (Travancore) and the adjacent border districts of Karnatak and Madras. The Chenchus, known in the south as Irulas or Irulagas, and the Paniyan of the Wynayad plateau occupy most of the former area. The numerous tribes of the latter area are divided into two main groups: a mountain jungle ridge group – the Muthuvan, Mannan and Pulayan of the high ranges and Cardamom Hills; and a highland valley cluster – the Malapantaram along the Pampa and Achankoli Rivers, the Urali of the Periyan forests, the Paliyan in the foothills of the Vandanmet range, the Kurumba in Pampa, the neighbouring Kannikaran and some twenty or thirty smaller groups.

To these groupings, some would add as northern extensions the Khonds of Orissa – most of whom now speak Mundari dialects – and the Male of Andhra. The Chenchu of Andhra, numbering nearly 20,000, and their counterpart the Irula of Madras and Kerala, totalling nearly 75,000, are sufficiently numerous to be studied separately; the populations of the southern mountain cluster of eastern Kerala number less than 100,000. Of these, the Palayan comprise more than half and the Pardhan, Malayarayan, Kannikaran and Mukuvan nearly one-third. The smallest groups are the Kadar and Malapantaram with less than a thousand each. The Veddas of Ceylon, described in detail by the Seligmans [334], have frequently been grouped biologically with the Malapantaram, a comparison referred to in Chapter 24.

PART IV

THE EASTERN QUADRANT

The Chinese Colossus and its Eastern Neighbours

15

South-east Asia: a Human Kaleidoscope

Eastern Asia as defined here includes south-east Asia, China, Japan and Korea, excluding inner Asia, the peripheral territories of greater China of imperial days: Tibet, Sinkiang, Mongolia and Manchuria. South-east Asia is extended westward to include most of Assam and the intermontane regions of the Himalayas in Bhutan, Sikkim and Nepal but omits the pockets of Tibeto–Burman populations in the uppermost valleys of the Ganges and Sutlej Rivers west of Nepal. The inclusion of the intermontane groups is based upon biological comparisons which link them more closely with the peoples of south-east Asia, although many of the cultural links are with Tibet and India.

Eastward, the line fails to coincide with geographical or political boundaries and has been subject to change. Southward, it includes the Andaman, Nicobar and Mergui archipelagos and the offshore islets of Indo–China, but it excludes the larger archipelagos (Indonesia and the Philippines) except for the prehistoric periods. In general, the boundaries are expressed in human rather than geographical or political terms, in populations rather than terrain, and at no specifically fixed time level. For these reasons they are neither precise nor stable.

In the eighteenth century the name Indo–China was used to designate the entire region of competing influences of the two great civilizations, Indian and Chinese. It included Thailand, Burma and sometimes Assam, in addition to the later French Indo–China – Cambodia, Laos and Annam – and much of the East Indies. Had European imperial rivalry been initiated three centuries earlier Indo–China would have included also the wan-ing Shan kingdom of Nan-Chao, which extended over most of Yunnan and other parts of south-west China. Although there were no empires in south-east Asia comparable to those of the Turks, Mongols or Arabs, there were maritime interests – Indian, Arabian, Chinese and Malayan. Their power was often as effective, but seldom as ferocious.

The post-Magellan maritime conquests of the European powers have masked these earlier influences and their impact on the densely populated trading lands of the monsoon belt was quite different from that of the Russian encroachments in Central Asia and Siberia or the European conquests of Africa, Australia and the New World. Competition in south-east Asia was at the administrative, entrepreneurial and exploitative levels rather than in direct agricultural pursuits. Furthermore, the administrative controls of the two great Asian nations were in the hands of semi-alien dynasties: Mughal in India and Manchu in China. The primary differences between Indian and Chinese civilizations strongly affected events that determined the genetic structures of the various populations of south-east Asia.

During early historic times most of the significant contacts and pressures from the Indian side were by sea, except in Assam; whereas many of the westward ventures of the Chinese and Shan were by land. In previous chapters references were made to the Munda-speaking peoples of India and to the relationships between the Munda and Mon–Khmer languages now classed together as Austro–Asian – Austronesian in insular Asia and Oceania. The relationships appear to be very old and fundamental to the entire southern and south-east Asian theatre, as well as to large areas of Oceania. If the Dravidian speakers of southern India actually acquired their languages from intrusive cattle breeding peasantry and élite of the Indus Valley and the adjacent plateau, then presumably most of the peoples of south India would also be included. This argument is related to the notion that the megalithic builders of south India may have been seaborne from the west; but there are many valid arguments relating them also to south-east Asia.

Very ancient south Asian populations were probably speaking Austro–Asian languages when they moved into south-east Asia and Sundaland as long ago as palaeolithic times, and they must certainly have travelled by land. Following the earliest moves eastward, there were probably several counter-moves westward from south-east Asia including the carriers of shouldered celts of the mesolithic–chalcolithic period, and possibly also Bronze Age celts, in the second and first millennia before Christ – or even earlier, if conclusions concerning the new discoveries in Thailand are validated.

The earliest protohistoric trade contact eastward from India appears to have been during the Maurya period (413–185 BC) when there was also extensive trade with Rome. There are references to visits along the Burma coast and to a Tibeto–Burman people called the Pyu who had established a centre at Pagan and controlled the northern half of the Irrawaddy Valley – a region already largely pre-empted by Mon speakers. Today the Mon-speaking Talaing still occupy parts of southern Burma.

There were further contacts by Indian traders in the second century AD, but the major period of intrusion began in the fifth century when Buddhism was introduced at Thaton in Mon country and a Buddhist-ruling dynasty was established. In the eighth century a southern capital was established at Pegu, and soon after the south extended its conquests to the central Irrawaddy basin.

Not long afterwards from the Chinese side began the first of the Thai–Shan incursions by the highly sinicized kingdom of Nan Chao. Pressure continued throughout the ninth century, and by the beginning of the eleventh century Nan Chao had taken control of Pagan and had begun expanding southward. Towards the end of the century it was strong enough to attack and defeat the southern Mon kingdom and to destroy Pegu and Thaton. The conquest was brief. Nan Chao and Pagan were soon defeated by the Mongol–Chinese armies of Khubilai Khan although Sino–Mongol occupation lasted only about thirty years.

For the next five hundred years Burmese history is largely concerned with wars between the north and south and against Thai–Shan incursions from the east. During the following century, a centralized government was established at Ava and a series of punitive wars waged against Thailand. Most of Assam was also conquered but was later lost to British–Indian forces, and Burma itself was ultimately incorporated into the Indian empire.

In recent centuries Assam has been closely related to India, although the mountainous terrain has been a deterrent to easy conquest. The Assamese language is Indo–Aryan and reflects the influence of the Hindu Kamrup dynasty which attracted riverine settlers from Bengal. Migration may have begun in the first millennium BC, but biologically the marginal Assamese-speaking populations resemble the substratum of Burmese speakers of the Irrawaddy more than they do the Bengali. It follows that the old Assamese population very likely formed part of the basic Mon–Khmer-speaking continuum which even today connects the Mundari speakers of the Deccan linguistically with the Khmer speakers of south-east Asia. The Mon-speaking island of Khasi in the Khasi and Jaintia hills is a reminder of this continuum and it may be suggestive that the Tibetan name for several of the river valleys on the Indian side of the eastern Himalayas is Monyul ('Mon Country').

Periodically Assam was attached to Bengal and there have been powerful Hindu and Islamic influences from the west, but in the thirteenth century the Shan kingdom of Ahom (Assam) – a corruption of the name Shan – was established in the central Brahmaputra Valley with an elaborate highly urbanized wall-enclosed capital.

Westward in the 'intermontane wedge' between the outer and central Himalayas, most of the ethnic groups were politically under Indian Rajput or Tibetan lamaist control for centuries. Some have become Hindu, others Tibetan Buddhists; still others maintain the older Tibetan Bön religion. In addition, there are local syncretic cults with strong Tantric influences from India and shamanistic practices from south-east Asia.

The non-Indo–Aryan languages of the intermontane populations are classed as Himalayan Tibeto–Burman by Grierson [136, p. 55], who distinguished between a western pronominalized group and an eastern non-pronominalized. He noted that, in those features in which the Himalayan languages differ from Tibetan, they are similar in all respects to the Munda group. He also found the pronominalized group to be more similar to Mundari than to the non-pronominalized. He posited a migration from Tibet; the possibility of an influx from the east apparently never occurred to him in spite of the obvious language ties with Burma.

Included in the pronominalized Himalayan group are the Manchati (Patni) of Chamba in Himachal Pradesh; the Bunan,

Tinan and Kanashi in Lahul, Kangra district, east Punjab; and the Kanauri (Kinauri) in the Sutlej Valley of east Punjab. Isolated extensions (Rangkas, Dharmiya, Chaudangsi and Ryangsi) exist in Almora district, just west of Nepal in the source tributaries of the Kali. Near Askot Jangli is presumed to be a related dialect.

Of the eastern pronominalized group Thami, Rai and Limbu in Nepal are the largest and best known. The non-pronominalized group includes the more familiar languages spoken by the Khas (Gurkhas – Magar and Gurung) of Nepal and by the Lepcha in Sikkim.

Thailand, the largest of the Thai ('Free') or Shan states (conventionally, the people are referred to as Thai and the language as Tai), today forms a wedge between the predominantly Mon regions of Burma and Assam and the Khmer regions of Cambodia and Annam. The current name Vietnam ('Southern Yuët') betrays the latter's Mon–Khmer origin, in spite of enduring close ties with China. Until the seventh century AD only scattered colonies of Thai–Shan had drifted south from Yunnan. Later, while Nan Chao was resisting Chinese aggrandisement, Thai peasants and petty chieftains were slowly penetrating southward. The Khmer kingdom of Cambodia was dominant at the time but the dynasty was more concerned with regal affairs than with Thai–Shan encroachments. By the thirteenth century the numerically superior Thai–Shan immigrants had established their own kingdom, a process assisted by the defeat of Nan Chao by China in the north and the flight of refugees southward.

Malaya remains in a category by itself. The oldest records relate to Hindu-influenced petty kingdoms of the second century AD which were successively dominated by Cham, Srivijaya, Sukhotai and Ayuthia. The rise of the port of Malacca during the fifteenth century encouraged the dissemination of Islam, and by the end of the sixteenth century, although Malacca had come under Portuguese control, the older states had already established their separate sultanates.

The present kingdom of Laos was developed during French administration through the consolidation of a number of Thai-related petty Laotian states which had accepted Teravada Buddhism at the state level.

The story of Cambodia in early historic times is connected in a rather extraordinary way with the overseas expansion of Hinduism rather than with Buddhism. The Pallavas had established their Hindu Brahminical cult in Cambodia in the fourth century AD, but during the ninth to twelfth centuries the Khmer state was in competition with the Sumatran Hindu state of Srivijaya. Cambodia meanwhile had reached its Golden Age with the building of the temple–palace complex at Angkor, near the lakeside of Tonle Sap. The Khmer downfall occurred in 1385 when Angkor was sacked by the Thai kingdom of Sukhotai.

It is difficult to be precise about the people and history of Annam ('peaceful south'), now known as Vietnam. The ruling family claimed descent from the ancient imperial lineage of the Chou dynasty of China. In Han times the northern half was overrun by Chinese forces and incorporated into the Han empire under the name of Yüeh (Yüet). Most of the south meanwhile was under the domination of the Malayan–Hindu and Islamic state of Cham (Fulan in Chinese), with ties linking it to Sumatra and Malacca. Towards the end of the tenth century the Chinese were ousted temporarily from the north, but returned in the early part of the fifteenth century. In the meantime the Cham empire had been weakened by encroachments from the north and by internal dissensions. By the time Annam had finally regained its independence in the sixteenth century from both China and the Cham, the northern and southern spheres (Tonkin and Cochin) had developed such distinctive differences, even with a centrally and neutrally located capital at Hue, that they were never completely reconciled to each other. North Vietnam remains today strongly influenced by ancient Confucian values, just as the south has been influenced not only by Khmer and Cham Hindu and Buddhist values but by Islam as well, and by ethnic ties with the older Khmer populations of the south.

The majority populations of the seven present states of continental south-east Asia – Assam, Burma, Thailand, Malaya, Cambodia, Laos and Vietnam – represent distinctive mixtures of populations which have contributed to the respective gene pools, but bear only indirect relationship to the populations of the hinterland forested areas and mountainous perimeters of the interior. Some are exceedingly old, others are recent immigrants from neighbouring regions. There are also a few refugee groups which arrived by sea. The story of the peopling of the seven lands and adjacent areas can be reduced for convenience to the language groups with which they are associated; but the populations of China south of the Yellow River must be included in any discussion of south-east Asia prior to the fifth century BC.

This date marks the first phase of Chinese expansion, which began during the feudal period of the Chou dynasty when there were half a dozen tributary states in the Yellow River basin. Chou had also extended its control northward over the barbarian state of Yen – probably Tungusic – in the region of the present Peking; south over the states of Ch'u and Wu in the Yangtze Valley; and further south over Yüeh, which then extended northward to Hangchow. The people of Wu were probably speaking a dialect of Chinese; but those of Ch'u, in the area of the present Hupeh and southern Honan, were mainly Tai–Shan and Miao speakers or mixtures of both. The Chou dynasty was forced out by the semi-Turkic Chinese dynasty of Ch'in, which took control over the feudatory states and consolidated them for the first time into a unified empire, and incorporated also the barbarian states of Pa in Szechuan and Shu in the mid-Yangtze region.

A characteristic of Chinese civilization has been its emphasis on the 'family system' which should more correctly be called the system of interrelated lineages and branch lineages: *tsu* and *feng*. Chinese society consisted traditionally of one hundred lineages, each with its own surname, ancestral founder and 'clan' ancestral hall, genealogical records and membership rolls. As the lineages expanded, branches were established and separate ancestral halls built. The proliferation continued over the centuries, and groups of families began moving southward to establish the nuclei of new villages. Protection was afforded for pioneering colonies until a new district office could be established and the local lineages registered. Frequently *feng* units moved together to form 'multi-clan' villages, with newcomers added in junior status.

Lineages were patrilineal, so that all males and unmarried children in 'mono-clan' villages had the same surname, but wives were secured from neighbouring villages with different surnames. Exchanges of brides frequently took place between specific villages, and cross-cousin marriages became a preferred form of mate selection. As the nation expanded in population and territory, new surname lineages were added and today there are over five hundred old line families. Many were drawn from the ranks of non-Chinese – Thai, Moi, Miao, Tibetan, Tungus and other 'barbarian' sources – or through the addition of occupational or place names. Through the operation of such a closely knit kin network collective action and mutual protection became traditional, and the society maintained over the centuries a solidarity based on the teachings of Confucius, the integrity of the lineage and the sacredness of the 'five relationships' – parent–child, husband–wife, sibling–sibling, elder–younger and friend–friend.

The differences in social structure between the Indian caste-oriented and the Chinese lineage-oriented societies were reflected not only in characteristically divergent forms of colonies but in their ties with the homeland and places or origin. Wherever Indians colonized, ties with the homeland remained primarily economic and social and were not concerned with the ancestors. In the religious realm matter and soul were separable and what happened to the corpse was of little consequence; it was usually consigned to some process of rapid disintegration and the organic remains – generally ashes after cremation – were available again for regenerative use. The soul achieved spiritual continuity either through rebirth (karma) or the attainment of a state of blissful non-existence (nirvana). The body had no intrinsic value except for the symbolic or magical efficacy of some ashes, a tooth or a wisp of hair. Contrarily, wherever Chinese civilization penetrated, except when influenced by Indian ideas incorporated into Buddhism, there was a close relationship between the spirit of the departed and the corpse. It hovered about until properly cared for, so that its preservation in ancestral surroundings became an overriding obsession. Burial in the lineage cemetery and maintenance of ties with the departed spirits were matters ritual as well as economic and social.

At the administrative levels there was little difference in the manner in which colonies were formed, but at the mercantile, peasant or artisan levels there were usually radical differences. It was imperative for splinter migrations to maintain close ties with the parent lineage centres even after branch halls had been established. Chinese expansion generally involved either complete assimilation of the non-Chinese or sharp differentiation between the two, and social relationships were more on a horizontal than vertical plane. When marriages and intermixtures occurred, the offspring were usually absorbed into Chinese society within a few generations.

The southward expansion of the greater Chinese society was into the lower riceland valleys and at the expense of the 'barbarian' populations. Those not absorbed were usually displaced to higher slopes. Exceptions were the Thai–Shan, Palaung and a few other groups who either contested the taking over of the ricelands or allied themselves to such enterprises. Frequently Thai–Shan élite families were elevated to chieftain status and maintained administrative supervision over alien Tibeto–Burman, Mon or Miao–Yao villages and districts [119].

Degrees of political complexity and differences in social structure characterize the linguistically identifiable ethnic groupings throughout south-east Asia [206]. So scattered are the language groups and so complex their intermixtures and relationships that one or more representatives of all of the three major groups – Austro–Asian (Munda, Mon–Khmer and Malay), Sinitic (Chinese, Tai–Shan and Kadai) and Tibeto–Burman (including Miao–Yao and Karen) – are found in each of the seven political states comprising south-east Asia. Within the Chinese and Thai–Shan are various subunits. The Chinese include Han officials, scholars, merchants, artisans and peasants and nearly a third of a million Yunnanese Muslim Hui or Hwei and about a thousand Pantha (Panthe) in Burma, who serve mainly as muleteers. In Thailand and Laos are also small colonies of Haw or Ho, upland farming colonies speaking south Chinese dialects. The Hakka were originally north Chinese refugees who fled south in the face of barbarian conquests during the period from the Wei to the end of the Sung dynasty.

Among the Thai–Shan are many more subdivisions. According to a recent review [206, part III], there were by the late 1960s some thirty million Tai speakers whose ancestral homeland was probably in the region of the Red basin of Szechwan, while the Han Chinese were still limited to the Yellow River basin. As the Chinese moved in, the Thai became sinicized or migrated slowly southward and became an elite class which gradually assimilated the previous non-Thai inhabitants. The mixtures with the non-Thai groups created several distinct Thai and Thai-related splinter groups. The entire complex is so confusing and often contradictory that the precise identity of many of the existing populations is impossible. The reference cited above provides only a general regional classification of the Thai–Shan; western, southern, central Mekong, central upland and eastern. It is not consistent either culturally or biologically. The Kadai have been added as a closely related sixth grouping.

The western group includes the Ahom of Assam, linguistically related to the Khamti of the old Shan state of 'Mogaung' in north Burma; the hundred thousand or so Shan Tayok in the Irrawaddy Valley, related possibly to the Pai-Y of China; and the million or so Shan in eastern Burma – a western extension of the Chinese Shan.

The southern group is a collective term applied to the majority Thai population of Thailand. Totalling nearly nineteen million, they are divided into northern, central and southern divisions. Exceptions are the Khorat Thai of the east central region, thought to be descendants of Siamese soldiers and Khmer women, and the Pak Thai of the south who are said to be mixed with Malays and Semang–Senoi.

The central Mekong groups totalling five million or so include the Nö (Nüa) and the Chinese Lü or Pai-Y of south-west Yunnan. Related to the latter are the Khün (Hkün) of north Thailand and neighbouring Kentung in Burma. More distant are the Chuan of eastern Thailand, close cousins of the Laotians of Laos and Thailand.

The central upland group is defined by river basin homelands into the Black, White and Red Thai, and three small splinter groups known as Neua, Phuan and Phuthai. The distributions are quite independent of state borders; scattered in parts of Laos, Thailand, Vietnam and China, they total probably less than half a million.

More than ten million Thai-Shan still remain in their original homeland, China. Of these the Chuang, Tho or Tu-jen, numbering over seven million, are mainly in Kwangsi; about a million and a half Chung-Chia, I-Chia (Pu-yi) and Shui are in Kweichow; nearly a million Tung-Chia (Kam) are in Kweichow and Kwangsi. Southern extensions include the Tho, Trung-chia, Nhang, T'ou Lao and Pa-di of Vietnam. The Kadai are widely scattered and mixed – the Li on Hainan Island, the Kelao in Kweichow, the Laqua in Vietnam and the Lati on the Yunnan border. The entire group does not exceed a quarter of a million.

Of the three major migrations into south-east Asia the Chinese has been the latest, most powerful and most numerous; the Thai–Shan, which commenced sometime after the eighth century, the next oldest; and the third, or Miao–Yao, appears to have been more or less continuous over a long period – never in large numbers – and is still continuing but chiefly at higher elevations above the more densely populated riceland plains.

Linguistically the Miao–Yao, who have been tentatively linked with the Tibeto–Burman speakers, occupy mainly the eastern sector of south-east Asia, while the main Tibeto–Burman group occupy the western and northern sectors.

The two and a half million Chinese Miao (Meo in Vietnam) are wet rice cultivators and swidden farmers. Their settlements range from valley bottoms to 3000 feet. Their domestic plants and animals are similar to those of the Chinese and Thai but a major difference is the addition of high-altitude hunting with the crossbow. The Miao–Meo are so fragmented that the major subgroups number several score. Many of the Chinese divisions – over ninety per cent – survive today under their earlier Han dynasty names: Pai ('White'), Hua ('Flowery'), Ch'ing ('Blue'), Hei ('Black') and Hung ('Red') [217].

The Yao are linguistically linked with the Miao but total less than a quarter of a million in China and fifteen thousand in Thailand and Vietnam, where they are known as Man or Mien.

In uncertain language status are the half million or so Karens. With few exceptions their territories are in Burma. Their language has been classed as independent although related to Tibetan, Mon–Khmer and Tai–Shan. Most of the Karen – Sgaw and Pwo – are now lowlanders living among the Burmese and speaking Burmese. Known as the 'White' Karens, they share a mixed genetic heritage with the Burmese and have little in common with the 'Red' or hill Karenni of the eastern plateau.

The Tibeto–Burman group as a whole is sharply divided between the lowland Burmese of the central Irrawaddy basin and the upland groups – western and eastern. Of the upland groups, the western extends eastward as far as the Yangtze and the eastern stretches westward into Assam. The latter includes the intermontane populations of the Himalayas.

In the panorama of several hundred ethnic groups in south-east Asia, the six major lowland valley populations – Assamese,

Burmese, Thai, Cambodian, Vietnamese and Malayan – are all extremely mixed biologically and show clearly that they share in part a common genetic inheritance, but with differing degrees and kinds of subsequent admixtures. Additions from upland groups and neighbouring lowland populations are detectable but not necessarily indicative of ancient trends. The mixtures may have been quite recent. The seventh major population, the Laotian, is as much an upland as a lowland cultural and biological complex. Possibly the most difficult to explain biologically are the Burmese, the only population of significant size among those classed linguistically as Tibetan-related (see Chapter 25).

Over the past several hundred years there has been a steady but slow movement of all Tibeto–Burman groups into south-east Asia. Among the more fanciful ideas concerning human migrations has been the notion that they streamed directly southward from the Tibetan plateau along the great river valleys in successive waves. The authors of such statements seem quite unaware of the nature of the terrain, or the facts of history. The major river valleys – Salween, Mekong and Yangtze – are not traversable over many stretches. As for the Tsangpo, which leaves the Tibetan plateau as the Dihang and turns westward as the Brahmaputra, no one has ever followed its course through the deepest gorges.

Between Bhutan and Atunze in Yunnan, the only practical migration route southward is from Zayul in south-eastern Tibet, westward down the valley of the Lohit to the Brahmaputra; but the route has been used almost exclusively by hunters, pilgrims and traders. North–south migrations from the plateau have always been extremely limited and confined almost exclusively to grazing and limited agriculture in the high grassland meadows just below the crests of the high ranges. Tibetan economy and technology have not been adjusted to altitudes lower than about 10,000 feet. Even more important has been the Tibetan reluctance to leave the highlands. Except for the pocketed petty enclaves of Lomed and Pemakö along the middle course of the Dihang, the only permanent colonies below this level until the recent overflow of refugees into India and Nepal have been at lamaseries and trading posts or as the ruling élite in Sikkim and Bhutan.

Most of the Tibeto–Burman migrations have been from the foothill districts of Szechwan and Yunnan in a south-westerly direction across the high mountain ranges flanking and parallelling the Salween. The infiltrations of the Shan were also from west China into the Irrawaddy between Sadon and the Shan plateau. Once in Burma, movements were in two directions: north into the valleys of the Nmai and Mali tributaries (the 'Triangle'), where they are still identifiable as the Khamti; and westward across the Patkai hills into the Brahmaputra Valley.

Only within Burma, south-west China and northern Thailand have there been direct movements on to the Shan plateau. As the Thai–Shan were primarily lowland wet rice cultivators, whereas the Tibeto–Burmans were upland dry farmers and hunters, the movements of the two groups were seldom in conflict, usually complementary and not infrequently symbiotic. This is especially true of the respective migrations of the two eastern upland groups, which parallelled each other for centuries.

The northern half of the eastern uplands group includes the Lutzu (Chu-tzu), who occupy a high mountain pocket on the upper Salween–Irrawaddy watershed; the Nakhi (Lühsi), referred to frequently by their Chinese name Moso or Mosu; the Minchia (Chinese 'Families of Peoples') who occupy a block of upland terrain west of Tali-Fu: all in Yunnan. In Burma are the Kachin in the northern hills and the Achang (Maingtha), Hpon and Kadu (Sak) in three enclaves surrounded by Tai–Shan groups in the north. The last three are possibly unassimilated remnants of older migrations. Geographically these groups are relatively compacted although internally the Kachin and Minchia have numerous subdivisions. The language of the latter may be related to the Mon–Khmer group.

The subdivisions of the Kachin or Jingpaw (Chingpaw) – Singpho in Assam – include the Hkaku, Gauri, Atsi, Lashi, Nung and Maru. The names are not necessarily consistent. Many individuals claim to be Kachin; others disavow any connection. As pointed out by Hanson [146], the disclaimers may interpret Kachin as a corruption of Hka Khyen, the Burmese rendering of Ye-Jen (Chinese 'Wild Men'). It is certainly alien to the Kachin, who usually refer to the subdivisions. The Maru refer to themselves as Lawng Waw.

In the southern half of the eastern uplands are the Lolo, Noso, Woni, Lisu, Lahu and Akha. The Lolo (Hei-I, I, I-chia) are by far the most numerous and may total as many as three million, of whom the majority are in Yunnan and Kweichow. The greatest concentration known as the Independent Lolo, numbering possibly half a million, occupy the Ta-Liang ('Great Cold') range of western Szechwan. Unlike other Lolo groups, that of Ta-Liang maintained a stratified society: a Black Bone élite and a servile White Bone sector, a distinction no longer officially recognized [249, 374].

The southern Lolo tend to be scattered, often living in isolated villages in otherwise Miao, Thai or Han Chinese territory. There is strong awareness of ethnic identity but society tends to be village- rather than group-centred. Bilingualism is common and accepting wives from outside not infrequent. Even renting lands from Han landlords is quite common, or in turn renting to outsiders or participating in festivals and 'country rituals' [206, pp. 14–24].

The Lahu, Lisu (Yawyin) and Akha (Kaw) who straddle the Sino–Burmese and Thailand borders are often grouped together with the Lolo. All are similar in language and social structure, which has a segmented patrilineal system. The village is the unit and the focal point of political as well as social significance [205]. Another common trait is the almost universal fear of *nats*, the spirits of deceased mortals, not necessarily ancestors, who require constant propitiation.

The western upland groups (Naga and Chin) are also hillside farmers and hunters, but in the north – the Patkai and Naga hills – the villages are uniformly on the high crests of mountain ranges because the valley walls are so steep-sided and the bottoms generally so tortuous as to be uninhabitable. The collective term Naga may be derived either from a word meaning 'hill men' or from *nok* meaning people, and bears no relationship to the serpent worship of India. There are nine major Naga groups totalling a third of a million. A peculiarity of all groups is the *morung* or young men's dormitory. There are no comparable young women's dormitories, but groups of girls are accommodated in private homes where courtship often commences. Mate selection is left to individual choice and young couples have ample opportunity for pairing off and lovemaking, a common characteristic of most upland groups throughout south-east Asia.

South of the Naga, the Chin include the highly hinduized Kuki Chin or Meithei (Manipuri) of Manipur state, which at one time played a conspicuous role in Assamese history; and to the south are some forty or fifty other groups totalling over a quarter of a million.

Finally, the Garo (Mande or A'chik) of the Garo hills, west of the Khasi, are a separate group whose background is unusual. Numbering about a third of a million, their descent system is matrilineal, a trait they share with their Mon-speaking neighbours, the Khasi. Young men's dormitories are also a feature. Of importance to their biological heritage is the differentiation between the upland villages – up to 4000 feet – and the plains villages, which are interspersed among those of the Bodo–Kachari language group. The latter include the Koch–Kolita, who occupy an island area largely surrounded by non-Tibeto–Burman peoples, but their social structure, especially the descent system, may imply more than simply borrowing from their upland neighbours. The largest of the Tibeto–Burman-speaking groups of the Northeast Frontier Administration (NEFA) are the Mishmi, Abor, Dafla and Apa–Tani, each with numerous subdivisions; confined mainly to the river valley outside of the administrative area are the Miri.

If the Tibeto–Burman ethnic groups and subgroups and their alternate designations seem confusing, the speakers of Austro–Asian languages are considerably more so, especially the upland Mon–Khmer speakers. Apart from the Mon-speaking Talaing of Burma and the Khmer of Cambodia, other major lowland populations are the Vietnamese or Annamese, whose language is tonal and strongly influenced by Tai and Chinese, both of which are also tonal. The closely related Muong live in the northern foothills.

Of the northern upland groups the only one in Assam is the Khasi, whose eastern origin has been fairly firmly established. They are linked with the Jaintia (Pnar or Synteng), Bhoi, War and Lynngam, although the latter may be mixed with the Garo. By far the largest concentrations of the remaining northern group are the Palaung-Wa in Burma. Totalling over half a million, the Palaung occupy the lowland regions in close contact with the Shan, while the Wa remain more isolated in their own upland state territories. The Khmu and Lamet of Laos are apparently linguistically affiliated.

The remainder of the northern upland groups are mainly in

Laos and Vietnam. All are Mon–Khmer speakers but some have Tai admixtures or are occasionally bilingual. Of the more than forty listed, only a dozen or so range in size over ten thousand. Of the south-eastern upland Mon–Khmer group, numbering a dozen, all are in Vietnam and comprise the majority of peoples collectively referred to at times as 'Montagnards'. Seven have populations ranging from eight to forty thousand [153].

The south-western upland group of Mon–Khmer speakers is in Cambodia or on the Thai–Cambodia border. The Kui, numbering over 100,000, are by far the largest. The others number less than 2000 each and intermix freely with Cambodians.

Finally, among the Mon–Khmer speakers are the Senoi and Semang of Malaya. Located mainly in Pahang, Perak and Kelantan, the two are sometimes bracketed, but this is mainly to distinguish them from their Malayan neighbours.

In earlier classifications [353], now outdated, three aboriginal groups were distinguished: Semang, Sakai and Jakun. Biologically, the Semang (who number only about 2000) were termed Negrito, the Sakai Veddoid or 'Dravido–Australoid', and the Jakun proto-Malayan. The term Sakai ('hill men') is merely a pejorative Malayan name for the Senoi, who number over 25,000. Linguistically, the Semang and Sakai were given independent status, but today both are classed among the Mon–Khmer speakers and the Jakun are among the Malayans.

The Malayan–Polynesian linguistic groups may be separated into Cham speakers and Malayan speakers. The former includes a lowland group in southern Vietnam and Cambodia and nine upland groups, of whom the largest is the Jarai with nearly a quarter of a million. The second most numerous are the Rhade with 60,000, and the remainder range from 6000 to 40,000.

Most of the two and a half million Malayan speakers are in Malaya, with about ten per cent in peninsular Thailand. The remaining Malayan speakers apart from Jakun 'hill men' are the Moken or Orang Laut 'sea gipsies' of the Mergui archipelago. Over fifty per cent of Malaya's continental population are non-Malays: nearly 300,000 Indonesians and other south-east Asians, two million Chinese and half a million Indians. For a description of the relationships of the minorities to their central governments the reader is referred to Kunstadter [196].

16

Eastern Asia in Prehistory

GREATER SOUTH-EAST ASIA

A great deal of interest has been aroused lately by new discoveries in south-east Asia, south China and Japan which might revolutionize our current ideas on the origins of agriculture and even on the commencement of the age of metals. They suggest the possibility of a realm of independent origin of plant and animal domestication and the 'domestication' of metals in south-east Asia and the now-inundated Sundaland.

The excavation of Spirit Cave in western Thailand, initiated by Gorman [133] in 1967, is especially important. The cave is in a limestone outcrop overlooking the Salween near the Thai–Burmese border and has not been occupied since 5600 BC. The oldest levels reveal Hoabinhian-type polished stone tools dated by carbon–14 from 10,000 to 6000 BC. There were also carbonized broad beans, peas (?), water chestnuts, pepper, gourds, Chinese olives, candlenuts and cucumbers, as well as bone fragments. The food could have been stewed in large bamboo sections, as is done commonly in south-east Asia today. At the 6000 BC level were sherds of burnished, incised, cord-marked ware associated with partially polished stone tools, slate knives and burnt clay pellets for use with the pellet bow. Pottery associated with Hoabinhian tools was first discovered at the type site of Hoabinh [233] in Vietnam in 1920, but was assumed to be intrusive [356]. The occurrence of food plants from 10,000 BC raises anew the question of early cultivation, as proposed by Sauer [330] in 1952.

The development of polished stone tools, which came to play such an important role throughout eastern and southern Asia in the Neolithic and later periods, was associated with the beginning of horticulture, the domestication of animals and, soon after, the invention of pottery.

So far the oldest pottery in eastern Asia came from Japan and dates from 10,000 BC. This is very old by European standards, possibly the oldest discovered anywhere, and it is associated with incipient horticulture. It is unlike any pottery of western Eurasia and is referred to as cord-marked: twined fibres were either rolled across the surface, or the walls were impressed with cord mesh before firing. The ware is relatively abundant in the so-called 'cord-marked pottery horizon'.

At Ta-pen-k'eng in north Taiwan and Feng-pi-t'ou in the south, cord-marked ware assemblages somewhat later than those of Japan were associated with pollen-dated charcoal fragments. They suggest the existence of forest clearings and horticulture by 5000 BC [219]. Other early sites, as yet undated, have been located along the coast in south China and Vietnam. Chang [50] is of the opinion that the Hoabinhian cord-marked ware of south-east Asia may have been contemporary with the early Jomon of Japan and also with the Chinese corded ware and stone tools of the Wei Valley tributary of the Yellow River, the oldest of the proto-neolithic finds in China. He adds that the later Yangshao and Lungshan specializations in China, the Sa–Hyunh of south Vietnam and Laos and the Ban Kao-Gua-Cha of central Thailand, as well as the Jomon, may all have developed from a common base in south China or south-east Asia.

Among early cultivated food plants from these areas Chang [50, table 1] lists taro, yam, rice, gourds, oranges, lemons, tea and pepper, as well as some fifteen other vegetables and fruits, and such vegetable products as cassia, cotton and Chinese jute.

The faunal complex has not been as fully documented, but food animals certainly included domestic fowl, pig, dog, deer and somewhat later goat. From a mound excavation at Non Nok Tha in the Chi River basin of central Thailand, Solheim [256a] reports humped cattle and rice cultivation by the sixth millennium BC, and a variety of fish, molluscs, crustaceans and small game animals from several south-east Asian sites.

Dugout canoes may have been used as early as the fifth millennium BC and the outrigger possibly by the following millennium. By the third millennium there was sea contact with Taiwan, Japan and Indonesia, when pottery designs and cultivated plants were introduced. Malayan outrigger voyages to Madagascar and the introduction of south-east Asian plants to East Africa may have started before the Christian era [356].

The oldest determined dates for bronze axes from Non Nok Tha range from 2600 to 2400 BC [20], but a number of bronze artefacts have been recovered from earlier levels, and sandstone axe moulds have been dated at over 4000 BC. Even if this early date is substantiated, it does not necessarily prove sea contact between south-east Asia and western Asia. Somewhat in favour of local invention is the fact that copper is readily accessible in Burma, Thailand, Vietnam and Yunnan, and tin and other alloys are in abundant supply. There is considerable argument among archaeologists as to whether bronzes in east Asia first went from north to south or the reverse. The best of the Dong Son bronze vessels are clearly Chinese in origin. On the other hand, the earlier axe forms are closer to neolithic stone axes of south-east Asia. There was certainly trade back and forth, but based on skeletal evidence the gene pools of the major regions had already been largely determined before the beginning of the Bronze Age. Such movements as did occur in late prehistoric times and throughout the Chou and Han periods indicate a later southward trend from China. There seem to have been earlier movements from south-east Asia northwards as well as southwards into Indonesia and Oceania.

CHINA

Unlike south-east Asia and south China, which have retained their moist tropical climates and forest coverage, the Yellow River basin and the desert and steppe regions of Inner Mongolia and most of Manchuria underwent dramatic climatic and vegetational changes at the end of the Pleistocene. In early Holocene times the entire area was parkland, while to the south the Yangtze basin was a region of extensive forests and tall savannas, with elephants, rhinoceros, bison, tapir, water buffalo and deer.

During this relatively warm moist period conditions were favourable for the extension of mesolithic and early neolithic cultures northward into areas that could not sustain settlements in the later neolithic and early historic periods. As animals of the arctic tundra type moved northward after the last (Tahi) glaciation, mesolithic hunters followed them.

There may have been two separate mesolithic facies [49, pp. 72–3]: one of dune inhabitants and oasis-dwellers in Mongolia; the other of a forest-dwelling population in north China and Manchuria. The former was characterized by an extensive use of ostrich shell rings but no projectile points and the latter by an exact reversal of the artefacts. In both areas microliths belonging to the Turkestan and Siberian horizons were in use. South of the Yellow River basin the mesolithic artefacts are of a wholly different character.

Recently, various mesolithic and early neolithic cave sites have been excavated in south China. In 1956 choppers, quartzite flakes, charred bones and part of a human skull were found in a yellowish breccia matrix at Lai-pin-hsien in Kwangsi. In a rock shelter in Yunnan were found flints, charcoal ash and the bones of dog, bear, felines, deer, bovids and monkey. Other similar caves have been located in western Kwangtung. The skull fragment from Kwangsi is badly fragmented but seems to fall well within what is commonly termed the mongoloid range.

The Neolithic of central China has been the subject of considerable debate. According to Watson [395], there seems to be a relatively abrupt transition to the Yangshao, a sudden appearance of wheat, painted pottery and other signs which point to Anau in Turkestan, western Asia and Baikalia. The implication is one of culture contact and not necessarily of migration, of which there is no certain evidence. The current view of most Chinese scholars emphasizes the continuity of the underlying early Neolithic, which was largely innovative. It developed into the full Neolithic of the Lungshan in the lower sections of the river, from where it spread northward into Amuria (Manchuria) and southward at least as far as Canton.

There appears to be a fundamental similarity between the earliest Neolithic of central China and the rest of east Asia and Siberia. However, there are no sites in the Yellow River basin in which corded ware and polished stone artefacts appear except in association with later Yangshao assemblages, whereas wholly corded ware horizon level sites are general in the rest of east Asia. The Neolithic continues late in central China, ending about 2000 BC, only a short time before the beginning of the full-blown Bronze Age of the Shang dynasty.

The central Chinese Neolithic could have developed independently, and the Lungshanoid presumably developed from this base with many innovations, especially in ceramics. These include the *li* tripod vessel with hollow legs, *ting* vessels, various amphorae, pedestalled stands, perforated flat rectangular polished stone knives, sickles and ornaments. It is possible that the Yangshao continued while the Lungshan was developing.

Although reports on human remains are inadequate, brief references indicate no major difference between the neolithic population of the Yellow River basin and the respective present-day inhabitants. There were doubtless local migrations from the Yangtze basin northwards, followed by later migrations southward from the Yellow River, but most of the alterations in artefact assemblages are probably the result of diffusion and trade. Such skeletal data as exist tend to confirm a common gene pool throughout the entire Yellow River basin from the Neolithic into the Bronze Age (see Chapter 25). The cultural borrowings, transitions and innovations seem to have been tremendous, whatever the local directions of human movement may have been. The Yellow River was definitely 'Chinese' biologically by the end of the Neolithic.

At the height of the Yangshao Neolithic, as typified at the site of Pan-p'o in Shensi, farmers were living in fairly large village communities, of which some three hundred have been located and partially studied. The huts were semi-sunken with pillared roofs covered with reeds and clay. Crops consisted of foxtail millet and domestic animals included pigs, dogs, sheep and goats. Among the tools were grooved, polished neolithic knives or sickles and polished stone axes – oval in cross-section and rounded at the end. The same type is found at apparently the same horizon in the central Yangtze basin and in Szechwan, where it occurs mixed with thin flat axes, apparently westward extensions of the southern Lungshanoid industry [395, p. 21].

Chang [50, p. 206] believes the Hoabinhian substratum spread northward from south-east Asia but not necessarily in conjunction with cord-marked pottery. The main north China food plants include broom-corn millet or *kaoliang* and foxtail millet, as well as numerous vegetables and fruits. Plant products include also varnish (*lac*) and hemp.

THE AMUR BASIN: MANCHURIA AND THE MARITIME COAST

The Amur basin has become an area of increasing significance to north-east Asian prehistory and possibly also to the peopling of the New World. Western Amuria in the Upper Palaeolithic was a zone of fusion of two distinctive industrial techniques and artefact assemblages. One was an upper palaeolithic blade tool industry reminiscent of some of the south Siberian industries and of cave sites in north China and open or rock shelter sites in the Ordos, parts of inner Mongolia, Manchuria, the middle sections of the Yellow River basin, the Wei Valley and parts of the central Yangtze Valley. The second was the south-eastern Hoabinhian edge-ground stone and wooden tool industry complex.

A major environmental distinction can be seen between the area of internal drainage (the Ordos excepted) and the more saline lacustrine areas of inner Asia, including the Gobi Desert on the one hand and the sweet water fluvial regions on the other. These include both the Yellow River of the north-west and the lacustrine areas of the Yangtze to the east and south. The faunas of the two regions were different and may have influenced the technologies of their hunters. The settled populations of the border zone – the Ordos basin and the Upper Cave dwellers of Choukoutien – may well have hunted in both regions.

A third area in the north central plain near An-Ang-hsi (Tsitsihar) in northern Manchuria includes sites with Baikal-type microliths, triangular knives, long rectangular blades and well executed arrowheads. The pottery is of the corded variety with simple incised bands [395, p. 28]. Finally, in the north-east and the lower reaches of the Amur were settled fishing communities with thick ground stone axes, jade rings and tubular jade beads.

The advanced Neolithic seems to have been influenced by a direct movement north into Jehol and Liaoning from central China through Shansi and Hopei, with influences from the eastern Lungshan complex. The latter may have been derived from an Amurian hunting and fishing community base to which was added farming from the Yangshao area. Trait stimuli may also have been derived from Baikalia and the south [395, pp. 37–43].

After the evolution from Yangshao into Lungshan had been completed, the Neolithic was carried northward into Manchuria and southward along the coast to Anhui and Kiangsu, but the complex did not advance much beyond the redeposited loess area until the beginning of the Bronze Age. In the later phases the advanced ceramic techniques of the coastal south were carried north with the burnished black ware and white bone geometrical decorative ('lattice-work') design of the Lungshan.

In the Amur basin quite extensive permanent settlements, sometimes numbering several hundred semi-subterranean houses, were established at strategic points along river courses and sea coasts to take advantage of the annual fish runs and mammal and bird migrations. Agriculture and animal breeding were introduced from the Yellow River basin long after the settlements had been established. The general economy and industrial techniques, however, were those of the north Asian Mesolithic characterized by the absence of polished stone tools and the presence of north Asian 'grooved' pottery. Bronze and iron artefacts were acquired incidentally through contact with Chinese centres in the Yellow River, and without reference to any special horizon sequence.

Both the Liaoning and west Manchurian artefact assemblages of the circum- Gobi 'black earth' region were part of the link between north China and the Selenga–Baikalian regions of northern Mongolia and south-central Siberia. The eastern corridor carried trade and culture contact artefacts between the Angara–Minusinsk area and the late Neolithic–Bronze complex area of north China.

KOREA–JAPAN AND THE RYUKYUS

The discovery of a rich Pleistocene fauna, including such continental mammals as the mastodon, in Korea and throughout Japan and the Ryukyus as far south as Okinawa is evidence of dry land extensions to the very rim of the continental shelf.

Korean prehistory, although distinguishable in detail from that of Manchuria, belongs to the same general province. An exception is along the north-east coast, which falls within the shell-mound area of the Maritime Province, parts of Sakhalin and Japan. Another exception is the south-west region, which became the kingdom of Paekche, the region where irrigated rice and taro were introduced from south-east Asia. The particular assemblages of these southern elements, combined with the Manchurian Neolithic and later Bronze Age additions, are recognizable later in Japan as the Yayoi.

Archaeological interest in Korea has centred largely on the rich sites of early historical periods, in particular on the relative profusion of mound burial sites now classed as national treasures. There are some twenty or more royal burials in the south alone.

Man must have reached Japan before post-glacial times – possibly as early as the middle Pleistocene. Thus far, however, the only clear evidence of human presence prior to 15,000 years ago are a few artefacts and bone fragments dating from about 30,000 BC. Japan was not subjected to ice sheets, and the habitable areas during glacial periods were far more extensive than they are today. The islands were connected to the mainland where big game was plentiful, so that continuous cultural and migrational contact must have existed between the Maritime Province and the entire archipelago.

Many thousands of prehistoric and proto-historic sites, mostly Mesolithic and Neolithic [179], have been identified in the Japanese archipelago and on the two festoons of minor island chains that tie them to Kamchatka in the north and Formosa in the south. The northern chain – the Kuriles – is broken by stretches of dangerous open seas and there is nothing to indicate their settlement until the last two or three thousand years; but the southern chain, the island links in the Tsu strait, connecting Kyushu with Korea and Hokkaido–Sakhalin with maritime Siberia, have been channels of migration and trade since at least late third interglacial times.

Neither the 'aceramic' (*mudoki*) blade and flake industries of the Upper Palaeolithic nor the oldest ceramic industries of the Mesolithic carry any hint concerning the biology of the populations. No certain skeletal remains have been recovered from periods earlier than the late Neolithic Jomon dating from about 2000 BC. Of the several hundred skeletons that have been studied in detail conclusions differ as to possible origins, just as they differ concerning the genetic structure of present-day Japanese.

For nearly a century, ever since publication of Morse's [248] classic study of the late Jomon shell mound site at Omori (within the limits of Tokyo), there has been heated debate concerning the identity of the human populations of the Jomon period. Some contend that they were southern; others that they were Ainu. Cord-marked pottery dating from 10,000 BC has been established from Kyushu – which tends to confirm either a southern origin or a later extension northward into the Amur basin – with an expansion of the associated shell mound culture into Hokkaido and Honshu from the north or by direct dugout canoe passage to Honshu. There is an interesting thesis that early storm-driven fishermen of the Jomon culture might have drifted across the Pacific by the northern arc route to South America as early as 3000 BC. The Valdivia pottery of Peru, which is C14-dated at 3000 BC, is surprisingly similar to the rare red slipped ware with a unique rim style and decoration of the late-early Jomon of Kyushu [239]. Proof of deep sea fishing in early Jomon times exists and a journey of eight thousand miles would not have been impossible, but the thesis remains unproven. A fascinating feature of late Jomon pottery was that, though coiled and hand-beaten, the rim was elaborately scalloped with highly intricate filigree appliqué designs and frequent additions of human or monkey heads and faces and serpentine bands.

In the early period food was primarily marine, with the addition of land molluscs, small mammals and plant foods including wild tubers and berries. There is some question about garden products which might link the economy more closely to that of south-east Asia. Semi-pit dwellings, *magatama* 'jewel' stones, perforated crescentic polished stone 'knives', pulley-wheel-shaped lip and earlobe plugs and clay human figurines (*haniwa*) suggest connections with the east coast continental province.

The Yayoi culture began in Kyushu and spread eastward and northward, mixing with the earlier Jomon to produce a wide range of local cultures which survived in attenuated form in northern Honshu for centuries. The Yayoi-type site carries the name of a city block in the heart of Tokyo, part of the grounds of the University of Tokyo. The Yayoi culture introduced highly developed wet rice cultivation and wheel-turned thin-walled ceramics related to Lungshanoid forms, but more specifically forms familiar to south-west Korean coastal sites. This is their presumed initial source, although there is evidence of later additions from coastal China – especially Shantung – and ties with the Ryukyus and Formosa. Taro, sweet potato, squashes and beans were the primary crop plants but some scholars contend that the first two were earlier introductions.

A sequence of incursions must have taken place during the early centuries of the Christian era and culminated in the invasion of a sophisticated horse-riding military aristocracy, introducing in the third century AD what is called the Tomb Culture period. The name is derived from burials which were either of two large urns placed mouth to mouth and encasing the corpse or of rock tombs: coffins made out of stone slabs or chambers cut into rock-faced slopes. Burial artefacts included riding equipment, protective helmets, greaves and armour, lances and other military gear strongly reminiscent of Manchurian and Korean prototypes which appear to have been influenced from two directions – the Yellow River basin and Baikalia.

Egami [100] has recently traced Scythic influences in the Tomb Culture of Japan of the third and fourth centuries after Christ and in the strongly Chinese and Korean-influenced brilliantly coloured frescoes and murals depicting courtly and heavenly scenes.

To recapitulate, after the upper palaeolithic phase there was an early shell mound culture introduction from the Korean and Maritime coasts which extended far south into southern Honshu. This remained a hunting and gathering culture even though it acquired cord-marked pottery, the literal translation of the Japanese *jomon*. Very likely earlier pottery will be found in some other area of the Hoabinhian proto-neolithic polished stone and cord-marked pottery complex which will suggest that it reached Japan from the south during the early Neolithic [395, pp. 109–20]. The hunting and gathering culture, with the addition possibly of yam and taro, continued until the third century BC. It was superseded by irrigated rice agriculture with hoes and adzes, double urn burials, some early bronzes and probably ramie fibre textiles, and a variety of Lungshanoid wheel-turned pottery vessels.

Contacts with south China and south-east Asia were continuous and cultivation of garden plants provided economic and technological advantages and stimulated trade and probably migration. There must have been considerable gene flow from southern sources into Japan, and the languages of the historically chronicled Kumaso and Hayato of Kyushu seem to point in this direction.

A sudden alternate trend developed, however, in the third century BC with the explosive intrusion of migrants from Korea and the neighbouring Chinese coast. The population of the forest hinterland and remote coastal regions of Japan must have retained much of the old Jomon heritage, but the later intruders – both Yayoi and Tomb Cultures – quickly expanded and mixed with the diminishing and technically less sophisticated 'aboriginal' Jomon population to form a number of discretely different local populations and artefact assemblages. Additions from the hinterland were continuous, as were expansions and assimilations northward as far as the Tokyo area.

The Yamato culture and the Japanese or Wa people might be described, then, as having a partly southern and partly coastal-derived (Jomon) substratum mixed with later intruding east coastal (Yayoi) farming population and a still later northern (Tomb Culture) aristocracy who introduced the highly sophisticated arts and crafts of Korea and China. Numerous petty states were established but neither genetic nor cultural stability had been achieved before a coalition engineered through the leadership of the imperial line and under the protection of the Sun Goddess achieved hegemony over the Yamato plain – the heart of what developed eventually into the Japanese Empire.

The prehistory of the Ryukyu Islands – of which Okinawa is the largest – merits far more space than can be given in this study. There are shell mounds with associated pottery similar to Jomon but of a distinct type which could have been initiated either from Japan or carried northward by migrants from the south in large dugout canoes similar to those found in archaeological sites along the entire east coast of Asia. They survived into recent decades among the Ainu and along isolated coasts of Indonesia.

While the south Ryukyus continued to trade with Taiwan, Okinawa and the northern chain received the Yayoi culture and undoubtedly migrants also from Kyushu. The Tomb Culture as such, however, apparently never reached the island. Trade and migration continued between Okinawa and Japan, but during the millenium from the sixth to the sixteenth centuries trade and political ties were developed with China. Both the people and the culture developed along independent lines, however, and it was not until the early seventeenth century that vassalage to China ended and the islands were brought under the control of the fiefdom of Satsuma in feudal Japan [324].

17

Chinese, Koreans and Japanese

CHINA AND THE CHINESE

From the earliest period of Chinese history it was customary to confer symbolic titles with cosmological, directional or geographical significance on the various parts of the realm. It was plain to the Chinese that Heaven was above China, and to the sages and geomancers, who had discovered the compass and were obsessed with directions on a four-cornered flat earth, that the people who occupied the centre were on a direct line between Heaven and the underworld. China was the place of union between the forces of Heaven and Earth and the essences of the male and female principles, the Yang and the Yin.

As the empire expanded, it was to be referred to as Chung Kuo – the 'Middle Kingdom' – although 'Central Country' might be a better rendering of the original Chinese. This is still the name for China, although when it was first used the Yellow River was the central part of the land and the capital was in the river's middle section. The region to the north became known as Hopei ('River North'), and to the south Honan; the mountains to the east were called Shantung ('Mountains East'), and those to the west Shansi. Historically, the Yellow River has remained the heart of China, although after the T'ang dynasty the economic centre shifted to the Yangtze basin. Geographically the Yellow River has become north China, and it is customary to think of the Yangtze as central China and the West River (Pearl River at the mouth) as south China with its seat of government at Canton. Such is the historical and administrative approach. In literary and allegorical terms, China is referred to as the 'brilliant' or 'flowery' land, much as one might refer to Albion, Hibernia or Iberia.

The classical philosophical view of the universe called for a spirit of humility and responsive obedience on the part of the emperor to the Will of Heaven – hence obedience on the part of the people to the emperor's command. Peoples and nations on the fringes should recognize the special place of China in the universe and act accordingly. So obvious did this fact appear that a standing army was not deemed necessary and in fact was not developed until the T'ang dynasty. Previously China had depended almost solely on border and palace guards, on mercenaries and on the raising of a militia as occasion demanded. Just as the children of Israel considered themselves the chosen people of God, so the children of Han were equally conscious that they were the chosen people under Heaven. Furthermore, theoretically, if the celestial son was unable to prevent disorder and discontent, then Heaven would determine a successor; if barbarians managed to seize the throne, that was further evidence of Heaven's displeasure.

Another special aspect of Chinese history has to do with its 'cyclical' character, both calendrical and social – periods between the conjunctions of planetary circuits and between socioeconomic upheavals, juridical procedures, dynastic policies and the opening and closing of the land to alien influences. The latter part of the Shang and early Chou was undoubtedly such a period, as was the Han and more spectacularly the T'ang. The Wei (Toba), Hsi-Hsia (Tangut), Yuan (Mongol) and Ch'ing (Manchu) dynasties were all of alien origin.

There are today nearly eight hundred million people living within the limits of the imperial China of the Ming and Ch'ing periods, an area about the size of Europe. About ninety-four per cent speak dialects of Chinese; they are concentrated mainly in about one-quarter of the total land surface – known in English as China Proper – the land of the eighteen provinces and its recent extensions northward. The remaining six per cent, roughly fifty million non-Chinese, have been organized within the Peoples' Republic of China into three major nationality populations: Tibet; the Uighur (Turkic) Republic of Sinkiang; and the Chuang (Tai–Shan) Autonomous Region of Kwangsi Province. In addition, as of 1960 there were twenty-nine ethnic groups or 'nationalities', each with its territory designated as an autonomous district (*chou*) in nine different provinces. Of the nationality districts, nine speak standard Tibetan or Tibetan dialects, five speak Mongol or Turkic, one Korean, four Miao, three Yi (Lolo), two Tai, one Pa-y (Tai–Shan), one Pu-yi (Tai–Shan) and one Lisu (Tibeto–Burman). Excluded are the million and a half Mongols of the independent Peoples' Republic of Mongolia, and what remains of the Manchus.

When the Manchu dynasty was established in the early seventeenth century there may have been as many as a million and a half Manchus. During the period of their rule, so much of their population strength was required to meet military and administrative needs that, by the time of the dynasty's downfall in 1911, there had been little change in size – if anything, it had probably decreased and was mixed with Chinese. Subsequently, when colonization was legalized and migration spurred by the construction of a network of Russian, Japanese and Chinese railways, the native Manchurian population was soon completely inundated and assimilated. By 1950 less than 200,000 returned themseves as Manchus; today fewer than two hundred speak the language and in a generation or two it will probably become extinct. Some half-million Japanese colonials were enticed to settle in Manchuria before the Second World War. By now almost all have returned and form a substantial part of the postwar population of Hokkaido.

The non-Chinese are now identified by the names of their respective autonomous regions and *chou* just as the Chinese are identified as the people of the Middle Land, although formerly at the local level where they were neighbours of non-Chinese they used to be called Han-jen or 'People of Han'. The name originated in the Han River tributary section of the Yellow River basin and was perpetuated historically through the establishment of the Han dynasty, which endured for half a millennium.

Numerous efforts have been made to relate existing minority groups to those recorded in historical records, but the task has not proven very rewarding. Chinese scholars have been particularly active and Eberhard [97] has brought their efforts to the attention of European readers. The 800 and more groups have been subdivided into 80 northern, 345 western and south-western and 290 southern. The remainder are assigned to the prehistoric and mythical past. Chinese historians, though renowned for their descriptive accuracy, were none the less at fault on two major counts. They often omitted important ethnographic information and tended to copy descriptions from revisions of dynastic histories regardless of acculturational and name changes. When military campaigns were launched, known minorities were often described as new groups with new names without reference to past identities. Fortunately, the systematic groupings by Chinese historians coincide more or less with current classifications.

Of the western and south-western groups, Eberhard suggests that the 62 Ch'iang can be identified as Tibetan Tangut; the 47 Fan and Hsi Fan as Tibetan; the 93 Wu–Man as Lolo. In the larger southern divisions, he lists 39 Yao, 65 Miao and 3 Tan, which he refers to as palaeo–Austronesian (Austro–Asian), and 25 Chuang as Thai. The 17 Yueh are Mon and the remainder variously mixed: 5 Li, 17 Ch'i-lao, 8 Liao, 11 Pa and 44 Pai–Man or indefinite.

The process of sinicization followed much the same pattern as that of arabization. Conquered populations gradually adopted Chinese culture and in time the term Chinese came to have far more cultural than biological significance, especially during the period of greatest expansions southward from the latter part of the Chou dynasty to the end of Han.

Corroboration of this observation lies in the fact that biologically the primary line of demarcation between the northerners and the southerners follows the classic division between north and south – between the Yellow and Yangtze basins. Part of the process of sinicization was the adoption of a claim to descent from the Yellow Emperor, Huang-Ti – a claim parallelled by the neo-Muslim descent from the semi-mythical Arab progenitor Qais. As for names, there may be some question concerning Hsu Sung-shih's interpretation [399] that the original Chinese *man* ('barbarian') became corrupted into Miao, Ma, Meng, Min and Ming and that these can be equated with Mon, the major linguistic grouping of much of south-east Asia. The suggestion that *min* (Chinese for 'people') might also be from the same source seems even more untenable.

No population statistics are available for any period prior to the Ch'in dynasty but, based on the sites and the average number of households per site, the total population of the petty states recognizing the Heavenly Mandate of Shang probably did not exceed two million. By the end of the Chou dynasty, and during the period of consolidation under Ch'in, the figure may have doubled but it is doubtful if it exceeded thirty million by late T'ang [64]. The rough figure of fifty million is given for the Yüan or Mongol period of the thirteenth century; by the mid-seventeenth century possibly as much as four-fifths of China proper was inhabited by the people of Han, and the total population had risen to seventy million. Since then, it has more than doubled each century and in the past twenty years has soared to over 750 million. From these statistics it is impossible to distinguish between the descendants of the original Chinese, the true Han-jen, and those who have been assimilated from non-Han sources. Such detailed demographic analyses still remain speculative, but undoubtedly differential fertility favoured the intensive agricultural rice-growing communities more than the upland swidden-farming populations.

The demographic parallels seem to be with India. In China, as in India, the greatest concentrations have been in two separate river basins, one arid and the other moist. The dry rivers (Indus and Yellow), the oldest centres of the respective civilizations, lie along the north-western frontiers adjacent to mountain escarpments through which, at fixed points, invading armies and migrant settlers periodically entered the riverine lowlands. The moist river basins (Ganges and Yangtze), though frequently subjected to uncontrollable flooding, were later to become the major regions of economic growth and cultural development. Both nations border on the Tibetan plateau and on the rich monsoon ricelands of south-east Asia. Both also have southern upland plateaus, largely occupied by unassimilated 'tribal' populations.

Beyond these basic similarities it is possible to equate the emergence of India from European domination in the twentieth century with the contemporary escape of China from the gradual encroachment of a European–American–Japanese consortium. In other respects, especially political, social and religious institutions and in the linguistic field, the differences are tremendous.

Scholars fail to agree on the number of dialects apart from Mandarin, the accepted national language and primary language of nearly three-quarters of all Chinese. Mandarin is spoken in the Yellow River basin, Manchuria, the Yangtze area from Szechwan almost to the delta, most of Kweichow, Yunnan, northern Kwangsi, western Hunan, most of Hupeh and southern Shensi and by the Chinese of inner Asia. Differences of minor consequence characterize local dialects throughout this area.

Some ten major dialects are spoken in the rest of the country: (1) Wu or Soochow (Kiangsu, Chekiang and eastern Kiangsi); (2) Hsiang (central Hunan); (3) Kan (Lake P'o-yang area of Kiangsi); (4) Hakka (scattered throughout the south); (5) Yüeh (Cantonese, scattered intermixedly with Hakka); (6) Min (Fukien, Taiwan, Hainan, Amoy, Swatow); and four others in southern Anhwei, Hunan and Kwangsi. The majority of overseas Chinese in south-east Asia speak Cantonese (Yüeh) or Fukienese (Min).

Throughout China's history the terms 'China' and 'Chinese' have been applied as much to the civilization as to the nation or the geographical region. It was used initially by Europeans during the Ch'in dynasty, and hence the name.

Chinese traditional history begins with a series of mythical sovereigns or culture heroes whose life spans match the celestial dimensions of their divine and semi-divine origin. The first historical Hsia dynasty must have endured for several hundred years during the early part of the second millennium BC but the archaeological evidence is still sketchy. The Shang (Yin) dynasty (1523–1027 BC) on the other hand, is traceable through a list of kings verified from the caches of bamboo analects excavated from one of the capitals, An Yang [49, pp. 209–11].

Bronze Age artefacts and historical documents are relatively late in comparison with western Asia, but their lateness is deceptive. The social differentiation between the peasantry and the élite, the architectural sophistication of the palace structures, the archival system of tax tallies and labour services and the technical superiority of the bronzes, ceramic wares and gemstone treasures indicate a much longer tutelage than is apparent from archaeological sources.

Although the current Chinese view supports the notion of rapid but independent development, the standard European interpretation is that bronze was introduced at an advanced stage from Turkestan, or by way of Baikalia to the Ordos and central China, and that China's superior ceramic firing techniques made possible a rapid improvement in smelting so that Shang bronzes very quickly achieved a perfection unmatched in the west. The most perfect Shang bronzes were made not by the *cire perdue* or lost-wax method, but by direct casting. Proof rests in the lack of tell-tale traces usually left by the lost-wax method. The best Shang bronzes are thin-walled, with detailed relief ornamentation 'surpassing anything' even from Turkmenia [395, p. 40]. They spread rapidly northward into the Minusinsk area and from there westward to Turbino and central Europe. The most characteristic and unique Shang artefact was the socketed celt which spread throughout Europe; and there is no need to dwell upon the numerous varieties of *cloisonné*, porcelains and other chinas which have made chinaware a household word throughout the western world.

The earliest attempts at writing, which appear about 1300 BC, are pictographic and associated with divination and ritual. There are no equivalents elsewhere, and they soon began to assume hieroglyphic and ideographic significance. The earliest legible inscriptions are on deer scapulae and long bones, and later on tortoise carapaces. All are connected with oracles. Questions were incised and the bones held over red coals; the replies were interpreted from the manner in which cracks appeared.

Oracle bone inscriptions were undoubtedly a source of Chinese ideographs, but questions remain concerning the possible stimulus diffusion of the pictograph and hieroglyph concept from western Asia. By late Shang, pictographs were gradually replaced by early forms of ideographs appearing in stylized form on bronze vessels and knives. By middle Chou the conventionalizations approximate the seal-style, which continued into Han times and survive today in modified form.

Because of the large number of homophones and dialects in Chinese, there are many advantages to a script emphasizing visual distinctions and capable of multiple permutations and groupings of elements. There are some thirty to forty thousand ideographs but roughly sixty per cent are highly esoteric and may have been used only a few times or in special contexts. The average literate Chinese commands no more than two or three thousand, but can appreciate the nuances of many more thousands regardless of their specific meanings.

Another feature of the Shang and Chou dynasties was the royal burials with horse-drawn chariots and accompanying furniture, and the decapitated bodies of accompanying slaves and consorts destined to comfort the deceased during the tedious journey to the nether world. Some of the elaborate cruciform pit burials are not unlike those of the Kuban in Caucasia. Others are dolmen-covered and surrounded by circles of upright stones. Eastward a succession of modifications led to the evolved dolmens of the early Korean kings of the Paekche and Silla kingdoms. In turn these Korean dolmens were the prototypes of the early imperial burials of the Japanese Yamato emperors.

The formation of the north Chinese population remains highly speculative. The Yellow River basin was a zone of pressure and stimulus contact between the peoples of the north and south. Northern pressures appear to have been the oldest and most pervasive until well into the neolithic. The skeletal materials from the Yellow River are poorly studied, but such studies as have been made suggest closer affinities with the northerners than with the inhabitants of the Yangtze basin. By the Bronze Age skeletal remains seem possibly to approximate those of the Yangtze Valley more closely, especially in Szechwan.

According to Li Chi [215], who depends heavily upon an analysis of the twenty-four classic histories, the Chinese population was stabilized and there were no barbarians in the Middle Kingdom in 246–222 BC. By AD 40, after the Ch'iang tribes had been subjugated and moved about, the population came to be quite mixed. By AD 299 half of the population of political China was non-Chinese and there were, in addition, several thousand descendants of the Hsiung-nu and several thousand Koreans. The effect of the Jurchen invasions was not so much an addition of Tungus speakers to the gene pool as a moving about of peoples within the empire and a devastation of the countryside. There appears also to have been a considerable drop in population owing to plague or other natural causes. Another factor relating more to gene flow than to numbers was the flight of the Chinese southward as refugees during the Wei and Sung dynasties, their places often being taken by Tungusic and Manchu–Liao tribesmen.

Li estimates at least a ten per cent genetic influx from the north during the days of barbarian control. However, while each of the barbarian invasions added to the gene pool, the difference initially between the northern Chinese and the northern barbarians was probably no greater than that between the dwellers in the

Yellow River basin and those of the Hoabinhian areas of the Yangtze basin and the south.

Contact between the Chinese and the northern barbarians in the Yellow River basin resulted in cultural as well as biological mixtures. Scapulomancy is definitely northern; whether the Will of Heaven can be added is debatable. The claim has been made that Chinese *t'ien* and Mongol *tengri* (both meaning 'heaven') and their related Altaic equivalents are from a common source. The uses of the horse and wheeled vehicles from the north from very early proto-historic times were undoubtedly contributory factors in the consolidation of power and development of centralized authority. The enormous advantage of the extremely fertile valley of the central and lower Yellow River basin, and later the acquisition of the ricelands of the Yangtze – combined with technical superiority – conferred upon the dwellers in the Middle Kingdom a special advantage leading eventually to a decisive alteration in the course of history, especially in the Chou, Han and T'ang dynasties.

The peopling of China and the development of their civilization has been studied by scholars for centuries, but its outlines are still indistinct. Much of the uncertainty is due to the fact that major sites have been flooded by the Yellow River, but the efforts of Chinese and foreign scholars since the turn of the century have added much to our knowledge.

The overriding question of primary origins remains unanswered. There seem to be three major theories. The first is that the prehistoric population of the Yellow River basin was ethnically more close to the proto-Altaic and Tungusic groups than to those of historic south China and south-east Asia; and that the development of the early Hsia and Shang civilizations (the formative period) was strongly influenced by contact with western Asia and central Eurasia. The second theory is that Chinese civilization developed its own local high civilization *sui generis* and, though influenced somewhat by western and southern contacts, was the main centre of inspiration for transformations of neighbouring cultures. The third is that, while the early Yellow River cultures had strong ties with the northern sphere in the beginning and were undoubtedly influenced by contact with the west, the main inspiration – especially in agriculture and metallurgy – was from south-east Asian sources.

KOREA AND THE KOREANS

Unlike Japan, the peninsular tie of Korea to the continent favoured an early introduction of Chinese civilization. Steep cliffs and sharp escarpments outline most of the east coast, but the mountainous terrain slopes gradually downward to sea level along the west coast facing China, providing relatively easy passage around the gulf of Chih–Li (P'o–Hai) and across the Liaotung peninsula to the Yalu River.

In the second century BC, during the early Han dynasty, the Chinese occupied the northern two-thirds of the Korean peninsula. They established a colony at Lo–Lang or Nang–Nang in the neighbourhood of Pyongyang, which later became the capital of Koguryo and is now the capital of the Peoples' Republic of North Korea. Though the Chinese relinquished their control within a century, they subsequently occupied the land again during both the T'ang and Yuan dynasties. Korea was also invaded twice by Japan prior to the thirty-five-year period of recent administration which was terminated in 1945.

In spite of these periods under alien domination, there was less permanent genetic impact by invaders than might have been expected, and the civilization, though deriving much from China, maintained its independence. In the postwar period North Korea chose to retain its classical and Chinese-oriented name – Chosön, usually translated 'morning calm' – while South Korea has reverted to the ancient name of Han. Written with a nominal or designation ideograph, it is not to be confused with the Han dynasty ideograph or the Han people of China; the ideographs are different, although it is conceivable that the two names might have derived from an ancient common source. The name Korea is an anglicization of Koryo, the name of the northern dynasty which united the three kingdoms of Koguryo, Paekche and Silla in AD 936.

Had Korea been less mountainous it might have been absorbed within the expanding Chinese nation, the fate that overtook Manchuria. It is estimated that when the Yi (Li) dynasty assumed control in AD 1392 the population was less than half a million. Two hundred years later it was about a million and a half, and by the beginning of the nineteenth century it had risen to over seven million. Today it stands at about thirty-five million, of whom only a few thousand are Tungusic-related tribes who survive in the north. In addition there are 200,000 or more Koreans on the Manchurian side of the Yalu River border, and a sizeable colony remains in the Maritime Province of Siberia. A larger colony was transferred to Soviet Central Asia under Soviet supervision.

During the Japanese occupation (1909–45) nearly a million Japanese, apart from military garrisons, migrated to Korea as officials, merchants, businessmen and landlords. During the same period a million and a half or more Koreans were sent to Japan, mainly as labourers, the majority from north Korea. After the war the Japanese were all returned to their homeland, but over a million Koreans still remain in Japan. Most of the latter continue to work as labourers and they retain their alien status unless they opt to become Japanese. The genetic exchange through marriage in both directions has been estimated at no more than about five per cent.

Although Korea owes a great deal to China in the fields of scholarship, religion, administrative techniques and the fine arts, the material culture – especially dress and house types – remains distinctive and the social structure was less influenced than might be expected. The traditional Chinese four-fold division of society may have been introduced in Nang-Nang during the Han dynasty, but the classic examination system which encouraged social mobility seems never to have become general. Ultimately a two-class social system came to prevail and was crystallized during the Yi dynasty into the *yangpan* – 'gentry–élite' or 'nobility' – and the *sangnom* – 'commoners'. There were also slaves who might be liberated at the discretion of their owners and outcastes similar to, but less variegated than, those of Japan: leather-workers, butchers and, interestingly, the *mutang* or female shamans, who still retain their importance in rural communities.

The rural–urban cleavage is probably accentuated by the fact that the strongholds of Buddhism and the cult of Confucian ancestor reverence are primarily urban. On the other hand, Shamanism and animistic spirit worship are more prominent in the rural areas as well as other practices reminiscent of the Tungusic regions to the north: the importance of bear spirits; the tying of blanket-wrapped children's corpses to the limbs of trees; and the ancient custom of exposure of adult corpses in coffins for several days before burial.

Ki-ja, the traditional founder of the first dynasty, was reputed to have been a Chinese refugee minister of state who fled China in the Shang dynasty and organized a city–state with its capital in the north. During the Ch'in dynasty, towards the end of the third century BC, when the earlier Chou aristocracy were being persecuted, several thousand Chinese families are known to have taken refuge on the peninsula. Again, in the late T'ang dynasty, when Buddhists were under similar pressure, both monks and lay adherents sought refuge in the Buddhist strongholds of the Korean south. The refugees, however, were concentrated largely in the urban centres and along the western sea coast. In the rest of Korea, both the biological and mythological–shamanistic ties are closer to the ancient Tungusic strongholds of the north.

Korea shared with Manchuria the acquisition of the full Neolithic and the earlier northward extension of the Lungshanoid culture, as well as the expansion of bronze during the late Shang and Chou dynasties. Like Japan, Korea adopted the Chinese script, but instead of devising a syllabary, an alphabet known as *hangul* was conceived by an ancient sage, inspired possibly by – but unrelated to – the neighbouring alphabetical script of the Manchus.

Among the Amur tribes of historical importance to Korea were the Mahan (Maguk) in Kyonggi province, and east of them the Yehan (Yeguk) – rival tribes whose later merger provided the basis for the northern kingdom of Koryo. The multiplicity of the Tungusic tribal and confederacy names that characterize the ancient chronicles of Korea is probably not of major genetic significance.

A number of ancient Korean traditions concerning the bear and the tiger strike a familiar chord in old Japanese fables, as well as the persistence of the female *mutang*, whose role is not unlike that of the *noro* priestess of Amami and the central Ryukyus. In the ancient folklore of the Tungus tribes of northern Korea and the Amur are numerous myths highly suggestive of those in the ancient mythology of Japan. The spirit gate and effigies at the entrances to villages in northern Korea are very much like those in the mountain districts of central Honshu; the sister guardian spirit in parts of northern Korea survives in memory in the Ryukyus. Brother–sister marriages were reported in ancient Ryukyu; they exist in Japan's mythology, and were standard among the ruling family of the Koryo dynasty [269].

Biologically, the Koreans seem to have retained their genetic ties more firmly with the Tungusic tribes than did the Japanese. Skeletal data are not as abundant for Korea in the mesolithic and neolithic periods as they are for Japan, but what is available points towards remarkable continuity and relative homogeneity with low standard deviations.

JAPAN AND THE JAPANESE

Japan is referred to classically as Nihon or Nippon – different readings of the same Chinese ideographs meaning 'Sun Source'. The name 'Japan' is a corruption of the Portuguese Zipangu, the terminal *gu* an abbreviation of *kuo* (Chinese 'country'). The Portuguese rendering is closer to the original Chinese than either of the Japanese versions, illustrating the dilemma the Japanese have faced since they first began to absorb Chinese scholarship at the end of the third century AD.

Sporadic references to the land of the 'one hundred communities' [324, vol. 1, p. 15] can be found in the writings of Han travellers of the first century AD, but not until the later Han and Wei, or Turkic Toba, dynasty of the third century are there reliable accounts. By the end of the third century AD some thirty of the one hundred petty chieftains of northern Kyushu were formed into a confederation under a queen named Pimeko – probably a corruption of the Yamato *hime-ko*, 'princess'. The secret of Yamato and the great Wa queen power may have lain in a Chinese trading centre in northern Kyushu through which technological and possibly mercenary assistance and advice could be secured. References to neighbouring confederations on Kyushu and at Izumo on Honshu indicate considerable rivalry among the Wa groups.

Some scholars believe that Izumo was actually a petty Korean coalition. There are accounts of campaigns against the Kumaso and Hayato in southern and western Kyushu – pocketed enclaves of Malayo–Polynesian (Austronesian) speakers, whose languages were probably related to those of mountain tribes of Taiwan and the Philippines. The local Satsuma dialect of south Kyushu today contains several hundred words that are not in the Yamato vocabulary and are traced mainly to southern sources.

During the third century the expanding Yamato confederacy was strong enough to establish a minor dependency outpost

(Mimana or Karak) in southern Korea between the states of Paekche and Silla and, by the end of the fourth century, had expanded eastward along both shores of the Inland Sea to the plain just south of Kyoto, appropriately naming it Yamato. It is this region that the Japanese have come to consider the homeland of their civilization.

The three sacred treasures that are enshrined in the sanctuary to the Sun Goddess at Ise, south of Kyoto – the mirror, the sword and the *magatama* or curved jewel – are all characteristic of the eastern seaboard cultures from the Yellow River to Manchuria. The emphasis on the Sun Goddess, ancestress of the imperial line, is significant and has its echoes in myths and legends of the northern forested lands. In classic Chinese legend the sun is derived from the right eye of the expiring original creator – P'an-ku – and the moon from his left eye. The Japanese version combines Chinese cosmology with that of earlier Shinto: the heavenly bodies are deified and their sexes reversed. The goddess Amaterasu, the sun, emerges from the left eye of Izanagi and the Moon God from his right eye. In the Chinese myth P'an-ku acts as the sole creator; in the Japanese the task is divided between Izanagi and his sororal consort Izanami. This heavenly pair was responsible not only for the creation of the heavenly bodies but for the Japanese isles and all living beings thereon. The question then is, 'who were the people of Yamato?'

Apparently referring originally to a petty clan-dominated state in northern Kyushu, the name is believed by some to have been derived from a sacred mount Yamatai. But Japanese scholars are not agreed on the identity of the mountain or even on a Yamato people there. The name is probably from *yama* (mountain) and *to* (east), but Chinese ideographs bear no relation to the word Yamato either in sound or meaning. The characters would normally be read *daiwa* or 'great Wa' in Japanese – the old Yamato name for themselves. This would be something like writing 'Great We' in English but consistently reading it as 'British'. The riddle might be explained by the fact that early Japanese records were all written in Chinese with the addition, when necessary, of Yamato words, and they were written with ideographs which might be used either for their sound values or their meanings.

Development of the Japanese language is sometimes compared

to that of English: Anglo–Saxon–German with a Celtic substratum and massive borrowings from gallicized Latin and Greek. Comparably, the Japanese language – apart from several thousand recently acquired European loan words – has a basic mixed vocabulary of Tungusic–Altaic and Austro–Asian (Malayo–Polynesian) words and a vast classical vocabulary (roughly two-thirds of the dictionary) derived from Chinese. The Sino–Japanese words came both from the north by way of Shantung and Korea and also from the south: sometimes the same word came from both directions with different readings. But Anglo–Saxon, Celtic, Latin and Greek are much more closely related to each other than Japanese is to Chinese. The Yamato language, although mixed, is structurally related to old Korean, old Manchurian and ultimately old Tungusic – all of the Tungusic group. Sometimes the etymologies are hard to trace because of the numerous substratum words from south-east Asia and place names from the Ainu language, but like many ethnic groups the history of the Japanese is remarkably revealed by their language.

The language dilemma stems from a variety of conflicts: the morpho-phonemic structure of Chinese is completely different from Japanese; Chinese is non-inflecting and depends heavily on idioms for syntax and particles to express tense, case, mood and person; Chinese is tonal and the vocabulary is composed entirely of monosyllabic words or their compounds. Japanese (Yamato), on the contrary, and apart from its phonemic and morphemic peculiarities, is highly inflecting; has quite a complete syntax; is non-tonal; and most of the basic words are polysyllabic. An added peculiarity of Chinese is that the written language depends on vision and abstract concepts – ideas – rather than phonetic symbols and consequently there is no means of anchoring sound values except by use of special phonetic components or by substitution of homophones. For these reasons, while the Japanese maintain a high degree of respect for classical Chinese scholarship and creative genius, oral communication has always been difficult between the two peoples. Because of radically differing value systems, there is more cleavage between Yamato and Chinese meanings of basic words than in their artistic expressions, where remarkably creative and ingenious fusions of the two cultures are so tangibly visible.

From the circumstances of Japan's early history and civilization it is clear that the Wa of Yamato were not the relatively homogeneous people they appear to be in historical accounts. There is no documentary record concerning the Wa prior to Chinese sources from the Han and Wei dynasties, but there is archaeological evidence of constant contact between Chinese trade settlements in Kyushu and Bronze Age centres in Shantung and south Korea as early as the third century BC. Sites in Kyushu and coastal areas around the Inland Sea indicate the local manufacture of military equipment such as lances, spears, continental bows and arrows and horse trappings. There were also palace compounds and distinctive burial sites for a military élite class and a peasantry. This population complex, both military élite and agricultural peasantry, were presumably the Yamato, but the people identifiable ethnically as the Japanese derive their origin from additional sources.

The most significant characteristic of traditional (feudal) Japanese society, which has its roots in the ancient *uji* (clan) system of the élite aristocracy, was the separation of the so-called *bushi* or military aristocracy from the peasantry. In this it resembles the two-fold class system of Korea. In Japan, only the *uji* clan leaders (later lords) and the special craftsmen (*be*) were permitted to have surnames. Peasants were identified by the names of their dwellings and surnames were not allowed among the peasantry until late in the feudal period, some not until a century ago with the beginning of post-feudal modern Japan.

In the latter part of the ninth century, when the T'ang dynasty was at its peak, Japanese interests turned largely to the main source of high civilization – China – instead of maintaining dependence solely on Korea. The capital was moved from Nara to Kyoto and was modelled after the T'ang capital of Chang An. Chinese families were induced to come to Japan as scholars and specialists in the manufacture of sophisticated porcelains and textiles much as Koreans had been invited at an earlier period. The descendants of many of these early specialists in Kyoto maintain traditions of their Chinese – less often Korean – origin to this day and their names confirm these traditions.

The origins of the so-called outcastes are traceable to the period of early contacts with Korea and the introduction of Buddhism. Biologically, no significant differences are detectable between outcastes and other 'commoners'. Many were, and continue to be, leather-workers from Korea (Koma). Others are possibly Jomon or Yayoi survivors who were never completely incorporated and continued to hunt and fish or to eat the flesh of four-footed animals. In the stricter Buddhist areas, such diets would automatically be construed as anti-religious and anti-social.

Japanese scholars have listed as many as three or four hundred categories of outcastes of whom the Eta form the largest single group. Others include grave diggers, preparers of corpses, wandering minstrels, certain categories of wood carvers, basket makers, smiths and a variety of herbalists, story tellers and acrobats. While totalling at most a million and a half when last tabulated, no census is now taken of the *shin hei min* or 'new commoners'. Many have flocked to the cities where they are accepted as hairdressers, factory workers and civil servants.

For earlier periods population estimates vary considerably. At the end of the Jomon there were probably less than 100,000. At the founding of the Yamato empire in the third century estimates vary from a quarter to a half million. By the eighth century the figures may have risen to as high as five million. The population was about thirteen million in the twelfth century and remained between twenty and twenty-seven million during the feudal period (1598–1868) – a period fraught with abortion and infanticide in the face of stringent laws to the contrary, an indication of the economic plight of the peasants.

Japan's population todays stands at about one hundred and eleven million; it has trebled since the turn of the century and quadrupled since the beginning of the modern period (1868) – a result mainly of industrialization and trade. Life expectancy matches that of the most highly industrialized nations of the west.

PART V

THE NORTHERN QUADRANT

The Oasis-Dwellers and Nomads of the North

18

Life in the Desert, Steppe and Woodlands

The northern quadrant, which encompasses over fifty per cent of the land surface of continental Asia, divides conveniently into three ecological zones: northern – tundra, taiga and eastern forest; central – steppe, desert–steppe and desert; southern – high plateau. Ethno-linguistically, except for areas occupied by recent eastward-moving Europeans and northward-moving Turkic and Tungusic herders, the three zones correspond roughly to major language areas: (1) Uralic (including Samoyedic), Palaeoasiatic and Eskimo; (2) Altaic (Turkic–Mongol–Tungusic); (3) Tibetan (Sino–Tibetan). The Turkic-speaking Yakuts and several Tungusic tribes have migrated into regions formerly occupied almost exclusively by Uralic and Palaeoasiatic-speaking hunters. Historically and geographically, the three subregions are Siberia and Hokkadio, Inner Asia and Tibet (which is usually considered a part of Inner Asia).

The most fascinating aspects of Asia's northern half are the vastness of its arctic tundra, the seeming endlessness of its forests, steppes and deserts; the grandeur of its snow-capped ranges and swampy river basins teeming with fish and game; the treachery of its deep river gorges; the brilliance of its winter skies; and, on the human side, the persistence of a wide range of subsistence economies: hunting, fishing and gathering, and the close husbanding of natural resources.

Prior to intensive European colonization, native populations were conditioned to maintaining economic and political independence. The tremendous distances between camp settlements fostered a spirit of self-reliance and a close symbiotic relationship between man and his animals. The northerners depended far more upon this alliance than on trade for life's essentials. Except in the desert oases, the people were traditionally pastoral nomads or engaged in semi-sedentary pursuits, shifting camp with the seasons. Their animals provided food, fuel and shelter, guided them both in this world and the next, and helped them in their daily tasks. Everything about them was animate and only the fine line of visibility separated them from the surrounding spirit world.

In southern lands, the fickleness and whim of deities controlling natural disasters – floods, droughts, diseases and locusts – were to be feared more than human attacks. Separate deities had to be appeased, temples built, festivals held and prayers raised in propitiation. But in the northern expanses life meant constant exposure to more earthly dangers. In the larger river-supported desert settlements there was always the possibility of destruction of dikes and levees and the loss of fields and orchards won through years of toil and patience: water supply networks were exceedingly vulnerable and could be lost beyond retrieval by shifting sands and water-courses. Much of western Asia even today depends on oases kept alive by wells, artesian springs and underground reservoirs, but Inner Asian settlements depend mainly on surface networks fed by melt-waters flowing from the mountainous hinterlands.

Among the steppe herders were also the dangers of stock diseases, drought and overgrazing; the deadly sandstorms of summer and blizzards of winter; and in their wake the wandering packs of half-starved predators. Well-trained mastiffs provided reasonable protection against rustlers and pillagers, but constant alertness was the rule. Sometimes security could be purchased; otherwise, skilled horsemen and powerful kin alliances were the most dependable deterrents against attack and the surest guarantees of revenge. Settlements were strung together like beads on a necklace with fixed staging accommodation along the sandy or rutted trails; but across the open steppes staging areas were usually simple camping grounds where only grazing, water and fuel were available, or the courtyard and commissary of an occasional monastery which might provide additional facilities.

Further north among the hunters, fishers and herders fear of fellow beings was less urgent than the need for collective protection against natural dangers: floods, iceflows and avalanches, or the lurking threat of predatory beasts and the unpredictable acts of malevolent spirits.

The inhabitants of the northlands existed, in fact, in a climate of tension and uncertainty, with economies adjusted to mobility in a constant search for greater security. The gradual imposition of Chinese and Russian political controls has had a stabilizing effect, but the greatest impact has been demographic.

For centuries the greater societies peripheral to China had been developing their own high civilizations, their own centres of learning and pilgrimage, of literature and the fine arts, and their own administrative systems. Living in contact with both China and the Byzantine world, they had long been schooled in the wisdom of the ancients, and, for a time at least, each had maintained dynastic control over all or part of the Middle Kingdom: the Tibeto–Turkic Tangut (Hsi–Hsia), the Turkic Toba (Wei), the Mongol (Yuan) and the Manchu (Ch'ing). After the great Khubilai ('Kublai') Khan's first major triumph in the Middle Kingdom, it is said that only the wise counsel of his advisers dissuaded him from putting the cities to the torch and the people to the sword, and converting the fields to grasslands – 'For how else can a pastoral nomadic sovereign rule except from the saddle?'

For Chinese settlers, adjustment to life in the grasslands meant sacrificing silks and cotton goods for hides and coarse woollen garments, and the substitution of parched barley, curds and cheese for rice and vegetables; of mutton, yak meat and game for pork and fish. Only the oasis centres provided some balance to the privations to be endured.

Manchuria was closed to colonization until after the fall of the Manchu dynasty in 1912, but since the lifting of the ban the Chinese population has increased from less than a million to over forty million, and Inner Mongolia from a few hundred thousand to five or six million. Nearly five million now live in Sinkiang and several hundred thousand migrated to the Tibetan plateau. The men of Han now completely dominate the territories politically and eclipse numerically the former native populations, except in parts of Tibet and in (Outer) Mongolia, a land that achieved independence fifty years ago.

Even more impressive has been the role of Russia. One of the most glaring differences between the demography of northern Asia today compared to that of AD 1500 is the overwhelming preponderance of Europeans. Siberia is no longer merely an Asian wilderness. Except for the autonomous republics, all of the Soviet sphere territories – some sixty to seventy per cent of the land surface – have been incorporated within the Russian Soviet Federated Socialist Republic. For all practical purposes most of Soviet Asia has become a part of Europe, and gradual absorption of the remainder seems inevitable. The ethnic watershed of Europe has shifted back again from the Urals eastward even beyond the ranges of the Lake Baikal faultline which marked the general frontier zone of the Upper Palaeolithic.

The peopling of Siberia by eastern Europeans since the end of the fifteenth century is reminiscent of the settlement of North America. There were the same exploratory expeditions; the battles with the natives; the era of cross-country portaging, prospecting and shouts of gold; the settling of prairie lands; the building of a transcontinental railway; and finally the construction of vast industrial complexes. But the contrasts were possibly even greater. For Siberia there was no voyage of discovery and crossing of a vast unknown ocean. There were no major rivalries among contending European powers, nor was there the same kind of refuge for the religiously and politically oppressed. The very name Siberia conjures up the opposite impression. It was largely a land of exile and enforced isolation.

There are other reasons why the settlement of Siberia has been so different. For a full millenium prior to 1500 the Slavs themselves were victims of numerous invasions of 'fierce barbarians' from the Asian steppelands, and there were few allies whose aid could be counted on in times of distress.

It was not until after the acquisition of firearms that Europeans were able to withstand the sieges of the steppe barbarians, but when the shift in power finally occurred it signalled one of the greatest turning points in history. The horse, which had been a military mount, was turned around in its tracks and became again, as it was in the early Bronze Age, a draught animal drawing the ploughs and carts of the peasants eastward as they trekked across the same steppe–prairies that had previously been the thoroughfares for their destruction.

The Chinese had provided Europeans with the secret of their means of defence and ultimately of aggression – gunpowder. It was not until shortly before 1500, however, at the dawn of the Renaissance, that the European nations began to realize the full extent of the power they commanded. Before this time, emigration along the Russian border had been discouraged. People were needed on the land and for the development of mercantile trade. A few frontier colonies had been established on the eastern slopes of the Urals and in the Ural River basin between the eleventh and fifteenth centuries, but their existence was precarious and dependent on trade. Even as late as the early seventeenth century there were only some twenty thousand Europeans beyond the 'Wall of Stones' (the Urals), and colonization was not encouraged until the reign of Catherine the Great. At that time, some thirty thousand dissenters and other undesirables were banished to the Baikal area. Others were to follow: conservative Orthodox believers (starovyers) who refused to cut their beards; raskolnik dissenters; 'spirit warriors' or Dukhobors; *stundists*, who spent hours in devotions; vegetarian *molokans* or 'milk drinkers'; *khlyst* flagellants and *kamenshchiki* hermits. Some five thousand Cossacks were sent to protect them and a string of *ostrogs* or forts was established along the steppe–prairie corridor to the headwaters of the Ob. The majority were males and many of the descendants of these Sibiriaks, in particular those of Cossack ancestry, are still recognizable by their physical features.

No two characterizations of the Cossacks agree. Some were refugees who had settled in the Kuban basin to escape the rule of Peter the Great. Others were Robin Hood-like outlaws, freebooters and highwaymen. All shared a common bond of mutual protection and a bravado seldom matched in the annals of history. Feared for their ferocity and admired for their courage, they became both a defence against the later Khanate hordes and dependable mercenaries in the early period of settlement. Even the name of the land was a reminder of Cossack destruction of the Tatar stockade at Sibiri in 1581.

With the exception of the southernmost republics, the European population of Soviet Asia has grown until today over ninety per cent of the nearly forty million inhabitants are of European extraction, and nearly half of the remaining ten per cent are of mixed ancestry or are thoroughly russianized. About seventy per cent of the Europeans were from greater Russia, the remainder from the Ukraine, Byelorussia, Poland, Hungary, Armenia, the Caucasus and the Baltic states – Estonians, Lithuanians, Latvians and Finns. Nearly a million Volga Germans were also transplanted to the borders of Kazakhstan after the First World War, and an autonomous Jewish state was established in the province of Birobizhan on the lower Amur. Russianized Tatars and splinter settlements of Chuvash, Mordvins, Pechenegs, Chermiss and other minorities – some of them Asians who had settled centuries before in Europe – were moved back again to constitute most of the remainder. Finally, to safeguard the eastern frontier, some 200,000 Koreans were transferred from the Maritime Province to Kirghizia, and several thousand Chinese Muslim Tungans on the Sinkiang border were moved further westward. As an added precaution, the government has been assisting European settlers to homestead in the open lands of the east coast, in particular along the Chinese frontier.

In Soviet Central Asia the percentage of Europeans and displaced Asian settlers and migrants from other parts of the continent is considerably less, but increasing. In 1926 it varied regionally from ten to thirty per cent in Turkmenistan, Tajikistan, and Uzbekistan. Today the average is nearly fifty per cent. By the end of the century it may well approximate that of Siberia.

In spite of their numbers, Europeans occupy no more than about twenty to twenty-five per cent of the land. Settlement has been mainly along the crucial steppe-corridor which was converted to farmland and cattle ranges, along the waterways which provide transport and power, and near the mineral-rich ranges of the heartland.

The Europeanization process has been rapid and has stimulated intensive archaeological and ethnological research. Among the more startling discoveries have been those revealing the early penetration of northern Asia by Indo–European- and pre-Indo–European-speaking populations prior to the westward sweep of the nomadic hordes. These archaeological revelations had been foreshadowed by the earlier linguistic identification of the Scythians and Tochari as Indo–European speakers, but they scarcely equal in importance the corroborative evidence provided by Chinese historians for the crucial millennium 500 BC to AD 500.

19

Siberian Prehistory and New World Origins

The possibility that man might have roamed across northern Siberia or even migrated into the New World some time before the final glacial period is intriguing but as yet unproven. Conditions were favourable for such movements in the Yenisei and Lena basins during the latter part of the third interglacial, and passage across Beringia (the Bering Strait land bridge area), could have been made perhaps by the beginning of the last glacial period some fifty thousand years ago [260]. Most of the north was ice-free and the taiga was largely replaced by tundra which extended far south across the plains of the present temperate zone; there was ample forage for the now extinct big game which at that time ranged across the northlands – arctic reindeer, mammoth, woolly rhinoceros, musk-ox, glutton, lemming and, in the higher lands, marmots and goats [273]. Temperatures were as warm there as in central Europe, where man was already at home.

It remains a mystery why no definite traces of man have yet been discovered north of the central plateau barrier before the height of the fourth glaciation. Man could have taken the Pacific coastal route northward along the Maritime Province, but this also remains unproven. The answer may lie hidden under the present coastal waters.

Man was presumably in continuous or periodic occupation of the region south and east of the great mountain barrier from *Homo erectus* times onward. The chopper-type palaeoliths found near Vladivostok prove that he had penetrated that far north and possibly into Inner Mongolia during the middle Pleistocene (late second interglacial to early fourth glacial). During this time span of 300,000 years, however, the population concentrations were probably mainly in the warmer tropical regions of southern and south-east Asia and Sundaland. There may have been little need or attraction to move into the northern hunting grounds until after the climate had changed and recessions of the shoreline had encouraged a return to former more northerly habitats.

In a challenging article Müller–Beck [251] points out that early migrations across Beringia would have been possible between 28,000 BC and the end of the Pleistocene excluding the so-called Two Creeks Marine Transgression period between 23,000 and 13,000 BC. Because of local climatic variations between Alaska and eastern Siberia, a realistic view would limit to three separate periods the time spans during which such migrations would be plausible: before 35,000 BC; from 26,000 to 21,000 BC; and from 11,000 to 8000 BC. The breadth of the land bridge corridor must have varied, but a drop in sea level of at least forty metres from its present level would have been required to provide reasonable passage.

One of the puzzling problems about the earliest peopling of America is that nothing older than 6000 BC has been positively dated in the Bering Strait area, whereas absolute dates as early as 13,000 BC have been established for the Llano complex of Arizona. The nearest prototypes of its characteristic fluted projectile points are found in Kostyenki in the Ukraine. Some possible dates, however, range as far back as 25,000 years and recently – using a new method of dating referred to as racemization which depends upon amino acid deterioration – Bada [11] has determined the age of human bones excavated from a site in southern California at 20,000 years. Using the same technique on specimens excavated several years ago in a nearby site, he derived a figure of 40,000 years. The artefacts are reminiscent of the chopper-type tools found in north China and the Maritime Province, but the age claims have been greeted with mixed reactions on the part of anthropologists and it may be some time before a final verdict is reached.

Early man's progress eastward from Europe seems to have been stalled beyond the Baltic–Black Sea line until towards the end of the third interglacial, about 70,000 years ago, and beyond the Volga until the latter part of the fourth glacial period some

40–30,000 years ago [260]. The fog-bound lake and marshlands of the Ob basin of western Siberia were still too inhospitable. The larger tundra and steppe fauna of the central regions – man's greatest potential food source – could not have moved into the area until considerable shrinkage of the wetlands had occurred. The expansion of man's habitat by way of the Caspian corridor south of the Urals apparently did not take place until the beginning of the Upper Palaeolithic.

Movement north from Turkestan might have been possible at a much earlier date, but with the possible exception of a few Soan-type chopper-like artefacts of uncertain age from that area there is no evidence of man's having reached the steppe corridor earlier than 40,000 years ago.

SIBERIAN PALAEOLITHIC AND MESOLITHIC

Two major problems concerning man's primary migrations have yet to be resolved: one concerns the time and identity of the first migrants into the New World; the second, the related problem of the first encounter of people moving eastward from the desert–steppe corridor and the migrants moving northward from north China. It does not follow that the two problems are interrelated.

Artefacts of the Levalloiso–Mousterian tradition associated with neanderthaloid remains similar to finds from Irania and the Crimea have been found in Uzbekistan and even in Ferghana; but there is no proof of man's presence in Kazakhstan before about 30,000 BC. There may have been migrations across or around Sinkiang into the Yellow River basin somewhat earlier: artefacts of the same general type have been found in the Ordos and even south of the Tsinling range, suggesting that they were carried eastward, north of the Tibetan massif, rather than by the southern route through India and China.

The populations of Kazakhstan appear to have mixed cultural traditions which were overtaken by locally modified aurignacoid 'projectile-point' industries which reached the Lake Baikal area by about 13,000 BC. Distinguishing features of the Aurignacian are the relatively large numbers of blade tools, bone points with split bases and well carved figurines [251, p. 387].

Upwards of two hundred advanced palaeolithic riverine sites have been located in the upper valleys of the Ob and Yenisei, the main valleys of the Angara and Selenga south of Lake Baikal, and the Lena leading to the Arctic Ocean. There is a fairly continuous sub-arctic zone of aurignacoid industrial techniques from the Baltic to the Lena, and traces of it have been identified in locally modified assemblages across Beringia into the New World.

It would appear that the encounter between migrants from central Siberia and those from the Yellow River basin would not have taken place until towards the very end of the last glacial period. The former migrants were still in an Upper Palaeolithic stage, whereas the latter had already moved into the Mesolithic. If the so-called 'chopping tools' of the New World prove to be genuine artefacts and as old as at present conjectured, they could have been carried up the coastal route in delayed and attenuated form during the early phases of the final glacial period.

The Siberian Upper Palaeolithic can be divided into three phases [34, pp. 188–92]. The first is the eastward extension of the European Aurignacian from roughly 18,000 to 13,000 BC. The second – from 13,000 to 10,000 BC – is reminiscent of the earlier assemblages from Uzbekistan, although the Siberian complex is distinctive and considerably later. The third stage is post-glacial [52].

In the second stage the fauna includes the mammoth, and the artefacts are massive. A characteristic spear point or 'dagger' and various tools reminiscent of the chopping-tool tradition were found at the site of Malta, west of Lake Baikal. Man lived in skin-covered, semi-subterranean dwellings and had sophisticated hunting equipment and clothing comparable to that of the Eskimo of today. At Afontava Gora on the Yenisei and Buret on the Angara the most typical artefacts are discs and side scrapers, large blades, borers and burins, some of which are duplicated in the Ordos at Sjara-osso-gol [34, pp. 202–3]. Many of the artefacts of the Irkutsk area and Transbaikalia generally, including the Selenga basin, are virtually identical with those of the upper cave site at Choukoutien. This evidence, as well as part of a cranial vault described as 'Mongoloid', suggests the earliest fusion of the Siberian and east Asian traditions. The biological evidence is not very conclusive, and the time discrepancy presents problems in rationalizing the connection of the chopping tool artefacts of Siberia with earlier east Asian counterparts.

In the third – post-glacial – stage, ranging from about 8000 to 6000 BC, characteristic artefacts of temporary hunting encampments include Azilian-type harpoons and bifacial laurel leaf blades.

To summarize, it would seem that man first moved from western Asia into the Aralo–Caspian basin about 40,000 years ago, extending his hunting range as far northwards as the upper Yenisei in the course of the next 10,000 to 20,000 years. Somewhere in the corridor region he must have encountered an eastward migration from Europe south of the Urals, and by about 15,000 years ago a third migration entered the Baikal area from the east, probably moving around the eastern fringe of the Gobi into Transbaikalia before 8000 BC.

The fact that 10,000 to 15,000 years ago there were cultural ties with Europe points to migratory populations derived from that source as well as from the west Asian gene pool. It might be assumed further that east Asian man, with 'Mongoloid' traits, began moving westward from the upper regions of the Amur, and that the first encounters between the western and eastern gene pools took place in southern Siberia.

By mesolithic times three distinct provinces and time phases are recognizable: Central Asian, south Siberian and Amurian. The Central Asian is distinguishable by about 6000 BC; its main connections are with the Iranian plateau sites of Dan–Dam Chashma, Kailiu Cave and Hodja–Su I, and an extensive Caspian cave group correlated with the Zarzian of Iraq Kurdistan of the seventh millennium BC [200]. There are paintings in Shakhta cave showing dogs assisting in the hunt. The absence of sickle blades and domestic plants suggest a stage prior to that of the earliest Jeitun (late Neolithic of Turkestan) and a technology less sophisticated than that of contemporary sites of the Zagros group such as Jarmo and Tepe Giyan. Again there is a lack of skeletal material, but probably genetic ties were closest to the populations of Anatolia and the Caspian area. Steatopygic and pendulant-breasted female figurines which matched those of the so-called 'Venuses' of central and eastern Europe provide a suggestive hint.

To the north along the steppe–woodland corridor in Kazakhstan the third phase of the Upper Palaeolithic merges with the Mesolithic; the time span is brief in comparison with that of the east Asian province. Part of the reason seems to lie in the changing environment. Until Holocene times large sections of the Gobi and Takla Makan Deserts were marshy with interspersed lakes; it was not until the end of the Upper Palaeolithic that the region became habitable. By about 8000 BC the lakes and marshlands had given way to vegetation attractive to big game, and a broad rocky passageway had opened up between the uppper tributary expanses of the Yellow River and the southern watershed of the Selenga basin which at that time extended considerably further south into Mongolia [395, p. 2].

In the so-called Sino–Siberian Upper Palaeolithic culture microlithic industries spread rapidly from the steppelands of the Irtysh into the great river basins of the north along the steppe–woodland corridor. Migrations were also taking place through the Tarim basin, Zungharia and Mongolia into the Tsaidam and Ordos regions of the Yellow River, and doubtless hunters of east Asian traditions were taking advantage of the same hunting grounds. Man's technological achievements had reached a high level of efficiency. As in the case of the European prototype, micro-blades were used mainly as insets in bone fishing spears. Harpoons were probably used as well so that full advantage could be taken of the huge preserves of megafauna: wild cattle, horses, reindeer, mammoths, the woolly Siberian rhinoceros and, in the Tsaidam and Kokonor, both wild asses and yak. To these were added in season a variety of plant products and, with refinements in trapping techniques, fish, waterfowl and small mammals.

To the east, in the Amur–Manchurian province, a highly evolved series of mesolithic cultures was also in progress and had been for several millennia. The domesticated dog seems to have been as early here as anywhere in Europe [260, p. 27]. In the west it was not until the third millennium that the mesolithic hunting and fishing cultures of northern Europe, with their emphasis on animal head carvings in wood, bone and slate, and wooden vessels and ladles, made their appearance. Proof of their European inspiration rests in the pit-ornamented and comb-impressed ceramic wares similar to those of the Volga area [288, p. 267].

THE NEOLITHIC AND BRONZE AGE

In some respects the Neolithic of northern Asia is even more confusing than the previous rather indefinite Mesolithic. There is a time lag of roughly three thousand years between the Neolithic of Mesopotamia and that of the Caspian basin, and two thousand more years passed before it reached Baikalia.

The fishing, hunting and gathering cultures continued in the woodland–steppe regions from the Volga to Lake Baikal considerably longer than they did in eastern Europe, from whence they probably came. They are followed by a series of 'sub-neolithic' cultures [288, p. 268] beginning some time in the fourth millennium BC. They acquired this qualified designation because, although the assemblages include pottery and other characteristically neolithic artefacts, the people were not producers. They continued their fishing, hunting and gathering economies and added a number of neolithic artefacts to their mixed cultures which extended across Siberia from the Ob to the Amur; the transition to metal was also varyingly mixed from region to region.

The Siberian Neolithic began early in the fourth millennium before Christ and spread rapidly into the upper Yenisei and Baikal region. Several cultures reveal exchanges both with Europe and east Asia. The earliest, known as Isakovian, is characterized by terraced slab grave sites concentrated on the Angara tributary of the Yenisei [260, p. 20]. The burials contain the bones of game animals, bone spear points, flint blades, serrated flakes, arrowheads, a simple type of bow, polished adzes, women's knives of nephrite, bone needles and comb-marked pottery, all of which suggest adjustments to a hunting and gathering economy, but there is no trace of agriculture.

During the Serovian period, from the fourth to third millennium BC there are marked improvements in ceramics, stone tools and hunting equipment, such as the addition of harpoons; but most important is a wide range of art forms – carvings of mammals and fish, and human figurines. The art styles and motifs are surprisingly similar to those of the Tungusic and palaeo-Asiatic tribes of eastern Siberia, but this should not be taken necessarily as implying migration. The skeletal remains of both periods appear to be of European and west Asian type and indicate little, if any, admixture from east Asia.

In the succeeding Kitoyan period of the third millenium there is a sudden rash of fish hooks, some of the composite type. Burials were more ritualized: the head was covered with red ochre, and the grave frequently filled with red ochre mixed with sand or earth. Green nephrite ornaments were common but metals were still absent.

The first Bronze Age is identified with the type site at Afanasyevo in the Minusinsk basin of the Yenisei. It began in the second millennium as an outgrowth of the third phase of the Neolithic, with characteristic polished adzes and flaked knives and the addition of needle holders and strap bindings for wooden vessels. Its influence may have extended into Sinkiang and to the Burzahom site in Kashmir. The most important innovation was the introduction of domestic animals: sheep, horses and cattle. Burials contain pendants of animal teeth and bloodstone red colouring and comb-marked pottery with pointed bases.

By the next or Andronovo stage (1500–1200 BC) metal had almost completely eclipsed the use of stone, workmanship had improved, and local mining and smelting had become important. From this time on, the Altai region rapidly became the most important centre for metal casting between the Caucasus and China, and it could conceivably have been the centre from which, at an earlier time, the first of the animal art styles reached the Yellow River. Settlements contained rectangular semi-subterranean houses supporting straw and turf roofs on wooden posts, with accompanying corrals for horses, cattle, sheep and goats. The presence of querns, sickles and scorched wheat grains indicate the spread of agriculture from Turkestan. Skeletal remains of Kitoyan, Afanasyevo and Andronovo periods are all 'Europoid' [260, p. 47] and similar to those from burials in the Volga–steppe area.

The following Karasuk period, about 1400–800 BC, centres primarily around the Minusinsk basin. The camel is a sure indication of contact and trade with the Caspian region and Iran, and identical artefacts discovered in Turbino in Russia and Yakutia in central Siberia suggest a degree of east–west traffic. A chiselled representation of a four-wheeled cart and a *kibitka* or yurt on wheels imply nomadism, and caches of bronzes, including a wide variety of knives, celts, daggers, sickles and body and harness ornaments indicate considerable commercial activity.

The discovery of Shang-style Bronze Age burials containing the typical socketed celt and 'Mongoloid' skeletal remains of the fourteenth century BC in the Minusinsk basin is undeniable evidence of Chinese contacts. They seem to have been 'colonists' who had reached the Yenisei, but there is no evidence of 'Mongoloid' admixture in the European skeletons of the Andronovo period burials. Earlier burials with funerary Shang pottery and 'black pottery' of the preceding Ch'eng-Tz'u-Yai period have also been found in the Fofanovo sites on the Selenga in Baikalia. Among the most interesting objects were south sea shells which must have come from the Moluccas or the Ryukyus.

During the following Tagarian period (*c.* 1000 to 100 BC), bronzes of typical nomadic animal style made their appearance throughout much of southern Siberia including Minusinsk, but they are sufficiently distinctive not to be termed Scythic [260, p. 58]. It was in the high meadows of the Altai Mountains that the now famous Pazaryk tribal chief burials of this period were first excavated by Rudenko in 1928 and continued in 1949. The embalmed and tattooed human remains have clearly European features, according to Okladinkov [260, p. 68], while the clothing and art styles, textiles and horse trappings are 'Scytho–Sarmatian'. He believes, however, that chiefs or leaders were of some Massagetae tribe which he equates with the Yüechih.

It is still too early to write a satisfactory account of the identities and movements of the early European populations in the central regions of Eurasia. Many of the answers must lie hidden in the Black Earth country of the Ukraine and the lower Volga basin. The immigrants may or may not have been Indo–European speakers. There is no certain evidence of the latter before about 3000 BC, and it seems more likely that the earlier movement could have been by speakers of the Uralic group, to which the Indo–European languages may be distantly related [69, p. 223].

The Bronze Age had already developed a highly stylized animal art in the Maikop burials of the Kuban Valley on the north slopes of the Caucasus before the end of the third millennium BC. The style shows resemblances with Anatolia, and, while this was doubtless linked with trade, there appear to have been movements of peoples along the eastern Black Sea littoral. Copper was mined both in Anatolia and in the Urals. The origin of the Lurs is still a puzzle, but they may either have been Hittites who fled to the Zagros with the advent of the Cimmerians in Anatolia about 1200 BC, or they may have learned bronze casting from the Cimmerians who shared the art with the Scyths. The animal style of the Lurs is distinctive but reminiscent of the Scythic, and

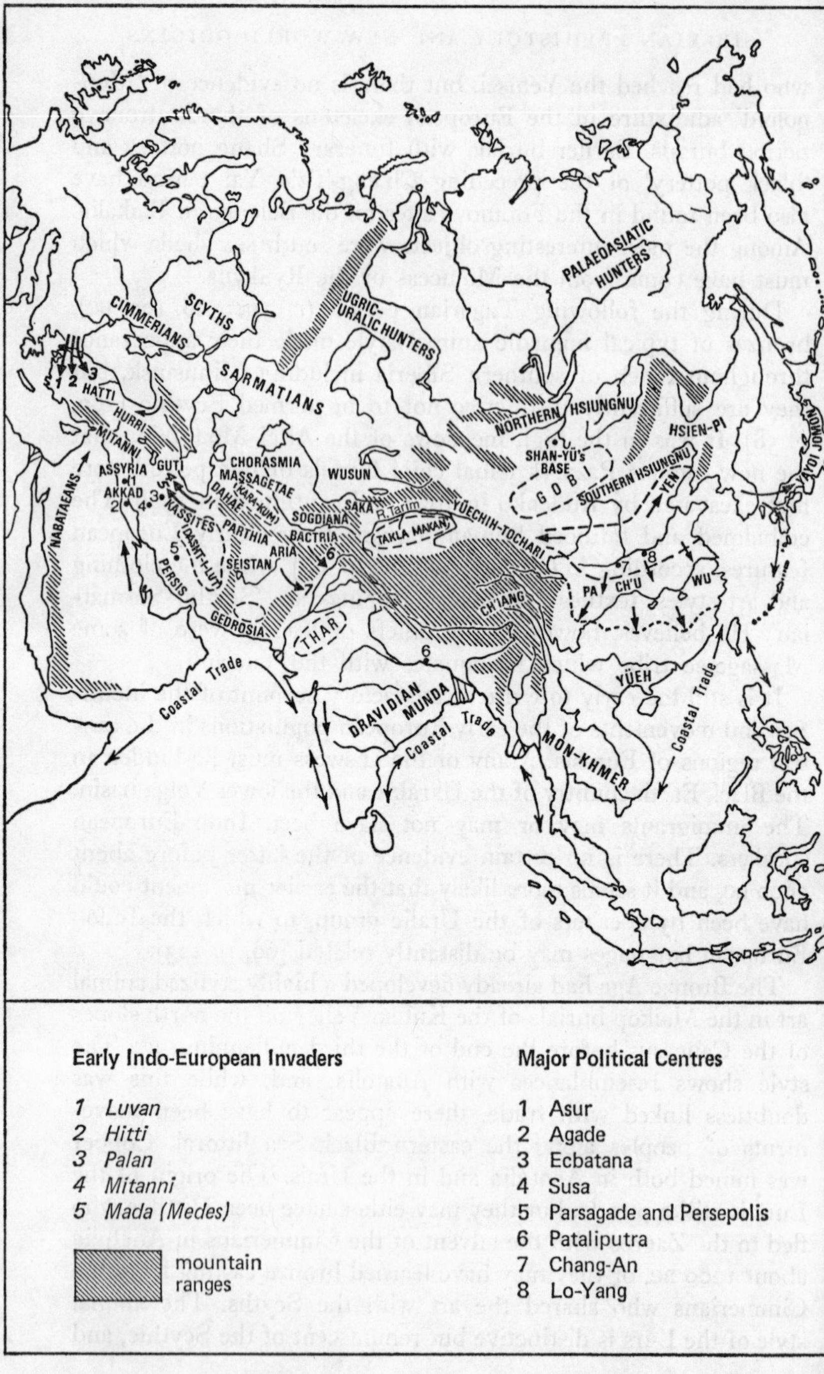

Map 6 Migrations and expansions, from 1500 BC to the Han dynasty

there was certainly an interchange between the Luristan bronze makers and the craftsmen of the steppes. The precise time and place of origin of western bronze making has not been determined. It may have been in Caucasia, Urartu or Armenia. Apparently it preceded the Scytho–Sarmatian movement from the Kelteminar culture of the Aralo–Caspian region to the Minusinsk and Altai River area where the oldest bronze period was the Afanasyevo.

The inhabitants of the Black Earth country can be traced in their movements westward and southward into central Europe, the Balkans and Anatolia by the third millennium before Christ. They are identifiable both skeletally and by their artefacts, and emerge in history as the earliest Indo–European migrants. Many of the same artefacts and skeletal resemblances can be traced into the regions east of the Caspian and Siberia, and on this basis it is possible to postulate the infiltration of Indo–Europeans or Uralic speakers several thousand years before the movements of the Scyths.

It might be appropriate to refer to these migrants as the 'chariot users'. They were certainly associated with horses, but as charioteers, not riders. It has sometimes been said that man is best known by the animals he keeps; an amendment might be that he is best known by the *uses* of the animals he keeps. The Scyths are known primarily as horse-riders. Chariots were definitely of secondary importance, if used at all. It was their predecessors who were the charioteers and users of carts and sledges.

The horse and its substitutes – the ass, the onager and the camel – have assisted man in a number of unique ways: as transport and riding animals, sources of food and shelter, friendship and recreation and, most important of all, by increasing man's energy output. Horses added a quantum dimension to his engineering potential. The onager was domesticated perhaps as early as 5000 BC; but the horse, which is not native to western Asia, was first used as a traction animal in the steppes of central Eurasia by about 4000 BC. A thousand years later came the horse-drawn cart, which spread southward on to the Anatolian plateau and reached the Fertile Crescent by the middle of the third millennium.

More than any other animal, the horse has shaped the course of human history. Without it the great chariot empires of the

Hittites, Hyksos, Persians, Greeks and Romans could never have developed. In a sense one might say that what the dog was to the human family, the horse – and its inorganic counterpart, the sail – was to society down through the ages until the advent of the steam engine.

The only true surviving wild equine is the Prejwalski horse of south-western Mongolia and the Tsaidam. All others are feral, domesticated animals which have reverted to the wild state in behaviour but not in anatomy. It is doubtful if such 'wild' horses would ever revert morphologically to the state of the first tamed horses of the Neolithic, although careful back-crossings have produced approximations of the tarpan, the extinct wild horse of the east Russian steppes. The steppe horse, like its modern descendant, the Mongolian pony, was bred as an all-purpose animal, as important to the steppe nomad as the camel to the Bedouin.

In China, the horse was known as a food but not as a traction animal during the Lungshan Neolithic of the third millennium BC. The war chariot was used by early invaders who raided China's north-west frontier before the Erh–Li–Kang phase of the Shang dynasty about 1450 BC [49, pp. 230–8]. Horse trappings are all of the traction type, and there is no evidence of riding until several centuries later.

To summarize, and ignoring minor regional and time phase differences, it is possible to distinguish three major technological and economic stages among the European immigrants to Asia. First were the upper palaeolithic and mesolithic hunters and gatherers, who had spread beyond Lake Baikal into the Lena basin before being overtaken by the second stage. This consisted of sedentary and semi-sedentary neolithic communities with polished stone artefacts, some use of copper and early bronze, wheel-turned ceramic wares, mixed agricultural and stock-raising economies and the use of traction animals, with chariots for warfare and burials. Thirdly came the Bronze Age stock-raising nomads, with highly stylized animal motif decorative art, associated with horse-riding and the use of elaborate wheel-based, yurt-like mobile dwellings – the Scytho–Sarmatians of the steppes.

20

Tibetans, Turks and Mongols

THE HIGH PLATEAU AND ITS INHABITANTS

The powerful deflecting effect of the high plateau upon human migration and trade was mentioned in Chapter 2. The outer slopes of the encircling mountain flanks were undoubtedly part of man's hunting and collecting preserve from as early as palaeolithic times, yet surprisingly there is no archaeological evidence that the heart of the plateau was reached until neolithic times. The first penetration seems to have taken place along the northeastern (Mongol–Kansu) border, very likely by peoples speaking an archaic Sinitic language. As yet there is no definite evidence of access northward from India across or around the Himalayas before the third millennium before Christ.

Almost certainly man must first have found his way from the swampy but game-rich Tsaidam south to the plateau grasslands of Amdo (Chinese Ch'ing-hai or 'Blue-Green Sea'; Mongol Kokonor). Very likely they were reached during the recession phase of the fourth glaciation. The plateau itself was not glaciated but heavy icecaps covered all of the encircling mountain perimeter, and temperatures must have fallen to arctic depths while heavy mists hovered over the coarse tundra covering. Along the eastern border, the snowline had dropped to the plains of China; in the south to the Punjab foothills; and in the north and west to the Tarim basin. The Pamir ranges were sealed off by a solid icecap. There is no evidence that any of the cold fauna of the Gobi ever reached the high plateau. The clue to man's entry lies very largely in the peculiarities of the environment.

More than half of the Chang Tang ('Northern Plain') has

always been uninhabitable. Like the Takla Makan and Lop Nor Deserts to the north – lands of internal drainage – the Chang Tang is scattered with numerous brackish lakes and patches of crusted soda and potash. Even today only the hardiest of animals can survive, and then only because they can reach the sweet grass below the snowline during the spring and summer months.

So many features about the land and people of Tibet are unique. Although much of their economy and many of their cultural values are associated with the animals of the north, nearly ninety per cent of the inhabitants are sedentary agriculturalists living in scattered hamlets along the main valleys and side streams of the upper Indus, the Tsangpo (upper Brahmaputra) and the great rivers that flow into China and south-east Asia. Primary dependence is on irrigation agriculture, with secondary emphasis on transhumant pastoralism – the seasonal herding of sheep, goats and yak to the upper meadows in late June and returning to the winter corrals in late autumn. True nomads are only in the north-east, bordering China, in the province of Amdo; on the northern slopes of the inner Himalayan Tangla ('Range of the Plains') bordering the Chang Tang; and in parts of south-eastern Ladakh. Even so, most of the flocks of sheep and goats and the herds of yak and *dzo* (yak–cattle crosses) of the Chang Tang are owned by the sedentary landed nobility and prebendal church estates of the south.

The peoples of the high plateau include many more than those claiming to be Tibetan. The Balti of Baltistan, who occupy the westernmost section, speak a Tibetan dialect but are mostly Shiite Muslims, having been converted to Islam in the fourteenth century. In the higher valleys are pockets of Dards, who share with the Purik Balti of Kargil the region along the present demarcation zone between Pakistan and India. The cease-fire line itself follows roughly the ethnic border between the Muslim Puriki and Balti in the west and the predominantly Buddhist Ladakhi, whose language is considerably closer to standard Tibetan.

In 1841 the kingdom of Ladakh was formally annexed to Jammu and Kashmir and has remained politically within the borders of India, but ecclesiastically under the jurisdiction of Lhasa. Commercial ties have existed with India, Sinkiang and Tibet and genetic admixtures are traceable from all three directions. In the urban centres are colonies of Indian, Tibetan, Chinese and Turkic merchants and artisans.

To the north of Ladakh and Baltistan, the high Karakoram range sharply divides the Tibetan-speaking plateau-dwellers from the nearest Turkic-speaking settlements in the Tarim basin. On the Indian side, before the recent refugee movements, Tibetans had settled across the mountainous Himalayan border and established a number of colonies in the higher grassy valleys of the central range, in Himachal Pradesh, and in the *pahari* regions of the Punjab. Tibet (Tö–Böd, 'Land of the Bö'), east of Ladakh, divides into five provinces: nGari in the west; Tsang and Ü in the centre; and two in the east which have been under Chinese control since the thirteenth century: Amdo in the north-east and Khams in the south-east.

South of the plateau on the Indian side and along the Chinese border is a continuous series of forty or fifty Tibetan and linguistically related petty states or former states and scores of minor detached settlements under Indian or Chinese administrative supervision. Some are of strategic importance dating back a thousand years and more; others have served as refuge areas for even longer periods.

On the Indian side all of the Rajput states [159] except Nepal have been absorbed politically by India. The populations of these states remain highly mixed but tend to fall into three parallel ethnic zones determined by altitude: (1) Tibetan settlements of the highest meadows; (2) greatly mixed Bhotia of India and Gurkhas of Nepal in the upper intermontane valleys and valley slopes; (3) scattered intrusive pre-Rajput, Indo–Aryan and Mon-related populations in the valleys and on the outer foothill slopes.

Traditionally, the major population distinctions of Tibet have been between the settled agriculturalists of the five provinces and the nomads (*drokpa*) of the adjacent sections of the Chang Tang grazing lands. Mongol nomads occupy the lands north of Lake Kokonor in the Tsaidam; to the south are Tibetans and tibetanized Mongols.

For the Tibetans religious issues were far more important than linguistic. The schisms that tore the country apart periodically during the past millennium caused numerous human dislocations and created various politico–religious factions. The strongholds of the pre-Buddhist Bön worship, which incorporates much of

Indian Tantrism, were mainly in the deep river gorges along the Szechwan border. Those of the heterodox Red Hat Lamaist sects were in parts of Khams and Tsang under the authority of the Panchen Lama, and of the reformed or orthodox Yellow Hat sects – mainly in Ü, Amdo and parts of Khams – under the Dalai Lama in Lhasa. Until recently, a theocratic form of dyarchical government had maintained a complex balance on the one hand between the landed estates of the nobility and the prebendal estates of the church, and on the other between the vested interests of the heterodox Red Hat sects – favouring China – and the orthodox Yellow Hat sects – leaning toward India.

The traditional division of Tibetan society into a landed nobility and a serf–tenant peasantry traces back to the earliest records of the fifth century. Many institutions doubtless date back to the earliest known trade with China in the Han dynasty but influences from India may have been just as old. Buddhism and writing were introduced from the south in the fourth or fifth century and ever since there has been rivalry between factions supporting close ties with China and India respectively, but always so as to retain a considerable degree of autonomy.

In classical Chinese history Tibet had been viewed for a thousand years as the moon satellite of the sun, China; Tibet was the younger brother, China the elder. In the seventh century the kings of Tibet and Nepal are said to have married Chinese princesses. Fine arts and luxuries of the Chinese gentry class became status symbols of the Tibetan nobility and Chinese astrologers were attached to the royal court. In spite of the proximity of Tibet to India, and the introduction of Buddhism and a Sanskrit derived alphabet from that source, ethnic ties have remained closer to China. The Chinese and Tibetan languages have a common source in basic structure and vocabulary, and during the Yuan dynasty, when the great khans extended their empire across China into western Asia and Europe, Mongol troops were stationed in Lhasa, and Mongol, Turkic and Chinese families were established in the capital. A certain amount of intermarriage seems to have taken place among the élite, and the continuing penetration of Chinese merchants and officials along the eastern border has had its genetic impact [103].

Until the recent communist upheavals, Tibetan bureaucracy had changed little since the thirteenth century when the theocratic regime was established. Every household was expected to provide a child to the church, but in fact noble families usually preferred to subsidize the church and train their sons for civil office. It followed that the clergy were drawn largely from the peasantry rather than the nobility.

The power of the church as a marriage deterrent has probably been exaggerated. Celibacy was demanded of the Yellow Hat sect monks, but many of the Red Hat sects permitted and even encouraged marriage; probably no more than ten per cent of the total population was celibate. Tibet was famed also for polyandry which was invariably of the fraternal type and associated with inheritance [284, 229].

Fringing the entire eastern perimeter of the plateau between Kansu and Burma, the buffer 'tribal' states were recognized by the Chinese during the Sui and T'ang dynasties but not incorporated into the empire until the Manchu period. The northernmost may have been a part of the Hsi–Hsia or Tangut empire, whose armies defeated the Chinese and burned the T'ang capital in AD 763. Collectively the tribal confederacies and petty principalities were referred to as the 150 Ch'iang (Chiang) tribes. The ideograph means simply 'sheep-raisers', and their land was called the 'grass country' (*t'sao-ti*). White stone-worshipping Ch'iang, who claim to be the pastoralists of Chinese history, still survive near Li–Fan on the edge of the plateau.

South of the Ch'iang were eighteen principalities whose hereditary rulers were granted the title of *t'u-ssu* or 'local chief': five Hor, ten Gya-rong (Chin-chia-lung) and three Tibetan. The Hor-pa (Hor people), who speak an eastern Tibetan dialect, may be mixed descendants of Turkic Hu or Hur refugees from Sinkiang. Peoples of the Gya-rong petty states spoke archaic Tibetan-related languages linked possibly to Lolo.

North of the Gya-rong are several groups of Tibetan-speaking Hsi-fan ('Western Barbarians'); and on the Kansu frontier are the nGo-lok (Golog) or 'Robber' Tibetan nomads who raid caravans on the trade routes to Lhasa and compete for grazing rights with the Amdo nomads.

TURKESTAN – LAND OF THE HUNS AND TURKS

There are today some seventy million speakers of languages classified as Turkic, but the majority are descendants of converts who became Turkic speakers during the course of the past three thousand years.

The name 'Turk' first appears in its Chinese form T'u-chüeh, which Grousset [137] derives from *türküt*, the Mongol plural of *türk* (strong). The reference dates from the sixth century after Christ, when the Juan-Juan Mongols were attempting to consolidate their hold over their western vassals in the region of the Altai mountains. According to Chinese sources, the ancestral tribes were in the Tarbagatai–Altai region by the end of the second millennium before Christ. At that time they were not organized to cope with the mounted horsemen of the steppe zone, but were capable of causing havoc in the Chinese frontier settlements. If Eberhard [98] is correct, the founders of the Chou dynasty may actually have been Turkic; they overcame the Shang dynasty in 1028 BC and introduced many new Turkic and Tibetan culture traits into the fast-changing character of the new state [98, p. 29].

The barbarians who occupied the Altai complex were known to the Chinese as the Hsiung-nu. Some scholars refer to them as generalized Altaic rather than Turkic or proto-Turkic: the name Hsiung-nu means simply 'Nomad' [295]. It first appears in Chinese chronicles of the third century BC, but may be the same as the earlier Hsiun–Yün [137, p. 19] and still earlier Hsiun–Yü or Hu (Hur).

The Hsiung-nu were in Zungharia and western Mongolia by 500 BC during the Chou dynasty. Very likely they acquired the art of horse-riding from their southerly neighbours, the Indo-European-speaking Yüechih–Tocharians who were then in the Yumen–Ordos area of eastern Sinkiang and Ningshia, or possibly from the Scytho–Sarmatians on the borders of western Sinkiang. With the development of cavalry as an effective military device, they were quick to seize the initiative and created the first truly Asian nomadic empire. It was their pillaging of the frontier Chinese settlements that led to the building of the Great Wall – an undertaking not completed until the brief but fiery reign (222–206 BC) of the first unifier of China, the mighty Ch'in Shi Huang-ti, the Yellow Emperor. The Chinese also attempted to placate the marauders and to secure their collaboration against their common foe, the Yüechih, by conferring on their leader the title Shan-yü ('Supreme Ruler') of the Five Hordes.

The Hsiung-nu responded by turning their attention from border pillaging to control of the oasis trade route in the early part of Han about 200 BC. Under the leadership of Shan-yü Mao-tun ('Supreme Ruler Vast One') they defeated the Yüechih–Tochari, who at that time controlled the Tarim basin to the Kansu border, and expelled their leaders from eastern Sinkiang. Forced to retreat, the Yüechih–Tochari leaders and their loyal retinues attempted to seize control of the rich Issyk Kul grazing lands of the Ili Valley, which were then held by the Wu-sun. The oasis settlements remained primarily Indo–European-speaking, but had received admixtures of sedenterized Hsiung-nu and possibly some Chinese. Failing in their purpose, the Yüechih–Tochari leaders were eventually forced out of Sinkiang and settled in the Ferghana Valley (Ta-yuan), the eastern part of Sogdiana, the land of the Iranian Saka. A splinter group is said to have fled into northern Tibet, but later identification of this refugee remnant remains uncertain. In Sinkiang the Iranian and other Indo–European-speaking settlements survived as oasis city-states until well into the sixth century, and there remain to this day genetic reminders of these early European populations in the Turkic-speaking western oasis settlements and the old Iranian communities near the Pamir border.

The ethnic composition of Sinkiang (Chinese Turkestan) during prehistoric times is still far from clear. Indo–European-speaking Tochari, known to the Chinese as Yüechih, were in the Tarim basin, Zungharia and the Kansu border at least by the beginning of the Bronze Age (2000 BC). Probably the inhabitants, especially in the west, spoke an early Iranian satem language, as well as the centum Tochari. There was undoubtedly a mixture, but ecological logic would support a stronger infiltration from the desert and steppe areas of the west by peoples familiar with a comparable environment rather than neolithic infiltrators moving in from the Yellow River basin.

Bronze Age chariots of the Shang dynasty have been found associated with artefacts and human remains of European origin in burials in the Tarbagatai and Altai ranges, and Bronze Age artefacts connect the region of the Baikal faultline with the Ordos and early Shang sites of the Yellow River. However, the harnesses, trappings and construction of the chariot burials of the middle Shang period are distinctive and may be a result of stimulus diffusion rather than invasion [49]. The human remains are clearly attributable to the east Asian gene pool.

As the Hsiung-nu empire continued to expand throughout Mongolia, Sinkiang and parts of Manchuria, the Han rulers were forced to greater efforts to defend themselves and garrison the silk route. During early Han the throne had become so weakened by internal revolts that a takeover by the Hsiung-nu would have been possible, but the Shan-yü may have avoided the temptation in the belief that conquest would only serve to alienate them completely and that permanent control would be impossible. The Shan-yü may not have been quite so astute, but all alien powers that have gained the Chinese throne were either forced to retreat or were eventually assimilated.

Toward the end of Han, the loosely organized Hsiung-nu empire fell apart through over-extension and internal dissensions. The northern faction broke away to appear later in the Orkhon–Selenga region, while the southern faction fled further southward. The northerners were shortly faced with the emergence of the Hsien-pi, who became powerful contenders for control of the northern steppes. For a time they held their own, but eventually they were forced to retreat westward. The defeat of the northern Hsiung-nu and their flight to Ili, the land of the Wu-sun – whom they defeated – marks the beginning of the western Hunnic empire and the pillaging of Europe under Attila in the fifth century AD.

The identification of the Hsiung-nu as the Huns has long been a matter of debate, but there seems little doubt that both were at least Turkic-speaking, or more correctly proto-Turkic, and there is persuasive evidence that they were the same people. Roman historians describe the Huns as stockily built, with long arms and short legs, tremendous round heads, flattened noses, high cheekbones, sunken eyes and relatively beardless chins [137, pp. 74–5]. The portrayal matches that of contemporary Chinese historians. The Roman descriptions suggest traits similar to those of the modern Turkic Kazakhs, whose mean head size is the largest in the world and whose bodies are stocky and short-legged. The description of their facial features matches those of the so-called Mongoloids.

The place of origin of the Hsien-pi as a political force was in the Khingan range area of the upper Amur basin, in a region inhabited later by speakers of Tungusic languages; for this reason it was assumed that they also were Tungusic, but more recent research links them with the Mongols [137, p. 53].

Having defeated the northern Hsiung-nu in AD 166, the Hsien-pi shifted to the Orkhon–Selenga basin just west of the Amur in northern Outer Mongolia. There they formed the nucleus of what became within a few centuries the Mongol empire. Just as the control of Sinkiang shifted from Indo–European speakers to the Turks with the defeat of the Yüechih–Tochari between 174 and 161 BC, so the control of Mongolia switched from the Turks to the Mongols.

Meanwhile the southern Hsiung-nu had been forced south-westward into the Alashan–Ordos region of Inner Mongolia, where for a time and through mutual self-interests they collaborated with the Chinese in stabilizing the western border. For the Chinese the bargain may have been ill-advised, but possibly was inevitable. The Han dynasty had been crumbling from within, and with each unfavourable shift the throne had been forced to depend increasingly upon the expanding protection of the Hsiung-nu. Finally in AD 312 the Shan-yü in a whirlwind onslaught burned the capital and captured the Han emperor. The Ch'in line reoccupied the celestial throne, but within a few years the Hsiung-nu returned and the Ch'in emperor was forced to flee southward. He established a new seat of government at Nanking (southern capital) and consolidated his hold over the lands south of the Yangtze, while the Hsiung-nu took control of most of north China.

North China remained partly or entirely under barbarian rule for more than six hundred years during the first millennium AD, and the whole of China was under alien domination for another four hundred years in the second millennium. The distinction between the periods of partial and total control has to do with a fundamental weakness of barbarian power. Their strength was in their command of highly mobile horsemen with fire arrows; their weakness was inadequate stabling and pasturage, and the *ennui* which inevitably overcame the garrison forces. These weaknesses were constant threats to the success of prolonged sieges or the maintenance of permanent administrative controls.

During the next two hundred years the lower part of the Yellow River basin came under siege at the hands of a succession of petty Turkic–Mongol chiefs. As told by Wittfogel [400], the chronicles of the time make fascinating reading to anyone interested in methods devised by barbarian nomad rulers to trick their rivals and assert their control over the peasants. Few conquerors could resist the temptation to engage in acts of terrorism and demonstrate their disdain for the urban effete. Two of the Han emperors were summarily executed after a year's service as personal cup bearers to the Shan-yü. An even more bizarre deed was conjured up by one of the Shan-yü, who is said to have served up at table as a garnished dish the prettiest of his Chinese concubines [137, p. 58].

China, whose classical moral code called for humane treatment, exemplary behaviour and harmonious existence, was characterized at times by treachery, barbaric cruelty, terrorism and wholesale manslaughter – the reaction possibly of a nation so often the victim of steppe barbarian conquests. The result was an entrenchment of practices alien to Confucian, Taoist and Buddhist principles.

Among the significant contributions of the Turks was the establishment of the sinicized Turkic Wei dynasty of the late fourth and early fifth centuries – more familiarly known as the Toba dynasty and to the Turks as the Tabgatch. The earlier Wei emperors espoused the cause of Buddhism, organized monasteries, encouraged the establishment of different sects and spread the light of Buddha to the contending kingdoms of Paekche and Silla in southern Korea. Also during the Toba dynasty accounts of the Isles of the Hundred Petty States (Japan) were first officially chronicled. Toward the end of Toba rule, when the policy of encouragement to Buddhism was reversed and monks were persecuted, some took refuge in Korea. Historians attribute the decline of Turkic rule in north China to their espousal of Buddhism and their over-sinicization in matters politic. At best their hold was at the administrative level and they did contribute, though not significantly, to China's genetic heritage.

By the beginning of the sixth century after Christ the western Hsiung-nu, or Huns, as they may now be called, were in the ascendancy in Europe. In Mongolia the Hsien-pi had been renamed and reorganized as the Ju-Juan (nicknamed by the Chinese the 'Juan-Juan' – 'Wriggling Insects' or 'Worms'). They formed the first Mongol empire, which stretched from the borders of Korea to the Urals.

Toward the middle of the sixth century, about the time of the collapse of Turkish rule over north China, there developed in the Altai region a short-lived nomad empire whose territory extended at one time from the borders of Mongolia to the Aral Sea. The Hephthalites or White Huns were Mongol in leadership but the rank and file seem at first to have been a mixture of Turks and Mongols. They moved into Sinkiang but their hold over the Tarim basin proved ephemeral and they continued southward. After establishing themselves in Bactria they added an Iranian element and moved on to exploit the riches of India.

The entire steppe country from northern Manchuria to the Don was now under the domination of the three Turco–Mongol empires: the Huns in the west, the Hephthalites in the centre and the Ju-Juan Mongols in the east. Turkic power was concentrated only in the north-west in the region of the Altai and in north-west China, where the last of the Toba rulers was still holding court. The northern Turks, now identified as the Tü-Chüeh, had developed smithing to a fine art, supplied by the rich ore deposits of the Altai and Tarbagatai ranges. By combining forces, the two Turkic armies were ultimately able to defeat their common enemy, the Ju-Juan, and force their retreat south of the Gobi. Later the Tü-Chüeh temporarily defeated the Khitan, another Mongol-related tribe. In recognition of this service, their leader was confirmed as *yagbhu* or *khagan* (khan) of the northern Tü-Chüeh by the Chinese, and among the Persians the western Tü-Chüeh came to be known as Turks.

At its height towards the end of the sixth century the dual Turkic empire became a highly co-ordinated world power, which controlled not only the desert–steppe trade routes but virtually all of the steppe zone from Manchuria to the Volga and dominated the Indo–European-speaking oasis settlements.

Shifting from steppe nomadism to semi-nomadic transhumance and sedentary life in the Altai and Tarbagatai ranges, with associated mining, smelting and agriculture, had prepared some of the Turks for adjustment to settled oasis existence. Having wrested the ancient Mongol homeland and western territories from the Ju-Juan Mongols, the northern Tü-Chüeh Turks consolidated their domains from the upper Orkhon, the strategic and spiritual base of all ancient steppe empires of the east. Zungharia and parts of the Irtysh basin became their headquarters. From there they engaged their Mongol and Tungusic foes in conflict and expanded across Inner Mongolia into Sinkiang. The western Tü-Chüeh moved southward into Sassanian Transoxiana and Irania at the expense of the defeated Ju-Juan and Hephthalites, who collectively appear in European history as the Avars. They attempted to control Sogdiana and Bactria (Turkmenistan, Tajikistan and northern Afghanistan) while maintaining headquarters in the steppe country to the north. The extent of the western thrust is indicated by the fact that the leader, Istami – who was later remembered in the renaming of Constantinople – was in touch with the Byzantine government, with whose interests he soon came into conflict.

The partnership between the northern and western empires did not endure long. As the west grew more powerful the break became inevitable, and in AD 588, encouraged by the Chinese, the west challenged the authority of the north and the leader declared himself the true *khagan*. The rift marked the end of Turkish hegemony, and by the end of the seventh century the western confederation itself had fallen apart. The central group of Tü-Chüeh remained in Sogdiana, where they gradually became iranized, but the three vassals re-established their separate controls over their respective regions: the Uighur between Kobdo and the upper Selenga in western Mongolia; the Karluk in the Ili Valley between the Tarbagatai range and the Issyk–Kul; and the Basmil in the vicinity of Kuchen. Taking advantage of the rift, the Chinese were able to re-establish their hold over the trade routes. It was this rift more than any other single event that enabled China, first during the Sui dynasty (AD 518–618) and later during the T'ang (AD 618–907), to become the greatest empire on earth. China had entered its Golden Age.

During the eighth century the entire continent of Asia reached a crucial period in its history. In the west, the Arabs extended their hold over most of Iran and Afghanistan and were preparing to seize Transoxiana. In the east, the Chinese were at the height of their power and were determined to strengthen their hold over Zungharia and the trade routes to Byzantium. At one point Chinese forces even crossed the Pamirs into the Yasin Valley of Gilgit and were threatening Kashmir. The Arabs were unable to dislodge the Chinese from Sogdiana and were forced to call upon the Turks for assistance. The final defeat of the Chinese was at the hands of the Karluks in the battle of the Talas in 751. Barthold, the great Russian historian, considered this defeat the turning point in Asian history. Central Asia, instead of being converted to Buddhism under T'ang aegis, remained under Arab–Turkic control and was eventually converted to Islam. This also marked the high point of the Arabs' advance; in spite of the estimated 200,000 'Arabs' in the region at the time, their influence rapidly disappeared. Gabrieli concludes: 'The only lasting heritage the Arabs left was Islam' [123].

In the north, meanwhile, the Uighurs were strengthening their position in Mongolia and established their capital at Karabalgasun on one of the upper tributaries of the Selenga. By AD 763 they were able to provide aid to the T'ang government against the Khitan who had recommenced their border harassment. By a peculiar combination of circumstances, the Uighur entered a new phase which completely altered their future role. In the course of freeing Loyang from Khitan control, the Uighur *khagan* met some Sogdian Manichaean missionaries stationed in the western T'ang capital and was not only converted to the faith himself but brought his people into the fold of that rather strangely syncretic Mazdeo–Christian faith. The Uighur khanate's court assumed a semi-ecclesiastical atmosphere. The Sogdian alphabet, a derivative of the Syriac–Aramaic or earlier Phoenician script, became the official vehicle of transcription, and white-robed priests played a prominent role in court and state affairs.

The next act in the drama was the emergence of a new Turkic power – the Kirghiz – whose home territories had been in the upper Yenisei tributaries. In AD 840 they defeated the Uighur and took control of Mongolia, but within a few years lost their hold. The defeated forces retreated into Zungharia and to the oasis settlements of Kara–Khoja (Turfan), Besh Baliq (Kuchen) and the Kansu corridor settlements as far east as Kanchow. At this stage they adopted Tocharian art of the Kuchen–Kizil school and are said to have helped to preserve the local Tocharian language. Over the course of the next few centuries, until converted to Islam, they served as scribes and intermediaries among the Chinese, Turks and Mongols.

The leaders of the northern Turks, who had been weakened

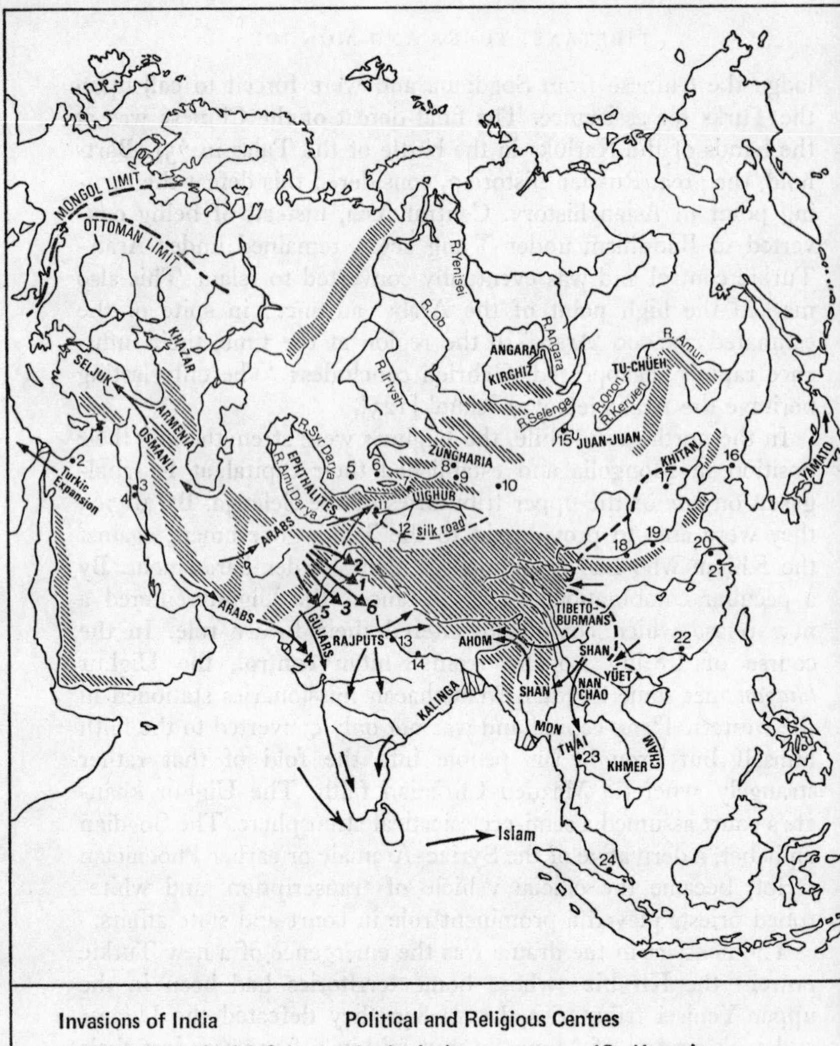

Invasions of India

1 *Yüechih-Tochari & Saka*
2 *Kushan*
3 *Ephthalite (Hunna)*
4 *Arab-Turkic*
5 *Timur (Tamerlane)*
6 *Mughal*

Political and Religious Centres

1 Antioch
2 Jerusalem
3 Baghdad
4 Seleucis
5 Talas
6 Balassagun
7 Kizil
8 Kuchen (Besh-baliq)
9 Turfan (Kara-Khoja)
10 Hami
11 Kashgar
12 Khotan
13 Kanauj
14 Benares
15 Khagan Court
16 Lo-Lang (Nam-Nam)
17 Peking
18 Chang-An
19 Lo-Yang
20 Nanking
21 Hangchow
22 Canton
23 Ayoudhya
24 Malacca

mountain ranges

Map 7 The changing world from the Han dynasty to the age of exploration

by their struggles with the Hsien-pi of the upper Amur and later by the Mongol Khitans, were forced to flee to China and they seem never to have retrieved their lost power. Their home territories were brought under the control first of the Uighurs and then of the Kirghiz. A century later, the Kirghiz were in turn driven out of the Selenga basin by the Mongols and returned to their former lands in the upper Yenisei. Later they migrated to the T'ien Shan area, although earlier Kirghiz settlements are known to have been in adjacent western Zungharia.

Contemporaneously, Transoxiana in the Aral basin was under Persian Abbasid and Samanid domination. The Seljuk Turks were active in Anatolia and, as Persian power waned, their influence extended eastward to appear in Afghanistan under the mottled banner of the former Turkish slave Mahmud of Ghazni who penetrated as far as the Indus. Other Turks were active in the regions south and east of the Urals. The Khazars had established an empire reaching from the Caucasus to the Crimea, but were finally defeated by the Russians and continued their move steadily westward to Moldavia and Bessarabia in the Carpathians. The tale of their ultimate defeat, first by the Byzantines and then in 1065 by the Oghuz Turks, belongs more properly to the European scene.

By the end of the ninth century China was in turmoil. The Khitans, an early Mongol confederacy, ultimately captured Loyang and their leader assumed the dynastic name of Liao. When the T'ang dynasty finally collapsed in 904, the Khitans seized control of the entire Yellow River basin. Beyond the safety of the Yangtze, the new imperial court of the Sung dynasty was established in Hangchow and set about trying to regain the north. With the aid of the Jurchen Tungusic tribes of Manchuria they achieved this goal, but their success was short-lived. At first they were forced to share control with their barbarian allies and then to relinquish it entirely. The Jurchen could not resist the temptation to play the nomad ruling game themselves and finally established their own dynasty, the Chin ('Gold') in Chinese annals.

After their defeat by the Jurchen Tungus most of the Khitan remained in the Liao Valley, but some moved west to the Tarbagatai and established the nucleus of a new Mongol confederacy with headquarters near Chuguchak in Zungharia. From this base, and with the help of their eastern allies, the Khitan ousted the

Karluk Turks from their stronghold at Balassagun, west of the Issyk-Kul. The leader, who assumed the title Gur-Khan ('King of the World'), began extending his control over all of the Turkic-speaking territories from Hami to the Aral Sea. Thus the first Mongol empire, the Kara–Khitai ('Black Khitai'), highly sinicized and largely Buddhist, was established in the early part of the thirteenth century. It paved the way for the next Mongol empire initiated by Temüjin on the Onon and Kerulen Rivers in the watershed area of the upper Amur.

The territories of the Kipchak ('Nomads'), as the desert–steppe Turks came to be called, and most of the oasis dwellers had been islamized before they were overrun by the Mongols in the thirteenth century. It might be said that the twelfth and thirteenth centuries belonged to the Mongols, and even that during that period the *world* belonged to the Mongols. It was not long, however, before all Mongols outside of Mongolia had been converted to Islam and largely absorbed into the Turkish population. Previously, the Mongols had accepted the lamaist form of Buddhism from Tibet – the continuing religion of Mongolia. From the beginning, while the Mongol khans were the nominal rulers, the power was largely in the hands of Turkish governors. Timur, a Turkish governor in Transoxiana and the celebrated Tamerlane of history, after gaining control of the Golden Horde soon built a world empire which extended in the south to Delhi, in the west to Baghdad, Aleppo and Damascus, and across most of Anatolia. But this vast empire, too, proved ephemeral. In less than a century the Mongols had lost effective control, and by the beginning of the sixteenth century it was the Turks again – the Uzbeks – who were in the ascendancy throughout all of Turkestan until stopped by the forces of a reawakened Europe – the Cossack vanguard of czarist Russia.

Turkic languages are spoken today in scattered areas across the entire continent from within three hundred miles of the Bering Strait to the heart of eastern Europe and from the Arctic to the Indian Oceans. The sequences from ancient Hunnic to modern Turkic have been defined into six interrelated language groups with designated antecedents. The following is a modification of the lists cited by Krader [190]:

Western

(1) Bulgar (ancient – Volga Bulgar and Khazar; modern – Chuvash).

(2) Oguz (ancient – Oguz, Pecheneg, Uz, Seljuk and Osmanli, modern – Turkmen, Gagauz, Turkish and Azerbaijani).

(3) Kypchak (ancient – western Golden Horde Tatar, Polovtsian, Kuman and Nogai; modern – Tatar, Bashkir, Karaim, Kumyk, Kazakh and Karakalpak).

(4) Karluk (ancient – Karakhanide and eastern Golden Horde Uzbek; modern – Uzbek, Uighur and Salar).

Eastern

(5) Uighur (ancient – Orkhon-Tü-Chüeh and Uighur; modern – Tuvinian Soyot or Soyon, Karagas or Tolfar, Yakut, Dolgan, Hakas, Kamasin, Shor, Tuban and Kumandin).

(6) Kirghiz-Kipchak (modern – Kirghiz, Altaian, Teleut and Telengit).

The geographical relationships of the six language groups reflect fairly accurately the origins and spread from a common source. All are believed to stem originally, but with subsequent admixtures, from their homeland in the Altai range complex [296].

The Bulgar group took little part in the affairs of the Turks of Turkestan after their migration into southern Russia. The second group were all originally part of the Oguz or Uz confederacy which occupied the Syr–Darya region by the tenth century. One branch, the Pechenegs, moved west into Europe; the Seljuks were enslaved or moved into Anatolia; another group, the Osmanli (Uzmanli) followed a century or two later. The Gagauz and Azeri were the latest to move south around the Caspian, while the Turkmen remained in Turkestan as the heart of the old confederacy, acquiring their name upon conversion to Islam. Today there are still over a million in the Turkmen Soviet Socialist Republic; over half a million live across the Oxus in Afghanistan, and some seventy thousand have settled in Iran. (For a general account see Czaplicka [75].)

The term Turkmen (Turkomen) dates from after the tenth century when they were recognizable as one of the tribal confederacies referred to in history as the Oguz. The original Oguz were from the Issyk–Kul and Ili Valley region of Zungharia in western Mongolia. As they moved southward through Turkestan other tribes were encountered, incorporated and included in the blanket designation Oguz, thus masking the internal weakness of former political ties.

The Turkmen in closest geographical contact with the most

'mongolized' Uzbek and Kazakh clans reveal 'Mongoloid' traits most markedly, as might be expected, but evidences of admixtures decrease southward and are almost completely absent in many sections. Some scholars identify the antecedents of the Turkmen with the Scyths, others with the Sarmatian–Alans [25]. Supporters of the former view cite as evidence skeletal comparisons with the human remains in datable Scytho–Sakian burials from the second millennium BC [91].

Barthold [190, pp. 57–69], citing accounts of Eratosthenes and other Greek writers, separates the ancient Iranians living south of the Hindu Kush and Kopet Dagh from the Turi or Saimiri–Sarmatians of the Aralo–Caspian basin. The Turanians would be a Scytho–Sarmatian tribe inhabiting Turkmenia prior to their turkicization and miscegenation with east Asian 'Mongoloid' invaders. The Turkmen south of the Kopet Dagh he identifies with the Parthians. Documents pertaining to the latter have been discovered in the last few years: they were written in Aramaic script but the language was Iranian.

Speakers of the Kypchak* group are split between Europe and Asia. As a result of pressures, the Tatars are widely dispersed and many, if not most, speak only Russian. In Asia the greatest concentrations are along the main steppe corridor across the heart of Siberia. The Karaim are in the Kuban Valley of northern Caucasia and the Kumyk and Nogai live along the Caspian Sea coast just north of the Caucasus range and next to the Iranian-speaking Tay or Talyshes. Only the Kazakh and Karakalpak remain in the Aralo–Caspian basin and steppelands to the north.

Originally the Kazakh had been part of the Uzbek nation but they broke away in the eleventh century as a result of internal dissensions. The name means simply 'steppe-riders', a term appearing in Turkish records and used later by the Russians in the sixteenth century. The Russians, however, call the Cossacks 'Kazaki' – a name derived possibly from the same source although biologically and ethnically the two are quite unrelated. In order to distinguish between them the Russians generally refer to the Kazakh as Kirghiz–Kazakh, but this has only added to the confusion. The Turkic Kazakh formed a substantial part of the Kipchak tribes of the Golden Horde. In the fifteenth century

* 'Kypchak' is used for the ancient language group, 'Kipchak' for the modern peoples.

they were organized into three and later four Hordes: the Great Horde around Lake Balkash; the Middle Horde in the central region of Kazakhstan; the Lesser Horde in the lower Ural basin and the Caspian Sea area; and, as a segment of the latter, the Inner Horde between the lower Ural and Volga basins – a region they were later to contest with the intrusive Zungharian Kalmuk Mongols.

Today there are nearly four million Kazakhs, of whom all but a small number are in the Kazakh Soviet Socialist Republic. Ismagulov [163] traced the ancient 'core' population to the 'early Europoid Bronze' and 'Usun' (Wu-sun) or late Saka period – third to fourth century BC. He concludes from the fairly extensive skeletal material and artefacts from these periods – when allowance is made for successive Mongoloid admixtures from the Huns to the present – that a 'preponderance of both early and late Bronze Age Europoid components' are still recognizable in the modern Kazakh. He supports his argument with craniometric comparisons of collections from six different time periods and traces specific cranio-facial dimension changes: 'From the Bronze Age to the present day, the cranial index has grown by seven units (75–82%) with an average increase of two units every thousand years. A similar picture is to be observed in the cheek-bone breadth and the upper height of the face. These characteristics have increased, on the average by five millimeters with the period under examination' [164].

The significance of these new data are two-fold. Not only do they demonstrate specific changes over time – in this instance three and a half millennia – but they give detailed information on the precise manner in which changes have occurred in the gradual gene flow between early 'Europoids' and 'Mongoloids'. Furthermore, the figures are given as populations and not as scattered specimens. They include 29 crania of the Bronze Age and 184 of this century. They provide also precise information concerning origins of the highly distinctive morphological traits of the Kazakh, whose features have been noted from classical Greek and Chinese times to the present.

When the Kazakh established their separate identity from the Uzbek they had already acquired a distinctive economy centring round 'tent-wagon' encampments, and their internal socio-political structure was unique. They were mainly nomadic in contrast to the majority of Uzbek who had settled in the oasis centres. In many respects their genealogically based political structure is similar to that of the Mongols, but they never emerged as an empire-building nation – a reflection perhaps of their more limited mobility. Another factor was doubtless the developing power of Russian expansion with which they were challenged.

Biologically, the Kazakh had acquired more Mongoloid admixture through incorporation of a greater proportion of disbanded Mongol hordes and fragmented clans than either the Uzbek or the Kirghiz.

In a somewhat equivocal status are the Kara-Kalpak ('Black-Caps'), who are today as mixed as the Uzbek. Their eponym originated while they were still a part of the Pecheneg nation in the Dasht-i–Kipchak. Upon the breakup of the Pecheneg confederacy they moved south in the middle of the sixteenth century.

Based on ethnological studies and archaeological excavations, it is thought that the 'core' of the original inhabitants of the Kara–Kalpak oasis settlements were the Massagetae or 'marsh Sakae' with later additions of splinter groups of Sarmatian Alani and disbanded Hephthalites. The mythological tale of the Amazons and their queen is supposed by some [273] to refer to the reputedly matriarchal Sakae–Sarmatians.

The present Karakalpak of the lower Oxus oasis settlements inherit the same name as that applied later to the Pechenegs although they are allied more closely to the Kazakhs. Some are descendants of part of the Greater Kazakh Horde and many trace their ancestry to the period of the Khwarizm (Khorezm or Chorazm) empire, which originated in the Aral Sea basin and enjoyed a decade of supremacy over most of Iran in the thirteenth century when it disavowed its vassalage to the Kara–Khitai empire. There are today less than a quarter of a million Karakalpak Turks, confined almost exclusively to their own autonomous region.

Speakers of the Karluk group are split between Soviet and Chinese Turkestan (Sinkiang) and are limited today to the modern Uzbek, the Uighur of Sinkiang and the pocket of Salar speakers near Sining in a tributary valley of the Yellow River which marks the border between Amdo province of Tibet and the Kansu corridor.

The Uzbek seem to indicate by their name '*Uz-beg*', or Uz-

'noble', their former status as rulers of the Oguz confederacy, although the majority were known as Karluk during the T'ang dynasty. They acquired their name only after they had absorbed a number of splinter tribes – notably the Semiz, Kesamir and Musa–Barzai – and became an empire after the collapse of the Mongol khanates in the late thirteenth century. Some scholars consider the Lokai, who originated in the Issyk–Kul region, to be the nomad precursors of the Uzbek.

Growing in numbers and strength, the Uzbek moved southward across and around the Kara–Kum Desert, incorporating alien tribes into their own political structure. All had originated in the same Semirechie ('seven rivers') region of the Issyk–Kul and had preceded them southward. The first to reach the interfluvial basin were the Karluks who migrated south as early as the sixth century and within two hundred years had established their capital at Balassagun. In time, the Karluk penetrated Tokharistan where today many speak Tajik and intermarry freely with Tajiks [273, 2(3):8]. The majority remain incorporated within the Uzbek nation but retain their separate identity as Karluks. They are the least 'mongolized' biologically of all the Uzbeks and may even have retained some of the old Bronze Age European–Mongoloid mixture of the upper Yenisei–Minusinsk basin population.

Succeeding the Karluk were the Barlas, also an ancient Turkic population, who are considerably less mixed with the local Tajiks. In the thirteenth century they became closely identified with Mongol-speaking tribes during the period of Chingis (Genghis) Khan's rule. Although they were gradually turkicized, many joined the Mongol invasion of India where today, in the Doab near Amritsar, some fifteen thousand continue to preserve a distinct identity [273, p. 9]. The Barlas are much more Mongoloid in morphological traits than the earlier Karluk, but the next Turkic nation to develop in the Dasht-i-Kipchak – the Kazakh – was even more so.

The Uighur of Sinkiang are no less confusing. The modern Uighur are survivors of the struggle between the Uighur and Kirghiz of the ninth century who migrated to oasis settlements in the Kara-Khoja (Turfan) area and mixed with the remaining earlier Indo–European speakers. The Uighur language is spoken in the original Uighur territories in the upper Irtysh–Yenisei tributaries. A sharp linguistic division exists today, however, between this northern group – in which the separate languages are mixed with Samoyedic–Uralic – and the southern group, which is closer to Mongolian and Tungusic.

The group known collectively as the Khakas (Hakas) are in two large concentrations east of the Kazakh. Known earlier as the Sagay, they moved north-eastward into the upland meadows of the Kuznet and Abakan ranges west of the Minusinsk area. They were partially responsible for the turkicization of the second concentration – the Tuvans or Tuvinians of the Tannu Ola and Sayan ranges – who were formerly Uralic speakers.

In the Altai region today speakers of the northern group include the Shor, Chelkan, Kumandin, Tubalar and Tolfar (Tolofar) and the geographically distant Dolgan of northern Siberia.

In the Yakut ASSR of east central Siberia, an area equal in size to Soviet Russia, the Yakut comprise nearly ninety per cent of the half million inhabitants, although they started from inconspicuous beginnings in the early centuries AD. The Yakut are a mixture of Tungusic, Palaeoasiatic and Turkic speakers who extend from their original Baikalian homeland to the Arctic Ocean.

The Kirghiz traditionally derive their name from *kyrk* ('forty') and *kyz* ('daughters'), whom they claim as their ancestors. In the T'ang dynasty they were in the Abakan steppe in the upper Yenisei. After defeating the Uighur in Mongolia, they returned to the Yenisei and remained until forced south to the T'ien Shan complex in the seventeenth century. Some authors believe that the Khakas were the original Yenisei Kirghiz who remained behind. This would explain the apparent Uralic–Kirghiz mixtures, both cultural and biological, which characterize the Khakas and Shor populations of the northern Altai. The Kirghiz-related Teleut and Telengit are located to the north and south respectively of the Tuvinian or Tuvan Altaians (Soyot or Soyon) in the meadowlands of the upper Yenisei tributaries between the Tannu Ola and Sayan ranges.

From the above discussion, the term 'Turk' appears almost as confusing as 'Arab'. It may be used politically of the peoples of Turkey, or of the Turks of Cyprus; ethnically, it may refer to all peoples speaking Turkic languages and, by extension, to the

Tatars of the Caucasus and eastern Russia. It has come to be largely dissociated from its biological connotations except in Turkestan and the immediately adjacent areas. Turkicization at the height of the Ottoman sultanate extended from Tangier to the Arctic Circle and from Serbia to Kansu.

In spite of Iranian resistance, Turkish influence became irresistible. Among other developments were the establishment of the Seljuk dynasty; the caliphate of Baghdad; the conquest of the Turkish trained Kurdish Ayyubite empire under Saladin, who held off the crusaders; the Mameluke sultanate of Egypt; the Ottoman empire which stretched as far as Tunis and Algeria; Tamerlane's conquest of India; the Safavids of Persia; and finally the Turkish conquest of the Balkans. The list is a long one and this is only south of the great mountain barrier. Even the scintillating century of Mongol supremacy was a momentary interlude. Most of the Mongols who remained in Turkestan were converted to Islam and otherwise assimilated. Though the former vast empire of the Ottoman sultanate has been contained, Turkish influence is still powerful, a heritage that has endured for a thousand years throughout a large part of the Muslim world.

From an ethnic point of view, the prominence given to the Mongols seems highly overrated. It was largely an accident of history that it was the Mongols rather than the Turks who cut such a swath across Eurasia, just at a time when it looked as if Europe might be able to break out of its encirclement. Suddenly, without warning and with unprecedented ferocity, the barbarian Mongol hordes (Mongol *ordo*, 'ten thousand') came thundering across the steppelands into the heart of Poland and to the very portals of Vienna. Only the death of their leader, the waters of the Danube and the lack of grasslands saved the rest of Europe from the fate of Moscow. Less than eight hundred miles separated the furthest point of earlier Moorish advance in the west from that of the Mongol penetration in the east. On the battlefield and amid the ruins of burning cities they left a trail of blood and massacre, and in their quieter movements wherever they swaggered – as the Chinese described their own experience – the garrisoned soldiers in their sheepskin garments left in their wake the stench of sheep dung and rancid butter.

The origin of the Mongols is strangely no more definite than that of the Turks or the Tungus. All three developed in the woodland–meadow border separating the taiga from the steppelands between the Irtysh and the Argun. The territorial homeland of the Hsien-pi, the reputed ancestors of the Mongols, is thought to have been somewhere near the source of the Kerulen River. The home of the Mongols was probably in the same general area between what was Turkic territory – the Selenga basin – and the Argun tributary of the Amur at the western extremity of the territorial nucleus of the Tungus.

Linguistically, Mongolian, Tungusic and Turkic are all Altaic, but Mongolian – although it borrowed heavily from the other two – retained many distinctive features. Borrowing is also suggested in their material culture and social organization, although in time both came to develop their own specializations. As to the name, there is no agreement. Some suggest that it may come from *mong* ('brave') others that it is from the Chinese Mon-wu, a tribal name from the fourth century AD.

The secret history of the Mongols traces the ancestry of Temüjin to the lineage of Börte Chino, the 'Blue-Grey Wolf', who descended from heaven to Mt Burkhan Khaldun at the source of the Onon. A more earthly derivation places his birth in AD 1167. The story of Temüjin's fortunes and rise to power as Chinggis (Genghis) Khan, 'Ruler of the Universe', needs no repetition. It is told in Howorth's classic [157] and in many other versions. Of more significance is the possible genetic impact his empire might have had in the ethnic 'fallout' following the division of his empire among the lineages of his three surviving sons: Chaghadai, Ögödei and Tolui. The secret of the fantastic military exploits of a people who could not have numbered more than a million but who gained dominion over most of Eurasia lay in organization, strategy and speed, and in the ability to secure the allegiance of allies, mainly Turkic. Even today those who speak Mongol or lay claim to Mongol heritage total no more than a few million. Though concentrated in political Mongolia and its immediate environs, remnant pockets can be found stretching as far as Pakistan, Afghanistan and Iran, and from the Ukraine and the Caucasus to Siberia and Manchuria.

At its peak the empire was divided into four great khanates: (1) the Great Khanate of Ögödei and his sons, Möngke and Khubilai – rulers of Mongolia, Manchuria, China, Tibet, Korea and the continental south as far as the heart of Burma; (2) the

Chaghadai Khanate of Zungharia, Sinkiang, Kazakhstan and most of Turkestan; (3) the Il–Khans of Persia from Damascus to Karachi and from the Caspian Sea to Kabul; (4) the Kipchak Khanate (the Golden Horde), including most of Russia, the steppelands as far as the Yenisei and the Aralo–Caspian basin.

The memory of these khanates lingers on in legend and place names, and more especially in the military structuring of society in the banner system in modified form, echoed in the systematic groupings of 'ten thousands' which the Mongols took over from the Turks and perfected; and the kin group variously styled as Obok, Oboh or Abok [10].

Today the Mongols within the borders of the Great Khanate comprise numerically nearly ninety per cent of the total population. The Khalka are the most numerous and occupy the heartland of Outer Mongolia. At the time of the fall of the Manchu dynasty in China, which they supported, they were divided into four *aimaq* or territorial units. Each *aimaq* included a number of temple lands and was divided again into *usu,* or 'banners'. Each banner had its own prince or *jasak,* and all had their respective lineages tracing back to the Great Khan [275a].

East of the Khalka are the Chahar of Inner Mongolia and the Ordos, the Dagur or Dagor of northern Manchuria, and the Mongols of Tsaidam and Kokonor districts on the border of Amdo in north-eastern Tibet. Several families in Lhasa and other parts of central Tibet trace their lineages to the period of Mongol occupation in the thirteenth century. Ever since this time there have been close ties between Mongolia and Tibet, although conversion of Mongolia to Lamaism did not take place until the sixteenth century under the Khutuktus, at about the time that the Dalai Lama line was initiated in Tibet.

Within the limits of the former Chaghadai Khanate, the largest concentration of Mongols is in Zungharia ('Left Hand'), a part of the present Sinkiang autonomous region and the adjacent Soviet districts of Oirot and east Kazakhstan, although the people known as Oirot are Turkic-speaking.

In the former territories of the Il–Khans of Persia, the best known are the mixed Hazara of the region known as Hazarajat in south central Afghanistan and the four *aimaq* of north Afghanistan (see Chapter 4). Today most of the Hazaras speak Persian, the rest mainly Tajik Iranian. The justifiability of their claim to Mongol ancestry is uncertain, but according to Schurmann [332] this varies from district to district. The only Mongols who still speak Mongolian and whose claims can be documented are the Mogholi in two small cryptic enclaves in south Hazarajat [165] and in the north near Balkh. Finally, there are the few hundred Torgut who have made their refuge home in one of the hidden valleys of the Hazara district in northern Pakistan.

The only people speaking Mongolian in the former lands of the Golden Horde are the Buddhist Kalmuk of the Volga basin, although the word 'Kalmuk' itself may be of Turkic origin. Originally the Kalmuks were in Zungharia, where they were known as the Dörbön Oirat: the Zunghar, Torgut, Koshot and Dörbet. The four Kalmuk, however, were not identified as such when the Great Khan's army of a quarter of a million won him his empire. They were late migrants in the sixteenth and seventeenth centuries from the upper Yenisei basin, who had moved to the T'ien Shan area. They were later forced out under Chinese pressure and settled in the Volga basin. Many of those have since returned to Zungharia, but two groups deserve special mention: a military detachment who moved into western Europe as part of the Russian forces occupying Germany and Austria at the end of the Second World War; and the community of Torguts. The majority of the detachment returned to their homeland while some defected in France where they now live; others went to the United States where a small colony exists in New Jersey and maintains a lamasery. As for the Torgut, a large part of the population of nearly half a million migrated in 1771 some three thousand miles back to the T'ien Shan Mountains bordering southern Zungharia to escape the proselytizing efforts of Catherine the Great. Later, in the middle of the twentieth century, some of this group trekked on across the Tsaidam and Amdo in eastern Tibet, wintered in the Chang Tang and then continued through Tibet and Nepal to India where they were finally permitted to settle in what is now northern Pakistan.

The formative process of the Buriat, as revealed through Russian sources, is an excellent illustration of the amalgamations that characterize many of the peoples of the taiga, tundra and steppe. According to Dolgikh [96], when the Russians reached eastern Siberia (Transbaikalia) in the mid-seventeenth century, there was a small core of tribal clans referred to as Buriat [96,

p. 109] speaking a Mongol dialect. But the ancestors of the majority of the present-day Buriat were then speaking a variety of Turkic–Tungusic dialects. Reflecting the paramount political pressure still being exerted by the Mongols, these non-Buriat tribal groups were gradually incorporated into the expanding Buriat nation and simultaneously assumed the Buriat dialect of Mongolian – which in itself was being modified through contact with the local Turkic–Tungusic dialects. The actual incorporation of the non-Mongol tribal groupings was accomplished by increasing with each new addition the number of eponymous ancestral sons of the prodigiously prolific mythological ancestor of all Buriats, 'the grey bull' – Bukha-noyon-baabay.

The estimated total Buriat population based on clan name lists and paying tribute (sable-skin tax) rose from 25,000 in 1640 to 157,000 in 1823 and over a million by 1950, a forty-fold increase in three hundred years. To what extent the gradual imposition of Russian controls may have hastened the consolidation is problematical, but the same pressures existed throughout the entire sphere of Russian penetration.

While the meteoric rise of the Mongols was due to their mastery of military and political strategy, the secret of their power was the deadly accuracy of their mounted archers, who could strike terror into the ranks of their enemies by shooting the leaders at distances of from two or three hundred yards. There was no comparison between the effectiveness of the mounted bowmen and the earlier mounted spearmen and lancers. The Mongol bow was also of a special order: it was triple-curved and sinew-backed, giving its user a tremendous advantage over the conventional weapon of the times. The ponies were also of an especially sturdy breed. Taking note of the all-purpose usage of the Mongol pony in which mares were preferred, one historian is said to have described the Mongol horseman as being such an acrobat that, when in need of sustenance, he could remain astride his mare, swing under her belly and suckle from her udder; he suggested that possibly this was the way in which the Mongols acquired their flattened nose!

Archery and lancing from the saddle and horse racing are still among the favourite contests of skill, but wrestling is possibly an even more popular sport the Mongols share with the Turks. Many of the world's greatest wrestlers and weight-lifters, even in the modern arena, have been Turks and Mongols; and the memory of their skills lives on in spectacular festival pageantry among the Japanese, in a land the Mongols never succeeded in conquering. Three times the armadas of the great Khan Khubilai ('Kublai'), which had stripped Korea of its best timbers in the construction of their vessels, had attempted to conquer the 'land of the dwarfs'; but each time Heaven (or the Sun Goddess) came to the rescue and with a 'divine wind' (*kami-kaze*) sank or scattered the enemy's fleets. Periodically the scene is re-enacted today in northern Kyushu, where the landings – once partially successful – were attempted. Mounted archery contests after the Mongol fashion are held annually at the great shrine of the war god – Hachiman – in Kamakura near Tokyo.

21

Hunters and Herders of the Taiga and Tundra

THE URALIC SPEAKERS

The question of cognatic relationships between the Uralic and Altaic languages has been a thorny one but the two appear to be distinct groups in spite of similarities [298]. The Uralic languages are old in northern Europe and they may share a common source with ancient Indo–European languages of the southern steppes and the Black Earth country. All of the western or Finno–Ugric branch remains European except Ostyak and Vogul and a fragment of Komi on the eastern slopes of the Urals.

On the Asian side of the Urals the eastern or Samoyedic group includes the Nentsi and Entsi Samoyeds, Yuraks, Tavgins (Nganasans) and Selkup Samoyeds. Until the eighteenth century, Samoyedic was also spoken in the Sayan range by the Tofalars (Karagasy), Motors and Koybals (Kamasins), most of whom have been turkicized. To these some scholars would add the Kets: structurally their language is allied to the extinct Kott which is probably Palaeoasiatic. It is closest to Yukaghir, although many words are Samoyedic or Tungusic [59]. The ancestors of the Kets must have played a part in the original peopling of the northlands.

According to Soviet historians [294], the eastward extension of the west Uralic speakers – the Khanti and Mansi (Voguls and Ostyaks) – were descendants of the horse-breeding Yugric or Ugri (Ugral) of the Aral Sea steppe region during the late Neolithic and transitional Bronze Age (*c.* 3000–2000 BC). During the first millennium BC they infiltrated northward into the marshy basin of the lower Ob east of the Urals, which bears their name.

In their new environment, unfavourable to horse breeding, most of them switched to the hunting and gathering economy of their Palaeoasiatic neighbours. In due course the eastern Ugri, who were herders, became mixed with the palaeo–Asiatics to create the Samoyedic-speaking groups, while the Kets retained their identity as part of the earlier Tyma and Taz Palaeoasiatic inhabitants.

The Ugric herders learned to depend heavily on raw or dried fish with secondary dependence on meat, berries, wild onions and tubers. Although nominally christianized in the eighteenth century, they continued their bear festivals, ancestor propitiations and belief in animal spirits. They used reindeer for clothing, shelter and as pack anmials, and dogs and dugout canoes for additional transport.

The northern Samoyedic Nentsi (Nenets), Entsi and Nganasans are tundra reindeer breeders, fishers and hunters of marine mammals and migrant birds; they live in conical tent dwellings made of poles and reindeer skins. The turkicized southern Samoyeds, the Karagasy (Tofalars) and Soyots of Uriankhai, who refer to themselves as Tuva (Tuvans or Tuvinians) are reindeer breeders in the marginal taiga and steppe–woodland meadows, moving freely into the adjacent grazing lands of Mongolia.

THE TUNGUSIC HERDERS OF THE NORTHLANDS

The Tungus tribes today are divided loosely on a regional and linguistic basis into two groups: the northern Evenk and Even (Lamut) of Siberia and the upper Amur basin; and the southern Nanay (Goldi), Ulchi, Oroch (including Udege), Orok, Negidal and Solon. To these some would add the Dahur, who are generally classed with the Mongols. In a special category are the Manchu and ancient tribes of the lower Amur, some of whom appear later in history as the Koreans and as part of the ancestral population of Japan.

The origin of the Tungus is closely related to the east coast neolithic province which spread southward into the Yangtze basin and northward into the Tung–Pei ('East–North') – the basins of the Liao and Amur. The Amur or Hei-lung ('Black Dragon') basin forms the northern third of the Chinese neolithic culture area of the second millennium. With the commencement of the Chinese Bronze Age Tung–Pei became the land of the

Tung or 'eastern' barbarians. The term Manchuria has been applied only since the emergence of the highly sinicized Manchus, successors to the earlier Jurchen Tungus who ruled China as the Kin or Chin dynasty [214].

The earliest Chinese reference to the inhabitants of Tung–Pei is to the Su–Shen of the second millennium BC, the ancestors apparently of the I-lou. By the time of the Han dynasty the I-lou were located in eastern Manchuria. They seem to have combined cattle, horse and pig breeding with millet and wheat agriculture. They lived in semi-subterranean houses with corridor entrances, wore hemp and shredded tree-bast garments and enjoyed falcon hunting [261, pp. 84–201]. The economy is similar to that of other sedentary Tungus tribes of northern Korea of approximately the same time.

By the fifth century AD the I-lou are referred to as the Wu-chi or Mo-ho, who lived to the east of the Khitan. By the seventh century the Mo-ho were defending their territories against the neighbouring state of P'o-hai in Kao-li (Korea). The name Jürchen or Ju-chen appears among the lists of Mo-ho tribes who are known to be the antecedents if not the ancestors of the Manchus. During the three centuries of the Manchus' rule they became so highly sinicized both biologically and culturally that their identity as Manchus became largely reduced to the preservation of rites and rituals surrounding the throne and the panoply associated with officialdom.

The ideographs comprising the Chinese name Man-shu means simply 'abundant province', but it is the name of a dynasty and not a people. The Tungusic-speaking semi-sedentary, agricultural–nomadic nation was thrust into the limelight more by accident than by prowess. Without the assistance of their Mongol–Tungusic allies, the Manchus probably would never have achieved and maintained their elevated role in history. The title 'Dragon–Tiger General' bestowed on their charismatic leader Nurhachi by the Ming throne was responsible for the shift in symbolism from the celestial to the dragon throne – recognition of the power of the northlands, home of the dragon.

The Tungus (Evenk and Even) are the most numerous of the northern reindeer herders and breeders totalling, however, less than 100,000 in Siberia but occupying in their nomadic camp cycles all of west central and much of eastern Siberia, northernmost Mongolia and Manchuria, or roughly twenty per cent of the entire area. Until neolithic times they were largely confined to the Amur basin, and they began moving into basins of the Yenisei and Lena in the early centuries of the Christian era when these were largely occupied by Palaeoasiatic speakers.

Distinctions are usually made between reindeer herders or breeders and salmon fishers, between reindeer sledders and dog sledders, and between walkers and riders. Changes in economy may require only two or three generations and have usually been in one direction – from walkers with dog sleds to reindeer herders afoot, and from herders afoot to riders. Migration to a new environment and the sudden availability of a major new resource such as fish or marine mammals may also have had its effect.

During the past millennium the Tungus have gradually assimilated the earlier Palaeoasiatic-speaking populations, just as the Tungus have been turkicized and assimilated by the Yakuts of the Lena basin. The Dolgans near the Arctic Circle at the mouth of the Yenisei represent an extreme example of the process. Some of the southern Tungus herd or breed reindeer, but usually add fishing and marine mammal hunting. Much of their territory also was inhabited by Palaeoasiatic speakers, and most of the ethnic groups represent hybridizations or splinter groups of the two populations.

THE AINU OF HOKKAIDO, SAKHALIN AND THE KURILES

The problem of Ainu origins, both biological and cultural, has fascinated 'ethnic speculators' for hundreds of years. A voluminous literature exists on the subject in Japanese, and the Russians have contributed to it since the time of Peter the Great.

Today the Ainu are limited to the southern parts of Sakhalin, the Kurile chain and the island of Hokkaido, but historical Japanese sources place their known distribution as far south as central Honshu when their existence was first officially chronicled in the seventh century. Some historians and archaeologists claim that both in legends and artefacts their presence in prehistoric times can be traced as far south as Okinawa. They have generally been identified historically with the Yemishi, who are among the tribes with whom the people of Yamato contended for several centuries.

The name Yemishi is probably preserved in Yezo [325], the

former name for Hokkaido ('North Sea Territory'). Tales of the individual and collective struggles with the Yemishi remained largely legendary until the ninth century, when a string of defensive forts was built across the coastal corridor just north of Sendai. From this time on they have been referred to as Ainu ('Person' or 'People'), the Ainu name for themselves. Reciprocally, the Ainu use Wa, the old Yamato word for 'people', in speaking of the Japanese.

In encounters with the Japanese a thousand years ago the chief weapon was the bow, and the Ainu had the advantage of poison-tipped arrows. Horses were of little advantage in the rather heavily forested areas of northern Honshu where armour was the major defense. Progress northward to the strait of Tsugaru was slow, and the history of the campaigns is marked with temporary truces followed by banquet scenes from which the victorious Japanese alone emerged alive.

By the tenth century the Ainu on Honshu had been decimated and the remainder largely absorbed. Their genetic impact is traceable among the Japanese today, and their memory lives on in bear hunting methods, ghost legends and Ainu place names, especially those ending in *betsu* or *nai* (both meaning 'stream') and that of the sacred Mount Fuji ('Fire Goddess'). During the following centuries Japanese trading posts were established at strategic locations on Hokkaido and Sakhalin – some were later converted into feudatory estates – and the Russians established some coastal forts in the eighteenth century, only to lose them after the beginning of the Meiji era (1868).

The Ainu language is sometimes given independent status but it is agglutinative as are many of the Palaeoasiatic languages such as Gilyak and Chukchi (Chukchee) and in its morphemic–phonemic aspects it resembles them closely. Basic word lists also show close resemblance to neighbouring Palaeoasiatic and Tungusic languages, although many loan words have filtered in from Yamato. Mythology, art forms, material culture and many social institutions also suggest strong ties both with prehistoric and ancient Japanese and with adjacent continental populations.

THE PALAEOASIATICS AND ESKIMOS OF NORTH-EASTERN SIBERIA

The surviving ancient populations of north-eastern Siberia, speaking Palaeoasiatic languages, are limited to the Yukaghir of the Indigirka and Kolyma basins, the Chukchi of the north-east peninsula, the Koryak of the northern districts of Kamchatka, the Itel'men (Kamchadal) of the west coast of Kamchatka and the Nivkhi (Gilyaks) of northern Sakhalin and the lower stretches of the Amur. As a group the Palaeoasiatic peoples appear to have had linguistic and other cultural ties with the Eskimo and also with the Kets of western Siberia. They have retained an arctic hunting economic complex of tundra game, fish and berries, similar to that of the older economy of the Uralic-speaking Komi of north-eastern Europe. The latter, however, have been greatly influenced by their Turkic and Samoyedic (Saams) neighbours of the Ob basin in western Siberia.

In the seventeenth century, according to Russian documentation [260, p. 34], the Yukaghirs and Samoyeds were within less than 200 kilometres of each other at the mouth of the Lena, separated by an intrusive wedge of Tungusic speakers who moved into the region and reached the Arctic Ocean sometime during the previous century. The Yukaghir language has a number of dialects even among the fewer than 500 survivors and, while it is usually classed as Palaeoasiatic, it is today syntactically and in much of its vocabulary closer to Saams than to Chukchi or Koryak [260, p. 3].

East of the Yukaghir, the Chukchi – who number 12,000 – have acquired the art of reindeer breeding from the Chuvantsy, a highly mixed population on the Anadyr peninsula. The majority are nomadic hunters and a minority (thirty per cent) have learned to hunt marine mammals from the Eskimo and have settled along the coast. The dwellings are either conical skin tepees or yurt-shaped with a conical peak. Clothing is similar to that of the Eskimo; and for transportation they use sleds with either reindeer or dog teams for traction.

South of the Chukchi, the Koryak – who number about 6000 – are divided into interior reindeer breeders and coastal marine mammal hunters and fishers. Of the interior Koryak there are seven regional groups, each with its specialized mixture of reindeer breeding, with or without hunting or fishing. They have conical pelt tepees similar to those of the Chukchi, but the coastal settlements shift from summer skin houses on piles to semi-dugout dwellings with log roofs and corridor entrances in the winter.

The Itel'man of Kamchatka, who now number less than 1000, inhabited the entire peninsula in the eighteenth century. In economy they are similar to the coastal Koryak and the languages are closely related.

The Nivkhi or Gilyaks of Sakhalin are unique in many respects. Their language contains a number of Tungusic loan words, especially the mainland half of the less than 8000 total population. In material culture they differ considerably, the mainlanders making more use of salmon – even to using the skins for clothing – while the islanders are largely hunters. Houses in both areas are usually semi-subterranean with timber-corridored entrances and bark roofs. The house types and general economy are similar to those of the long since extinct neolithic population on the north coast of Hokkaido.

The Asian Eskimo, who are similar culturally to the Alaskan Eskimo with whom they are in annual contact, appear to be related also to Palaeoasiatic populations in economy, material culture and language, but the differences are too great to class them together. The population fluctuates seasonally with visitations to the Diomedes or Alaska, but the total never exceeds two or three hundred. The native peoples of the Komandorsky Islands off Kamchatka are Aleuts, but there appear to be fewer than 100 remaining in what is otherwise a largely Russian population.

PART VI

THE BIOLOGICAL ASSESSMENT

22

Population Analysis and Classification

In the latter part of the nineteenth century it was fashionable to compare body systems, organs and tissues. Such studies are still useful, but they provide little information about the processes of formation or the relative significance of differences. There followed a period of concentration on anthropometry and somatology – the study of body segments, head and facial measurements, pigmentation and similar traits. It was not uncommon to take thirty measurements and as many observations.

Statistically determined shape–size similarities were presumed to indicate degrees of genetic relationship and common heritage. There is no way yet of proving this, but the presumption is maintained with certain modifications. Stature, body weight and correlated measurements in themselves are known to be of limited genetic importance. There is a great difference between overall size and relative sizes and shapes of different segments. Malnutrition as well as extreme climatic conditions and hormonal deficiencies are powerful factors in reducing body size during growth. People living in the lower Ganges area are not necessarily 'racially' – genetically – different from those in the middle and upper stretches just because they are smaller.

Within a few score generations body shape and size can respond hereditarily to environmental pressures. Linear, tall bodies – ectomorphic, in somatotyping terminology – are best adjusted to arid, hot climates. The larger skin surface relative to body volume permits lowering of temperature through evaporation – sweating – even though it means loss of salt. Many Arabs, Syrians, Iranians, Pakistanis and some inner Asians approximate this optimal physique and those who do not have probably been culturally sheltered or are fairly recent migrants from more humid regions. Classification of physique on a three-fold basis dates to the Middle Ages, but in modern times has been developed into a quantifying technique.

Using a triangular grid and a sequential three-digit system, the extreme ectomorph is classified as 1–1–7; the extreme mesomorph, or medium-build, heavy-set, muscular type, as 1–7–1, and the endomorph or rotund individual often given to obesity as 7–1–1 [345].

Considerable somatometric data are now available for Asia and differences are generally positively correlated with environment. In Arabia, parts of Pakistan, India and south-east Asia, where climatic conditions induce linearity, the percentage of ectomorphs is higher than in most of eastern and northern Asia, which are predominantly mesomorphic [69, p. 83]. Endomorphs are more frequently encountered in the plateau region of western Asia. Diet and, indirectly, economic factors must be considered and the value of somatotyping appears to lie mainly in registering long-range responses to adaptive pressures rather than short-range secular changes.

The classic chi square (χ^2) method of determining similarity (square root of the sum of the squares of the difference between means) is still a common means of determining 'distance' between two populations, but neither it nor such devices as the coefficient of racial likeness (CRL) can eliminate the compounding effect of correlated size differences. For example, if stature is to be measured, then the inclusion also of limb lengths and other correlated body measurements will weight the results unduly. The same criticism applies to methods dependent on indices rather than measurements. Such direct methods of comparison have been largely abandoned in favour of new statistical procedures.

Relative significance of variables remains a problem. From the statistical point of view it would be helpful to know, for instance, if head length is more significant than nasal breadth, interorbital diameter or colour of the eyes. Current methods of determining relative importance are through the numerical strength and variability of the samples, determined mainly by the standard deviation.

Ultimately it may be possible to reduce the number of measurements to those that can be correlated with physiological processes. The four kinds of cell tissues (epithelial, connective, muscular and nervous) of which organs are composed yield highly informative histological data.

MORPHOLOGICAL DATA AND METHODS OF ANALYSIS USED IN THIS STUDY

Because of the unevenness in quantity and quality of Asian population samples, it has been necessary to eliminate hundreds of series and in a few instances to introduce data corrections. Eventually 519 male series were selected, each consisting of nine variables: stature, head length, head breadth, minimum frontal breadth, facial breadth, total facial height, mandibular breadth, nose length and nose breadth.* Unfortunately, owing to the paucity of female samples, study of comparative sexual dimorphism has not been attempted.

Ideally a series should be a true random sample and the group recognizable as an ethnic entity maintaining itself as a breeding unit, but in highly urbanized concentrations the number of discrete genetic isolates is exceedingly limited.

The 519 series were clustered into groups with the aid of the 'Nature's Group Programme' [171], a form of multivariate analysis involving the discriminant function procedure – in this case computerized. The clustering method is based upon the premise that similar ethnic groups are likely to be near each other geographically; accordingly, computer cards containing the biometric data were arranged sequentially as a compromise between ethnic (cultural) similarities and geographical proximity. Principal components' scores rather than raw data measurements were used as variables in the clustering process, eliminating the correlated size factor by transforming measurements into uncorrelated variables. As a comment on the importance of correlated size: 48 per cent of the variance of the entire series – 111,533 indi-

* In instances where nose height has been taken from the nasal bridge root (sellion) instead of nasion (fronto-nasal suture) 3 mms. have been added and, when minimum frontal or bigonial diameters are missing, it has been necessary to insert the means of the respective clusters as substitutes.

viduals – was mainly in stature; nearly 30 per cent in head length and breadth; and 22 per cent in facial measurements.

The first step was to determine the generalized (biological) distance between two series using the refined D^2 (distance squared) procedure [223]. The computer scans the entire card deck, searching out the most-alike series to form pairs and most-alike pairs to form clusters and groups. As each pair is formed, the computer selects one of the two to form a second pair with the next closest series, returning to the starting point each time the end of the deck is reached until eventually the total deck is exhausted. The next step is to describe the pathway followed so that the sequences of matched pairs can be strung together in the right order and finally clustered. This method is highly accurate in the first two or three runs but the picking and choosing process becomes erratic as the deck shrinks.

To reduce error, separate decks of cards were fed into the computer on an overlapping basis beginning with Arabia and moving counter-clockwise south of the central mountain massif, through south and east Asia then westward north of the central massif to the northern rim of Irania. Final cluster determination was arbitrary, with cut-off points based on statistically significant differences. There may still be up to 5 per cent error in the results; nevertheless, the advantage of using the computer is enormous, permitting escape from the restrictions of geographically confined groupings and limitations of hand sorting.

PIGMENTATION

Owing to the complex factors involved in eye colour – number, location and concentration of pigment granules in the iris, cryptic structure and reflectance angles of the striae, etc. – no single apparatus has yet been devised to determine varietal distinctions with any degree of accuracy. Absence of pigment in the surface layer of the iris results in a bluish colour, and if the influence of refraction could be eliminated such eyes would be regarded not as blue but as 'non-brownish'. Females seem to be dominant in the brown eyes and tend to have darker eyes than males. This poses the problem of determining the difference between a 'racial' and a sex-linked character. Furthermore, after the age of about sixty the outer perimeter of the iris may become clouded with a ring called the *arcus senilis*. Not infrequently, especially among hunting populations whose eyes are constantly exposed to camp fires, the deeper pigment layers may be superficially concealed. Under field conditions, therefore, determination of eye colour can be even more subjective than that of hair or skin colour. Colour photography with controlled light has proven to be fairly reliable, but few studies using this method have yet been conducted on sizeable populations.

In the case of skin and occasionally hair colour, spectrophotometric techniques are used to determine the percentage of light reflected throughout the visible spectrum. In skin colour, factors that must be considered are density and location of pigment granules, amount of adipose tissue and degree of surface vascularity. For most populations the data are still limited to subjective evaluation.

OTHER MEANS OF CLASSIFICATION

Monogenic traits are in many ways more satisfactory than polygenic biometric measurements because they relate to single gene loci and chromosomes; they can be precisely identified and their hereditary patterns more specifically determined. In practical application it might be possible to determine most genes, whether 'structural', 'regulating' or 'operating', by their molecular structure, but it is usually easier to determine variability by chemical reaction as in the case of blood group antigens or types. The ultimate object is to determine gene frequency distributions or group levels of variability in relation to physiological homeostasis or internal dynamic equilibrium.

The search is primarily for alternative hereditary forms (polymorphisms), especially those that are sufficiently stable to be maintained in balanced genetic homeostasis, and to eliminate transient genes. Exclusion arbitrarily drops all very low gene frequency alleles of less than 1 per cent of the sample, but in large populations if the frequency of an 'abnormal' allele is constantly present even below 1 per cent it is likely to be relatively stable and hence of potential long-range significance [47a].

The problem of understanding and classifying man's populational varieties becomes a matter of locating and identifying those substances that are most essential in determining his distinctive hereditary characteristics. Much has been learned about monogenic inheritance such as blood types, taste and secretor factors, but little about polygenic traits which constitute those observable in the phenotype. The precise genetic basis for and origin of such traits as skin colour or hair form still remain uncertain, but the weight of evidence for the latter favours local mutational derivation.

At present the most useful comparative studies are limited primarily to blood group systems, serum proteins, certain glandular secretions and a limited number of enzymes. Fields for future intensive study include the biophysical and biochemical mechanics of growth in which enzymes have specific catalytic roles as 'body-builders'. Another intriguing thesis is connected with steroids: the functions of several hormones or endocrine secretions still remain unknown. It has also been conjectured that some enzymes in the cryptoplasm might be self-perpetuating and interact with gene-controlled enzymes [275].

RED CELL PROTEINS: THE BLOOD GROUP SYSTEMS

Among the best studied polymorphisms (gene markers) are the various blood group systems whose inheritance patterns are now fairly well established. They can be identified and quantified with relative accuracy and serve as agents of selective change or as catalysts in tissue-building, immunization and metabolism. Until recently it was assumed that they had no selective value, but it is now clear that most if not all are associated with immunological resistance and therefore are subject to selection. Their taxonomic significance may be indirect, but they are valuable indicators of time depths relating to filiation, genetic distance and hybridization. Most studies have concentrated on frequency gradients in continental or global perspective, with the implication that systematic balances must exist between the protective roles of antibody proteins and their destructive roles in tissue-building.

Several hundred blood 'factors' have been detected, but most of them are localized or insufficiently tested so they have little current value except as clinical anomalies. Ten systems have been fairly well established although not all are independent: ABO, MNS, Rh, Duffy, Kidd, P, Lutheran, Kell, Lewis and Diego.

Many of the human blood group systems are found in other primates. Since primates have the ABO system, for instance, it is highly improbable that the allele for type B was a relatively recent mutation. This refutes the argument that antigen B must have originated in some human populations in Asia – possibly in India or inner Asia where the proportions are high – and from there spread to other parts of the world. Many significant associations have now been discovered between ABO phenotypes and diseases of the gastro-intestinal tract. Blood type O individuals are suspectible to various ulcers and carcinogens, and type A is associated with cancer of the stomach and pancreas. More recently, their association with other diseases has been noted: pernicious anemia, rheumatic fever and certain types of poliomyelitis and diabetes, to mention only those most carefully studied. It has been shown, for instance, that mortality rates for smallpox in Bengal and Bihar were significantly higher in A and AB-type persons than in those of the B and O groups [386]. One interpretation of the relationship between the ABO system to specific diseases is that it is not so much the disease itself as individual physiological factors that condition susceptibility. Some diseases, however, affect people past the breeding age, thus minimizing the influence of selection.

By itself the ABO system is a poor indicator of 'racial' differences, but its relationship to the MNS system is unusual. Although the precise immunological significance of the MNS system is not clear, the proportion of M and N in populations seems to relate to a range of diseases and incompatibilities as in the case of the ABO system. The antibodies of M and N have not been found, but discovery of the associated antigen S and its allele s has greatly increased the number of possible combinations, and other rare antibodies multiply the possibilities even further. There are subdivisions of A in the ABO system: some people produce in their body cells the same group-specific substances as are found in the blood, one of which is similar to but distinguishable from A, which is thus divided into A_1 and A_2. Another substance is found in secretions. Tests are determined by saliva, and secretors are distinguished from non-secretors by the symbols Se and se.

The Rhesus system is probably more informative than any other single blood group system. It was first discovered in clinical cases of haemolysis in newborn infants which sometimes arises when the mother is Rh negative (r or cde) and the father positive (R). The gene frequency distributions of the Rh system indicate that it too has been subjected to intensive selective pressures. One of the highest concentrations of the Rh− allele is in the Pyrennees (40–50 per cent); in south-east Europe it decreases by 10 per cent and in western Asia by another 10 per cent. The decrease continues into southern Asia and throughout most of the eastern and northern quadrants where frequencies are generally below 10 per cent and in many populations reach zero. The system is phylogenetically significant but highly complex. There are some twenty variants, and over thirty combinations have been identified, but many are rare and only eight or nine are sufficiently generalized for comparison on a world-wide basis.

Other blood group systems whose immunological roles are less clearly understood are linked either to each other or to the Rh and ABO systems. As yet their distributions are less well known in Asia than in other continents.

HAEMOGLOBINS, RED CELL ENZYMES AND SERUM PROTEINS

Blood serum carries a tremendous variety of proteins serving a wide range of functions. All known gene action appears to be carried out through the control and catalytic action of the serum proteins which synthesize other proteins and complement the protective immunizational role of the antigens on the red and white cells.

Proteins are identified as simple, compound or derived – determined by their solubility and other physical properties. There are seven groups of simple proteins of which three are most useful: albumins, globulins and globins. The commonest way to distinguish between varieties is by electrophoretic chromatography or electrophoresis – the fractional salting out which causes differential migration in an electrical field.

Albumins, which are the fastest moving, are thought to differ varietally ('racially') and to reflect differing capacities for protein intake. Four globulin fraction proteins are especially significant: the alpha–1, alpha–2, beta and gamma. Over the centuries diet and disease have exercised powerful effects on populations, detectable by percentage differences of the globulins within the groups. In the alpha–2 group the haptoglobins perform the important function of binding the oxygen-carrying haemoglobin of red cells; among the beta globulins, the transferrins are distinctive. Even more so are the slow-fractioning gamma globulins and inhibitors.

GLANDULAR SECRETION POLYMORPHISMS FOR THE WHOLE OF ASIA*

PTC The percentages of PTC (phenylthiocarbamide) 'tasters' (T) drops from over 90 per cent in Europe and western Asia to a range of 60–70 per cent among the southern Semites and Indo-Aryan caste populations of northern India [24]. The lowest figures are in southern India where they reach 41 per cent among the Tamils [265]. There is a clinal rise from west to east in south-east Asia; among the Chinese and Japanese the frequencies rise to 80–95 per cent, but they drop to 60–70 per cent in Inner Asia and even lower in parts of Siberia.

Se In Europe and west Asia the percentages of the Se (secretor) gene, which controls the ability to secrete ABH substances, ranges from 60–75 per cent. In south Asia there is a steady decline from 60 per cent among Punjabi [343] to 23–60 per cent in Bengal and Gujarat and 51 per cent in Madras [42]. There is a further drop of 10 per cent or more in different parts of south-east Asia and a rise to 55 per cent in Japan [369] and 66 per cent in Tibet [14].

BAIB and the Amino Acids Amino acids and related chemicals are excreted in the urine and provide many useful telltale markers, especially alanine, lysine, leucine, histidine, tyrosine and uric acid and a substance called B-aminoisobutyric acid – BAIB for short. These vary in detectable amounts. East Asians excrete larger amounts of all of these substances than Europeans but the latter excrete more BCG (bromocresolgreen) basic (.32) and BCG acid (.90) [367]. West and south Asians are varyingly intermediate between the two major populations.

Cerumen or Ear Wax Another rather unusual glandular secretion trait is cerumen or ear wax. It is probably appropriate that Japanese scientists should have been the first to note that east Asians have exceptionally high percentages of dry cerumen: 90 per cent among the Japanese, 96 per cent among the

* Mourant [250] is the reference except where specific sources are cited.

Koreans and 98 per cent among the Chinese. In Europe the percentages drop to 50–60 per cent in northern Europe and less than 20 per cent in France. Similarly there is a clinal drop from east Asia southward to 52 per cent in Thailand and less than 40 per cent in India. The percentages in west Asia match those of northern Europe, but in Africa and Australia they drop to below 10 per cent [286]. The Ainu fall into the European range with 37 per cent [236].

GLOBINS, GLOBULINS AND ENZYMES

Abnormal Haemoglobins The sickle cell gene (HbS) reaches its highest frequencies as expected in the malarially infested, circum-Mediterranean lowlands – 2 per cent among the Arabs and coastal Iranians – and in the tropical coastal and peninsular regions of south and south-east Asia. Among the Indo–Aryan caste populations of the north it is virtually absent, but among the west tribal groups it ranges from 2–17 per cent [389] and among the east tribal groups 23–29 per cent [344]. The percentage drops steadily in an easterly direction. Interestingly it is absent among the Andamanese and virtually so in the rest of the Malayan peninsula.

The thalassemia gene (ThT) is also concentrated in the same general circum-Mediterranean and tropical regions of south and south-east Asia, but is not as common in tropical Africa. Conversely it is more prevalent in south-east Asia where it is associated with other haemoglobin anomalies, notably HbE and several other highly localized rare mutants.

HbE is extremely rare in northern India, but it reaches 1 per cent in Bengal [58] caste populations, rises among the east tribal populations and reaches a peak in south-east Asia: Thai 8 per cent and Burmese 15 per cent [216]; Khmer 21 per cent and Stieng Mon of Vietnam 36 per cent [39]. It is absent in Japan and China and in all recent immigrants from central and north China into south-east Asia [120].

The rare HbD gene which occurs in Bengal [337] is absent in east Asia. Among Koreans and Chinese several haemoglobin variants of HbG seem to associate east Asians with American Indians [29].

SERUM PROTEIN HAPTOGLOBINS AND TRANSFERRINS

The iron-binding alpha–2 globulin haptoglobins are of special interest in south Asia because of the low frequencies. The Hp^1 gene range is from 26 per cent [99, pp. 357–94] among the Arabs to 29 per cent in Iran, percentages slightly below the European range of 30–40 per cent. The Hp^2 gene accounts for all but a fraction of the remaining percentages; the Hp^1 gene drops to 20 per cent in the Punjab [183] and among the Tamils to 9 per cent. The lowest figure in Asia is 7 per cent among the tribal Irula [183]. Among the cattle breeding Toda of the Nilgiri Hills of western Madras it reaches 35 per cent and on the basis of this and related monogenic gene frequencies Kirk *et al* [183] postulate that this Dravidian-speaking group may be a surviving remnant of the ancient cattle-breeders of pre-Aryan days who once ruled the south. An outstanding feature of their culture is the revered status of their cattle, and the sacred nature of their dairy barns which serve as temples [378]. Unfortunately, their total population size is so small – less than 600 – that statistically satisfactory samples for anthropometric study are not available. They are reminiscent, however, of some of the north-west border tribal Pathan or Punjab tribal castes.

Among the eastern tribes of Orissa the Hp^1 frequency rises to 15 per cent among the Oraon [182] and in south-east Asia the range is from 20–24 per cent. Among the Chinese it reaches 34 per cent with the Japanese and Thai virtually the same: 23 per cent and 24 per cent respectively. In Okinawa the frequency is almost the same as among the Chinese – 32 per cent. By way of contrast with Asian percentages, the Hp^1 frequencies range up to 80 per cent in Melanesia and Hp^2 is virtually absent. The Ainu figure is extremely low – about 10 per cent [244].

The TfC (transferrin) gene is present in most of Eurasia in ranges exceeding 85 per cent, but the rarer genes are significant. The allele TfD_1, though entirely absent in Europe and most of west Asia, occurs in 2–3 per cent of the north Indians, 3 per cent of the Oraon and Chenchu and in 6 per cent of the Veddas [201]. It drops to less than 1 per cent among the Sinhalese but ranges from 2–3 per cent among the Malays, Thai and Japanese and rises to 4 per cent among the Chinese [201]. In the last group there is a rare D chi gene which reaches 6 per cent; it is present in 1–2 per cent of the Japanese and is slightly higher among the Ainu and Ryu Kyuans [268].

G6PD Enzyme Deficiency This gene was first noted among Negroids and it is not unexpected, therefore, that it should be present in western Asia. Most pronounced among males, percentages of this deficiency run as high as 28 per cent in parts of Africa and 20 per cent in some circum-Mediterranean groups. Its absence in the Samaritan isolate is striking and adds to the probability that their ancestors were from Armenian or Caucasian regions where frequencies are low. It averages 6 per cent among the Greeks [180] and drops to 9 per cent among the Iranians [38], matching percentages in central Europe. Further east it drops to 3 per cent in India and rises again to 5 per cent in the Philippines, 7 per cent in Malaya and 14–17 per cent in Thailand, but drops to 2 per cent among the Chinese and is absent in Japan and northern Asia. The percentages may not be reliable as time depth markers if it has as high a mutation rate as has been suggested [180].

Lesser Known Enzymes The possibilities for comparative studies of catalyst polymorphisms appear unlimited, but as yet only some twenty to thirty have received much attention. Among the most intensively studied is the red cell acid phosphatase group. The gene ph^C appears to be limited to Caucasoids and west Asians. It reaches a 3 per cent level of frequency in Iran but does not appear in India or east Asia, where percentages are limited to ph^A and ph^B, but frequency variations may be of limited significance [392].

Intermediate Alpha-2 Polymorphisms Among the newer serum protein markers are ceruloplasmin (Cp), glycoprotein I (Bg) and the protease inhibitor (Pi) and their variants. As is so often the case, it is the rare localized alleles which are important and offer clues to past origins. The data are far too incomplete for more than general comparisons but a few trends are indicated: in west Asia, Cp^A frequencies are within the European range – up to 2 per cent; in Pakistan and India they drop to less than 1 per cent but exceed the east Asian percentages. Cp^C is present in frequencies of less than 1 per cent in Europe and east Asia but is absent in India. Low Bg^N frequencies in east Asia also appear to be significant as well as the absence of both Pi^F and Pi^S [393].

COLOUR BLINDNESS

Colour blindness or red–green vision defect, which afflicts males more than females, is of particular significance in greater Arabia and Irania where there seems to be a clinal gradient ranging from 12 per cent among Arabs to 6 per cent among Iraqi and Irani. The scattered Hebrew communities in the Yemen and in Palestine range from 5–9 per cent. The highest frequency is among the Samaritans with 28 per cent. In south and south-east Asia percentages decrease sharply. In Japan the incidence is below 2 per cent and it is very rare (.054 per cent) among the Ainu [267].

THE GAMMA GLOBULINS

The gamma globulins have attracted considerable attention because of the large number of distinctive polymorphism phenogroups or haplotypes. They seem to fluctuate less than the haptoglobins, transferrins or blood antigens so their use in tracing migrations and mixtures may be more feasible [73].

Table 3 reveals progressive increases in the Gm^a frequencies and decreases in the Gm^b commencing in western Asia and moving eastward to Japan. The south Indian Tamils fall more closely into the east Asian orbit while the Oraon occupy a distinctive intermediate position.

Table 3. *Gamma globulin polymorphism phenogroups*

		Gm^a	Gm^{ax}	Gm^{ab}	Gm^b
West Asia	Irani [13]	0.18	0.08	—	0.75
South Asia	Punjabi [387]	0.37	0.08	—	0.55
	Toda [387]	0.20	0.04	—	0.76
	Tamils [387]	0.60	0.16	—	0.24
	Kurumba [387]	0.39	0.07	—	0.54
	Oraon [387]	0.18	0.02	0.50	0.30
East Asia	Okinawans [255]	0.66	0.20	0.14	0.26
	Japanese [360]	0.67	0.33	0.10	0.30

Table 4 adds a number of south-east Asian samples, but they were tested also for Gm^g and are not, therefore, directly comparable. The numerical superscripts follow the recently approved

World Health Organization listing of over 30 haplotypes which have been substituted for the older alphabetical designations. With so many new haplotypes the number of possible combinations has become virtually limitless and it is quite beyond the

Table 4. *Gamma globulin polymorphism phenogroups*

	Source Tables	$Gm^{1,21}$ (Gm ag)	$Gm^{1,2,21}$ (Gm axg)	$Gm^{1,13,15,16}$ (Gm abst)	$Gm^{2,21}$	$Gm^{1,4,5,13}$ (Gm afb)	In*.1
*South-east Asia**							
Karen	(5b)	0.01	0.01	0.05		0.92	0.11
N. Thai	(4b)	0.02	0.02	0.02		0.94	0.20
Lisu	(5b)	0.13	0.16	0.15		0.56	0.41
Meo	(5b)	0.21	0.04	0.02		0.74	0.48
S. Chinese	(6b)	0.15	0.06	0.05		0.74	0.30
C. Chinese	(6b)	0.33	0.18	0.07		0.42	0.37
*East Asia**							
Okinawan	(9c)	0.48	0.15	0.29		0.07	0.28
Japanese	(9c)	0.47	0.17	0.28		0.08	0.31
Koreans	(8)	0.51	0.21	0.14		0.14	0.30
N. Chinese	(6b)	0.55	0.10	0.12		0.22	0.34
Ainu†		0.56	0.09	0.05	0.25	0.04	0.22

* Modified from data obtained in Schanfield [331].
† Misawa *et al.* [244], p. 284, table 4.1–20 (5 phenogroups).

scope of this brief survey to cope with the mass of detail opened up by this plethora of polymorphisms. The table shows, however, a constant pattern of increasing $Gm^{1,21}$ frequencies starting with the Karens of Burma and moving in an easterly direction to the Chinese, Koreans and Japanese and a corresponding decrease of $Gm^{1,4,5,13}$ frequencies. In the Gm–Inverted series (Inv.), or kappa light chain immunoglobins, there is a similar increase commencing with the Karens and moving northward to the Koreans in the Tungusic area.

The recent Ainu study [244, p. 284, table 4.1–20] appended for comparative purposes, shows frequencies closely matching those of the Japanese, but lists $Gm^{2,21}$ frequencies which are not present in any other Asian series and are apparently unique to the Ainu. It demonstrates also that at least in Gm frequencies the Ainu are quite distinct from either Australoids or Caucasoids. This is only one of more than 20 rare phenogroups identified among 'Asiatic Mongoloids'.

DERMATOGLYPHS, HAIR WHORLS AND PILOSITY

Dermatoglyphs Finger, palmar and solar prints, which first gained world-wide usage for forensic purposes in India nearly 200 years ago, have more recently demonstrated their value as comparative polygenic traits. Although data are still inadequate for a full scale continental survey, the ridge count percentages in the following table will give some idea of their comparative significance.

Table 5*. *World distribution of digital ridge count percentages by categories*

	Whorls	Loops	Arches
Africans south of the Sahara	24	64	9
Europeans	35	60	4
South Asians (Indians)	43	54	3
East Asians (Orientals)	47	52	2
American Indians	43	52	5
Australian Aboriginals	53	46	1

* Modified from [290], table 12.

Hair Whorls Another genetically significant trait has received considerable attention in India – the hair whorl or 'cowlick' at the back of the head. Among Europeans approximately 20 per cent have a single counter-clockwise whorl; among Japanese and Chinese the percentages rise to 36 per cent and 40 per cent respectively. In south and south-east Asia they are variable between these extremes and among Tibetans it is 20 per cent [280]. In the foothills of north India there is a rare double whorl which occurs in percentages up to 10 per cent [194].

Hypertrichosis and Midphalangeal Pilosity The tufting of hair along the upper rim of the ear is a common hereditary trait in up to 10 per cent among males in the upper Indus, the Pamirs and adjacent areas of the Punjab. A possibly related trait is the abundance of hair in the mid-sections of fingers and toes, which reaches frequencies ranging up to 20 per cent in south Asia.

23

West Asia in Biological Perspective

Many scholars continue to use such terms as Caucasoid, Mongoloid and Negroid although they are confusing because of their association with stereotypes. The genetic meaning is imprecise because it is constantly changing; the morphological meaning overprecise because it is too rigid and arbitrary.

Morphologically most west Asians have been classed as part of the 'Mediterranean race' or a subdivision of the Caucasoids, but this represents a type and not a people; individuals so classified are present in most of the populations of Europe. The greatest concentrations extend eastward across the Iranian plateau into India and parts of central Asia. The conceptual type is of medium stature and slenderly built; the head is long (dolichocephalic), the mid-facial region relatively long and narrow, the lower jaw proportionally small; the brow ridges only slightly developed; the nasal bridge usually straight and the chin pointed. Skin and eye colour are light to dark brown, hair colour dark brown to black, hair form straight to deep wavy or curly.

Another Caucasoid type – the Armenoid of south-eastern Europe – is distinguished by a marked posterior (occipital) flattening of the skull with consequent high ranges in the cephalic index. The nose is highly arched and convex, a characteristic often but incorrectly termed Jewish or 'Semitic' – a nose is not religious, nor does it have a language. Arabs as well as Jews are Semites; furthermore, if the Bible is correct, the Hebrews were originally from eastern Arabia, and the 'Jewish nose' is rarer in eastern than in western Arabia. It is also more of a rarity than a commonplace among Mesopotamian and Palestinian skeletal remains of the third millennium BC. Far more likely this mid-facial appendage was carried southward by migrants from the Anatolian and Armenian highlands. Its occurrence among Jews from Long Island to Leningrad is probably the result of conversions of northern Aramaic peasants to Judaism during the later Helladic–Seleucid period and of later intermarriages in the north Anatolian Ashkenaz district during the early Diaspora.

Of some 300 morphometric series from west Asia, 111 were selected for intensive analysis. Satisfactory samples are not available for much of Iran and southern Arabia, but in spite of these shortcomings the results are striking. They tend to confirm the conclusions of many earlier localized studies despite the methodological differences: in this study stress has been placed on collective or clustered distance relationships of ethnic groups scattered throughout a huge region.

There were 19 fairly distinctive clusters recognizable in west Asia. The number of series in a cluster, however, varied from a single highly divergent population – the Ossetes – to as many as 14 – a mixed collection of Turkic–Iranian–Afghan Hazaras and Turkic–Arab Syrians. The clusters separated into four distinctive groups. The ethnic populations and clusters comprising the groups are listed in Table 6; their geographical locations marked on Map 8; and the means of the raw measurements and indices seriated in Table 7. The four-fold grouping and the compositions of many of the clusters conform in general to archaeologically and historically based expectations.

GROUP I: WEST ARABIA, EAST IRAN AND SOUTH AFGHANISTAN

The western Arabs, whether sedentary (Yemeni) or Bedouin (Beni Sakhr, Howeitat and Rwala), reveal a remarkable degree of morphological similarity and resemble more nearly many of the eastern Iranians and some of the Tajiks – even Turkic speakers in Afghanistan – than they do such Syrian Arabs as the Akeydat and Mawali or the sedentary Arabs of Iraq. This may be due in part to the arabization of Syrian villagers, but the primary reason is probably the penetration of southern Iran and Baluchistan by Arabs ever since the seventh century and probably earlier. Today there are Bedouin and settled Arabs on the borders of the Khorasan Desert in eastern Iran, Turkestan and western Sind, and mixtures have a longstanding history.

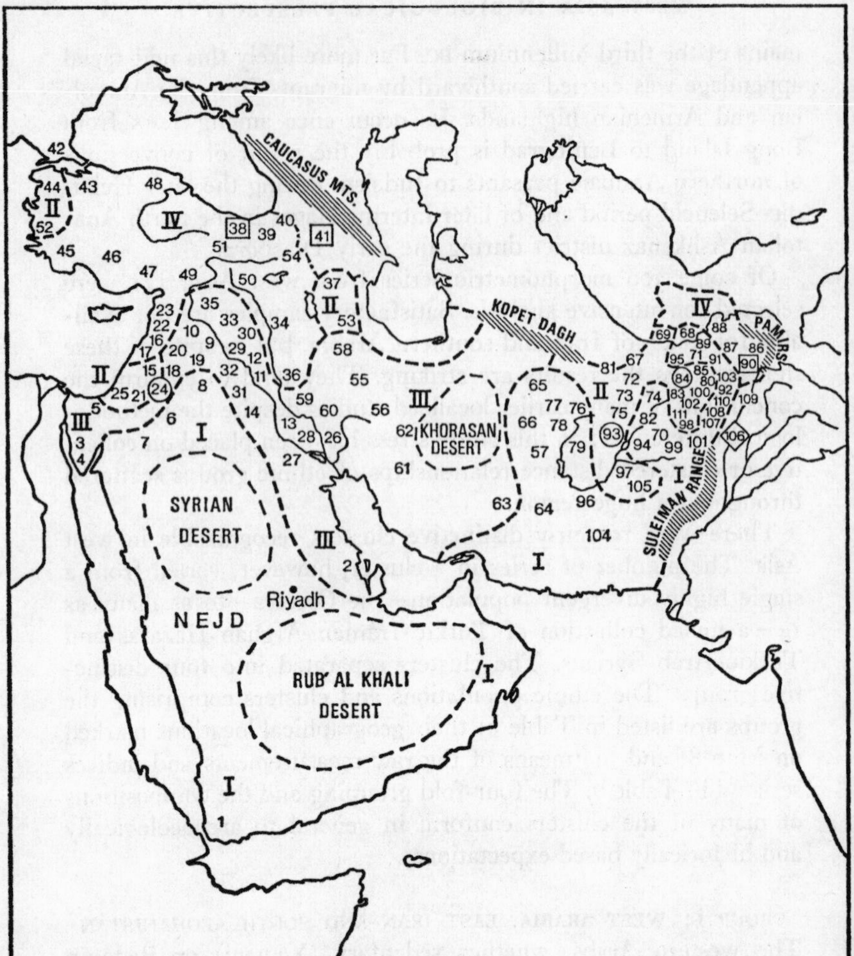

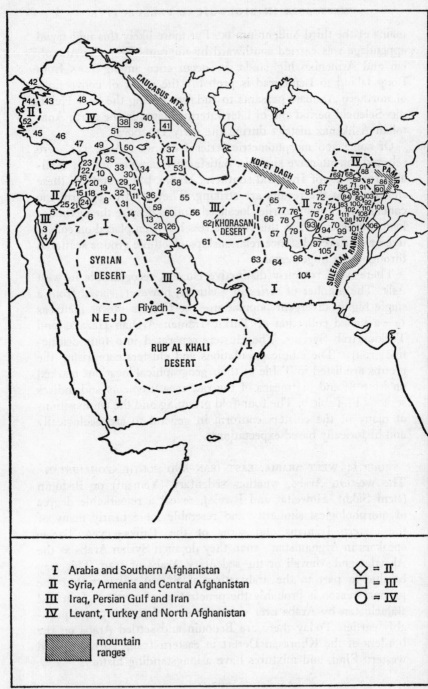

Map 8 West Asia: regional divisions based on morphologically determined groups

Table 6. *West Asia: morphologically determined groups and clusters*

Group I Arabia and Southern Afghanistan		
(1)	1 Yemeni [69, pp. 407–8]	7 Howeitat Bedouin [342]
	6 Beni Sakhr Bedouin [342]	8 Rwala Bedouin [339]
(2)	57 East Irani [94]	79 Jamshedi Irani [94]
	64 Afghan Irani [94]	94 East Afghan Parachi [94]
	65 Afshar [94]	104 Baluchi, 2 s.c. [94]
	70 Afghan Qizilbash, 2 s.c.* [94]	
(3)	66 Kang River Irani [94]	95 Durrani Afghans [94]
	78 Afghan Taimuri [94]	103 Kunar River Gujari, 2 s.c. [94]
	89 Pashai Tajiks, 3 s.c. [94]	109 Kohistani [94]
	91 Kati Kafiri [94]	110 Kafiristan Nari [94]
	92 Ashkun Valley Kafiri [94]	
(4)	68 Turkmen, 4 s.c. [94]	82 Ghazni Tajiks [94]
	71 Mogholi, 2 s.c. [94]	96 Wardak Pashto, 2 s.c. [94]
	74 Besud Valley Hazara [94]	99 Kush Pashto [94]
	76 Aimak, 2 s.c. [94]	101 Tirahi Pashto [94]
	77 Taimeni [94]	
(5)	107 Afridi Pathan [35]	108 Mohmandi Pathan [35]
Group II Syria, Armenia and Central Afghanistan		
(1)	15 Syrian Arabs [336]	73 Panjao Valley Hazara [94]
	21 Syrian Hijane Villagers [341]	75 Uruzgan Valley Hazara [94]
	44 West Turks III† [1]	81 Northeast Afghan Tajiks [94]
	53 Azerbaijan Azeri [92]	83 Charikar Hazara [94]
	67 Afghan Uzbeks, 6 s.c. [94]	85 East Afghan Tajiks, 2 s.c. [94]
	69 Afghan Arabs [94]	106 Khatak Pathans [35]
	72 Doshi Valley Hazara [94]	111 Ormuri Dards [94]
(2)	37 Anatolian Armenians [158]	52 Anatolian Greeks [69, pp. 606–9]
(3)	25 Samaritan Jews [125]	100 East Afghan Pashto, 3 s.c. [94]
	80 Parsivani Tajiks [94]	102 Ghilzai, 2 s.c. [94]
	97 Zabul Pashto, 4 s.c. [94]	105 Brahui, 2 s.c. [94]
	98 Central Afghan Pashto, 3 s.c. [94]	
Group III Iraq, Persian Gulf and Iran		
(1)	2 Bahrein Arabs [116]	62 Isfahan Jews [116]
	31 Iraq Assyrian Aisors [116]	63 Iran Baluchi [114]
	58 Iran Kurds [109]	
(2)	9 Akeydat Bedouin [340]	19 Mharde Villagers [341]
	10 Mawali Bedouin [340]	20 Hama Villagers [341]
	18 Hafar Villagers [341]	
(3)	11 Anaze (Anaiza) Bedouin [110]	28 Iraq Al-bu-Mohammed Villagers [111]
	12 Sulubba [112]	
	14 Shammar Bedouin [112]	29 Iraq Tribal Dulaimi [111]
	26 Iraq Amara Arabs [111]	
(4)	33 Iraq Yezidi [112]	56 Kinare Villagers [109]
	35 Iraq Turkmen [112]	59 Khursamabad Lurs [116]
	55 Iran Yezd-i-Khast Villagers [109]	

(5)	3 Sinai Bedouin [115, p. 237]	5 Taamre Dead Sea Bedouin [383]
	4 Jebeliyah Bedouin [115, p. 237]	90 Nuristan Kafiri [148]
(6)	41 Ossetes of the Caucasus [113]	
(7)	13 Jazirah Bedouin [110]	27 Kish Iraq Villagers [111]
(8)	30 Iraq Mandeans [111]	60 Iran Lurs [116]
	32 Iraq Assyrians [112]	61 Iran Bakhtiari [116]
	38 Laze Caucasians [257]	

Group IV Levant, Turkey and North Afghanistan

(1)	16 Bekaa Valley Villagers [341]	36 Iraq Jews [112]
	17 Mitwali Mountain Villagers [341]	42 West Turks I [1]
	23 Alouites of Latakia [341]	49 East Turks VIII [1]
	24 Druzes [168]	50 East Turks IX [1]
	34 Iraq Kurds, 3 s.c. [112]	51 East Turks X [1]
(2)	22 Syrian Alawiya [335]	87 Ishkashimi [94]
	45 West Turks IV [1]	88 Zebaki [94]
	48 Central Turks VII [1]	93 Afghan Parachi [94]
	86 Wakhi of Afghanistan [94]	
(3)	39 Anatolian Circassians [257]	47 Central Turks VI [1]
	40 Abkhaz Caucasians [257]	54 Trans Caucasus Jews [257]
	43 West Turks II [1]	84 East Afghan Tajiks [94]
	46 West Turks V [1]	

* Number of combined series.
† Roman numerals indicate Afet's group designations [1].

Numerous authors refer to Negroid-appearing individuals among these south coastal Arabs and attribute their presence to centuries of slave trade with East Africa. The presence also of 'elements' identified as 'Veddoid' has been attributed [69, p. 403] to migrants from south India, but there may have been a late neolithic influx of Dravidian cattle raisers from the Iranian plateau rather than a direct migration from India. The possibility remains of movements across the plateau in both directions. Such 'Veddoid' traits as dark pigmentation, curly hair and deep-set eyes occur in scattered pockets along the entire coastal rim from Malabar to the Horn of Africa and are evidently very ancient.

More puzzling is the inclusion in group I of the Kati and Ashkuni Kafiri of eastern Afghanistan and the Kohistani and Nari Dards of the Afghan–Pakistan frontier. Early travellers' accounts of blue eyes and blondism among the Kafiri appear exaggerated, and certainly evidences of Greek biological heritage cannot be specifically determined. The percentages of blondism [134, 94] are no greater than among the Yemen élite or the Khyber Pass Pathans. Their separate identity appears to be more cultural than biological, and such differences as exist can be explained as well by drift as by common ancestry.

In the overlap computer runs with the populations of Inner Asia it is striking that the border Pathans, especially the Afridi, are closer in some respects to the Yomudi and other Turkmeni than to the Pashto–Afghans, an indication of considerable admixture.

Most of the west Arabian and east Irano–Afghans have longer heads and narrower foreheads than those of other groups. In these traits they differ markedly from the east Arabs, who have relatively short heads and broad foreheads. The west Arabs especially have relatively narrow faces, noses and lower jaws; the east Irano–Afghans share these features to varying degrees.

Light reflectance studies of pigmentation are still inadequate for most populations, but both the Bedouin and sedentary west Arabs have percentages of blondism higher than are usually assumed, negating the picture of universal curly black hair and dark brown eyes so commonly ascribed to them. In the composite study of four Bedouin series by Shanklin [339], 10 per cent had mixed blue-grey to bluish-brown eyes; 3 per cent had red hair, 12 per cent reddish-brown and 11 per cent medium brown hair; skin colours ranged to as high as 25 per cent light brown while 20 per cent were light brown tinged with yellow. Only a quarter were classed as curly-haired, one-half had low to deep wavy hair and the remainder straight hair. While the percentages were based on subjective evaluation, they are indicative of considerable admixture, especially among the Bedouin bordering southern Syria and Palestine. There is some correlation between pigment factors and hair form but the figures for nasal profile are more striking. Over 90 per cent have either straight or convex noses and fewer than 10 per cent have saddle-shaped or concave noses and no more than 1 per cent have traces of the inner epicanthic eyefold or show a slight degree of 'shovelling' of the incisors – common east Asian traits.

Except among the Kafiri and a few Pashto groups, the east Iranians and Afghans of group I have lower percentages of light skin and hair pigmentation than the west Arabs. In skeletal features also most of the Iranian and Pashto–Afghans, including the Pathans, are very nearly identical with the west Arabs, and those who differ in pigmentation or hair form approximate closely

Table 7. *Morphological measurements and indices by groups and clusters*

Group	Clusters	Region	Local populations or ethnic groups	No. of series	Stat. (cm)	Hd.L. (mm)	Hd.br. (mm)	Frhd.* br. (mm)	Face* br. (mm)	Face ht. (mm)	Lower* jaw br. (mm)	Nose ht. (mm)	Nose br. (mm)	Ceph. ind. (%)	Fac. ind. (%)	Nasal ind. (%)
I	(1–5)	W	Arabia & South Afghan	31	166	192	145	104	135	124	105	56	36	75	91	65
II	(1–3)	W	Syria & Central Afghan	23	167	186	152	105	139	125	107	56	37	82	90	66
III	(1–5, 7, 8)	W	Iraq, Persian Gulf, Iran	32	167	189	144	112	134	123	107	56	35	77	92	64
III	(6)	W	Caucasus Ossetes	1	170	188	158	119	144	123	118	53	33	84	85	62
IV	(1–3)	W	Levant, Turkey, N. Afghan	24	165	183	153	108	139	123	107	53	35	84	88	66
V	(1–5)	S	Kashmir, Punjab & Pahari	47	165	191	141	103	133	120	101	54	37	73	89	67
V(a)	(6)	S	Pahari Bhotia	10	160	186	139	101	132	116	100	52	37	75	88	72
VI	(1–3)	S	UP Castes & Tribes	22	162	189	138	103	132	116	99	49	37	73	88	76
VI	(4–7)	S	Bihar & Bengal	21	162	183	141	102	129	115	102	51	37	77	88	72
VII	(1)	S	Orissa Castes	5	165	187	143	105	133	117	105	49	36	76	88	73
VII	(2, 4, 5)	S	C & E Tribal Gond, Oraon, Munda	28	159	184	139	103	131	113	101	48	38	75	86	80
VII	(3)	S	S. Deccan Tribal & Vedda	5	155	184	136	102	128	111	97	49	37	75	87	78
VIII	(1–5)	S	Gujarat & Konkan Coast	30	165	184	146	106	134	115	103	52	37	79	85	70
IX	(1, 3–5)	S	Maharashtra Castes	43	163	183	143	104	133	114	103	50	36	78	86	71
IX	(2)	S	W. Tribal & Low Castes	11	160	180	138	102	129	111	101	47	36	77	86	77
X	(1–3)	S	Kerala, Madras, Sri Lanka	22	164	190	141	103	132	117	99	51	37	74	89	74
XI	(1–4)	SE	E. Himalayas & N. Burma	27	160	186	146	104	139	122	105	56	39	78	88	70
XII	(1–3)	SE	Assam, Burma & S.W. China	18	162	186	146	103	138	120	105	54	39	78	87	72
XIII	(1–4)	SE	Yunnan, Kweichow, Vietnam	19	159	185	146	104	136	118	103	50	39	79	87	78
XIV	(1–2)	SE	Laos, Thailand, Cambodia	10	162	179	152	101	139	118	106	51	39	83	85	77
XIV	(3–4)	SE	Malaya	5	157	181	144	104	135	112	103	48	40	80	84	82
XIV	(5)	SE	Onge Andamanese	1	148	172	143	98	131	105	97	46	38	83	80	83
XV(a)	(1–4)	E	Tibetan and Ch'iang	15	164	191	150	107	142	126	107	57	39	78	89	68
XV	(5)	E	East, West & South Chinese	8	163	188	150	103	140	122	106	55	38	80	87	69
XVI	(1)	E	North Chinese	2	168	189	153	103	144	127	110	56	38	81	88	68
XVI	(2)	E	Koreans	2	166	184	157	103	146	126	112	54	38	85	86	70
XVI	(3)	E	Japanese	6	160	188	152	104	142	124	102	54	38	81	87	70
XVII	(1–3)	N	Mongols, Kazakhs, Kirghiz	17	165	187	160	106	148	128	113	57	37	86	87	67
XVIII	(1)	N	Uzbeks & Karakalpaks	3	165	183	155	108	144	131	111	59	36	84	90	61
XVIII	(2)	N	Tajiks	5	165	185	155	108	143	128	107	57	36	84	89	63
XVIII	(3)	N	Turkmen	3	167	194	146	106	139	130	109	57	36	75	93	63
XIX	(1–3)	N	Urali & Tungus	17	160	191	156	106	147	127	114	52	37	82	86	71
XIX	(4)	N	Palaeoasiatics & Eskimo	6	162	191	154	106	146	129	118	57	38	81	88	66

* Minimum frontal, bizygomatic and bigonial diameters are abbreviated as forehead, face and lower jaw breadths.

the Bedouin of adjacent south Syria and Palestine. Account must be taken of mixtures with immigrants from Inner Asia who introduced traits traceable to recent Turkic–Mongol penetrations from the north. The percentages of concave noses are fairly uniform in all clusters – 1–9 per cent – but convex or highly convex profiles are rather unevenly distributed and generally correlated with increases in blondism. Such correlations are seen among the Kafiri, Kohistani and Afridi as well as in a few groups of Tajiks and some Pashto–Afghans.

Explanation should be inserted here concerning the positional relationships of the groups. When the computer proceeds sequentially through the deck (see Chapter 22 for details) it performs the task of selecting pairs from the entire range of west Asia. After finishing the first run, it starts again from Arabia with what is left of the deck and repeats the process. The result is that, while groups I and IV are differentiated from each other statistically, they differ in all measurements and indices except stature (see Table 7). In approximately half of the dimensions (head length, head, face and nose breadths) group III is closest to group I, while group II is more nearly similar to group IV. On the other hand, group III is closest to group IV in the remaining means (forehead breadth, face and nose heights and bigonial or lower jaw diameter). The overall picture is one of three gradients rather than four. To anticipate: the clusters in group II appear to be mixtures possibly of ancient Semites with ancient and modern Anatolians – Turks, Greeks and Armenians – whereas group III would appear logically to be mixtures primarily between Semites, Iranians and Caucasians.

GROUP II: SOUTH SYRIA, ARMENIA AND CENTRAL AFGHANISTAN

The most distinctive feature of group II is the conglomerate character of its composition and its great variability, not only in means of variables but in standard deviations and coefficients of variation.

An example of the peculiar combination is the inclusion in the sixth cluster of south Syrian villagers, Afghan Arabs, southern Pathans, Khataks, western Turks, Azerbaijani (Azeri) of Iran, northern Tajiks and Uzbeks and Hazaras of central Afghanistan. Distinguishing features of this variegated cluster – as of the two others in group II – are the high cephalic and facial indices and broad foreheads and, negatively correlated with these, a trend towards shortening in facial and nasal heights. In other metric features all clusters approximate the means of clusters in group I. A possibly over-simplified explanation for both the motley combinations and high variances is that they represent rather recent and continuing movements and mixtures and are therefore quite unstable genetically; the fact that the Anatolian Greeks and Armenians are closely bracketed with them is in accord with this view.

The Armenians have relatively short broad heads and flaring lower jaws (bigonial diameters); foreheads are narrow; noses are long and narrow – traits commonly viewed as 'armenoid'. A word of caution is necessary, however: cranial deformation was referred to even by early Greek historians, and there is skeletal evidence of its practice much earlier. The effects of cradling and binding have been demonstrated dramatically in the study by Ewing [106] of a series of 209 Lebanon-born Maronites who were cradled and swaddled in infancy compared with 180 American-born Maronites who had not been. The mean cephalic index of the former was 88.3 per cent and of the latter 79.2 per cent. The critical ratio (32.6) was ten times the minimum level of significance. Information on the extent of cradling in other samples is sparse but the likelihood of its occurrence cannot be discounted. It is certainly common among various Tajiks and Hazaras and is practised among other ethnic groups in the same cluster.

Cluster 3 is equally mixed: Samaritans, eastern Tajiks and central Pashto–Afghans, a Ghilzai series and a Dravidian-speaking Brahui sample from Baluchistan. The sample of Nazareth Jews (Samaritans) was originally selected because of its antiquity and uniqueness. The colony is probably the oldest known and best documented example of a highly inbred isolate – matched only by the sister colony of Samaritans at Nablus (Shechem), who number less than two hundred. Referred to by Bonne [32] as probably the only surviving remnant of the ancient Hebrews, the Samaritans are very tall, relatively broad-headed, and combine rather narrow and long noses with narrow faces – characteristics that relate them more to the Armenians than to the eastern Semites.

The morphological linkage of Pashto–Afghans with Samaritan

Hebrews can scarcely be construed as proof of the traditional Afghan claim to Jewish ancestry, but it does strengthen the argument for partial sharing of a common heritage.

In pigmental and other observed traits, clusters in group II have lower frequencies of lighter pigmentation in eye, hair and skin colour than those of group I, although the figures are very nearly matched among the Armenians, Greeks and Samaritans. The Pashto-speaking eastern Afghans and Ghilzai of group II fall into a lower-range category with reduced frequencies of blondism, and the Tajiks of central Afghanistan into a third category. Finally, the Hazara of the central river valleys have the lowest light pigment percentages. They also have the highest percentages of the inner epicanthic fold (average 18 per cent), straight to light wavy, coarse black hair (80–90 per cent) and concave noses (8 per cent) – all of which support the tradition of ancestry traceable to disbanded troops of the Mongol khanate of the thirteenth and fourteenth centuries.

Debets [94] and his Afghan associates, who measured nearly eight thousand individuals from eighty-six groups, point out that various Pashto, Afghan, Tajik and Hazara series are very mixed. Debets gives the following sequence of groups demonstrating directional trends from fewer to more traits commonly attributed to Europeans: (1) Brahui and Baluchi; (2) Jats and Gujars of Afghanistan; (3) Pashto–Afghans; (4) Tajiks; (5) Dards and Kafiri. He states that the Kafiri are skeletally close to Pakistanis and Punjabis and that blondism is probably due to isolation and drift. He also finds a positive correlation between increase in beard quantity and decrease in malar projection.

GROUP III: NORTH SYRIA, IRAQ, EAST ARABIA AND WEST IRAN

Unlike the ethnic populations of groups I and II, clusters of this group are almost all contiguous, the major exceptions being the Sinai and Dead Sea Bedouin [383]. The relative cohesion and homogeneity of these populations indicate considerable genetic stability. The results of the present study underscore one of Shanklin's [341, p. 405] most important observations: that biological similarity is more closely associated with geographical propinquity than with religious ties; he might well have added language and economy.

The obvious point of major interest in this large group is the close similarity between Syrian villagers and Semitic-speaking populations of northern Iraq and the Iranian- and Turkic-speaking populations of western Iran. The separate minor clusters, as well as the group as a whole, demonstrate how extensive and intensive the mixtures must have been to have created a total population with such surprisingly low variances.

The settled Arabs of the Persian Gulf and the eastern Bedouin of the Jazira – the Anaze, Shammar and Sulubba – are grouped rather distinctly with the west Iranian villagers and the Lurs, Kurds and Iran Baluchi – all speakers of Iranian languages. Collectively the eastern Arabs are more similar to the Syrian Bedouin groups such as the Akeydat and Mawaly and to the Syrian 'desert border-dwellers' – the Hafar, Mharde and Hama villagers – than they are to the northern Bedouin of the desert steppes.

The chief distinguishing trends of the group as a whole are the sharp increases in forehead breadths and decreases in facial breadths in proportion to facial height. The figures can be registered as clinal gradients commencing with the plains populations and moving progressively on to the plateau. The means and percentages of other measurements and indices (except those of the Ossetes) are more or less intermediate between those of groups I and II.

The position of the Caucasus Ossetes is anomalous. The sample was included to test the possibility of residual genetic impact of documented incursions of their ancestors, the Alani, into Anatolia during the sixth century AD (see Chapter 7). The results were negative or at best indefinite. The very high head and face breadths and excessive forehead fullness are markedly out of place in the plains and even in Anatolia. The Ossetes, although Indo-European-speaking, fall more closely into the Turkestan area and the steppe country of the northlands. The reason for marginal statistical inclusion in group III was doubtless elimination of the correlated size factor: they are very tall. Their mean stature (170 cm) matches that of the Khyber Pass Pathans. There are no significant differences from other clusters in the nasal index or in percentages of hair form from straight to curly.

Pigmentaion is more erratic than morphometric traits. In eye colour the north Syrian village populations average 25 per cent in the blue-grey or light mixed categories. They are followed in decreasing frequencies by the Sinai Bedouin, the Iraqi and Iranian villagers on both sides of the border and the eastern Arabs generally. Finally, the Iran Kurds, Lurs and Baluchi register the lowest percentages. Skin and hair colour follow much the same sequence, but on the whole hair colour is darker than in the second cluster. The Ossetes, again, are closer to the steppe and desert populations of Turkestan than to those of greater Syria or Anatolia.

GROUP IV: THE LEVANT, ANATOLIA AND THE PAMIRS

The fourth group is confined primarily to Anatolia* with extensions southward into the Levant (Latakia) and Lebanon in the west and Iraq Kurdistan in the east. There is a distinctive secondary cluster in the old Iranian Ghalcha-speaking populations of the high Hindu Kush and Pamir plateau – the Wakhi (Wakhani), Ishkashimi and Zebaki of north-eastern Afghanistan and adjacent Tajikistan and Chitral.

Pronounced brachycephaly with cephalic indices of 83–5 per cent characterize all three clusters in this group, a distinction owing more to shortened head lengths than to increased breadths. The slightly higher nasal indices are probably due to shortening of nasal height rather than to increase in breadth.

The three clusters of the Alouites–Druzes, Pamiric old Persian and the Caucasic complex are more similar to each other than to the other clusters, and an argument for genetic ties is plausible. The Alouites of the Levant, the Bekaa villagers and Mitwali mountain-dwellers of Lebanon, and the Druzes of Syria all have 10–15 per cent blue to light mixed eyes. Their bracketing with the populations of Anatolia rather than with northern Syria and Arabia accords with the findings of several authors [384]. They are undoubtedly very mixed, the result of miscegenation between old Syrian Aramaeans and intrusive migrants from Anatolia – old Indo–European, Armenian, Greek, Caucasic and later Turkic

* Among more recent studies of Anatolia are the comprehensive surveys of Afet [1] and a manpower survey conducted under the auspices of the Turkish Government. Both were concerned more with physique than with the more usual morphological traits and gene markers.

[51, 335]. The same might be said of the Alawiya, but their close clustering with the three Pamiric series is not so easily explained. Unfortunately, no satisfactory study has been made of the Burushaski-speaking Hunza, an unusual enclave of long-lived highlanders of the Gilgit Pamirs.

The distribution areas of the four groups of west Asia can best be interpreted in the light of history. The northward expansion of the Arabic-speaking southern Semites had powerful religious and political effects, and the spread of Islam since the seventh century has been a tremendous cultural force, but the numerical preponderance of the older Syrian (Akkadian, Amoritic and Aramaic) gene pool is evident. Of more lasting significance were the penetrations from the highland plateaus, first from the east and then from the north, but only the recent voluntary and involuntary shifting of colonies and major migrations are genetically traceable.

A number of general lessons can be drawn from the present populations of west Asia. First, the type of economy – pastoral, nomadic, pastoral sedentary or sedentary agricultural – is far more important in affecting gene flow than are religious, linguistic or other cultural considerations. Second, where empires are controlled from fixed bases in densely populated regions, the gene pools are little influenced by an alien aristocracy; substantial alterations result only from large-scale migrations. Third, coastal enclaves of alien biological origin may be explained more convincingly as the result of migrations over thousands of years rather than solely through the impact of local adaptive pressures.

As a test of the procedure used in this study, a second clustering was undertaken using raw data means as variables. Instead of four groups, only two could be determined: these corresponded more or less to combinations of groups I–II and III–IV. The use of raw data means is evidently not as satisfactory, primarily because it fails to eliminate secularly induced differences.

The immediate impact of diet, climate, disease, stress and radiation have apparently not been as intense in west Asia as in other parts of the continent. Nomads such as Bedouins, Yoruk Turkmen and most of the semi-sedentary tribes depend heavily on animals for food and shelter or for trade, but nearly eighty per cent of the total population of west Asia is rural and ninety per cent of the rural population sedentary. The diet of all except a small percentage of desert-dwellers consists of wheat, bulghur, barley and, in lesser amounts, maize, millet and rice. Other plant foods include dates, almonds, melons, broad beans, leafy vegetables and, regionally, citrus fruits and olives. These, combined with clabbered milk, curds, cheese and occasional meat, provide a relatively balanced diet. When deficiency diseases occur they are likely to be due primarily to famine and poverty.

Possibly it is because of these relatively favourable factors that coronary, circulatory and digestive ailments associated with high cholesterol levels and calcium intake are relatively less prevalent than skin diseases or those affecting eyesight and hearing – not to mention the constant threat of windblown viruses and water-borne micro-organisms. The percentage of body fat to volume is 9.4 per cent in Turkey and 12.3 per cent in neighbouring Greece, which has a fat rich diet [99]. Percentages of colour blindness, a polymorphic trait, are relatively high: up to five or six per cent in most of the region and over ten per cent in one or two genetic isolates.

RED CELL ANTIGEN SYSTEMS

Table 8 lists the gene frequency distributions of the ABO, MNS and Rh systems of selected west Asian populations. The reader is reminded that the use of gene rather than phenotype frequencies automatically eliminates the AB phenotypes.

In the ABO system there is both conformity and disconformity in the distribution curves. The northerners – Greeks, Armenians, Syrians, Samaritans and Turks – have high A (25–35 per cent) and low B (6–15 per cent) frequencies; the southerners – Arabs, Iraqi, Iranians and the Taimuri Afghans – have low A (9–21 per cent) and high B (12–25 per cent). The proportions of A_2 to A_1 are higher in the north than in the south and the O frequencies are rather erratically distributed.

If the high O frequencies are attributable to selection against A, as has frequently been suggested, then it might be assumed that smallpox could be a factor, as proposed by Vogel and Chakravartti [386, p. 147]. A careful study of clinal contours among cattle raisers and non-cattle raisers should prove interesting, especially in western, southern and Inner Asia. One of the major discoveries in medicine was the principle of vaccination, which is historically traceable to central Asian cattle herders long

Table 8. *Blood group gene frequencies: Western Asia*

		Somali* [132]	Greeks* [62]	Syrians [40]	Samaritans [33]	Hejaz Arabs [234]	Saudi Bedouin [234]	Iraqi [178]	Kurds (Jews) [143]	Irani [366]	Taimuri Afghans [405]
ABO	$(A_1)p^1$	0.14	0.20	0.26	0.04	0.08	0.10	0.06	0.32	0.14	0.17
	$(A_2)p^2$	0.04	0.07		0.08	0.08	0.07	0.03		0.06	0.04
	(B) q	0.08	0.11	0.12	0.06	0.09	0.10	0.15	0.17	0.23	0.25
	(O) r	0.73	0.62	0.63	0.82	0.74	0.72	0.75	0.51	0.57	0.54
MNS	MS	0.13	0.23	0.51	0.20	0.35	0.37	0.60	0.66	0.25	0.17
	Ms	0.39	0.31		0.20	0.39	0.41			0.38	0.49
	NS	0.03	0.11	0.49	0.22	0.06	0.07	0.40	0.34	0.10	0.10
	Ns	0.45	0.34		0.38	0.20	0.15			0.26	0.24
Rh	(Rz)CDE	—	—	—	—	0.01	—	—	0.09	0.03	—
	(R_1)CDe	0.13	0.45	—	0.43	0.42	0.41	0.44	0.53	0.41	0.61
	(R′)Cde	0.17	0.02	—	—	0.01	—	0.02	—	0.01	—
	(R_2)cDE	0.01	0.16	—	0.09	0.11	0.17	0.15	0.18	0.11	0.24
	(R_0)cDe	0.38	0.05	—	—	0.30	0.14	0.11	0.05	0.04	0.02
	(R″)cdE	—	—	—	0.06	0.01	—	0.01	—	—	—
	(r)cde	0.21	0.23	—	0.43	0.28	0.28	0.27	0.15	0.39	0 14
	cD^ue	0.07	0.10								
	CD^ue	0.03									

* Somali and Greek series included for comparison.

familiar with the fact that those closest to cattle were most immune to smallpox.

The MNS system also tends to approximate European figures and to fall into three groupings from north-west to south-east: (1) Greeks, Armenians and the Samaritan isolate, M = 40–55 per cent; (2) Syrians and Iranians, M = 50–60 per cent; (3) Arabs and Afghans, M = 60–70 per cent.

In the Rhesus system the percentages closely match those of European Mediterranean figures. Almost all groups fall within the range of 40–50 per cent Cde(R_1) and in cde(r) the majority are in the 20–30 per cent range. The rare cD^ue and CD^ue genes – which run as high as 10 per cent – are also characteristically Mediterranean. In Arabia there are other rare genes associating the marginal groups with Ethiopia, Somalia and even tropical Africa – reminders doubtless of human traffic in the past.

Among various Arab groups the P_1 gene averages 49 per cent and the Lutheran (Lu^a) is fairly consistently 1 per cent. The most erratic is the Duffy gene (Fy^a), which ranges from 5 to 26 per cent; Kell (K) is almost as irregular – 3–11 per cent. The erratic frequencies might be explained as a result of earlier African intrusions, but more indicative of the latter is the 6 per cent frequency of the rare African V gene [250]. In Syria the respective gene frequencies generally match those of south European groups and the Turks and Iranians reveal mixtures suggestive of both southern Europe and Turkestan.

To sum up: west Asians as a whole, in both monogenic and polygenic (anthropometric) traits, belong essentially in the European sphere, but hybridizations and in some instances common origins with Africans are traceable to neighbouring lands. Recent intermixtures with Inner Asians are clearly apparent in scattered populations in Iran, Afghanistan and Anatolia; and, as will be seen in the following chapter, south Asian populations can be traced in large part to common origins with peoples on the Iranian plateau and the Aralo-Caspian basin.

24

The Biological Complexity of South Asia

The chapters on south Asia in Part II emphasized some of the seemingly contradictory aspects of Indian society: (1) rules regulating mate selection are not guarantees against inbreeding or outbreeding; (2) castes grouped together as a class and sharing a common traditional ancestry may have quite different origins, both biological and geographical; (3) caste names may bear little relationship to occupations and both may be altered gradually in splinter groups or spontaneously by collective action; (4) social ranking may have little to do with religious identity, economic status or political activity.

These observations imply considerable social mobility and potential gene flow so it is not surprising that, except for stature, the standard deviations of all morphological variables of the 244 south Asian series were collectively lower than those of any other quadrant. This observation is dramatized in Table 9, which lists the raw data means and transformed standard deviations by quadrants and for the continent as a whole. The calculations were based on raw data means but, even when the correlated size factor is eliminated by transforming the means into principal component scores, the deviations follow the same general pattern, except that the face and nose heights of the south Asian series are slightly more variable than those of west Asia, but less so than those of the east.

The people of south Asia are surprisingly homogeneous – considerably more so than those of west Asia. The people of both east and north Asia are intermediate but less variable in the northern than the eastern part of the continent. These results tend to confirm two conclusions which have been noted in the past: (1) a high correlation exists between physique and environment – climate, radiation, nutrition and disease; (2) in south Asia particularly, variabilities are low in spite of existing social barriers which might have been expected to exert more effect on gene flow.

This last point has been demonstrated repeatedly in state surveys in Uttar Pradesh, Bengal, Orissa, Gujarat and Maharashtra. Differences may exist, even significant differences, at caste–class levels and possibly more so in the north and east Ganges area than in the west; but there may be greater differences between socially equivalent castes in neighbouring geographical areas than between different caste levels within a single localized region.

Such generalizations vary regionally in accordance with the effectiveness of culturally or geographically imposed barriers, but there must have been very considerable gene flow approximating panmixia at times, especially in the north-west and extreme south, where strictures on mate selection have been generally less rigid than in the Ganges basin. It seems likely that as each successive immigrant influx descended from the plateau to the plains or skirted eastward along the Makran coast into Sind it was quickly assimilated and gave a distinctive identity to the local gene pool.

In west Asia, where localized populations were not subjected to the pressures of caste endogamy and village exogamy, it is easy to think of local geographic and ethnic groups as breeding units, but in greater India only the tribal populations lend themselves to such relatively simple identification. Usually the highest castes secure mates from a distance because their numbers are limited; and the lowest castes are likely to migrate as colonies in search of economic security. It is the intermediate castes that are most consistently representative of local gene pools, as demonstrated in a recent sampling study of a rural multi-caste village near Calcutta; it was found that all of the tribal caste Santal and 70 per cent of the low caste Dom labourers were born outside of the village. Likewise, 50 per cent of the high-caste populations (Brahmin and Kayastha) – mostly wives – were immigrants. Of the intermediate group, only 33 per cent were outsiders. Such movements are confirmed by biological comparisons.

Table 9. *Pooled means, standard deviations and variances by quadrants*

(a) *Pooled means of measurements*

	No. of series	n	Stat.	Hd.l.	Hd.br.	Min. Fr.br.	Face br.	Face ht.	Bigon. br.	Nose ht.	Nose br.
West Asia	111	55,642	166	188	148	107	137	124	107	55	36
South Asia	244	21,732	162	186	141	104	132	115	102	51	37
East Asia	104	18,239	161	186	148	104	139	121	105	54	39
Inn. & N. Asia*	60	15,920	163	188	156	106	145	127	112	55	37
Total Asia	519	111,533	163	186	146	105	136	119	105	53	37

(b) *Pooled standard deviations*

	West	South	East	North*	Total Asia
Stature	2.21	3.23	3.88	3.333	3.18
Head Length	4.80	3.49	4.44	3.88	4.30
Head Breadth	5.05	3.73	3.78	3.96	4.13
Min. Frontal Dia. (Frhd. Br.)	4.33	2.00	2.71	2.58	3.26
Bizygomatic Dia. (Face Br.)	3.71	2.66	3.36	3.06	3.20
Total Face Height	2.64	3.51	4.99	3.45	3.65
Bigonial Dia. (Lower Jaw Br.)	3.12	2.68	2.78	4.78	3.34
Nose Height (Length)	2.43	2.78	3.40	2.94	2.89
Nose Breadth	1.37	1.30	1.71	1.25	1.41
Averages	3.29	2.61	3.45	3.25	3.15/3.26

(c) *Pooled variances*

	West	South	East	North*	Total Asia
Stature	4.88	10.17	15.06	11.09	10.30
Head Length	23.08	12.30	19.76	15.08	17.55
Head Breadth	23.51	13.96	14.25	15.71	16.86
Min. Frontal Dia. (Frhd. Br.)	18.78	4.01	7.34	6.68	9.20
Bizygomatic Dia. (Face Br.)	13.78	7.15	11.28	9.33	10.38
Total Face Height	6.97	12.93	24.87	11.93	14.17
Bigonial Dia. (Lower Jaw Br.)	9.75	7.20	7.73	22.85	11.88
Nose Height (Length)	5.91	8.19	11.55	8.66	8.58
Nose Breadth	1.88	1.69	2.91	1.56	2.01
Averages	12.06	8.62	12.75	11.43	10.66/11.21

While many inconsistencies and irregularities exist between morphological trait distribution curves and serological gene frequencies, one explanation for the discrepancies may lie in the time differentials for achieving genetic stability as between polygenic and monogenic traits. The dilemma is far from resolved. Many of the blood group systems are interacting so that analyses of their frequency distributions are conditioned jointly in relation to tempos of gene flow and substitution as well as the pathogens of the environment. As Sharma [344] points out, there is a high correlation between diseases and geography, and most of the biochemical factors are highly selective. Where tribes have been localized for long periods of time this is particularly true. Patterns change with migration and changing disease vectors. For instance, the introduction of tuber culture and rice paddies from south-east Asia with associated clearing of forest cover may have resulted in population expansion, but it must also have increased mosquito-breeding areas through the creation of stagnant pools which encouraged the spread of malaria.

In south and south-east Asia where tropical diseases are rampant, immunologically related blood group systems are likely to be of considerable significance in determining time depth of migration and mixture, but they are probably only indirectly related to the morphological characteristics. Many rare antigens have limited and highly localized significance, but serum proteins, on the other hand, especially those having to do with growth – shape, size and adaption to climate and soils – are more likely to relate directly to phylogeny and to the structural as opposed to the protective roles of the genomes.

MORPHOMETRIC DATA

In spite of relative homogeneity, analysis of the data on south Asia is considerably more complex than that on west Asia. The peculiarities of the social hierarchy pose one problem, but the main reason is due to the wholesale influx during the past five thousand years of such diverse populations as Indo–European, Semitic and Altaic speakers from the north-west and Austro–asian, Tibeto–Burman and Tai speakers from the east. Since mesolithic times greater India has been more of a recipient than a donor, a cul-de-sac rather than a corridor, and traces of immigrant populations are not hard to detect.

The relatively limited range of morphological and physiological characteristics, and the consistencies between shape–size, pigment and related visible features, are matched by the limited ranges of biochemical gene frequency distributions. This has made the problem of distinguishing the larger populations less certain than in the case of west Asia. Among the more recent attempts has been that of Büchi [43], who describes four 'groups' which he identifies as original (aboriginal or tribal), southern, western and north-western, although he stresses their continuous and overlapping character.

The original population, represented most clearly in the jungle tribes, is characterized as having very dark skin, deep wavy hair, short stature, long heads, low facial heights and relatively short noses. In the ABO blood group system, A is quite common, B is low in the eastern tribes and O has high percentages among all tribes; in the Rhesus system CDe has high frequencies.

The south Indians of the Dravidian area – mainly along the east coast – have brownish and often wavy hair, are of middle stature and mesocephalic, faces and noses of medium size. In the ABO group the A percentages are low but O and B are high.

In many respects the north-westerners of the Punjab and Sind are the polar extreme of the southerners. They are tall, light-skinned and long-headed. Their faces are markedly long and narrow and their noses relatively small. The ABO frequencies are quite different and variable, and in the Rhesus group the CDe percentages are lower, cDe higher. The westerners are round-headed and low-faced with intermediate sized noses. They are of middle stature, relatively light-skinned and wavy-haired. The A gene has high frequency and O is correspondingly low.

Although differing in details, this four-fold grouping may be equated with von Eickstedt's [102] earlier typological classification: Veddoids with aboriginals, Melanids with southerners, and Indids with north-westerners and northerners. The westerners would be intermediate between the Melanids and Indids. By whatever labels they are designated, if the east is added as a separate area, there appear to be at least five if not six major populations that are recognizable by varying percentages of distinguishing traits and gene frequencies.

GROUP V: THE INDUS AND UPPER GANGES (KASHMIR, PUNJAB AND THE HIMALAYAN FOOTHILLS)

A major gene pool in such a tremendous subregion as southern Asia cannot be clearly defined. The standard deviations and variances are relatively low but some populations cluster more readily with those at a distance than with those nearby. The Indo–Gangetic plain contains a series of intermeshed population networks having somewhat the appearance of a jigsaw puzzle. Six clusters have been identified in group V although none is sharply differentiated except cluster 6, the Bhotia. The first three are confined almost exclusively to Kashmir and the Pahari districts including the Punjab foothills and Himachal Pradesh.

The Khasa of Jaunsar in the foothills of Uttar Pradesh are significantly clustered with the Kashmir Pandits, a self-styled title of the Sikh–Brahmin élite mercantile class of the Vale of Kashmir, who are historically of Dogri origin from the neighbouring Punjab foothills of Jammu. The morphological similarity brings to mind the Indo–Gangetic tradition of the once powerful ruling class referred to as the Khas. No less interesting is the addition of the UP Chattri and Rajputs of Kinaur.

Linking of the rather distantly separated Kashmiri Muslim labourers with east Pahari populations is probably long-standing and may be due to plains Punjabi 'wedges' from the lowlands into the foothills at the time of Rajput conquests. Muslim Kashmiri woodcutters, labourers and artisans move seasonally back and forth along the foothills so that mixture is not surprising.

The 41 series in clusters 2 to 5 include Muslims, Sikhs and Hindus but the differences are mainly cultural, not biological. Much has been written about the tallness (172 cm) and excellent physique of the Sikhs, qualities often attributed to their well-balanced vegetarian diet. In part this may be true, but the Sikhs are matched in physique by several other Punjab populations – meat-eating as well as vegetarian, Muslims as well as Hindus. Some of the neighbouring Pathan tribesmen are even taller. The Sikh physique is probably due to the fact that many have entered professions that have given them an economic advantage over their compatriots, Indians or Pakistanis. A correlation between nutrition and physique holds throughout the entire subcontinent as noted in Table 11, but it may be more noticeable in the Punjab, where there is such a variety of merchants and traders

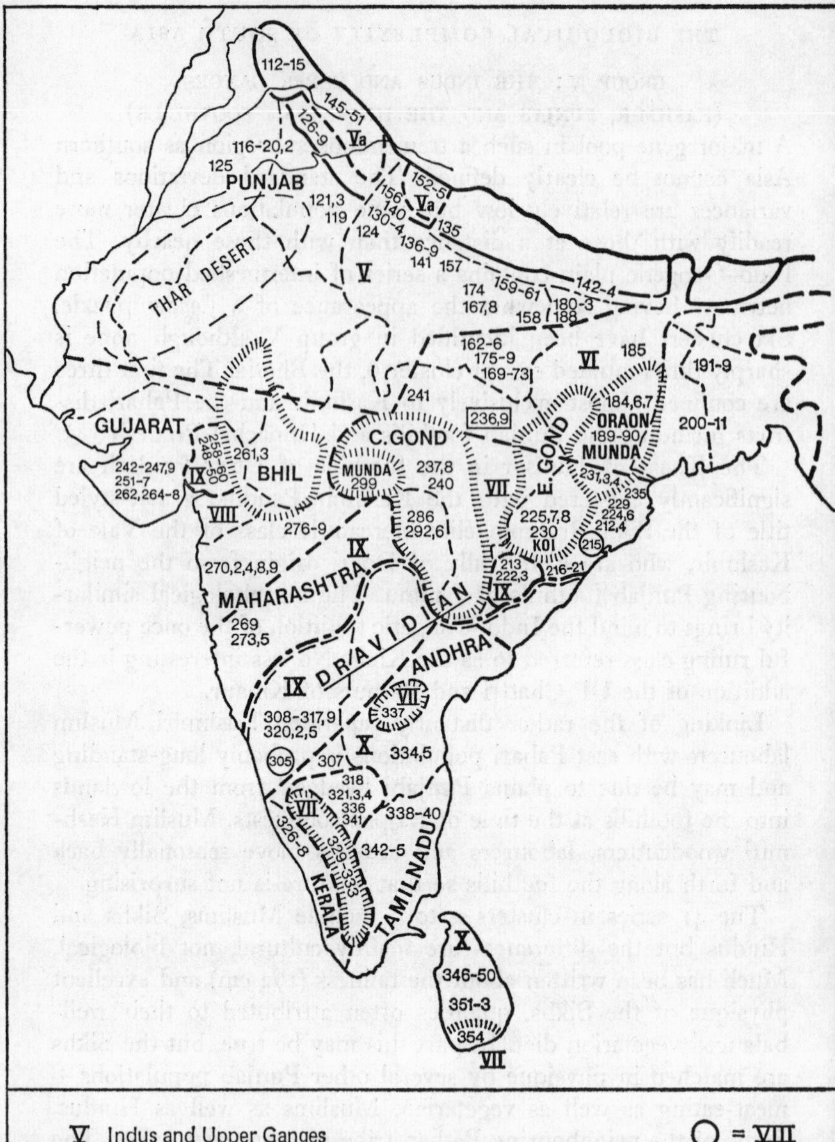

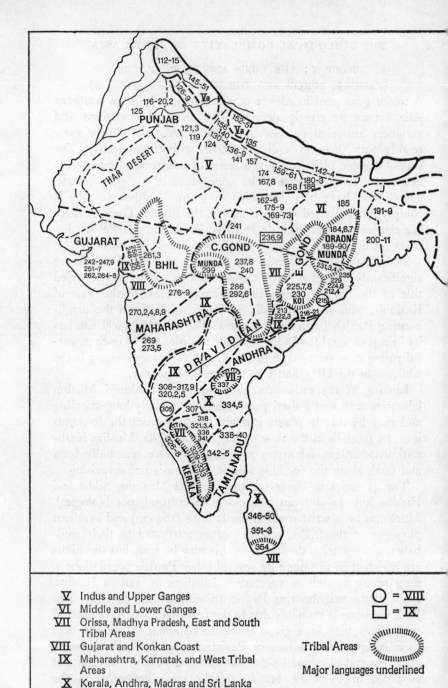

Map 9 South Asia: regional divisions based on morphologically determined groups

Table 10 *South Asia: morphologically determined groups and clusters*

Group V Punjab, Kashmir, Pahari Districts and Uttar Pradesh (Indus and Upper Ganges)

(1)	112 Pandits [311]	161 UP Chettri [226]
	139 UP Khasa [225]	180 Kanauj Brahmins [53]
	149 Kinauri [36]	181 Maithal Brahmins [53]
(2)	113 Kashmir Artisans [311]	137 Dom [380]
	114 Kashmir Labourers [35]	140 Kolita [225]
	115 Kashmir Muslims [172]	159 UP Rajputs [140]
	136 Danpuriya [35]	
(3)	116 Hindki [35]	122 Julaha [35]
	117 Punchi [35]	123 Doab Artisans [35]
	118 Jammu Dogri [35]	125 Jati [94]
	119 Gujari [35]	157 UP Brahmins [140]
	120 Punjab Muslims [101]	160 UP Agharia [226]
	121 Sikhs [101]	182 Bihar Kayastha [246]
(4)	126 Pahari Rajputs – West [35]	132 Pahari Scheduled Castes – Central [138]
	127 Himachal Pradesh Gaddi [35]	133 Pahari Rajputs – East [379]
	128 Kulu Kaneti [35]	134 Kumaoni [35]
	129 Pahari Artisans [35]	135 Nepal Dotiyali [35]
	130 Pahari Low Castes – West [35]	
	131 Pahari Rajputs – Central [138]	
(5)	124 Low Caste Purku [35]	156 Scheduled Castes Shilipkar [35]
	138 Raji [380]	167 UP Bhatu [226]
	141 Tharu [226]	168 UP Habru [226]
	142 Nepal Thakuri [35]	174 UP Jhansi Sahariya (Tribal) [15]
	143 Nepal Chettri [35]	183 Kurmi [246]
	144 Low Caste Nepali [35]	188 Pahira (Tribal) [300]

Group V(a) Pahari Bhotia

(6)	145 Lahuli (Upper Castes) [36]	151 Spiti Bhotia (Tibetans) [35]
	146 Lahul Kaneti [35]	152 Almora Bhotia [379]
	147 Lahuli (Low Castes) [36]	153 Johari Bhotia [35]
	148 Lahul Bhotia [35]	154 Dharmiya [35]
	150 Nyamkat Bhotia (Tibetans) [35]	155 Shokra [379]

Group VI U.P., Bihar and Bengal (Middle and Lower Ganges)

(1)	158 UP Basti Brahmins [226]	
(2)	169 UP Dom [226]	179 UP Kharwar (Tribal) [226]
	171 UP Bhil (Tribal) [226]	184 Hill Maler (Tribal) [327]
	172 UP Mirzapur Oraon (Tribal) [226]	185 Plains Maler (Tribal) [327]
		187 Ho (Tribal) [35]
	175 UP Korwa (Tribal) [226]	189 Munda (Tribal) [19]
	176 UP Chero (Tribal) [226]	207 Lodha (Tribal) [27]
	177 UP Majhi (Tribal) [226]	209 Santali (Tribal) [328]
	178 UP Pannika (Tribal) [226]	
(3)	162 UP Muslims [226]	166 UP Kahar [226]
	163 UP Ahir [226]	170 UP Chamar [226]
	164 UP Kurmi [226]	173 UP Rajwar (Tribal) [226]
	165 UP Artisans [226]	

(4) 190 Bihar Oraon (Tribal) [35]
198 Mahisya [246]
199 Goala [246]
201 Pod [138]
208 Bagdi (Tribal) [246]
210 Bengal Brahmins [138]

(5) 186 Singh Bhum Oraon (Tribal) [79a]
194 Rishi Kulna [224]
202 Muslim Mochi [230]
203 Rangpur Kshatriya [224]
204 Rangpur Muslims [230]
206 Malda Muslims [230]

(6) 191 Dacca Brahmins [224]
192 Baisya Brahmins [224]
193 Bengal Kayastha [224]
195 Sankhari [224]
196 Tili [224]

(7) 197 Kaibarta [224]
200 Namasudra [230]
205 East Central Muslims [230]
211 West Central Muslims [230]

Group VII Orissa, Madhya Pradesh, East and South Tribal Areas

(1) 212 Samaved Brahmins [175]
214 Orissa Kayastha [175]
216 Orissa Agharia [175]
218 Gwala Yadev [175]
221 Kumbhar [175]

(2) 219 Koivarta Keut [175]
220 Kolta [175]
233 Orissa Munda (Tribal) [175]
234 Orissa Oraon (Tribal) [175]
235 Savara (Tribal) [175]
286 Halbi [174]
292 Sonkoli [174]
296 Bhilla (Tribal) [174]
318 Ager [175]
321 Mukhri [175]
323 Jenu Kuruba (Tribal) [175]
324 Low Caste Kuruba [175]
331 Paniyan (Tribal) [57]
341 Shanar [265]

(3) 329 Kadar (Tribal) [326]
330 Kannikaran (Tribal) [54]
332 Malapantaram (Tribal) [57]
333 Urali (Tribal) [56]
354 Vedda (Tribal) [362]

(4) 217 Bhatra (Tribal) [175]
224 Binjhal (Tribal) [175]
225 North Bhuiya (Tribal) [175]
226 Bondo Porja [175]
227 Gadaba (Tribal) [175]
228 Orissa Gond (Tribal) [175]
229 Juang (Tribal) [175]
232 Koya (Tribal) [175]

(5) 230 Kondh (Tribal) [175]
231 Kharia (Tribal) [175]
237 Dorla Gond (Tribal) [297]
238 Dhurwa Gond (Tribal) [297]
240 Muria (Tribal) [297]
241 Bhatra (Tribal) [297]
299 Koraku (Tribal) [174]

Group VIII Gujarat and Konkan Coast

(1) 215 Baghel Rajputs [138]
243 Audich Brahmins [138]
264 Rabari [227]
267 Barsi Brahmins [174]
270 Deshastha Brahmins [138]
271 Chitpavan Brahmins [138]
272 Karhada Brahmins [138]
276 Prabhu [138]

(2) 242 Nagar Brahmins [138]
244 Kshatri Brahmins [138]
254 Kathi [138]
256 Jain Bania [138]
257 Parsi [227]
336 Madigar [142]

(3) 245 Gujarat Rajputs [227]
246 Luhana [227]
252 Memon [227]
253 Khoja [227]

(4) 266 Amraoti Brahmins [174]
268 Nasik Brahmins [174]
274 Khatri [174]
277 Vaishya Wani [174]
279 Twashta Kasar [174]
305 Havig Brahmins [175]

(5) 247 Bhadela [227]
249 Kunbi-Pattidar [227]
251 Miana [227]
255 Jain Oswali [227]
262 Mher [227]
265 Waghar (Tribal) [227]

Group IX Maharashtra, Karnatak and West Tribal Areas

(1) 250 Sunni Bora [227]
269 Yajurvedi Brahmins [174]
273 Sarasvat Brahmins [138]
275 Pathare [174]
293 Dhangar [174]
304 Rigvedi Brahmins [175]
306 Kodagu Brahmins [175]
308 Sadaru [175]
310 Devanga [175]
311 Ganiga [175]
313 Gauda [175]
315 Banajiga [175]
316 Lingayat Jangam [175]
317 Adikarnatak Holeya [175]
320 Panchamsali [175]
343 Kala [138]

(2) 222 Orissa Bhangi [175]
258 Gujarat Bhangi [227]
261 Bhil (Tribal) [227]
263 Other Bhil (Tribal) [227]
284 Agari (Tribal) [174]
295 Andha (Tribal) [174]
300 Koli Malhar [174]
301 Konkan Thakur (Tribal) [174]
302 Warli (Tribal) [174]
303 Katkari (Tribal) [174]
325 Sholega (Tribal) [175]

(3) 309 Agasa [175]
312 Vokkaliga [175]
314 Namdhari [175]
322 Harakantra [175]

(4) 213 Orissa 'Other Brahmins' [138]
223 Pana [175]
236 Malve Brahmins [138]
248 Gujarat Artisans [227]
259 Machi Kharwa [227]
260 Gujarat Koli [227]
281 Teli [174]
282 Maratha [174]
288 Kunbi [174]
291 Dhivar [174]
297 Maharashtra Gond (Tribal) [174]
298 Kolam (Tribal) [174]

(5) 239 Kol (Tribal) [55]
278 Sonar Ahir [174]
280 Shimpi [174]
283 Fulmali [174]
285 Bari Golait [174]
287 Maharashtra Koli [174]
289 Mang [174]
290 Mahar [174]
294 Vanjari [174]
319 Holer [175]

Group X Kerala, Andhra, Madras and Sri Lanka

(1) 327 Nayar [138]
334 Telugu Brahmins [138]
335 Telugu Non-Brahmins [138]
337 Chenchu (Tribal) [138]

(2) 326 Nambudri Brahmins [138]
328 Iluva (Tribal) [138]
338 Tamil Brahmins [138]
340 Vellaja [265]
344 Vannia [265]
345 Harijan [265]

(3) 307 Nadavara Bant [175]
342 Tamil Macouah [265]
346 Tamil Artisans [362]
347 Tamil Cultivators [362]
348 Tamil Fishermen [362]
349 Tamil Koviar [362]
350 Tamil Vellala [362]
351 Sinhalese Badulla [362]
352 Sinhalese Matara [362]
353 Other Sinhalese [362]
355 Maldivians [362]

engaged in commerce between the plains and hills and between the drier wheat regions of the north-west and the monsoon rice regions of the south.

Table 11. *Stature in relation to average daily food intake and nutritive values*†

(a) *Caste populations*

India by Regions*	Stat. (cm)	Calories (K Cal)	Protein (g)	Fat (g)	Carbo-hydrates (g)	Vit. B (I.U.)	Nicot. acid (mg)	Ribo-flavin (mg)	Vit. C (mg)
E. Punjab-Kashmir	168	3,196	92	49	628	341	12	387	31
UP, Bihar, W. Bengal	166	2,674	86	28	532	591	20	604	60
Deccan	165	2,789	70	25	571	795	11	247	45
South India	164	2,192	54	33	422	495	18	434	49

* Pakistan and Bangladesh not included.

(b) *Tribal populations*

	Stat. (cm)	Calories (K Cal)	Total protein (g)	Animal protein (g)	Vit. B (I.U.)	Niacin (mg)	Vit. C (mg)
Baiga	159	2,600	75	1.7	1.1	17.0	59
Muria	162	2,760	80	1.2	1.6	21.0	18
Urali	154	2,410	28	6.2	1.6	15.0	46
Muthuvan	157	2,640	44	2.5	2.3	11.0	3
Kanikkar	153	2,200	13	1.5	0.6	5.0	5
Malapantaram	156	1,850	13	0.3	0.6	6.0	16
Paniyan	160	1,975	53	3.1	1.5	21.0	44
Irula	162	1,860	50	9.0	2.0	13.0	52

† Modified from Malhotra [231], tables 3 and 4.

Tribal castes such as the cattle-herding Gujars and the mercantile and cultivating Agharia of Uttar Pradesh fall within the same cluster as the Dogri of Jammu and the Muslim low-caste Jullaha of the Punjab. The name Agharia is said to have derived from Agra, their reputed place of origin. They are variously classed with the Rajputs as Kshatriya or as upper Vaisya, claiming title to this status as descendants of Khatri women married to Sarasvat Brahmins. The inclusion also in group V of the Brahmins, Rajputs and scheduled castes of Uttar Pradesh and Bihar appears likewise to support their traditions of migration from the Punjab.

Table 7 illustrates the remarkable similarity of the means of the first five clusters: statures in the medium range; heads long and narrow with corresponding low cephalic indices – the lowest indices (72–4 per cent) in the subcontinent. Facial measurements are similar to most of the other regions, but noses are the longest and narrowest – with the nasal indices markedly lower than elsewhere in south Asia and approximating those of western Asia. The general biometric uniformity seems to be matched by the social organization of the countryside.

In a special category is the sixth cluster, composed almost entirely of west Pahari Bhotia. The Bhotia by name (Tibetan Böd) and other ethnic ties are associated with Tibetans of the high plateau and the highest meadows on the Indian side of the Himalayas (see Chapter 12). Morphologically, however, they are highly mixed. On the one hand, similarities exist with peoples of Kohistan, Chitral and the Burushaski speakers of Hunza – among some of the Manchati of Lahul cultural ties are apparent even in tradition, clothing and headgear. On the other hand, the Lahuli Bhotia from neighbouring northern Lahul might be mistaken for the Bhotia of northern Almora in Uttar Pradesh adjacent to Nepal: the Johari and Dharmia of the Milam Valley and the neighbouring Shokra. The Bhotia are so heterogeneous, in fact, that they can be classified only as a highly mixed cluster whose statistically determined similarities associate them with three distinct populations: the Tibetans of the plateau; the mixed Tibeto-Burman-speaking peoples of the central intermontane region of Nepal, especially the Gurkha; and the neighbouring Indo-Aryans of the foothills. A distinctive feature of all Bhotia populations is their segregation into valley isolates, usually separated from each other by geographical barriers which encourage development of many highly localized biological as well as cultural traits.

To untangle the morphological complexity of the Bhotia is a task for the future. In this study they have been lumped together as the last cluster in group V although statistically they should be considered as intermediate between the south and east Asians. The Tibetan speaking people of Spiti and the mixed Tibetan speaking Nyamkat – on the upper Sutlej in Himachal Pradesh – are prime examples.

GROUP VI: THE MIDDLE AND LOWER GANGES – UTTAR PRADESH, BIHAR AND BENGAL

The results of this analysis accord closely with earlier extensive studies by Mahalanobis, Majumdar and Rao [224] in Uttar Pradesh. When it is remembered that the computer has free rein to pick statistically similar pairs – in this case from among 244 series in south Asia alone – the parallels are even more remarkable.

In the first study, using the distance squared method and twelve variables, Mahalanobis determined three basic caste groups: (1) Brahmin (Basti and 'other'); (2) artisan (Ahir, Kurmi, Kahar and 'other'); (3) tribal (Chero, Majhi, Panika, Kharwar, Oraon, Rajwar and Korwa).

The first four clusters of group VI virtually match the three groups of the Uttar Pradesh study, but with many more series added. One minor exception, for reasons already explained, concerned the Agharia and UP Rajputs, who clearly belonged in group V. Cluster 2 is totally tribal and interestingly cuts across all language lines, demonstrating again how changeable language can be. Most important is the linking of the Dravidian speaking Oraon with the Kolarian (Mundari)-speaking Munda.

Variability in Bengal is remarkably low whether tribal, Hindu or Muslim, but there is a significant dichotomy between the upper and intermediate classes and those in the lower social brackets, including the tribes, in all clusters of this group which parallel the results of a separate study by Majumdar and Rao [230] and by Majumdar [226]. In both studies the Bengal Brahmins are clustered with the low caste Pod; the intermediate Mahisya and Goala castes with the tribal Bagdi.

GROUP VII: ORISSA, MADHYA PRADESH AND EAST AND SOUTH TRIBAL AREAS

Repeated overlap runs to determine clusterings that would include the northern half of India with the Deccan demonstrated consistently that there was a strong continuum from Bihar and Bengal southward through Orissa to Madras.

Among the caste Hindus of the first cluster, the Samaved Brahmins and upper-caste Kayastha were linked rather closely with the intermediate castes, Gwala and Agaria of Orissa – not to be confused with the Agharia in spite of their claim to a common identity. Constituting the majority of the remaining series are the aboriginal tribal populations ranging across the Deccan and Madhya Pradesh and bridging the distance from Orissa to Andhra and Kerala. The continuum was apparently initiated by the Keut and Sonkoli fishermen and cultivators.

Results of the anthropometric sorting were supported by a second sorting based on skin colour and 'Mongoloid' traits. In no ethnic group were the 'Mongoloid' trait percentages above the 15 per cent level. Skin colour and hair form varied more sharply, but the primary distinctions of almost all of the tribal populations were in their long-headedness and high nasal indices (78–82 per cent).

Students of the 'primitive' tribes disagree as to which is the most primitive and on the criteria to be used. Some apply a cultural slide rule; others cite the soft parts such as skin colour and hair form; still others turn to skeletal morphology or serological evidence. There is lack of agreement also concerning the mixtures that have taken place and even more on origins; but a close morphological distance comparison in this study suggests that cultural differences may be far greater than biological, and that forest tribes are biologically not clearly distinguishable either from each other or from the lower-caste populations.

One of the thorniest problems in the field of origins has been that of the so-called Negrito, a term applied rather loosely to all short, dark-skinned, frizzly-haired genetic isolates of south and south-east Asia, Melanesia, the Philippines and Indonesia. With these three characteristics and a general infantilism which usually accompanies dwarfism, the common traits are largely exhausted. In greater India the occasional occurrence of 'Negroid' traits – including lip eversion and prognathism – is probably attributable to Arab slave and mercantile trade around the Indian Ocean arc to Africa. Facial features of the few Kadars so designated are actually within the Veddoid and south Indian range, and the degree of hair frizzliness falls far short of acceptance within either the classification Negro or Negrito.

The only 'Negritoid' populations within or close to continental Asia are the Semang–Senoi of Malaya and the Andamanese off the coast of Burma, although frizzly hair is occasionally recurrent in some of the hill tribes of Burma, especially among the Chinbok and Wa [35]. The hair may be tightly spiraled, but none approximates the extreme form reached among some of the Andamanese or Semang–Senoi. Rather tightly curled hair is encountered among some Nagas and Mishmis of Assam and some ethnic groups in the foothills of south-west China. Early Chinese accounts refer to dwarf black-skinned barbarians with black, woolly hair who dwelt somewhere along the mid-course of the Salween River near the Burmese border.

The Andamanese The Andaman Islands lie equidistant between Calcutta and the Semang habitat in the forests of Malaya, some two hundred miles south-east of the Irrawaddy delta. The Andamanese (see group XIV, cluster 5) are biologically associable more with Burma than India, but administratively they fall within the jurisdiction of India. Following the establishment of a penal colony on the Islands shortly after the Indian Mutiny of the mid-nineteenth century, the Islands were included within the corporation limits of Calcutta. For this reason, the Andamanese appear in the Indian rather than the Burmese census, and owing to this historic fact students have usually considered the Andamanese as an Indian people. Studies of their biological affiliations have been carried out mainly under the auspices of the Indian or local Bengal governments and their biological traits are accordingly discussed with the south Asian populations in this study. Morphologically and genetically they are clearly linked with their south-east Asian neighbours.

The physical traits of the Andamanese are so outstanding that others that might be used for comparative purposes are all too often ignored. In skin colour, for instance, many populations in south India, Malaya and Indonesia register pigment intensities comparable to those of the Andamanese without manifesting other 'negritoid' traits such as hair form and dwarfism. In a stimulating article written some forty years ago Fischer [118] attributed the hair form of the Andamanese to mutational derivation probably in Malaya rather than to migration from Africa, Indonesia or Melanesia. The high percentage of the mongoloid inner epicanthic eyefold – a common trait also among the Semang–Senoi – supports this view.

Dwarfism, the occasional occurrence of steatopygia and the generally 'infantile' appearance of the Andamanese – as in the case of all other pygmoid populations – can be accounted for through adaptation to intensive environmental pressures. At birth the Bambuti Pygmies of the Congo are approximately the same size as European babies, but their growth is slowed through hormonal disturbances. Staffe [359] found that, where the iron content of soil and water in certain areas was high, the increase in porphyrin and haematoporhyrin underwent photosynthesis under intense sunlight and this induced mutation. Dwarfism is a common mutation in most mammals of the Cameroons; in the Andamans it occurs also among wild pigs. Growth retardation could also account for the bulbous foreheads [145], although the minimum frontal diameter (forehead breadth) is only 97 mm.

GROUP VIII: GUJARAT AND THE KONKAN COAST

The clusters in this group appear to be a compromise between the conclusions reached by Majumdar and Sen [227] and separately by Sanghvi [322] on the peoples of Gujarat, and those of Karve and Dandekar [174] in their survey of Maharashtra. Differences exist, but groups VIII and IX are statistically very similar – so much so that the first three or four clusters of IX could be included with the first three clusters of VIII. Elimination of roughly thirty per cent of the series would very easily reduce the two groups to a single large one in which there would be a realignment of some clusters and an amalgam of others. The mixing of series from the three states – Gujarat, Maharashtra and Karnatak – in various of the clusters in both groups should be interpreted in the light of the above explanation.

In Gujarat, for example, in group VIII the Meher (Mahar), Wagar (Wagher) and Miana are in one cluster, the Rajputs, Memon, Luhana and Khoja in another; in group IX the Koli are clustered with the Machi Kharwa and artisans, while the

Bhil and related west tribal groups are clustered with the scheduled caste Bhangi. These accord with the results of Majumdar and Sen.

In Maharashtra the main dolichocephalic group of Karve and Dhandekar includes the Maratha, Dhiwar, Gond and Kolam which are clustered together in this study in group IX. The overall conclusions of all studies are similar: (1) there must have been several migrations from the north and north-west; (2) there is close similarity among many of the upper-caste groups – Brahmin and mercantile – who are among the most brachycephalic in all India and are from both intrusive migrant and local sources; (3) the tribal populations are smaller-headed and more dolichocephalic than either of the major caste groups.

GROUP IX: MAHARASHTRA, KARNATAK AND WEST TRIBAL AREAS

The clusters of this group appear at first to be even more of a conglomeration than those of the previous group, but the separate clusters have their own rationale and approximate closely the studies initiated by Karve [174] and colleagues in Maharashtra and Sanghvi [322, pp. 305–28], Malhotra [231] and others in Gujarat which were reviewed in Chapter 9. All three authors noted that marked biological differences existed between the so-called subcastes, especially among the Brahmins and intermediate castes, and concluded, therefore, that the old notion that they were formed by the simple process of splitting or fission must be erroneous.

Recently Gulati [141] has continued the earlier studies initiated on Brahmins and Kumbhars (potters) in Gujarat. He found that there were significant differences between Kumbhars designated as big-wheel workers and stone-slab or small-wheel workers and that all Desashtha Brahmins were similar to some but not all groups in the so-called Maratha 'caste' – a collective term, actually incorporating many castes. Furthermore, some of the same Marathas and Desashtha Brahmins seemed more similar to some Kumbhars than to other caste groups. He concluded that various endogamous groups engaging in similar occupational activities might achieve comparable social rank and similar caste designations regardless of biological differences or time and place of origin. He proposed three or four major gene pools from which endogamous occupational castes have been derived; once occupational integration among castes from different gene pools has taken place – in some cases from the same parent heritage through fission – castes gradually acquired relative social equality regardless of origin.

These observations have led to the notion of various 'sets' of gene pools: (1) primitive – Warli, Bhil, Gond and Korku; (2) Kumbhar (both Gujarat and Konkan); (3) other caste groups such as the Brahmins, Marathas or Sonars. In the face of continuing evidence of complexity of origin and mixtures at all social levels, however, such a proposition will have to be demonstrated.

In Bombay, Sanghvi [322, p. 310] discovered that the rates of consanguineous marriages among the Brahmins and Prabhus were low, but among the Marathas and lower castes they were noticeably higher and cross-cousin marriages were relatively frequent. In Andhra Pradesh he found that as many as two out of every five marriages were either between matrilateral cross-cousins or of the uncle–niece type. Contrary to expectation, the figures for rates of morbidity and mortality of offspring are no higher than those of non-consanguineous parents. Sanghvi concludes: '. . . for a population such as that of Andhra Pradesh, which has had a high level of inbreeding presumably over a span of a hundred generations or more, the frequency of deleterious genes would have declined considerably' [322, p. 313]. He also noted that most genetically determined observations relate to immunological traits and that high selectivity rates are closely correlated with specific diseases, whereas other kinds of adaptive pressures are usually responsible for the induction of morphologically reflected variations. He concludes that morphological adaption to climate seems to be much slower than adaptation to disease [322, p. 306].

Although the first cluster of this group was initiated with the Sunni Bora of Gujarat the remainder of the cluster is quite mixed. Most are from Karnatak – both high and low caste and two tribal series – the Panchamsali Kuruba and Kalar. The latter provide transition to the major west tribal cluster – the Bhil and related Konkan Thakur and the Maharashtra Agari. Cluster 3 including the Agasa and Vokkaliga is closely related to the Sholega of the previous cluster.

In cluster 4 it is not surprising that the Kunabi or Kunbi and the Maratha – the two fastest-growing, highly mixed ethnic groups, who can no longer be referred to as castes – should be grouped together. Finally, the fifth cluster is composed largely of the lower and scheduled castes, whether from Maharashtra or Karnatak and the Kol from distant Madhya Pradesh.

GROUP X: KERALA, ANDHRA, MADRAS AND SRI LANKA

The position of this group is somewhat equivocal because of the linkage in the first series of the Telugu Brahmins and the tribal Chenchu both of Andhra with the Nayars of Kerala. The measurements are relatively close statistically and justifiable by the methods used in this study. Admittedly this is a weakness of the morphometric approach: they are not as close in monogenic traits. At the same time the morphological approach may be more telling than genetic serological comparisons when the series are numerically small and subject to intensive environmental pressures, as may be the case with the Chenchu. Possibly all three groups have a common origin; at least all are Dravidian speakers and from the same general area.

It is not surprising that the Nambudri would follow the Nayar, nor that there should be a close linkage between other castes in Karnatak with the Tamil speakers of Madras. The linkage of the Tamils of Sri Lanka is also understandable and possibly explains the closeness of the three Sinhalese series, in spite of language ties with the Indo–Aryan speakers of the Konkan coast. It accords with the ancient tradition of the islanders that the substratum population is descended from easterners rather than west coast Gujarati. A recent study [184] tends to support this latter argument.

BLOOD ANTIGEN SYSTEMS

In all of the antigen systems the main distinctions fall into the same general divisions noted in the morphometric data: northern, eastern, western among the Indo–Aryans, and southern or Dravidian. The tribal populations are sharply differentiated from each other as well as from the non-tribal populations.

In the Indus and much of the Ganges basins the A gene ranges from 17 to 22 per cent, the B gene is consistently 24–6 per cent, and the O range 53–8 per cent. In the east there is a slight de-

Table 12. *Blood group gene frequencies: Southern Asia*

		Punjabi [276]	Gujarati* [322]	Bengali [41]	Tamils [183]	Bhils [389]	Dorla Gonds [259]	Oraon [182]	Munda [195]	Irula [183]	Vedda [183]
ABO	$(A_1)p^1$	0.12	0.25	0.14	0.18	0.20	0.18	0.20	0.25	0.15	0.06
	$(A_2)p^2$		0.01	0.03		0.01	0.02		0.03		
	(B) q	0.26	0.12	0.23	0.19	0.25	0.19	0.27	0.25	0.23	0.25
	(O) r	0.61	0.62	0.60	0.63	0.54	0.60	0.53	0.47	0.62	0.69
MNS	MS	0.34	0.61	0.20	0.38	0.59	0.71	0.16	0.22	0.17	0.11
	Ms	0.31		0.39	0.32			0.46	0.50	0.55	0.29
	NS	0.14	0.39	0.13	0.13	0.41	0.29	0.18	0.11	0.03	0.14
	Ns	0.21		0.29	0.17			0.20	0.17	0.25	0.46
Rh	(Rz)CDE	—	0.005	0.02	—	0.02	0.02	0.01	0.01	0.03	—
	(R_1)CDe	0.61	0.53	0.66	0.64	0.67	0.81	0.85	0.79	0.49	0.77
	(R^1)Cde	—	—	0.03	0.03	—	—	—	—	—	—
	(R_2)cDE	0.10	0.13	0.08	0.06	0.01	0.08	0.08	0.07	0.17	0.04
	(R_0)cDe	0.05	0.06	0.04	0.01	0.12	—	0.06	0.08	—	0.20
	(R'')cdE	—	—	—	—	0.04	—	—	—	—	—
	(r)cde	0.24	0.27	0.18	0.27	0.14	0.08	—	0.05	0.31	—

* Vania caste.

crease in both A and B percentages which drop by as much as 3–5 per cent, while the O type rises to 63–5 per cent. The greatest irregularities occur in the west.

Among the caste groups of Gujarat, according to Sanghvi [322, table 2], the Brahmins have high A_2 and O frequencies: 2–5 per cent and 60–5 per cent respectively. The A_1 and B frequencies are lower – 17 per cent in both instances. These figures ally the Brahmins with the northern populations. At the opposite extreme among tribal populations, the A_1 frequencies run from 15 to 27 per cent and the A_2 are all lower than 2 per cent; B averages over 20 per cent and the O figures are under 60 per cent.

In the MNS system, the M gene among the Indo–Aryans drops from 65 per cent in the north to about 60 per cent in the east and west and rises steadily in the Dravidian south to 70 per cent among the Tamils. Among the east tribal groups M tends to be consistently higher than in the west where it averages less than 50 per cent.

Most revealing is the Rh group. The CDe (R_1) and cde (r) frequencies in the Punjab – 61 and 24 per cent respectively – shift to 66 and 18 per cent in Bengal and to 71 and 15 per cent in Madras. The trend is continued among the eastern tribal Munda to 79 and 5 per cent and among the southern Vedda to 77 and 0 per cent. Among the latter, cDe (R_0) rises to 20 per cent against a range of 2–10 per cent in all other populations.

Of the other antigen systems, the frequencies for Lu^a, K and Le are within the general ranges of western Asia for the Indo–Aryan-speaking regions. Among the Tamils, however, Lu^a is totally absent. They share the absence of this gene with the southern tribes. In fact, almost invariably when the Tamils and other Dravidian caste populations of the south differ from the caste populations of the north, the differences tend to favour approximation to the south tribal frequencies just as the Bengali differ in the direction of the eastern tribes, especially the Oraon and the Munda.

In the P system, where the west Asian range of P_1 was from 25 to 50 per cent among the Semites and Iranians, in western India it rises to 27–59 per cent among the tribes, although it drops to within the west Asian range among the caste groups [389].

25

The 'Mongoloids' – Eastern Third of Mankind

The visible traits that distinguish most of the peoples of east Asia are so distinctive and dominant that the biological demarcation line can be drawn more definitely along the eastern and northern borders of south Asia than along any other frontier. This was doubtless true before the Indo–Aryan-speaking populations began encroaching upon the Assam sector of the Brahmaputra some two thousand years ago, or even a millennium earlier when they commenced their eastward infiltration of the Ganges basin from the mid-courses of the Indus. There is archaeological, linguistic and historical confirmation of these movements, but much earlier – in post-glacial times, after the Assam cordilleras had become habitable – peoples of east and south-east Asian origin must have migrated westward from Burma into Assam, the Ganges basin and the Himalayan foothills.

The morphological characteristics of 'Mongoloids' have been summarized as follows: straight, coarse black hair; dark brown eyes; sparse beard; complete and sharp fold of the eyelid across the inner canthus and a tendency towards a medial downward slant of the palpebral opening; a frontal and lateral projection of the malars; shovelling or inner scalloping of the incisors; light tawny or yellowish skin colour; and round-headedness. A separation is usually made between a northern population, including the pre-European peoples of Siberia, most of Inner Asia, north China and Korea, and a southern population, embracing the peoples of the Yangtze Valley and south-east Asia. Von Eickstedt [102, pp. 27–30] suggested that the inhabitants of north-eastern Siberia might have been isolated by glaciers during the last glacial epoch and subjected to selective pressures favouring the intensification of Mongoloid traits – a thesis elaborated by Howells [155] and generally supported by Coon [70]. There seems to be no evidence, however, to suggest complete closure of the major corridors for long periods of time or that gene flow was ever discontinuous between the northern and southern gene pools. Nor does there seem to be definite proof of man's penetration into the great river basins of the north before an interstadial phase of the last glacial period.

Most of the characteristics associated with Mongoloids seem to be attributable to natural selection and recombination and to early, not recent, mutations. Body proportions such as linearity or stockiness, relative limb proportions, pelvic and pectoral dimensions, pelvic tilt, foot and hand morphology – as well as circulatory and nervous systems – are extremely variable. Brachycephaly is more common than in Europe or Africa, but the ranges in head form and size are as great and not infrequently associated with neoteny – retention of post-natal traits traceable to modifications in hormonal sequences and intensities. Finally there is the 'Mongoloid spot', a deeply pigmented patch commonly present in the sacral region which generally disappears soon after birth. It is noted in variable intensities in more than 80 per cent of east Asians but occurs also in roughly 10–15 per cent of both European and African populations.

East Asian populations are so heterogeneous that it may not be an exaggeration to say that there is no single monogenic or polygenic trait that is common to all so-called Mongoloids. The search is concerned with frequencies, not with exclusiveness. The only exceptions are mutations which have limited distributions: they are discrete but seldom if ever reach the level of 'racial' significance. Eskimos, for example, are generally classified as Mongoloids because a high percentage have straight black hair and many have the inner epicanthic eyefold and shovelled incisors. Most, however, are darker-skinned than Chinese or other northern Mongoloids and they are frequently long-headed or at least mesocephalic. Their nose forms are generally more like those of north Europeans – straight rather than concave in profile and narrow with compressed alae. In the serological field, also, they show few so-called Mongoloid markers: the Diego antigen and haemoglobin E are both absent, and antigen B is generally absent or the percentages exceedingly low. While the Eskimo example may be extreme, it is by no means isolated. In fact, no population exists which even approximates what might be construed as the ideal Mongoloid.

Based solely on the nine morphometric variables, east Asian samples separate into six groups which are geographically zoned and bear close association to historical traditions and plausible theories of migration and mixture.

GROUP XI: HIMALAYAS, NORTH ASSAM AND NORTH BURMA

The clustering of the Gurkhas (Magar, Gurung, Rai and Limbu) and the Sherpa of Nepal with the Nung and Atsi of north Burma may seem fortuitous, but the morphometric data are matched very closely by the percentage distributions of the soft parts – hair form, inner epicanthic fold and shovel-shaped incisors. The same close linkage holds for many of the other clusters, but not all – especially in Assam, where there are mixtures between the ancient populations of eastern India and intruders from south-east Asia.

Linkages between Burmese populations and those of Assam and the central and eastern Himalayas are characteristic of all but two of the clusters in groups XI and XII. There is no particular polygenic trait that distinguishes the Gurkhas from many of the other migrant populations from south-east Asia. The contrast is between Gurkhas and the Indian caste and tribal populations of the Ganges basin.

In the second cluster the northern Naga are linked to the Dafla and Abor, but the latter belong more properly in an intermediate position between the Naga and the two series from Sikkim. Similarly, the Lisu of Burma are linked only slightly more closely to the Sikkimese than to the Palaung of Burma. No explanation can be offered for the close association between the Paiwan of Taiwan and the Palaung.

The final cluster of group XI follows the same pattern as that of the first in linking the Bhutanese with tribes of Assam and Burma – notably the Maru and the Kachin.

GROUP XII: ASSAM, BURMA AND SOUTH-WEST CHINA

The most distinctive feature of these three clusters seems to be the composition of the second – Karen, Burmese and valley

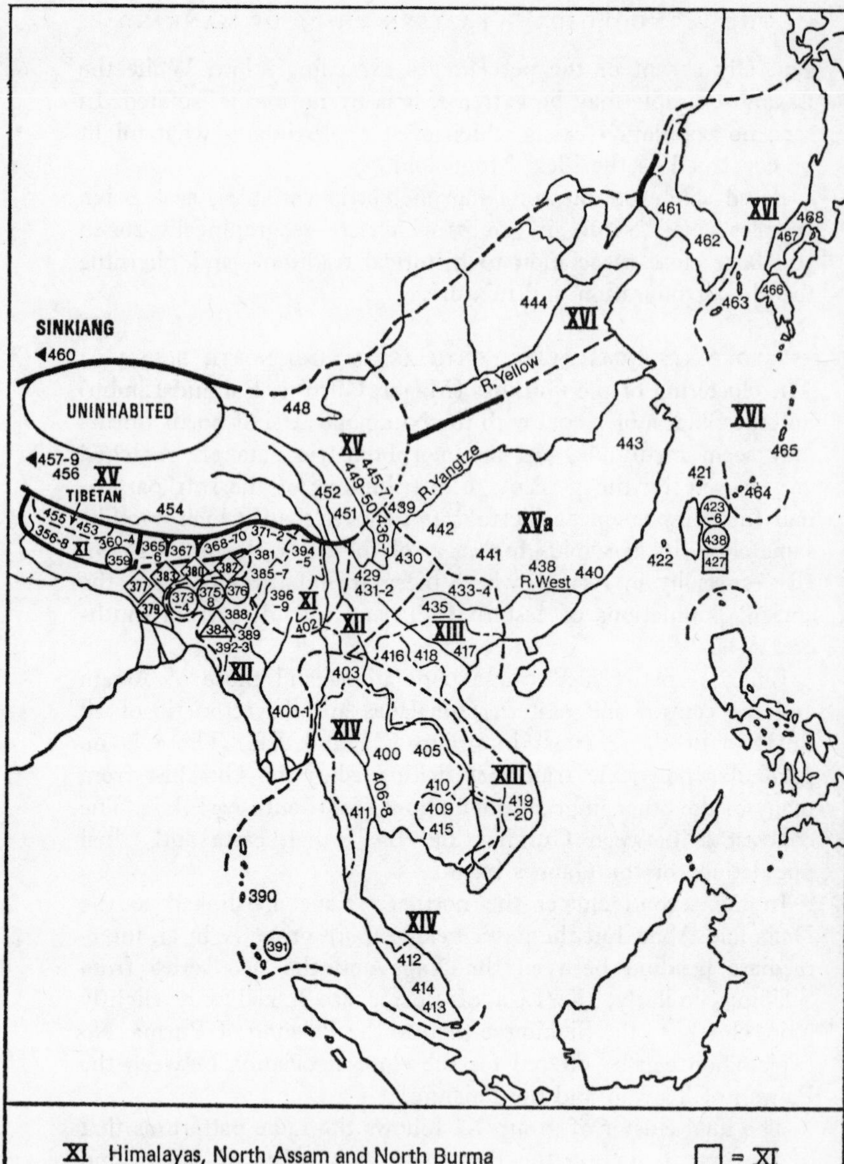

Map 10 East Asia: regional divisions based on morphologically determined groups

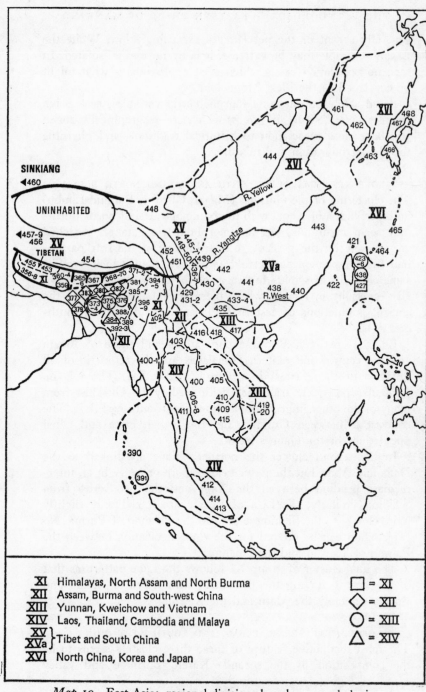

Table 13 *East Asia: morphologically determined groups and clusters*

Group XI Himalayas, North Assam and North Burma		
(1)	356 Magar [35]	362 Rai [35]
	357 Gurung [35]	363 Limbu [35]
	358 Tamang [35]	364 Sherpa [35]
	360 Newari [35]	394 Nung [35]
	361 Sunwari [35]	398 Atsi [35]
(2)	365 Lepcha [35]	370 Padam Abor [35]
	366 Danjong Sikkimese [35]	385 Konyak Naga [35]
	368 Dafla [35]	386 Ao Naga [35]
	369 Galong Abor [35]	396 Lisu [35]
(3)	402 Palaung [35]	427 Paiwan [48]
(4)	367 Bhutanese [35]	395 Maru [35]
	371 Mishmi [35]	397 Lashi [35]
	372 Miri [35]	399 Kachin [35]
	387 Angami Naga [35]	
Group XII Assam, Burma and Southwest China		
(1)	388 Kuki Chin [35]	392 Kamhau Chin [35]
	389 Lushai Chin [35]	393 Haka Chin [35]
(2)	380 Kachari [35]	383 Kaibarta [85]
	381 Mikir [35]	400 Burmese [35]
	382 Ahom [35]	401 Karen [35]
(3)	377 Kolita [83]	431 Shui-Hsi [374]
	379 Suri [81]	432 Lu-Jen [374]
	429 Chung Chia Shan [249]	436 Black Bone Lolo [249]
	430 Pai-Y Shan [374]	437 White Bone Lolo [249]
Group XIII Yunnan, Kweichow and Vietnam		
(1)	359 Thami [35]	433 Pa Miao [374]
	373 Hill Garo [82]	434 Chuan Miao [249]
	374 Plains Garo [274]	435 Ta Hua Miao [249]
	428 Ami [48]	
(2)	375 Khasi [84]	391 Nicobarese [139]
	378 Rabha [80]	
(3)	416 Cambodian [263]	419 Rhade [198]
	417 Vietnamese [262]	470 Cham [263]
	418 Vietnam Moi [263]	
(4)	423 Atayal [48]	425 Bunun [48]
	424 Saisat [48]	426 Tsou [48]
Group XIV Laos, Thailand, Cambodia and Malaya		
(1)	384 Tripura Riang [245]	406 Central Thai [6]
	403 Shan [35]	407 South Thai [6]
	404 West Lao [6]	408 Southeast Thai [6]
	405 East Lao [6]	
(2)	409 Mon [6]	415 Cambodian Khmer [263]
	410 Thai Khmer [6]	

(3) 411 Shui [6] 412 Malay [6]

(4) 376 Bhoi [84] 414 Sakai [333]
413 Semang-Senoi [333]

(5) 390 Onge Andamanese [140]

Group XV Tibet and Eastern Borderlands

(1) 457 Ladakhi [35] 459 Balti [35]
458 Puriki [35]

(2) 448 Amdo [285] 455 Ngari Tibetans [35]
453 Ü Tibetans [285] 456 Changpa [35]
454 Tsang Tibetans [285]

(3) 449 Dawo Horpa [285] 451 Markham Khampa [285]
450 Horpa [285] 452 Chamdo Khampa [285]

(4) 445 Bawang-Gyarong [35] 447 Minya [35]
446 Ch'iang [35]

Group XV(a) East, West and South China

(5) 421 Tachen Island Chinese [394] 440 Canton Chinese [202]
422 Pescadores Islands Chinese [63] 441 Fukien Chinese [249]
438 Kweichow Chinese [374] 442 Sinkang Chinese [35]
439 Szechwan Chinese [249] 443 Kwangsi Chinese [202]

Group XVI North China, Korea and Japan

(1) 444 North Chinese [361] 460 Tungan Muslim Chinese [243]

(2) 461 North Koreans [7] 462 Koreans [128]

(3) 463 Tsu Island Japanese [188] 467 South Honshu Japanese (5 s.c.) [161, 321, 414, 373, 177]
464 Hateruma Okinawans [253] 468 Oki Island Japanese [376]
465 Okinawans [364]
466 Kyushu Japanese (5 s.c.) [371, 247, 3, 410, 9]

Assamese – who are positionally intermediate between the Chin groups of the south Patkai hills of Assam and the Lolo and other tribes of south-west China.

The Kachari are very mixed and undoubtedly sampling would vary from place to place in this widely scattered population. The same comment might be made of the Karen, who are both lowlanders and highlanders, the two markedly different from each other. The few thousand Shan-speaking Ahom are so scattered and mixed that different series of the same nominal group might fit into any of the four groups of south-east Asia.

Attention has frequently been called to the similarity between the topknot hair styling and other cultural features of some of the Naga and NEFA (North East Frontier Administration) tribes and those of the Lolo and related tribes of south-west China and northern Burma, but there seems to be no need to call on cultural traits as evidence of common biological heritage. It may be necessary to point out, however, that the addition or subtraction of ethnic group series from the total used in the clustering process would change the compositions of the groups regardless of the statistical technique used.

The Nature's Groups Method used in this study is particularly vulnerable in this respect since it is set according to a fixed ordering of the series and the computer cannot 'turn back' to re-examine series that have already been paired. The only safeguard is to increase the number of overlap runs. This procedure was rigorously followed in south-east Asia especially and some minor differences resulted, but not of sufficient magnitude to warrant abandoning the original groupings. The real value of the present study, particularly in this quadrant, lies not in precision but in pointing out the existence of similar pairs in such widely separated areas as Nepal and west China; recognizing the power of cultural factors in altering migrational movements; and allowing permissiveness with respect to social class or group exogamy and to particular combinations that have occurred.

GROUP XIII: YUNNAN, KWEICHOW AND VIETNAM

The most significant feature in this group is the clustering of the Garo and Tami – both Tibeto-Burman-speaking – with the Miao series of China and the Mon-speaking series of Assam and peninsular south-east Asia. Another feature is that of the six tribal series from Taiwan – speakers of Indonesian languages – the Paiwan were linked with the Palaung, the Ami with the Miao and the remaining four – Atayal, Saisett, Bunun and Tsou – were set off as a separate cluster most nearly linked to the Rhade of Vietnam. This three-fold division might have some bearing upon their origins; it does not conflict with the findings in the excellent study by Chai [48].

GROUP XIV: LAOS, THAILAND AND MALAYA

The Tai-speaking series form a tight cluster as do the respective series in the other major language groups of the peninsula: the Mon and Khmer of Cambodia and the Malays and Malayan-speaking Shui.

The separation of the Sakai from the major Malayan population and from the Semang–Senoi is understandable, but the inclusion of the Bhoi presents a problem. They are Mon speakers, adjacent to the Khasi and Rabha of Assam (group XIII). The skin colour, hair form and eyefold percentages should probably associate them more closely with the Assam populations.

The Andamanese were included in this group because of their morphological and genetic linkages with south-east Asians (see Chapter 24).

GROUP XV: TIBET, WEST AND SOUTH CHINA

The people of the high central plateau present a problem, but ties with populations adjacent to Tibet would be expected. The Ladakh–Baltistan cluster is definitely mixed with Dardic and Turkic populations of Kashmir and Sinkiang respectively, while the main Tibetan clusters are more closely allied to the east Tibetan border 'tribal' groups – the Gyarong and Ch'iang – and to the Chinese as a whole rather than to Mongol, Uighur or Kirghiz populations of inner Asia, although the Tibetans of Amdo are secondarily linked with the Mongols. The metric data and percentages of visible Mongoloid traits follow the same general pattern.

GROUP XVI: EAST ASIA – NORTH CHINA, KOREA AND JAPAN (THE INTERMEDIATE POPULATIONS)

The classic division of Mongoloids into northern (Tungusic, Altaic, palaeo-Asiatic and north Chinese) and southern (south Chinese and south-east Asian) appears to be a most arbitrary procedure. Repeated overlap runs of all series (164) in the northern and east Asian quadrants reinforces the general impression of a genetic continuum extending throughout conventional north China, part of the Yangtze basin, Korea and Japan. Within this geographic range the Koreans and the Chinese of the Yellow and Yangtze basins appear to be genetically more stabilized than the Japanese. Overall, however, the populations cluster readily as a separate continental subregion roughly intermediate between the 'northern' and 'southern' Mongoloids. The designation 'east Asians' is possibly the most appropriate geographical label for this gigantic gene pool – the greatest in the world by far – but typologically they might appropriately be referred to as the 'central Mongoloids'. The populations certainly fit into an intermediate category.

NORTH CHINA

Within the Chinese population the northerners are intermediate between the southerners and the people of Sinkiang, Mongolia and the eastern woodlands. Their intermediate position is most clearly seen in the cephalic and nasal indices and corresponding measurements. The closest approximation seems to be with the Uighur and the Tibetans.

In pigmentation and other observable traits the north Chinese are also more similar to the people of Sinkiang and some of the Tungusic populations than to the southerners. In eye colour, 20 per cent are mixed grey-blue or grey-brown, 47 per cent light to medium brown and 33 per cent dark brown [35]. Skin colour is equally significant. Over 80 per cent have quite light pigmentation on the unexposed volar or inner surface of the arm, and the remainder are light medium brown – comparable to the majority of Chinese of south China. The yellowish tinge among most east Asians is due mainly to the number and position of pigment granules and only secondarily to variations in lipoproteins. Hair colour is over 95 per cent black and the remainder dark brown, but 31 per cent of the black hair is tinged with a visible reddish hue. In hair form, 95 per cent have straight hair and roughly 5 per cent have light wavy to deep wavy hair – the latter mainly correlated with other traits suggesting ancient admixtures. Among the Mongols, Vlcek [385] noted that almost all of his Khalka series had straight black hair while over 40 per cent had mixed grey-brown or grey-blue eyes and there were marked differences between unexposed and exposed skin colour – roughly the same as among the north Chinese.

Among other visible traits of the north Chinese, the inner epicanthic eyefold is absent in 11 per cent of the population and 7 per cent have no shovelling of the incisors. Over 40 per cent have straight nasal bridge profiles and in 20 per cent there is marked convexity. Southern Chinese approximate their non-Chinese neighbours – notably the Miao and Thai–Shan – more closely than they do the northerners.

KOREA

Prehistoric skeletal remains from Korea are few and not very helpful, but the close similarity between living Koreans and the older Chinese and Manchu populations of north China is striking. The peoples of Korea appear to be relatively the least changed of the three since neolithic times – far less so than the present-day peoples of Manchuria, who are overwhelmingly Chinese. The Koreans probably approximate quite closely the prehistoric Lungshanoid population of the lower Yellow River basin.

In both morphological and observed traits the Koreans as a whole are intermediate between the north Chinese and the Tungusic populations, but within Korea provincial studies [187] indicate a closer approximation of the west coastal inhabitants to the Chinese and the east coastal and northern inhabitants to their Tungusic neighbours of the lower Amur. The Koreans are positionally closer to the people of inner and northern Asia than to the majority population of Japan.

Straight black hair is characteristic of over 95 per cent of the Koreans; the inner epicanthic eyefold is absent in about 15 per cent and shovel-shaped incisors are absent in about 10 per cent. Probably Koreans as well as Chinese are undergoing secular trend changes similar to those of the Japanese.

JAPAN

The Japanese have always been conscious of their shortness of stature and smallness of body, in spite of the prodigious average size of the professional wrestlers, a select few who are recruited in childhood from promising candidates and entered into special schools which maintain strict dietary and training schedules.

In a recent article Kimura [181] has summarized the transformations that have taken place among Japanese since the turn of the century. The mean stature of male adult conscripts (aged eighteen and over) was 156cm in a government survey made in 1883. The mean stature today is approximately 168cm, or an increase of 12cm in less than a hundred years or roughly three generations. A graphed curve indicates an acceleration rather than a tapering off of the trend. The tempo of change now exceeds that among Americans of Japanese ancestry in Hawaii and California and even the general secular trend in the United States as a whole.

Simultaneously, according to studies by Suzuki [368] there has been a rapid trend toward increasing roundheadedness. He has traced the brachycephalization process since the Kamakura period – roughly six hundred years – and notes a rise in the cephalic index of roughly 3 per cent up to the Meiji period which commenced in 1868, and noted that the cephalic index of students at the University of Tokyo had increased from 80.8 per cent in 1917 to 84.1 per cent in 1944.

These stature and cephalic index changes are attributed by Japanese scholars to urbanization and modernization of living habits, including sports, nutrition and increased exogamy, implying heterosis or hybrid vigour as a result of outbreeding. In Europe and America diet, rather than living habits, is usually considered to be the primary factor inducing secular growth, and no satisfactory proof has been advanced supporting the argument for heterosis.

The results of many of these studies raise questions, however, about the value of direct comparisons between raw data sources. The use of transformed variables significantly reduces the impact of the size factor, but it was mainly to avoid undue skewing of statistical results from the changes that have been occurring that sample series were selected in the present study from areas less influenced by the modernization trend. The current mean national cephalic index compiled initially on a regional basis remains between 81 and 82 per cent for Japanese. It is possible that a special selection factor may be operating in the highly transient student population used in Suzuki's study.

The Japanese, like the Chinese and Koreans, have straight black hair in nearly 90 per cent of the population; 8–10 per cent absence of inner epicanthic eyefold; and roughly 15 per cent absence of shovelled incisors. These have not shown significant recent changes. Regional differences do exist, more so probably than in Korea or north China, but they may be attributable to secular trends and migration rather than selection.

In addition to the series of Japanese from Honshu and Kyushu, three from marginal territories in east Asia are added to this cluster: two from the Ryukyu (Okinawa) chain and one from the Tsu Islands. The fishing villages of Tsu have had a long history of ties with Korea, especially with Cheju (Quelpart) Island and the coastal strip of south Korea which, more than a millennium ago, formed the Japanese-administered region of Mimana. It is not surprising that the Tsu populations would be intermediate between the Japanese and the Koreans.

The Okinawans have been studied intensively but no firm conclusions have been reached. The population differs from island to island with a major divide separating the people of the central and north insular groups from the southern or Miyako population. The inhabitants of the northern and central islands are generally intermediate between the Japanese of Kyushu and populations of the east China coast, whereas the islanders of the southern group are morphologically and in genetic traits closer to the Indonesian-speaking tribes (Takasago) of the Taiwan mountainous interior.

Attempts have been made without much success to link the north Okinawans with the Ainu. In the ABO group, for example, the gene frequencies are: p 28 per cent, q 16 per cent, and r 57 per cent [254], which are fairly close to Ainu percentages, but in the MNS system they approximate the Japanese more closely. In pigmentation and hair form, inner epicanthic eyefold and related Mongoloid traits the Okinawans as a whole are very close to the Japanese.

BLOOD GROUP ANTIGENS

Only a few series have been selected from among the many available, but probably less is known about the non-Chinese populations of China and south-east Asia than about the eastern populations.

In the ABO system there is a high degree of consistency in the O gene, which ranges from 60 to 70 per cent in south-east Asia and drops to 50–60 per cent in the northern part of the continent. The B percentages are lower in south-east and east Asia than in India but rise to 37 per cent among the Mongols. Conversely, the percentages of A are relatively higher than B in east Asia but are not as variable. The range in all groups is 15–30 per cent.

In the MNS system M ranges from 57 to 66 per cent in south-east Asia and drops to 49 per cent among Koreans, 53 per cent among Japanese and 58 per cent among Chinese. Among the Mongols it rises to 61 per cent. The Rh system is more erratic. Among the Tibeto–Burman Riang of Assam 82 per cent are CDe (R_1) while cde (r) is absent. There is a steady decline eastward with lows of 62 per cent in CDe (R_1) among the Japanese, 58 per cent among Ainu and 51 per cent among the Mongols. Concurrently,

Table 14. *Blood group gene frequencies: Eastern Asia*

		Assam Riang [193]	Viet-namese [162]	Thai [287]	South Chinese [250]	Japanese [244]	Korean [401]	Ainu [244]	Kalmuk Mongol [291]	Tibetan [44]
ABO	$(A_1)p^1$	0.22	0.19	0.15	0.20	0.30	0.22	0.25	0.21	0.14
	$(A_2)p^2$				—		—		0.01	
	(B)q	0.33	0.13	0.26	0.17	0.16	0.21	0.16	0.37	0.21
	(O)r	0.45	0.68	0.59	0.63	0.54	0.57	0.59	0.41	0.65
MNS	MS	0.57	0.61	0.66	0.58	0.04	0.49	0.06	0.61	0.57
	Ms					0.49		0.40		
	NS	0.43	0.39	0.34	0.42	0.02	0.51	0.10	0.39	0.43
	Ns					0.46		0.44		
Rh	(Rz)CDE	0.03	0.05	0.02	—	0.003	0.01	0.003	0.05	—
	(R_1)CDe	0.82	0.76	0.75	0.74	0.65	0.62	0.58	0.51	0.59
	(R′)Cde	—	—	—	—	0.01	—	—	—	—
	(R_2)cDE	0.12	0.17	0.11	0.19	0.26	0.31	0.36	0.25	0.38
	(R_0)cDe	0.03	—	0.11	0.04	0.02	0.06	0.06	0.03	0.03
	(R″)cdE	—	—	—	—	0.03	0.03	—	—	—
	(r)cde	—	0.02	—	0.05	0.03	—	—	0.16	—

there are increases in cDE (R_2) from 12 per cent among the Riang to 26 per cent among the Japanese, 31 per cent among Koreans and 36 per cent among Ainu. Among the Mongols it drops slightly to 25 per cent but increases to a high of 38 per cent among Tibetans. The cde (r) Rh− negative gene is absent or registers less than 1 per cent in all groups except the Mongols, among whom it reaches a high of 16 per cent. In Assam and the Himalayan foothills all three antigen systems approximate in general the distributions of the Riang of Assam and the Vietnamese.

Information is quite inadequate for useful comparison, especially among the Tibeto-Burman and other minority populations of south-east Asia, but average frequencies among the larger populations – Thai, Chinese, Korean and Japanese – are instructive. P_1 drops to an extreme low of 17 per cent, Lu^a and K are totally absent, and the Lewis gene (Le) is 76 per cent – very close to the European figure. Duffy (Fy^a) rises to a record 90 per cent and Jk^a drops to 31 per cent. Characteristic of Asian populations is the Diego gene (Di^a), which ranges from 0 per cent to slightly over 10 per cent [124, pp. 45–7].

26

Gene Pools of Inner Asia* and the Northlands

It may appear over-ambitious to try to determine the gene pools of any of the subregions of the northlands or to equate them with populations. The term 'gene pool' itself may convey far too great a sense of genetic calm than seems likely to have existed in a region that has characteristically alternated between periods of violent warfare and temporary peace.

Around the perimeter the populations have become relatively stable, especially the Turkmen and Tajiks in the south-west, the Ainu in the east and the Eskimo, Koryak and Chukchi in the north-east. The greatest genetic disturbances have occurred in the central regions, where seasonal tides of nomadic humanity moved across the vast stretches of the steppelands and taiga or eddied into the foothill valleys of the mountain ranges and oasis trading centres.

That the zones of greatest variability have been in the vast central expanses is not surprising, nor that they should have been concentrated in the main areas of attraction: the ore-rich ranges of the Baikal fault-line; the game-rich forests of the taiga; the grasslands of the steppe country, and the booty-laden traffic lanes of the trade routes. It is these natural and artificial resources which have changed hands most frequently and been subjected to the dual processes of gene flow and acculturation during the three to four thousand years of spectacular conquest and exploitation that witnessed the rise and fall of the nomadic empires.

The majority of the 'Mongoloid' hordes who swept across half the known world were certainly not just Mongols but a medley

* With the exception of Tibet (see Chapter 25).

of assorted allies and mercenaries whose ethnic and biological heritages must have included a tremendous range from European to Chinese.

In spite of their close association during the past two millennia, there is no justification for concluding that a correlation exists between Mongoloid traits and grassland nomadism. On the contrary, pastoral nomadism was probably initiated by the early Indo–European-speaking populations of the Volga and Aralo–Caspian basins at a time when the 'Mongoloid' populations were confined largely to agricultural and hunting pursuits in the Yellow River basin and the forested regions of the taiga and eastern woodlands There is evidence that mixtures took place between these early northern migrants from Europe and the Palaeoasiatic speakers of central and eastern Siberia. Later there was a reversal of the eastward movement after considerable gene flow had taken place in both directions.

The fascinating task of unravelling the genetic threads of the past in an area twice the size of Europe but with less than ten per cent of the population has only just begun, but even in the little that is known many of the traces of man's ancient biological and cultural past – affecting the entire range of both the Old and New Worlds – are tangibly and often visibly present.

The fifty-one series selected for biometric analysis clustered into three groups – two concentrated almost exclusively in the 'intermediate desert–steppe zone' of Inner Asia, and the third mainly in the taiga–tundra zone.

Overlap runs to test the validity of the initial clustering of the Inner and north Asian series with those of west Asia revealed that, along the western border, the old Iranic-speaking Wakhani – who live in the gooseneck corridor between the Pamir ranges of Tajikistan and the Hindu Kush watershed – are very close morphologically to the Uighur of Sinkiang. Similarly, the Turkic groups of western Asia clustered with those of Turkestan. More interesting was the distant clustering of the Levantine Alawiya with the Tajiks of Tajikistan and of the Pathan Afridi with the combined Turkmeni. It might be speculated that these represent considerable gene flow between Anatolia and Armenia to the south and Turkmenistan to the north.

At the opposite extreme of the northern quadrant – Inner Asia and especially the region known historically as Central Asia –

the problem of sample series selection was exceedingly difficult. Many of the separate data series were so much alike that in a few instances combining was possible. In most cases selection was based on regional representation to achieve balanced coverage, or for some historic purpose as with the Tajiks of the Yagnobi Valley. Care was taken to select representative samples wherever possible, but the results can only be taken as tentative.

Unfortunately, few studies have been made of ethnic groups in political Sinkiang (Chinese Turkestan), whereas more than two hundred groups have been studied in the autonomous republics of Soviet Turkestan. The imbalance is the more distressing as it was precisely in the Sinkiang–Mongolian heart of Inner Asia that so much of the drama of the nomadic empires was enacted. There was also considerable movement and displacement of splinter groups in both directions across the Russian–Chinese border during the imperial days of the czars and the Manchu emperors and some exchanges have taken place during the past decades under communist regimes. Perhaps it will never be possible to reconstruct from existing populations the sequence of migrations in those areas.

In spite of these uncertainties, high correlations exist between the clusters and their language affiliations. Many apparent inconsistencies can be rationalized from archaeological data, historically documented migrations and wholesale language and religious conversions. All northern quadrant border populations touching on other major segments of Asia appear to be less differentiated than those of other quadrant borders.

GROUP XVII: SINKIANG AND MONGOLIA

In the first cluster of this group the close association of the Turkic-speaking eastern (Oirot) Kazakhs and Kirghiz of the Alai Valley in the Kirghiz Republic with the Mongol-speaking Buriats is in keeping with the history of the latter, who are a late amalgam of numerous splinter Turkic groups incorporated into the expanding Mongol Buriat nation. The inclusion of the Gilyaks, however, was unexpected and seemingly out of place, but may reflect possible ancient genetic ties with western Siberian populations. A possible rationale is given in connection with Ainu origins, summarized later in this chapter.

The second cluster is entirely Turkic-speaking and largely

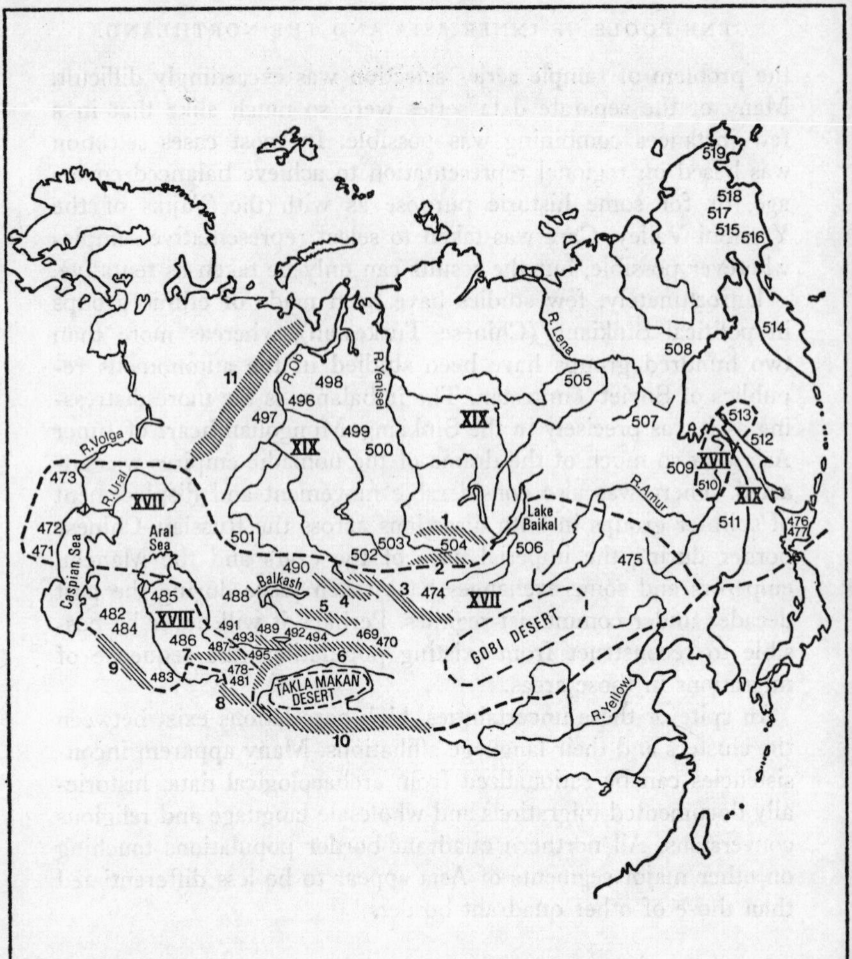

Map 11 North Asia: regional divisions based on morphologically determined groups

Table 15 *North Asia: morphologically determined groups and clusters*

Group XVII Mongolia, Sinkiang and Kazakhstan		
(1)	490 Eastern Kazakhs [128]	506 Buryat [417]
	495 Alai Valley Kirghiz [243]	513 Nivkhi (Gilyak) [210]
(2)	469 Aksu Raion Uigur [128]	489 Alma Ata Kazakhs [87]
	470 Alma Ata Uigur [207]	493 Ferghana Kirghiz [243]
	488 Steppe Kazakhs (3 clans) [87]	
(3)	471 Kumyk [242]	475 Eastern Mongols [203]
	472 Nogai [242]	492 T'ien Shan Kirghiz [243]
	473 Kalmuk Sarts [243]	494 Sayak Kirghiz [243]
	474 Khalka Mongols [417]	510 Nanay (Goldi) [203]
Group XVIII Turkestan and Tajikistan		
(1)	485 Karakalpaks [412]	487 Tashkent Uzbeks [271]
	486 Samarkand Uzbeks [271]	
(2)	478 Pamiri Shugnan Tajiks [272]	481 Surkhan Tajiks [252]
	479 Yagnobi Tajiks [272]	491 Kipchak Kirghiz [415]
	480 Karategin Tajiks [270]	
(3)	482 Yomudi Turkomen [413]	484 Total Turkomen [320]
	483 Merv Turkomen [273]	
Group XIX Siberia and Eastern Woodlands		
(1)	476 Central Ainu [189]	502 Altai Kizhi [243]
	477 Southern Ainu [256]	504 Telenget Tuvan [243]
	497 Mansi (Vogul) [60]	
(2)	496 Khanti (Ostyak) [88]	503 Khakasi [88]
	498 Nentsi (Samoyed) [88]	505 Yakut [208]
	499 Selkup [88]	507 Evenk [90]
	500 Ket [88]	508 Even (Lamut) [90]
	501 Barabinski Tatars [381]	511 Orochi Tungus [209]
(3)	509 Negidal [210]	512 Orok Tungus [365]
(4)	514 Itelman [90]	517 Reindeer Chukchi [90]
	515 Reindeer Koryak [90]	518 Coastal Chukchi [90]
	516 Coastal Koryak [90]	519 Anadyr Eskimo [90]

confined to Sinkiang and adjacent valleys and steppelands: two Uighur series, the Kirghiz of Alma Ata and Ferghana and the steppe Kazakhs.

The Uighur are the least studied biologically of all the major inner Asian populations, but their clustering with the Kirghiz was not unexpected. Some 8–10 per cent of the oasis populations of Sinkiang have light brown hair, long faces and straight to 'hooked' noses – descriptions common also among the Khakasi [292] and distinguishable among remains from the Afanasyevo–Andronovo graves of the late third and early second millennium.

The marked bimodality between the 'Mongoloid' and 'Europoid' Kirghiz serves as a striking example of the manner in which political, linguistic and other cultural associations can mask biological differences. Existing ethnic identities become meaningless unless understood in the light of history.

Soviet scientists claim that the Kirghiz have the highest percentages of blue and mixed eyes, blondism and fair skin. These characteristics have been cited as evidence that they incorporated the descendants of the 'blonde, blue–green-eyed' Tin Lin (Din Lin) of Chinese annals – which Debets [89] identifies as a tall, long-headed and straight-nosed 'Nordic' type. The presence of blondism is taken as an indication of north European origin as against the southern 'Europoid' ancestry of the Turkmeni and Tajiks. Skeletal remains identified as those of the Tin Lin are remarkably similar to those of the lighter pigmented Kirghiz. Presumably this blonde component (roughly 40 per cent) is to be associated with the same late Saka nomadic incursions into the Yenisei–Issyk-Kul region as was noted in the early formation of the Kazakhs. Today the blonde element is confined mainly to the settled communities of Ferghana, whereas the nomads of the T'ien Shan are quite Mongoloid with dark eyes, black hair and the epicanthic eyefold. Possibly a significant cultural factor identifying them with the Kazakhs is the use of homes on wheels (*kibitka*) – a legacy inherited probably jointly from the Scytho–Sarmatians.

The third cluster is largely Mongol and Mongol–Turkic and includes the Kumyk and Nogai of Caucasia along the western shore of the Caspian Sea; the western Mongols (Kalmuks of Zungharia); the Khalka of central Mongolia; the eastern Mongols of Manchuria; and two Turkic series from the western rim of Sinkiang (the Kirghiz of the Sayak Clan and the pastoralists of the T'ien Shan range). Rationale for inclusion of the Tungusic Nanay (Goldi) or Fish-skin Tatars may parallel that of the Nivkhi in the previous group.

Biologically there appears to be no single Mongol 'type' but the Khalka form a population with considerable genetic and morphological stability. In some regions the Mongols are also intermediate between northern Chinese and the Turkic populations of the Baikal faultline. Their story is well told by Lattimore

[204] in his analysis of their ability to assimilate from border populations.

There is little point in pursuing anything as elusive as a Manchu physical 'type' or even now a Manchu people. Not only is their spoken language virtually extinct, but what little is available in the way of biological studies shows them to be indistinguishable from any of the other Tungusic tribes of ancient Amuria.

GROUP XVIII: TURKESTAN AND TAJIKISTAN

This group is sharply differentiated from group XVII and has three easily distinguishable clusters: (1) the Uzbeks of Tashkent and Samarkand and the Karakalpaks; (2) the Karategin, Shugnan, Yagnobi and Sarakan Tajiks and a series of Turkic-speaking Kipchak Kirghiz; (3) several closely related series grouped together as a total Turkmen sample: Turkmen from the Merv oasis; the nomadic Yomudi and Turkmeni of Turkmenistan. This third cluster has the lowest variances of any in the entire northern quadrant, both as a separate series and collectively as a cluster.

In skeletal and soft parts the Uzbeks are much more heterogeneous than either the Turkmeni or the Tajiks, as revealed in distinct bimodalities or trimodalities of 'types' – Turkmen, Tajik or Mongoloid. The nomadic populations tend to be more Mongoloid with smaller percentages of the two 'Europoid' trait complexes, and the settled populations – especially the mercantile Sarts – are distinguished by social class or profession characteristics favouring Turkmeni or Tajiks. The oasis Karakalpaks are very similar to the settled Uzbeks, their separate identity stemming more from their traditional past than their biological traits of today.

Tajikistan – the north especially – is an ethnic and biological patchwork, both ancient and modern, of cultural borrowings and juxtapositions from varied time periods. The impact of external culture and biological factors was much less significant in the south, where most of the inhabitants remain Tajik and speak Tajik Iranian. The high mountain ranges which virtually enclose southern Tajikistan, except along part of the south-west border, provided sufficient isolation to preserve the biological and cultural heritages of the majority of the inhabitants. Based on skeletal remains from extensive burial sites at the foot of the

Hissar range, dating from the Bronze Age to the eighth century AD, Ginzburg [129] concludes that inhabitants of the northern part of ancient Bactria are indistinguishable from present-day Tajik populations. Similar skeletal remains have been found in neighbouring Sogdiana, although there the present inhabitants now have some Mongoloid admixture. Ginzburg concludes that the ancient Sogdians, whose documentary traces were first discovered by Sir Aurel Stein [130, 316] were similar biologically to the Tajiks of today.

When the first Turkic-speaking invaders began expanding from the Ili Valley westward across the central steppe (Dasht-i-Kipchak) and southward into the interfluvial area in the centuries just before and after the Christian era, they encountered two different 'Europoid' populations. One is identifiable today as the Turkmen in the central and western regions of Turkmenistan, and the other as the Tajiks in the eastern foothills.

Except for occasional blondism and other traits associated with north Europeans or those revealing distinct 'Mongoloid' admixture, the Turkmeni have very dark brown, slightly wavy hair, relatively light skin colour and medium to dark brown eyes. They are quite tall; their heads are medium-sized and long in proportion to breadth (dolichocephalic). Their foreheads are quite broad; faces and noses long and narrow; lower jaws of medium breadth. Nasal profiles are straight to convex with up to 40 per cent in this category. Much of this description would apply to a high percentage of Tajiks also – their chief distinguishing features centering around medium rather than tall stature; relative smallness and roundness of the head (brachycephalic); somewhat lighter hair, skin and eye pigmentation.

The Turkmeni preserve remarkably their biological heritage from a period prior to their linguistic substitution of Turkic for Iranian during the fourth and fifth centuries after Christ and their conversion to Islam in the seventh century. So distinctive are their visible traits that Deniker [95] characterized them as part of what he termed the Indo–Afghan race, occupying the area from Turkestan to the Indus. In Soviet literature this has been named the Trans-Caspian Dolichocephalic Europoid Khurasan race and is traced from south of the Caspian Sea to Azerbaijan in north Iran and settlement extensions in Iraq and Turkey. Apart from their marked longheadedness – which is in sharp contrast with the brachycephaly of the Tajiks – most of the distinctive traits are similar to those of the neighbouring Armenians.

GROUP XIX: SIBERIA AND THE EASTERN WOODLANDS

The first cluster is composed entirely of Uralic or former Uralic groups except for the Ainu, who are linked closely to the Mansi or Vogul of western Siberia and are the subject of a separate analysis. The Telenget (Tuvans) and Khizi were formerly Uralic speakers but are now Turkic-speaking. Their inclusion was to be expected.

The second cluster ranged across western Siberia from the Uralic-speaking Khanti (Ostyak), Samoyedic Nentsi and Selkup to the central Tungus – the Evenk and Even (Lamut) – and the Orochi of the Amur. To these were added the turkicized, mainly ex-Tungusic and Palaeoasiatic Yakuts who occupy most of central Siberia.

The Tungusic Negidal and Orok of the lower Amur and Sakhalin form the third cluster. The fourth is limited to five palaeo–Asiatic series: the Itelman of Kamchatka, the Reindeer and coastal Koryak, the Reindeer and coastal Chukchi and the closely related Eskimo.

Morphologically, the Tungus–Manchu populations have relatively light to medium skin colour; medium to coarse, straight to slightly wavy black hair; sparse beard and body hair; dark brown eyes with varying percentages of mixed to light brown shades and relatively thin lips. Stature is generally short to medium with relatively short limbs in proportion to trunk. Head form varies from mesocephalic to brachycephalic; malars (cheekbones) are prominent; the inner epicanthic fold is present in varying degrees from slight to pronounced and ranges in intensity from 60 to 100 per cent. The greatest variety is probably in length (height) of the face and nasal profile, characteristics which are expressed numerically in Table 7.

In spite of the general variety in morphological traits and genetic polymorphisms, there is a fairly distinctive difference between the desert oasis–steppe zone populations and the peoples of the taiga–tundra and eastern forestlands of the Siberia–Amuria zone. Levin [212] concludes that the biological affinities of the Tungus cannot be dissociated from their economic dependence on reindeer herding, which he believes was taken over from the horse-breeding complex of the steppe country. The Tungus centre of origin was in the southernmost zone of their present distribution, and their spread northward into the entire central Siberian area involved absorption of the previous Uralic and Palaeoasiatic-speaking populations and was assisted enormously by their reindeer herding economy. This process resulted in the creation of three distinct populations: Uralian in western Siberia, North Asiatic in the centre, and Arctic (Palaeoasiatic) in the north-east.

The older Tungusic-speaking populations in the Amur basin preserve to this day the physical traits of those who migrated northward and mixed with the earlier inhabitants of the area. As summarized by Levin [212], the Ural type is represented by the Khanti and Mansi but is found in mixed occurrence among the Selkup, Shor, Altai, Nantsi and Khakasi although it is not recognizable beyond the Yenisei. Westward it is recognizable in mixed form among such populations of the Volga–Kama region as the Komi, the Mari (Chernis) and Udmurts. The Kets are given distinctive recognition because of their deep pigmentation, scantier face hair and strongly convex noses, and are classed as a very ancient European–Mongoloid mixture.

In the Yenisei basin, an ancient palaeo–Siberian type is said to be still recognizable: a pre-Russian, European, early Mongoloid mixture referred to as the Baikal type. The hair is not as coarse as that of the later 'Mongoloids', pigmentation is relatively light, there is little facial prognathism but the malars are flaring, the nose concave with a very low bridge, and the inner epicanthic eyefold is strongly developed. The type is common among central and eastern Tungus – the Evenk and Lamuts and the lower Amur tribes, the Negidals and Oroks. The ancient palaeo–Asiatic-speaking Yukagir, who once occupied the entire central part of Siberia – especially the Lena basin – are also said to be of this type.

The Tuvans and southern Altai and the core population of Buryats are described as belonging to a mid-Asian type: darker pigmented than the Baikal type; coarser-haired; more heavily bearded; registering higher percentages and intensities of the epicanthic eyefold; broader and higher faces; high cranial vaults; moderate facial prognathism; considerable nasal convexity and medium lip thickness – characteristics associated with the present-day Mongols and noted among the Yakuts in mixed occurrence with the Baikal type.

The position of the Nivkhi or Gilyaks is intermediate between the Ainu and the Tungus–Manchu populations in almost all significant particulars. The Ainu, for instance, have the least malar prominence, face height and breadth; they have the highest percentages of straight noses, high nasal roots and the broadest noses, the greatest flare of the alae, the darkest skin colour and the coarsest and most wavy hair. The Tungus–Manchu, on the other hand, have the greatest malar prominence, face height and breadth, the lowest percentages of straight noses and least flare of the alae, the lightest skin colour and the straightest hair. In all these particulars the Nivkhi are intermediate, the only exception being in lip form: the Nivkhi have thicker lips, the Ainu are intermediate and the Tungus–Manchu are the thinnest lipped.

THE AINU

The puzzling status of the Ainu and debates about their origin have centred in the past mainly around three theories – one linking them with the 'Caucasoids', another with the 'Australoids' [412] and a third relating them to both through a common ancestry. The first two are based on impressions of external morphological similarities, which can be misleading. Many resemblances such as hairiness, general lack of the epicanthic eyefold, facial and skeletal features have been noted between individual Ainu and Australian aboriginals and the author has seen scattered instances of individuals in the western Himalayas, western Siberia and even parts of south-east Asia who were very Ainu in appearance. It is not unreasonable to speculate that genetic recombinations might be responsible for many of these instances, but resemblances require substantiation on a populational rather than individual basis.

Support for either of the first two Ainu theories is lacking. Furthermore, the term 'Caucasoid' is misleading: it is likely to be confused with the Caucasians and, if intended to be synonymous with 'European', it should be used only with reference to living populations. Objections that might be raised to the Australian argument are that the Ainu are generally quite stocky in physique while most Australoids are slender, or that most morphometric characteristics of the head differ considerably. Countering this argument is the rationale that adaptive pressures would favour selection toward stockiness in the colder regions and slenderness in a hot arid environment. A far more powerful argument is that many of the presumably most significant head and cranial measurements are statistically too different to permit a rational argument for a close common ancestry.

On the basis of morphometric data and gentic comparisons of living populations, data concerning the third theory – with an emphasis possibly on ancient Siberian sources – is divided, skeletal evidence leading in one direction and genetic in another. One of the most significant studies in support of ties with ancient Siberia is a craniometric comparison between a series of six eneolithic epi-Jomon crania dating from about AD 500 and thirty-three series of crania ranging in distribution from Europe to eastern Asia and Oceania. Using the Penrose generalized distance method, Yamaguchi [407] concludes that the epi-Jomon series most nearly resembles two of the Bronze Age (Andronovo and Afanasyevo) series from the Minusinsk basin of central Siberia and a neolithic series from southern Ukrainia. It is also very similar to present-day Ainu and to a neolithic series from northern Honshu, which at that time was outside the habitation range of Yamato Japanese. The greatest distances were from the 'Mongoloids' of north-east Asia. Australian, Yayoi Japanese and recent Japanese, Korean and various northern and European neolithic and Bronze Age series were intermediate.

In an osteometric study Yamaguchi [409] compared statistically adequate samples of both cranial and post-cranial skeletal collections using the Penrose method of calculating biological distance. He found that the Ainu clustered closely with the pre-Yamato Jomon population of Japan and the Maori of New Zealand, whereas the Australian aboriginals clustered most closely with the Melanesians of New Caledonia and New Britain.

Yamaguchi's conclusions concerning the Ainu generally corroborate the results obtained by Howells [156] using the multivariate craniometric method in which the Ainu were found to be distinguishable from neolithic Jomon populations but were more similar to them than to the Japanese. The Jomon were more variable than either the Japanese or the Ainu. Turner [382] also confirms the similarity of the Ainu to Jomon, based on ten dental traits, and adds pointedly that recent Japanese teeth are very similar to those of Shang dynasty Chinese.

Omoto and Harada [266] have presented some new data in the field of serum proteins. They compared a sample of 372 Hidaka Ainu schoolchildren, all of whom had more than half (average 68 per cent) 'unmixed' Ainu parentage, with two samples of Japanese totalling 577 and a check sample of 272 'Caucasoid' residents of Japan. Their tests included frequency distributions of the red-cell phosphatase P^a gene, the P^c gene haptoglobins and transferrins and the cholinesterases. They concluded: (1) that Australians and Ainu may each have a Caucasoid component, but that the Ainu component may be of northern origin; (2) that genes of the Rh system which are rare in Caucasoids are present in both the Ainu (r' and r'') and the Australian (R', R^z and r'); (3) that, since r' and r'' are present among certain south Indian populations, a gentic link may exist with south India. The conclusion accords in general with an earlier study by Simmons *et al.* [352] on blood antigens in which a possible tie with the Chenchu of south India is suggested.

In the other antigen systems the contrasts are quite marked. In the ABO, the Ainu frequencies virtually match those of various west Siberian series in which B is high (31 per cent), whereas it is absent in Australia. In the MN series the frequencies of the Ainu are intermediate between those of the Australians and north Asians generally. In the Lewis, Duffy, Kell and other systems there are marked discrepancies, but in all instances the frequencies are closer to continental Asian series than to Australia.

A team of Japanese scientists [244] has recently completed an exhaustive study of the few hundred relatively unmixed Ainu survivors. In almost all of their comparisons they concluded that the Ainu are closer in biological distance to present-day eastern and north Asians or some American Indians than to Australian aborigines. In a complex calculation using thirteen polymorphic loci (see Figure 1) and ranging through a series of red cell enzymes and serum proteins, they link the Ainu ancestrally with the Eskimo, Malay and Japanese.

The 'human tree' is one of many similar attempts to show relative distance among sample populations, and it should not be confused with a phylogeny. To create the latter would necessitate discovering all of the gene flow and drift that have taken place

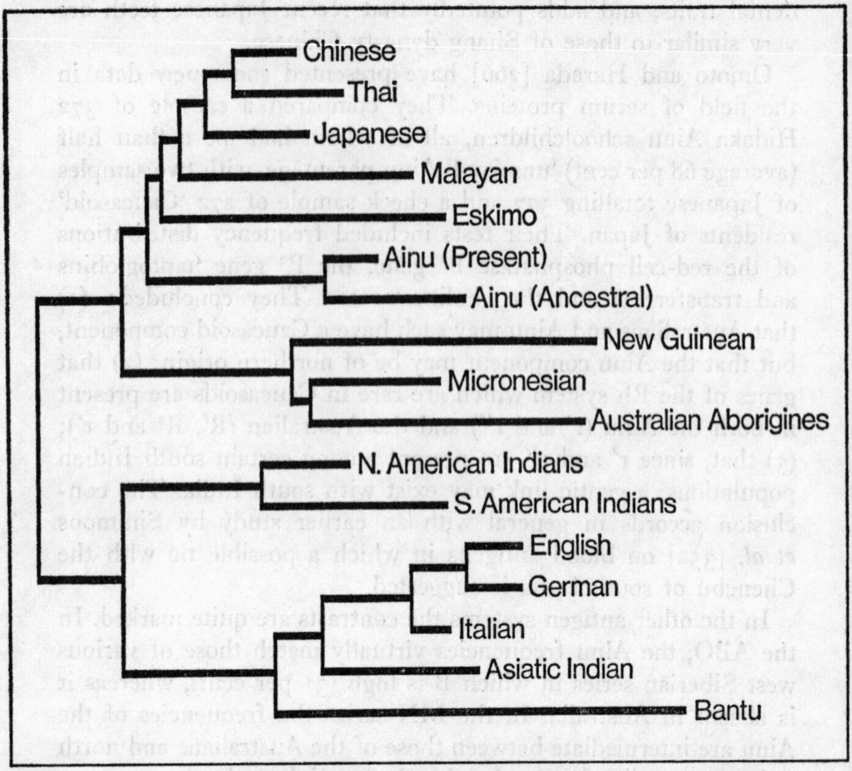

Figure 1 A phylogenetic tree constructed for 17 populations based on data for 13 polymorphic loci

in the past, not to mention the continuing impact of environment.

The close resemblances between the Mansi and Ainu were not observed by Yamaguchi [408] in his study of the Onkomai Ainu series. Admittedly, data used in the present study are limited to a few head and face measurements, but the differences between the Ainu and the Mansi are insignificant in comparison with those between the Ainu and the Australians or the Chenchu of southern India. Attention is usually called to the shortness of the Ainu face and nose but the facial and nasal measurements are extremely close to various west Siberians.

There may be some truth in the theory that the Ainu represent an old surviving remnant of a northern European population of the Mesolithic, Neolithic or Bronze Ages; or they could be a combination of Tungusic and other eastern and north Asian admixtures – possibly including mesolithic south-east Asian mixtures.

In the present study, with repeated overlap runs of both raw data and principal components, the Ainu were consistently clustered with populations of the Uralic series, especially the Mansi (Vogul), Khanti (Ostyak) and Kets, and secondarily with some of the older Altai Sayan groups adjacent to the Minusinsk basin of the upper Yenisei. If any genetic continuity exists between the present populations and the early Bronze Age Europeans, it could have survived among the Uralic speakers in the Minusinsk basin.

BLOOD GROUP ANTIGENS

Recent studies of the Siberian population have provided data on the ABO and MNS systems, but as yet little on the Rh system and no data seem to be generally available on the haemoglobins and serum proteins. Table 16 of ABO frequencies points to high O percentages ranging between 59 per cent among the Uralic speaking Khanti in the west to 65 per cent among the Palaeoasiatic Yukaghir and 62 per cent among the Siberian Eskimos. The B gene percentages are relatively low, ranging from 18 per cent in the extreme west (Nentsi) to 29 per cent among the Nanay (Goldi) Tungus of the Amur. The A gene has an equally low range from 13 per cent in the west to 28 per cent among the Yukaghir. Very low B gene – 6–9 per cent in the Palaeoasiatics – is in keeping with New World figures in adjacent North America.

In the MNS system the Tofalars and Tuvans of western Siberia – now Turkic speaking but formerly Uralic speaking – match the Lapp figures [250, table 17] closely and even some non-arctic European populations. The Rh system, on the other hand, appears to be intermediate between the north European and east Asian frequencies.

In a test to demonstrate that studies of genetic and morphological significance should prove to be corroborative, Malyutov, Passekov and Rychkov [232] conducted serological investigations in five Turkic speaking ethnic groups in the Sayan mountains, previously studied morphologically by Levin [211]. After taking into consideration the power of random genetic drift, they de-

Table 16. *Blood group gene frequencies: Siberia**

		Nentsi [318]	Khanti [318]	Selkup [318]	Telen-get [318]	Tuvan [318]	Evenk [318]	Buriat [318]	Nanay [318]	Negidal [318]	Yuka-ghir [416]	Chuck-chi [93]	Eskimo [93]
ABO	(A)p	0.13	0.22	0.15	0.22	0.20	0.13	0.15	0.11	0.15	0.28	0.23	0.20
	(B)q	0.18	0.19	0.10	0.19	0.13	0.15	0.21	0.29	0.21	0.06	0.09	0.18
	(O)r	0.69	0.59	0.75	0.59	0.67	0.71	0.64	0.60	0.64	0.65	0.67	0.62

		Tofalar [319]	Sayan Tuvans [319]
MNS	MS	0.28	0.39
	Ms	0.18	0.11
	NS	0.28	0.45
	Ns	0.26	0.05

		Tofalar [319]	Sayan Tuvans [319]
Rh	(Rz)CDE	0.11	0.17
	(R_1)CDe	0.11	0.17
	(R′)Cde	—	—
	(R_2)cDE	0.22	0.35
	(R_0)cDe	0.45	0.23
	(R″)cdE	0.03	0.05
	(r)cde	0.08	0.04

* See Table 14 for Ainu frequencies.

monstrated a high coincidence between the two approaches to distance analysis. On the basis of a highly complex statistical procedure, which took into account the probable impact of events extending back to the time of the Scyths some 2500 years ago, they concluded that the Tuvinians must approximate biologically the antecedent population of the region referred to by the Chinese as the Tu-po – their rendering of Tuva.

27
Conclusions

The identification of some twenty populations in this survey of the people of Asia has provided a number of suggestive results. Both the morphological and genetic approaches support most previous regional studies, contradict a few, and indicate current trends in population structure.

West Asia. Apart from the coastal zones of Arabia and Iran, where there has been considerable biological hybridization, the inland inhabitants of greater Syria–Arabia and Irania are demonstrably similar to each other and generally fall within the greater south-east European sphere. Recent and continuing migrational pressures from central Asia and the Caucasus on to the central highlands are apparent, as are movements from the highlands to the plains and from southern Arabia northward into Syria and Iraq. The present survey supports the evidence of history.

South Asia. Two conclusions may be inferred: the first is that changes in caste structure, social mobility and the processes of detribalization and Hinduization seem to have combined with differential fertility and internal demographic movements so as to gradually shift the total genetic structure. These changes have been in favour of the older substratum populations of the subcontinent, at the expense of those attributable to proto-historic and historic migrations and invasions from the Iranian plateau and south-east Asia. The second conclusion is that while some six or seven subregional population groups are recognizable, the differences between groups appear to be gradually decreasing. There is more of a trend towards genetic stability in the densely populated regions than in the peripheral hill tracts or the still relatively isolated pockets of forest tribal groups. This accords in general with the analyses of Sarkar [328] and Sanghvi [322].

Probably these changes will not be great enough to erase in the foreseeable future the characteristic differences distinguishing the people of the Punjab and Sind from those of Bengal, Gujarat or Madras, but the tempo will undoubtedly increase as modernization continues and social mobility is intensified.

East Asia. Regardless of political events, it seems likely that many of the processes which were initiated several millennia ago will be continued. The lowland or centrally located majority populations of Burma, Thailand, Vietnam and Cambodia will continue to expand at the expense of the surrounding mountain-dwelling minorities, just as the Indo-Aryan-speaking Assamese will increasingly dominate that state and the provinces of south China will become more Chinese. The future of the Malayan population is fraught with so many demographic imbalances and economic issues that its future is less certain. Far more predictable are trends among the northern nations of east Asia.

In numbers, the total population of China may well become stabilized before the turn of the century, but internally the dramatic population shifts which characterized China's past will doubtless continue. In recent decades nearly ten per cent of the population, mostly from north China, has moved into Manchuria, Inner Mongolia and Sinkiang and another ten per cent of southerners into the less densely populated parts of the southern provinces. Industrialization is likely to intensify these demographic shifts and with these changes there will probably be greater genetic stability in the north, where migrations have been into relatively unpopulated areas. In the south, however, past trends will continue – the sinicization, hybridization and ultimate assimilation of many of the local indigenous populations. Differentiation between northern and southern Chinese will consequently remain or be intensified. In Korea and Japan, where the assimilation of minority populations was virtually completed centuries ago, both populations are likely merely to attain greater genetic stability. Korea's ultimate political fate will have little impact on the issue.

North Asia. In the northlands the situation is quite different. As indicated in chapters 4 and 15, the overwhelming expansion of east Europeans across the entire northern half of the continent during the past half millennium has been fully as dramatic as the contemporary expansion of west Europeans throughout the New World. Most of these movements, however, have been into Siberia and only secondarily into the more arid regions of Central Asia, where the immigrants have been mainly at the official, industrial and entrepreneurial levels. The indigenous Turkic, Iranian and Caucasic speaking populations may become acculturated again as they were periodically in the past, but they are likely to retain their genetic ties which have stubbornly resisted major changes since they were first intensively settled. The genetic impact of the Centum-speaking Indo–Europeans, who moved into Sinkiang as far as the frontiers of China in the third millennium BC, has not yet been completely erased and in Tajikistan, Turkmenistan and Uzbekistan – especially among the Sarts – the genetic structure remains close to that of the ancient Scytho–Sarmatians, especially among the Tajiks and Turkmen, although many of the local populations may be Muslim and speak Turkic languages or even Arabic. The major genetic changes have taken place in the steppe and desert–steppe zone rather than in the oases outposts or in valleys where the economies are based primarily on plough agriculture.

The greatest changes have occurred among the nomadic herders. Effects of the migrations of Mongoloid populations of the desert steppes and marginal meadowlands of Amuria and Mongolia westward into Central Asia and eastern Europe have largely assimilated what had survived of the earlier migrations into those areas.

The future of the hunters and herders of the taiga and tundra is less certain. Regardless of the continuing numerical expansion of the European population, those who inhabit regions relatively free from Russian competition and encroachment are likely to survive in spite of acculturational changes, so long as their basic economies are not too seriously threatened by the growing industrial needs of the Soviet Union.

For the continent as a whole, in addition to demographic trends and accompanying changes in adaptive pressures and genetic structures, there are two other major observations. Firstly, while it is true that the inhabitants of pocketed high valleys in the Caucasus, Pamirs, Hindu Kush and Himalayas may be viewed historically as old, in terms of man's total experience they are relatively young. There is no evidence that these 'old' mountain populations pre-date the late Neolithic or Bronze Age, whereas the tropical forest-dwelling aboriginal tribal populations are by comparison very ancient, even though they may have been forced into their present refuge areas in relatively recent times.

Secondly, far more attention must be paid to the role of the central Tibetan plateauland and its encircling mountain perimeter than has been the case in the past. In deflecting migrations northward along the oases routes, steppe corridors or through taiga country, it has encouraged nomadic herding, migration and trade; whereas the southern regions with multiple peninsulas, mountain ranges and offshore islands have encouraged the development of a great variety of localized specializations, both cultural and biological.

Concerning the respective roles of Asian populations in the peopling of the New Worlds – America and Australasia – nothing new has been added. The survey emphasizes again the need for more intensive study of big game tundra routes along the arctic ocean and the offshore coastal route of eastern Siberia. In the south the need is for a more intensive study of Sundaland. More attention must also be paid to the antiquity of metallurgy and plant and animal domestication in the whole of east Asia, and the possibility of early trade and movement across the entire length and breadth of the Eurasian supercontinent. The time for reappraisal of man's innovative genius seems long overdue.

All of the world's major and many of the minor populations have demonstrated high levels of creative genius at different time levels although biologically they have changed relatively little. There were in the past the same hereditary controls and adaptive pressures as exist today. While these undoubtedly set limits on man's mental and behavioural capacities, the contrasts between his cultural accomplishments today and fifty thousand years ago are tremendous in comparison with the alterations in his biological structure. The latter have been only minor since man achieved modern status, and ancient man would probably be able to adjust to modern life as easily as any contemporary human being. Life's necessities have always been man's most important goal, but now he has acquired an insatiable curiosity and a desire to invent as well as to discover, to constantly expand his horizons and test the limits of his capacities.

Every continent and doubtless every ethnic group has added a part, no matter how small, to the accumulated store of human knowledge and experience. Possibly the people of Asia have even contributed the lion's share. While it might be said that Asia lost the lead with the commencement of the Renaissance, the age of discovery and later the industrial revolution, the people of that continent have already begun to meet the challenge of the modern world. There is no way of predicting in what directions and to what lengths their creative ingenuity may carry them, particularly if they heed the admonitions of many of the teachers and sages of Asia's great civilizations. Many times in the past the people of Asia have taken the leadership. There are signs that they could do so again in the future.

References

Abbreviations

AINA	Arctic Institute of North America
AJPA	American Journal of Physical Anthropology
BDA	Bulletin of the Department of Anthropology (Government of India, Calcutta)
FMNH,AS	Field Museum of Natural History (Chicago), Anthropology Series
ICAES	International Congress of Anthropological and Ethnological Sciences
JASB	Journal of the Asiatic Society of Bengal
JK	Jinruigaku Kenkyu (Kyushu University)
JRAI	Journal of the Royal Anthropological Institute
JZ	Jinruigaku Zasshi
KSIE	Kratkie Soobshchennia Instituta Etnografii (Akademi Nauk, Moscow)
PMP	Peabody Museum Papers (Harvard University, Cambridge, Mass.)
RTS	Russian Translation Series (Peabody Museum, Harvard University)
TIE	Trudy Instituta Etnografii (Akademi Nauk, Moscow)

1. Afet, M. (1940–41) 'Recherches anthropologiques sur 59,728 Turcs des deux sexes', *Arch. Suisses d'Anthrop. Generale*, 9: 79–192.
2. Agrawal, D. P. (1971) *The Copper Bronze Age in India*, (New Delhi), p. 91.
3. Akiyama, J. (1959) 'A Somatological Study on the Inhabitants of Onyujime Island, Oita', *JK*, 6: 493–532.

4. Al-Azzawi, Abbas (1951) 'Notes on the Yezidi' in Henry Field, *Anthropology of Iraq*, pt. 2(1): 81, *PMP*, 46(1): chapter 6.
5. Allchin, F. R. (1963) *Neolithic Cattleraisers of South India* (Cambridge University Press).
6. Andrews, J. M. (1939) 'Siam: Anthropological Survey' (Ph.D. dissertation, Harvard University).
7. Arase, S., Tabe, J., Kohama, M. & Takamori, I. (1934) 'An Anthropological Study of the Northern Koreans', *JZ*, 49.
8. *Archaeological Survey of India* (1953–4; 1961–2) Annual Reports – 'Indian Archaeology, A Review', cited in Fairservis, W. A. (1971) *The Roots of Ancient India* (New York: Macmillan), pp. 312–18.
9. Asakawa, K. (1954) 'Somatological Studies on the Inhabitants of Oshima Island', *JK*, 1: 52–219.
10. Bacon, Elizabeth (1958) *Obok: A Study of Social Structure in Eurasia,* Viking Fund Publications in Anthropology No. 25, (Wenner-Gren Foundation for Anthropological Research, New York).
11. Bada, Jeffrey (1975) in 'Coast Dig Focuses on Man's Move to New World' by Boyce Rensberger, *New York Times*, 16 August 1975.
12. Baden Powell, Sir Robert (1896) *The Indian Village Community* (London, New York, Bombay: Longmans Green), pp. 2–20.
13. Bajatzadeh, M. and Walker, Hubert (1968) 'Serum Protein polymorphisms in Iran' *Humangenetik*, 6: 40–54.
14. Balla, Vijender and Kaul, S. S. (1966) 'The ABO Blood Groups and ABH Secretions in the Tibetans', *AJPA*, 25: 315–18.
15. Banerjee, M. K. (1969) 'Anthropometry of the Saharya of Jhansi, U.P.', *Man in India*, 36(2): 92.
16. Barnett, L. D. (1914) *Antiquities of India* (London: Philip Lee Warner), p. 133.
17. Barth, F. (1958) *Nomads of South Arabia* (Oslo University Press; London: Allen & Unwin).
17a. Barthold, V. V. (1927) 'K voprosu o iazyke sogdiiskom i tokharskom (Problem of the Sogdian and Tokharian Language)', *Iran*, vol. 1 (Leningrad).
18. Basham, A. L. (1954) *The Wonder that was India* in *Evergreen Encyclopedia*, Vol. I (New York: Grove Press), p. 137.
19. Basu, P. C. (1932–3) 'Racial Affinities of Mundas', *Transactions of the Bose Research Institute*, 8: 214–47.
20. Bayard, D. T. (1972) 'Reports', *Science*, 176: 1411–12.
21. Bellew, H. W. (1880) *The Races of Afghanistan* (Calcutta).
22. Benvenite, E. (1952) 'Langues Asianiques et Mediterraneennes' in Meillet, A. and Cohen, M., *Les Langues du Monde* (Paris), p. 184.

23. Bernhard, Wolfram (1968) 'Human Skeletal Remains from the Bronze and Early Iron Age Cemetery of Timargarha (Dir State, W. Pakistan)' *ICAES*, VIII, (Tokyo and Kyoto), 1: 144.
24. Bernhard, Wolfram (1967) 'Die Häufigkeit der PTC Schmeckfähigkeit in Nordwestpakistan', *Anthropologische Anzeiger*, 30: 135–41.
25. Bernstham, A. (1962) 'On the Origin of the Kirghiz People' in *Studies in Siberian Ethno-Genesis*, ed. H. N. Michael, *AINA*, 2: 119–28.
26. Bharati, Agehananda – personal communication.
27. Bhowmick, P. K. (1956) 'Physical Affinity of the Lodhas of Midnapore', *Man in India*, 36 (2): 110–31.
28. Birdsell, R. (1967) 'Preliminary Data on the Trihybrid Origin of the Australian Aborigines', *Archaeology and Physical Anthropology in Oceania* (Sydney), 2(2): 103.
29. Blackwell, R. Q., Ro, I., Liu, C., Yang, H., Wang, C. and Huang, J. T. (1969) 'Hemoglobin Variant found in Koreans, Chinese and North American Indians', *AJPA*, 30: 389–92.
30. Blumenbach, J. F. (1795) *On the Natural Varieties of Mankind* (Göttingen).
31. Blumenbach, J. T. (1790–1828) *Collectionis craniorum diversarum gentum illustratae decades* (Göttingen).
32. Bonne, Bathsheva (1966) 'Are There any Hebrews Left?' *AJPA*, 24: 135–46.
33. Bonne, Bathsheva, Ada A., Ashkenazi, I. and Bat-Miriam, M. (1965) 'A preliminary report on some genetical characteristics in the Samaritan population', *AJPA*, 23: 397.
34. Bordes, Francois (1968) *The Old Stone Age* (New York: McGraw-Hill; London: Weidenfeld and Nicolson), pp. 77–136.
35. Bowles, G. T. (1935–7) Field data. Preliminary publication in Henry Field (ed.) (1970) *Contributions to the Physical Anthropology of the Peoples of India* (Coconut Grove, Florida: Field Research Projects), Appendix.
36. Bowles, G. T. (1943) 'Linguistic and Racial Aspects of the Munda Problem' in 'Studies in the Anthropology of Oceania and Asia' Coon, C. S., Andrews, J. M. (eds), *PMP*, 20.
37. Bowles, G. T. (1935) 'Racial Origins of the Peoples of the Central Chinese-Tibetan Border' (Ph.D. dissertation, Harvard University).
38. Bowman, J. E. and Hossain, Ronaghy (1967) 'Hemoglobin, Glucose-6 Phosphate Dehydrogenase Phosphogluconate Dehydrogenase and Adenylate Kinase Polymorphisms in Iran', *AJPA*, 27: 119–24.

39. Bowman, J. E., Corson, P. E., Frischer, Henri, Powell, R. D., Colwell, E. J., Legters, L. J., Cottingham, A. J., Boone, S. C. and Hiser, W. W. (1971) 'Hemoglobin and Red Cell Enzyme Variation with comments on the Malaria Hypothesis', *AJPA*, 34: 313–24.

40. Boyd, W. C. (1950) *Genetics and the Races of Man* (Boston: Little Brown), table 23.

41. Boyd, W. C. (1954) 'The Blood Groups in Pakistan' *AJPA*, 12: 393–412.

42. Büchi, Ernst (1954) 'ABH Secretion in India', *The Anthropologist*, 1(1): 3–8.

43. Büchi, E. C. (1968) 'Rassengeschichte des Indopakistanischen Subkontinentes' in *Rassengeschichte d. Menschheit*, pt. I, ed. Saller, K. (Münich & Vienna).

44. Büchi, E. C., Guibart, A. and Olivier, G. (1968) '*Anthropologie Tibetaine*' (Paris).

45. Burckhardt, J. L. (1830) *Notes on the Bedouins and Wahabys* (London).

46. Buxton, I. D. (1925) *The Peoples of Asia* (London).

46a. Campbell, B. G. ed. (1976) *Humankind Emerging* (Boston: Little Brown), pp. 201–21.

47. Caroe, Olaf (1958) *The Pathans* (New York: St Martin's Press), p. 44.

47a. Cavalli-Sforza, L. L. and Bodmer, W. F. (1971) *The Genetics of Human Populations* (San Francisco: W. H. Freeman and Co.), p. 118.

48. Chai, C. K. (1967) *Taiwan Aborigines: A Genetic Study of Tribal Variations* (Harvard University Press).

49. Chang, K. C. (1968) *The Archaeology of Ancient China* (Yale University Press), pp. 39–42.

50. Chang, K. C. (1970) 'The Beginnings of Agriculture in the Far East', *Antiquity*, 44: 175–85.

51. Chantre, E. (1895) *Recherches Anthropologique dans l'Asie Occidentale, Transcaucasie, Asie Mineure et Syria* (Paris).

52. Chard, C. S. (1969) *Man in Prehistory* (New York: McGraw-Hill), pp. 128–42.

53. Chatterjee, B. K. (1934) 'Comparative Study of the Somatic Affinities of the Maithal and Kanaujia Brahmin of Behar, *Anthropological Bulletin from the Zoological Society of India*, No. 2.

54. Chatterjee, B. K. and Kumar, G. D. (1952) 'Somatic Characters and Racial Affinities of the Kannikars of Travancore State', *JASB Science*, 18(1): 55–70.

55. Chatterjee, B. K. (1955) 'Racial Components of the Tribal Popula-

tion of India' (Presidential Address, Anthropology and Archaeology Section *Proceedings of the 42nd Indian Science Congress*).

56. Chatterjee, B. K. and Kumar, G. D. (1956) 'Somatic Characters and the Racial Affinities of the Urali of Travancore and Cochin States' *The Anthropologist*, 3(1&2): 1–22.
57. Chatterjee, B. K. and Kumar, G. D. (1957) 'A Comparative Study of the Somatometric and Somatoscopic Observations and their Racial Affinities of the Paliyans and Malapantarams of Travancore-Cochin', *JASB Science*, 23(2): 19–42.
58. Chauduri, S., Mukherjee, B., Ghosh, J. and Roychoudhury, A. J. (1969) 'Study of Blood Groups, ABH Secretors and Hemoglobin Variants in Three Upper Castes of West Bengal, India', *AJPA*, 30: 129–32.
59. Cheboksarov, N. N. (1952) 'Questions concerning the origins of the Finno-Ugrian language group' Sovetskaya etnografiya, No. 1, pp. 36–50 (in *AINA*, trans. from Russian, s.n. 2: 207–19).
60. Cheboksarov, N. N. and Trofimova, T. A. (1947) 'Mansi Data', *TIE*, vol. 1, table 2, p. 194.
61. Childe, V. G. (1960) *What Happened in History* (Harmondsworth, Middlesex: Penguin Books), pp. 195–7.
62. Choremis, C. (1953) personal communication, cited in Mourant, A. E. (1954) *The Distribution of Human Blood Groups* (Oxford; Blackwell).
63. Chou, F. S. (1956) 'Somatological Studies on the Peng-Hu (Pescadores) Islanders, Taiwan' *JK*, 3(3–4): 368.
64. Clark, Colin (1967) *Population Growth and Land Use* (London: Macmillan).
65. Clebert, J. R. (1967) *The Gypsies* (Harmondsworth, Middlesex: Penguin Books), p. 251.
66. Cohn, Victor (1976) '1.5 Million-Year-Old Skull is Found', *Washington Post*, 9 March 1976.
67. Coles, J. M. & Higgs, E. H. (1969) *The Archaeology of Early Man* (London: Faber and Faber), pp. 344 and 377.
68. Coon, C. S. (1951) *Cave Explorations in Iran, 1949*, Philadelphia, Museum Monographs (University of Pennsylvania Press), p. 3.
69. Coon, C. S. (1939) *The Races of Europe* (New York: Macmillan), pp. 27–8, 400–3.
70. Coon, C. S. (1962) *The Origin of Races* (New York: Knopf), p. 29.
71. Coon, C. S. (1965) *The Living Races of Man* (New York: Knopf).
72. Crookshank, F. G. (1924) *The Mongol in Our Midst* (New York: E. P. Dutton & Co.).
73. Curtain, C. C., van Loghem, Erna, Baumgarten, A., Golab, T., Gorman, J., Rutgers, C. F. and Kidson, C. (1971) 'The Ethnological

Significance of the Gamma-globulin (Gm) Factors in Melanesia', *AJPA*, 34: 259–72.

74. Cuvier, G. L. C. F. D. (1825) *Discours sur les Revolutions de la Surface du Globe* (Paris).

75. Czaplicka, M. A. (1918) *The Turks of Central Asia in History and at the Present Day* (Oxford University Press).

76. Dames, M. L. (1904) *The Baloch Race*, Royal Asiatic Society Monograph, vol. IV, (London).

77. Dani, A. H. (1967) 'Timargarha and Gandhara Grave Culture' in 'Ancient Pakistan', *Bull. Dept. of Archaeology*, University of Peshawar, vol. III.

78. Darwin, Charles (1859) *Origin of Species* (London).

79. Darwin, Charles (1874) *The Descent of Man* (New York and London).

79a. Das, A. K. and Raha, M. K. (1963) *The Oraons of Sunderban* (Calcutta).

80. Das, B. M. (1956) 'Physical Characters of the Rabhas of Assam', *Man in India*, 36: 92–9.

81. Das, B. M. and Mahapatra, U. D. (1960) 'Physical character of the Suris of Assam', *Journal of the University of Gauhati: Science*, 2(2): 87–98.

82. Das, B. M. (1960) 'Somatic Variations among the Hill and Plains Garo of Assam', *Man in India*, 40: 128–48.

83. Das, B. M. and Das, R. (1965) 'An Anthropometric Survey of the Kalita', *Man in India*, 45: 170.

84. Das, B. M. (1967) 'Etudes des caracteres anthropometriques des Khasi de L'Assam, Inde', *L'Anthropologie*, 71(1–2): 97–133.

85. Das, B. M. and Das, M. S. (1969) 'The Kaibarta of Assam', *Man in India*, 49(1): 49.

86. Debets, G. F. (1931) 'Eshche raz o belukuroi rase v Tsentral 'noi Azii', *Sovetskaia Aziia*, Nos. 5–6.

87. Debets, G. F. (1936, 1946) Tables 14–26 in Oshanin, L. V. (1964) 'Anthropological Composition of the Population of Central Asia and the Ethnogenesis of its People', *RTS*, 2(2).

88. Debets, G. F. (1947) 'Selkupi', *TIE*, n.s. 1–2, 103–45.

89. Debets, G. F. (1949) 'Paleoantropologiia USSR', *TIE*, 4.

90. Debets, G. F. (1950) 'Antropologicheskie Isoledovaniia v Kamchatskoi Oblasti, *TIE*, 17.

91. Debets, G. F. (1956) 'The Origin of the Kirgiz People in the Light of Physical Anthropological Findings', *Trudy Kirgizskoyeksped*, 1: 3–17 (also in *AINA*, 2: 129–43).

92. Debets, G. F. (1960) 'Anthropological Investigations in Daghestan', *RTS*, 1(2): 83–109.

93. Debets, G. F. (1961) Anthropological Investigations in Kamchatka, 1951, *TIE*, 17.
94. Debets, G. F. (1970) 'Physical Anthropology of Afghanistan, I–II', Henry Field, *RTS*, 5(1): 7 (table 3).
95. Deniker, J. (1900) *The Races of Man* (London) (ref. in Levin, M. G. (1963) 'Physical Anthropology of Northern Asiatic Peoples', *AINA*, 3: 21–7).
96. Dolgikh, B. O. (1953), 'Contributions to the History of the Buryat People', *Sovetskaya Etnografiya*, 1: 38–63 (in *AINA*, trans. from Russian, s.n. 2: 73–101).
97. Eberhard, Wolfram (1950) *Kultur und Siedlung der Randvolker Chinas* (Leiden).
98. Eberhard, Wolfram (1960) *A History of China* (University of California Press), p. 9.
99. Edholm, O. G. (1966) 'South-West Asia, with Special Reference to Israel', in *The Biology of Human Adaptability*, ed. Baker, P. T. and Weiner, J. S. (Oxford: Clarendon Press), p. 382.
100. Egami, Namio (1965) *Research on the History of Asian Cultures* (text in Japanese) (Tokyo).
101. Eickstedt, E. von (1920–21) 'Rassenelemente der Sikh mit einem Anhang uber Biometrische Methoden', *Zeitschrift fur Ethnologie*, 52–3: 317–94.
102. Eickstedt, E. F. von (1944) *Rassendynamik von Ostasien, China und Japan, Tai und Kmer von der Urzeit bis Heute* (Berlin).
103. Ekvall, R. B. (1939) 'Cultural Relations on the Kansu-Tibetan Border', *Univ. of Chicago Press Pubs. in Anth., Occas. Papers 1.*
104. *Encyclopedia Britannica,* 11th edn (1911) Article on the 'Bedouins'.
105. Esin, Ufuk and Benedict, Peter (1963) 'Recent Developments in the Prehistory of Anatolia', *Current Anthropology*, 4(4): 339–46.
106. Ewing, J. F. (1950) 'Hyperbrachycephaly as influenced by cultural conditions', *PMP*, 23: 2.
107. Fairservis, W. A. (1971) *The Roots of Ancient India* (New York: Macmillan).
108. Faris, N. A. (1944) *The Arab Heritage* (Princeton University Press), p. 27.
109. Field, Henry (1939) 'Contributions to the Anthropology of Iran', *FMNH, AS*, 29(1).
110. Field Henry (1940) 'Contributions to the Anthropology of Iran', *FMNH, AS*, 30, 1(1).
111. Field, Henry (1949) 'Contributions to the Anthropology of Iran', *FMNH, AS*, 30, 1(2).
112. Field, Henry (1951) 'The Anthropology of Iraq', *PMP*, 46(1).

113. Field, Henry (1953) 'Anthropology of the Caucasus', *PMP*, 48(1).
114. Field, Henry (1955) 'An Anthropological Reconnaissance in West Pakistan', *PMP*, 52.
115. Field, Henry (1956) *Ancient and Modern Man in Southwestern Asia* (University of Miami Press), p. 15.
116. Field, Henry (1956) 'Anthropological Reconnaissance in the Near East', *PMP*, 48(2).
117. Finegan, Jack (1946) *Light from the Ancient Past* (Princeton University Press), p. 27.
118. Fischer, Eugen in Sarkar, S. S. (1954) *The Aboriginal Races of India* (Calcutta), pp. 78–9.
119. Fitzgerald, C. P. (1972) *The Southern Expansion of the Chinese People* (London: Barrie and Jenkins).
120. Flatz, G., Pik, C. and Sringam, S. (1965) 'Haemoglobin E and B-Thalassaemia: Their Distribution in Thailand', *Annals of Human Genetics*, 29: 151–70.
121. Fürer-Haimendorf, C. V. (1945) 'The Problem of Megalithic Cultures in Middle India', *Man in India*, 25: 73–86.
122. Fürer-Haimendorf, C. V. (1948) *The Aboriginal Tribes of Hyderabad*, vol. III: *The Rajgonds* (London: Macmillan), pp. 1–2.
123. Gabrielli, Francesco (1968) *Muhammad and the Conquests of Islam* (New York: McGraw-Hill), pp. 219–20.
124. Garn, S. M. (1965) *Human Races*, 2nd edn. (Springfield, Illinois: C. C. Thomas Books), pp. 116–24.
125. Genna, Giuseppe (1936) 'Antropologia dei Samaritani', *Int. Cong. of Anth. & Prehist. Archae. (18th, Brussels)*, 128–35.
126. Ghirshman, R. (1954) *Iran from Earliest Times to the Islamic Conquest* (Harmondsworth, Middlesex: Penguin Books), p. 94.
127. Ghurye, G. S. (1950) *Caste and Class in India* (Bombay), p. 388.
128. Ginzburg, V. V. and Cheboksarov, N. N. (1947) in Oshanin, L. V. (1964) 'Europeoid Races of Central Asia and of Adjacent Countries of Iran and the Near East', *RTS*, 2(1).
129. Ginzburg, V. V. (1968) 'Anthropology of Present and Ancient Population of Soviet Central Asia', *RTS*, 3(2): 1–10.
130. Ginzburg, V. V. (1968) 'The Central Asiatic Interfluvial Race and its Origin', *RTS*, 3(2): 11–18.
131. Goldschmidt, Elisabeth (1963) *The Genetics of Migrant and Isolate Populations* (Baltimore, Maryland: Williams & Wilkins).
132. Goldsmith, K. (1952) (Ph.D. dissertation, University of London). Cited in Mourant, A. E. (1954) *The Distribution of Human Blood Groups* (Oxford: Blackwell).
133. Gorman, C. F. (1969) 'Hoabinhian: A Pebble-Tool Complex with Early Plant Associations in South-east Asia', *Science*, 163: 671–73.

134. Graziozi, Paolo (1964) 'Anthropological Research on Kalash, Katis and Chitrals' in *Italian Expeditions to the Karakorum-K² and Hindu Kush*, vol. 5 (Leiden).

135. Greene, John C. (1961) *The Death of Adam* (New York: Mentor Books).

136. Grierson, Sir George (1927) *Linguistic Survey of India*, vol. I, pt. 1: Introductory (Calcutta).

137. Grousset, Rene (1970) *The Empire of the Steppes* (New Brunswick: Rutgers University Press), p. 81.

138. Guha, B. S. (1935) 'The Racial Affinities of the Peoples of India', in *Census of India 1931*, (Simla, India) vol. I, part III-A, tables I–V, pp. 2–22.

139. Guha, B. S. (1953) 'Report of a Survey of the Inhabitants of the Andaman and Nicobar Islands during 1948–49', *BDA*, 1(1).

140. Guha, B. S. (1954) 'A Comparative Study of the Somatic Traits of the Onges of the Little Andamans', *BDA*, 3(2).

141. Gulati, R. K. (1970) 'Biological and Cultural Affinities', *The Eastern Anthropologist*, 23, (3): 236–7.

142. Gupta, P. & A. Basu (1960) 'Physical Characters of the Madiga of Guntur – A Pariah Caste of Andhra', *BDA*, 9(1): 53–60.

143. Gurevitch, J. and Margolis, E. (1954) 'A Further Report on Blood Groups among Kurdistani Jews', cited in Mourant, A. E. (1954) *The Distribution of the Human Blood Groups* (Oxford: Blackwell).

144. Haeckel, Ernst (1874) *Anthropogenie* (Leipzig).

145. Hanhart, E. (1925) 'Uber heredodegeneration Zwergwuchs mit Dystrophia Adipose-genitalis', *Archiv. Julius Klaus Stifft*, I.

146. Hanson, O. (1913) *The Kachin* (Rangoon), p. 18.

147. Herre, Wolf (1963) 'The Science and History of Domestic Animals', in Brothwell, Don and Higgs, Eric, *Science in Archaeology* (New York: Basic Books), pp. 235–49.

148. Herrlich, A. (1937) *Deutsche im Hindukusch* (Berlin).

149. Hitti, P. K. (1944) *The Arabs* (Princeton University Press), p. 44.

150. Hocart, A. M. (1950) *Caste: A Comparative Study* (London: Methuen), p. 67.

151. Holdich, T. H. (1910) Article on Asia, *Encyclopedia Britannica*, 11th edn. (New York).

152. Holdich, T. H. (1911) Baluchistan, *Encyclopedia Britannica*, 11th edn.

153. Hole, R. L. (1970) *The Montagnards of South Vietnam: A Study in Nine Tribes* (Rutland, Vermont: Charles Tuttle).

154. Howell, F. C. (1972) 'Recent Advances in Human Evolutionary Studies' in *Perspectives on Human Evolution*, ed. Washburn, S. L.

and Dolhinow, Phyllis (New York: Holt, Rinehart and Winston), vol. 2, p. 71.
155. Howells, W. W. (1960) 'The Distribution of Man', *SA*, 203(3).
156. Howells, W. W. (1964) 'Ainus in Prehistoric Japan: A Study in Discriminant Analysis', *ICAES*, VII (Moscow), 3: 23.
157. Howorth, H. H. (1927) *A History of the Mongols from the Ninth to the Nineteenth Century* (London: Longmans Green).
158. Hughes, B. O. (1938) 'The Physical Anthropology of Native Born Armenians' (Ph.D. dissertation, Harvard University).
159. Hutchinson, L. R. C. P. & S. E. and Vogel, J. P. (1933) *History of the Punjab Hill States*, 2 vols. (Lahore).
160. Ibbetson, Sir Denzil (1916) *Punjab Castes* (Lahore).
161. Ikeda, S. (1956) 'Aoshima Island, Yamaguchi Ken', *JK*, 3: 88.
162. Ikemoto, S., Watanabe, S., Ogawa, R. and Furuhata, T. (1966) 'Frequencies of blood groups among the Vietnamese', *Proc. Jap. Acad.*, 42: 975–9.
163. Ismagulov, C. (1968) 'The Process of Formation of the Kazak Type in Relation to their Ethnogenesis', in Abdushelishvili, M. G., Ginzburg, V. V., Miklashevskaia, N. N. and Trofimova, T. A., 'Contributions to the Physical Anthropology of Central Asia and the Caucasus', ed. Henry Field, *RTS*, 3(2): 129–33.
164. Ismagulov, O. (1968) 'The Origin of the Kazakh Anthropological Type', *ICAES*, VIII (Tokyo-Kyoto), 1: 137–9.
165. Iwamura, Shinobu and Schurmann, H. F. (1954) *Notes on Mongolian Groups in Afghanistan,* Zinbunkagaku Kenkyujo, (Kyoto).
166. Iwamura, Shinobu (1961) 'The Zirni' (manuscript) *Kyoto Univ. Scientific Expeditions to the Karakoram and the Hindukush* (Kyoto).
167. Iyer, L. K. A. (1928) *The Mysore Tribes and Castes*, vol. 1 (Bangalore), p. 129.
168. Izzedin, N. M. (1934) 'On the Anthropology of the Druzes', *ICAES*, I, (London): 131–2.
169. Jacob, Teuku (1966) 'The Sixth Skull Cap of Pithecanthropus erectus', *AJPA*, 25: 243–60.
170. Jacob, Teuku (1967) *Some Problems Relating to the Racial History of the Indonesian Region* (Utrecht).
171. Jones, Kenneth J. (1964) 'Nature's Groups Program', in the *Multivariate Statistical Analyzer* (Private pub., Cambridge, Mass), p. 125.
172. Kanda, Sanae (1966) 'Anthropometry of the Pathans and the Kashmirian in West Pakistan', *Medical Journal of Osaka Univ.*, part 1, 16(4): 235–9.
173. Karve, Irawati, (1948) 'Anthropometric Measurements of the Marathas', *Deccan College Monograph Series, No. 2* (Poona).

174. Karve, I. and Dandekar, V. M. (1951) 'Anthropometric Measurements of Maharashtra', *Deccan College Monograph Series, No. 8* (Poona).
175. Karve, I. (1954) 'Anthropometric Measurements in Karnatak and Orissa and a comparison of these two Regions with Maharastra', *Jour. Anthrop. Soc. of Bombay*, n.s. 8(1): 45–75.
176. Karve, I and Malhotra, K. C. (1968) 'A biological comparison of eight endogamous groups of the same rank', *Current Anthropology*, 9(2–3): 109–16.
177. Kasho, T. (1957) 'Doigahama, Yamaguchi Ken', *JK*, 4: 463.
178. Kayassi, A. (1949) 'The Rh Blood Groups of the Population of Baghdad', *AJPA*, n.s. 7: 549–51.
179. Kidder, J. E. (1959) *Japan before Buddhism* (New York: Praeger), p. 21.
180. Kidson, Chev and Gorman, J. G. (1962) 'Contributions of Red Cell Enzyme Deficiency Trait to an Understanding of Genetic Relationships between Melanesian and other Populations', *AJPA*, 20: 357–63.
181. Kimura, K. (1974) 'Growth Studies of the Japanese', *Japanese Committee for the International Biological Program, Synthesis*, 2(2): 15–32.
182. Kirk, R. L., Lai, L. Y. C., Vos, G. H. and Vidyarth, L. P. (1962) 'A Genetical Study of the Oraons of the Chota Nagpur Plateau (Bihar, India)', *AJPA*, 20: 375–88.
183. Kirk, R. L., Lai, L. Y. C., Vos, G. H., Wickremasinghe, R. L. and Perera, D. J. B. (1962) 'The Blood Serum Groups of Selected Populations in South India and Ceylon', *AJPA*, 20: 485–97.
184. Kirk, R. L. (1976) 'The Legend of Prince Vijaya – A Study of Sinhalese Origins', *AJPA*, 45: 91–100.
185. Koenigswald, G. H. R. von (1952) 'A Giant Fossil Hominid from the Pleistocene of Southern China', *Anth. Pap. Am. Mus. Nat. Hist.*, 43: 301–9.
186. Koenigswald, G. H. R. von (1962) *The Evolution of Man* (University of Michigan Press), p. 79.
187. Kohama, M. and Sato, M. (1938) 'An Anthropological Study on the South Koreans', *JZ*, 53(611): 419.
188. Kohama, M. (1957) 'Kaibogaku Zassi', *Acta Anat. Nipponica*, 32: 14.
189. Koya, Y. (1937) 'Rassenkunde d. Aino', *J. Ges, f. Förderung d. Wissenschaftlichen Forschungen* (Tokyo).
190. Krader, Lawrence (1963) *Peoples of Central Asia* (The Hague), pp. 33–50.

191. Kramer, S. N. (1963) *The Sumerians* (University of Chicago Press), p. 42.
193. Kumar, N. and Sastry, D. B. (1961) 'A genetic survey among the Riang; a mongoloid tribe of Tripura', *Zeitschrift für Morphologie und Anthropologie*, 51: 346.
194. Kumar, N. (1968) 'A Genetic Survey among the Rana Tharu of Nainital District in Uttar Pradesh', *Jour. Indian Anthrop. Soc.*, 3: 39–55.
195. Kumar, N. and Mukherjee, D. P. (1975) 'Genetic Distances among the Ho Tribe and Other Groups of Central Indians', *AJPA*, 42: 489–94.
196. Kunstadter, Peter (1967) *Southeast Asian Tribes, Minorities and Nations*, 2 vols (Princeton University Press).
197. Kürten, Björn (1968) 'Dating the Early Stages of Hominid Evolution', in *Evolution and Hominization*, ed. G. Kurth, (Stuttgart), pp. 75–81.
198. Lalouel, J. (1952) 'Les Rhades Protomalais-veddoides des plateaux indochinois', *Soc. d'Anth. de Paris Bull. et Mem.*, ser. 10, 3: 199–211.
199. Lamberg-Karlovsky, C. C. (1969) 'Excavations at Tepe Yahya, Iran (1967–1969)' *Am. Sch. of Prehist. Res. Bull.* 27.
200. Lamberg-Karlovsky, C. C. (1973) Review of Masson, V. M. and Sarianidi, V. I. (1972) 'Central Asia: Turkmenia before the Archaemenids' (Vol. 79, Ancient Peoples and Places Series, Thames & Hudson), *Antiquity*, 47: 43.
201. Lange, Volkmar (1966) 'Die Bedeutung d. Stärke-Gel-Hochspannungs Elektrophorese für die Humangenetische Serum Analyse', *Anthropologische Anzeiger*, 28: 181–221.
202. Lasker, G. W. (1945) 'Physical Characteristics of Chinese' (*Ph.D. dissertation*, Harvard University).
203. Lattimore, Owen (*c.* 1935). Unpublished data.
204. Lattimore, Owen (1962) *Inner Asian Frontiers of China* (Boston: Beacon Press).
205. Leach, E. R. (1954) *Political Systems of Highland Burma* (Boston: Beacon Press), p. 41.
206. Lebar, F. M., Hickey, G. C. and Musgrave, J. K. (1964) *Ethnic Groups of Mainland Southeast Asia* (New Haven, Connecticut: Human Relations Area Files Press), p. 187.
207. Levin, M. G. (1946) in Oshanin, L. V. (1964) 'Europeoid Races of Central Asia and of Adjacent Countries of Iran and the Near East', *RTS*, 2(1).
208. Levin, M. G. (1947) 'Anthropologicheskii Yakutov SSSR', *KSIE*, 3: 56–8.

209. Levin, M. G. (1947) 'Anthropologicheskie Tippii Oxotskogo Poberejhiya', *TIE*, n.s. 1–2: 84–102.
210. Levin, M. G. (1948) 'Antropologicheskie Isoledovaniia na Amure i Sakhaline', *KSIE*, no. 5 (1949).
211. Levin, M. G. (1954) 'K antropologii Yuzhnoy Sibiri: Predvaritelny otchet o rabote antropologicheskogo otryada Sayano-Altayskoy ekspeditsü 1952', *KSIE*, no. 20.
212. Levin, M. G. (1963) 'Anthropology of Northern Asiatic Peoples', *AINA*, trans. from Russian, 3: 1–7.
213. Lewis, G. E. (1934) 'Preliminary Notice of New Man-like Apes from India', *Am. Journ. of Science*, XXVII.
214. Li, Chi (1921) *The Formation of the Chinese People* (Harvard University Press), p. 268.
216. Lie-Injo, L. E. (1964) 'Haemoglobinopathies in East Asia', *Annals of Human Genetics*, 28: 101–09.
217. Lin, Yüeh-Hwa (1940–41) 'The Miao-Man Peoples of Kweichow (Annotated translation of "Ch'ien-nanchi-fang chi-lüeh", 1847)', *Harvard Journal of Asiatic Studies*, 5: 261–345.
218. Linnaeus (Linne, C.) (1735) *Systema Naturae* (Leyden).
219. Liu, Pin-Hsiung (1963) 'Excavations and Discoveries at Tap'enk'eng and other Prehistoric Sites in Pali District', *Asian Perspectives*, 7: 214–23.
220. Lloyd, Seton (1967) *Early Highland Peoples of Anatolia* (New York: McGraw-Hill), p. 54.
221. Lyde, L. W. (1933) *The Continent of Asia* (London: Macmillan), p. 26.
222. Madan, T. N. and Gopala, I. (1962) *Indian Anthropology* (London, New York and New Delhi: Asia Publishing House).
223. Mahalanobis, P. C. (1941) 'Historical Note on the D^2 Statistic', *Sankhya: The Indian Journal of Statistics*, 9 (2&3): Appendix 1, 237–9.
224. Mahalanobis, P. C., Majumdar, D. N. and Rao, C. R. (1949) 'Anthropometric Survey of the United Provinces, 1941. A Statistical Study', *Sankhya: The Indian Journal of Statistics*, 9.
225. Majumdar, D. N. (1940) 'The Racial Composition of the Polyandrous People of Jaunsar Bawar in the Dehradun District, United Provinces', *Jour. U.P. Hist. Soc.*, 13: 35–50.
226. Majumdar, D. N. (1949) U.P. Anthropometric Survey, 1941 *Sankhya: The Indian Journal of Statistics*, 9(2&3): 148.
227. Majumdar, D. N. and Sen, A. R. (1949) 'Anthropometric Status of the Castes and Tribes of Maha-Gujarat', *J. Guj. Res. Soc.*, II (3): 118.

228. Majumdar, R. C. and Pusalker, A. D. (1951) *The Vedic Age* (London: Allen and Unwin), p. 173.
229. Majumdar, D. N. (1950) *Himalayan Polyandry* (New York: Asia Publishing House).
230. Majumdar, D. N. and Rao, Radhakrishna (1960) *Race Elements in Bengal* (Bombay).
231. Malhotra, M. S. (1966) 'People of India Including Primitive Tribes – A survey on Physiological Adaptation, Physical Fitness and Nutrition' in *The Biology of Human Adaptability*, ed. Baker, P. T. and Weiner, J. S. (Oxford: Clarendon Press), pp. 329–56.
232. Malyutov, M. B., Passekov, V. P. and Rychkov, Y. G. (1972) 'On the reconstruction of evolutionary trees of Human populations resulting from random genetic drift' in Weiner, J. S. and Huizinga, J., *The Assessment of Population Affinities in Man* (Oxford: Clarendon Press), pp. 48–71.
233. Mansuy, Henri (1925) 'Contribution a l'etude de la prehistoire de l'indochine', *Mem. du service geologique de l'indochine*, vl. XII (III) (Hanoi).
234. Maranjian, G., Ikin, E. W., Mourant, A. E. and Lehmann, H. (1966) 'Blood Groups of Saudi Arabians', *Human Biology*, 38: 394.
235. Masson, Charles (1844) *Narrative of Various Journeys in Balochistan, Afghanistan, The Panjab and Kalat* (London), vol. 4, p. 4.
236. Matsunaga, E., Itoh, S., Suzuki, T. and Sugimoto, R. (1954) 'Incidence and inheritance of the ear-wax types', *Sapporo Med. J.*, 6: 368–71 (in Japanese).
237. Matsunaga, E. (1963) 'Selective Mechanisms Operating on ABO Blood Groups', *Homo*, 13: 7.
238. Mayr, Ernst (1963) *Animal Species and Human Evolution* (Cambridge, Mass.: Belknap Press), pp. 1–7.
239. Meggers, B. J. and Evans, Clifford (1966) *Scientific American*, 214: 28.
240. McGovern, W. M. (1939) *The Early Empires of Central Asia* (University of North Carolina Press), p. 95.
241. Mellaart, James (1965) *Early Civilizations of the Near East* (New York: McGraw-Hill), p. 13.
242. Miklashevskaia, N. N. (1953) 'Nekotorye Materiali po antropologii narodov Dagestana' *KSIE*.
243. Miklashevskaia, N. N. (1956) 'Kirghizskoi Arkheologo-Etnograficheskoi Ekspeditsii', *TIE*, 1.
244. Misawa, S., Hayashida, Y., Miki, T., Omoto, K., Harada, S., Matsumoto, H., Komatsu, I. and Hirai, M. (1975) 'Genetic Composition of the Ainu' in Anthropological and Genetic Studies on the

Japanese, ed. Watanabe, S., Kondo, S. and Matsunaga, E., *JIBP Synthesis: Human Adaptability,* vol. 2, p. 297.

245. Mitra, A. K. (1956) 'The Riang of Tripura' *BDA*, 1(2): 21–120.

246. Mitra, A. K. (1970) 'Anthropometric Data from West Bengal and Bihar', in Field, Henry, *Contributions to the Physical Anthropology of the Peoples of India,* Appendix N, pp. 245–55 (Field Research Projects, Coconut Grove, Florida).

247. Miyake, Y. (1959) 'Somatological Studies on the Inhabitants of Higashiseburi, Saga', *JK*, 6: 460–93.

248. Morse, Edward (1879) 'Shell Mounds of Omori', *Tokyo Univ., Mem. Coll. of Sci.*, vol. 1, pt. 1.

249. Morse, W. R. (1937) 'Schedule of Physical Anthropological Measurements and Observations on Ten Ethnic Groups of Szechwan Province, West China', supplement to *Jour. of the West China Border Res. Soc.*, vol. 8.

250. Mourant, A. E. (1954) *The Distribution of the Human Blood Groups* (Oxford: Blackwell).

251. Müller-Beck, H. (1967) 'On Migrations of Hunters across the Bering Land Bridge in the Upper Pleistocene' in Hopkins, D. M., *The Bering Land Bridge* (Stanford University Press), p. 383.

252. Nadzhimov, K. (1951–2) 'Tajiks of Surkhan Daria Uzbekistan Trudy', n.s. 143, *Biolovgicheskie Nauki*, vol. 35 (Tashkent).

253. Nagai, M. (1954) 'Somatological Studies on the Hateruma Islanders, Ryukyu', *JK*, 1: 304–22.

254. Nakajima, H., Ohkura, K., Imafuku, S., Ogura, Y., Koyama, T., Hari, F. and Takahara, S. (1967) 'The Distribution of ABO, MNS, Q, Lewis, Rh, Kell, Duffy and Kidd Blood Groups in Ryukyu, *Japanese Jour. Hum. Genet.*, 12: 29–37.

255. Nakajima, H. and Ohkura, K. (1970) Unpublished data, cited in Schanfield, M. S. (1971) 'Gm and Inv Antigens in Asia and Oceania' (Ph.D. dissertation, University of Michigan), p. 45.

256. Nakayama, E. (1937) 'Anthropological Studies of Ainu (Shiraoi)', *JZ*, 62(599): 336–53.

257. Natishvili, A. N. and Abdushelishvili, M. G. (1960) 'Preliminary Data on the Anthropological Investigations of the Georgian People', *RTS*, 1(2): 66–70.

258. Needham, Joseph (1962) *Science and Civilization in China* (Cambridge University Press), vol. 2, pp. 8–18.

259. Negi, R. S. and Ahmed, S. H. (1962–3) 'A Study of A^1-A^2 – B-O, MN, RH Blood Groups: A-B-H Secretion in Saliva and Colour-Blindness in the Dorla and Dhurwa of Bastar', *Bull. Anth. Survey. of India,* vols. XI, XII.

260. Okladnikov, A. P. (1964), 'Ancient Population of Siberia and Its

Culture', in *Peoples of Siberia*, ed. Levin, M. G. and Potapov, L. P. (University of Chicago Press), p. 15.
261. Okladnikov, A. P. (1965) 'The Soviet Far East in Antiquity: An Archaeological and Historical Study of the Maritime Region of the U.S.S.R.', *AINA*. trans. from Russian, 6: 24–42.
262. Olivier, G. (1951) 'Documents Anthropologiques sur les Mois D'Indochine (Montagnards de Type Indonesien)', *Bull. et Mem., Soc. d'Anth.* (Paris), s. 10, 2: 189–200.
263. Olivier, G. and Chagnoux, H. (1953) 'Documents Anthropologiques sur les Chams D'Indochine', *Bull. et Mem. Soc. d'Anth.*, s.10, 4: 499–514.
264. Olivier, Georges (1955) 'Les populations du Cambodge (anth. physique)' (Doctoral dissertation (Mimeo.), Lille University).
265. Olivier, Georges (1961) *Anthropologie des Tamouls Du sud de L'Inde* (Paris), pp. 233–8.
266. Omoto, K. and Harada, S. (1968) 'Red Cell and Serum Protein Types in the Ainu Population of Shizunai, Hokkaido', *ICAES*, VIII (Tokyo-Kyoto): 206.
267. Omoto, K. (1970) 'The distribution of polymorphic traits in the Hidaka Ainu. I. Defective Colour vision, PTC, taste sensitivity and cerumin dimorphism', *Jour. Faculty of Sci.* (Univ. of Tokyo), Sec. V, 3: 337–55.
268. Omoto, K. (ed.) (1975) 'Serum Protein Groups', *Japanese Committee for the International Biological Program, Synthesis,* 2(2): 145.
269. Osgood, Cornelius (1951) *The Koreans and their Culture* (New York: Ronald Press Co.), p. 189.
270. Oshanin, L. V. (1925) 'Ethnogenesis of the Highland Tadzhiks of Karategin and Darvaz' in Oshanin, L. V. [231].
271. Oshanin, L. V. (1929) in Oshanin, L. V. and Zezenkova, V. Y. (1953) 'Voprosi Etnogenesa Narodov Srednei Asii', *Isdatelstvo Akad. Nauk* (Tashkent).
272. Oshanin, L. V. (1937) 'Iranskie plemena zapodnogo Pamira (Iranian Tribes of the Western Pamirs) Trudy', *Uzbeck Institute of Experimental Medicine*, vol. 1 (Tashkent).
273. Oshanin, L. V. (1964) 'Anthropological Composition of the Population of Central Asia and the Ethnogenesis of its Peoples: III', ed. Henry Field, *RTS*, 2(1): 13.
274. Pakrasi, K. and Das, B. M. (1956) 'An Anthropometric Study of the Plains Mandes (Garos) of Assam', *Man in India*, 36: 100–09.
275. Papazian, H. P. (1967) *Modern Genetics* (New York and Toronto: Signet Science Books), p. 191.
276. Papiha, S. A., Roberts, D. F., Wigand, M. N. and Singh, Sarbjit

(1972) 'Red Cell Enzyme Polymorphisms in Punjabis in North India', *AJPA*, 37: 293–300.

277. Parapalo, A., Koskenniemi, Parpalo, S. and Aalto, P. (1969) 'Decipherment of the Proto-Dravidian Inscriptions of the Indus Civilization', *Scandinavian Institute of Asian Studies, Special Pub. No. 1* (Copenhagen).

278. Patai, Raphael (1959) *Sex and the Family in the Bible and the Middle East* (New York: Doubleday).

279. Patai, Raphael (1962) *Golden River to Golden Road* (University of Pennsylvania Press), chapter 8.

280. Patel, S. (1973) 'Study on Genetic Traits of Tibetans at Chandragiri, Dist. Ganjam, Orissa', *AJPA*, 38: 755–6.

281. Peake, Pasha (1958) *History of Jordan and Its Tribes* (University of Miami Press), p. 2.

282. Pehrson, R. N. (1966) *The Social Organization of the Marri Baluch* (ed. Barth, F.), Viking Fund Publications in Anthropology No. 43 (New York), p. 3.

283. Pei, Wen-chuang (1957) 'Giant Ape's Jaw Bone Discovered in China', *Vertebrata Palasiatica*, 2: 65–70 and *American Anthropologist*, 59: 834–8.

284. Peter, Prince, of Greece (1947) 'Tibetan, Toda, and Tiya Polyandry', *Man*, 47: 123–4.

285. Peter, Prince, of Greece (1966) 'Anthropological Researches from the 3rd Danish Expedition to Central Asia' ('Det Kongelige Danske Videnskabernes Selskab') *Historisk-filosofiske Skrifter*, 4(4): 1–76.

286. Petrakis, N. L., Pringle, Urmila, Petrakis, S. J. and Petrakis, S. L. (1971) 'Evidence for a Genetic Cline in Earwax Types in the Middle East and Southeast Asia', *AJPA*, 35: 141–4.

287. Phansomboon, S., Ikin, E. W. and Mourant, A. E. (1949) 'The ABO and MN Blood Groups of the Siamese', *AJPA*, n.s. 7: 563–8.

288. Piggott, Stuart (1952) *Prehistoric India* (Harmondsworth, Middlesex: Penguin Books), pp. 245–6.

289. Pilbeam, D. R. and Simons, E. L. (1965) 'Some Problems of Hominid Classification', *Am. Sci.*, 53: 237.

290. Plato, C. C., Cereghino, J. J. and Steinberg, F. S. (1975) 'The Dermatoglyphs of American Caucasians *AJPA*, 42: 195–214, table 12.

291. Pollitzer, W. S. (1962) 'Blood Types and Anthropometry of the Kalmuck Mongols', *AJPA*, 20: 11–15.

292. Potapov, L. P. (1964) 'The Khakasy' in *Peoples of Siberia*, ed. Levin, M. G. and Potapov, L. P. (University of Chicago Press), pp. 342–79.

293. Prabhu, P. H. (1958) *Hindu Social Organizaton* (Bombay), p. 295.

294. Prokof'yeva, E. D., Chernetzov, V. N. and Prytkova, N. F. (1964)

'The Khants and Mansi' in *The Peoples of Siberia*, ed. Levin, M. G. and Potapov, L. P. (University of Chicago Press), pp 511–46.

295. Pulleybank, E. A. (1962) 'The Consonantal System of Old Chinese', *Asia Major*, 9: 206 ff.

296. Radlov, W. (1887) *Etnograficheskij obzor tyurkskikh plemen Yuzhnoy Sibiri i Dzungaria* (Tomsk).

297. Rakshit, H. K. (1960) 'A Short Note on the Anthropometry of the Dorlas and Dhurwas of Bastar', *Man in India*, 40(1): 56.

298. Ramstedt, G. J. (1939) cited in Coon, C. S., *Races of Europe* (New York: Macmillan), p. 223. (Coon: #75)

299. Rawlinson, H. G. (1952) *India: A Short Cultural History* (New York: Praeger).

300. Ray, A. K. (1958) 'An Anthropometric Study of the Pahiras of Manbhum, Bihar', *Man in India*, 38: 129–37.

311. Raychoudhuri, T. C. (1961) 'The Pandit and Mohammedan of Kashmir: An Anthropometric Study' *The Eastern Anthropologist*, 14(1): 84–93.

312. Reed, C. A. (1960) 'A review of the archaeological evidence on animal domestication in the prehistoric Near East', in Braidwood, R. J. and Howe, B., *Prehistoric Investigations in Iraqi Kurdistan*, (Chicago University Press).

313. Ripley, W. Z. (1899) *The Races of Europe* (London), p. 436.

314. Robertson, Sir George S. (1896) *The Kafirs of the Hindu-Kush* (London).

314a. Robertson-Smith, W. (1885) *Kinship and Marriage in Early Arabia* (Cambridge), p. 18.

315. Roux, Georges (1964) *Ancient Iraq* (New York: World Publishing Co.), p. 98.

316. Rozenberg, F. E. (1925) 'Ancient Sogdian letters. A contribution to the early history of Sogdian colonies in Central Asia', *Izvestiia*, A.N., SSSR, vol. 7: *Ser. Obschehestveyynkh Nauk No.* 5 (Leningrad).

317. Russel, Hiralal (1931) 'Central India' in *Census of India, 1931*, vol. I, pt 3: Ethnographical, p. 75.

318. Rychkov, J. G. (1965) 'Peculiarities of Serological Differentiation in Siberian Peoples', *Voprosij Antropologii*, 21: 18–33.

319. Rychkov, J. G., Perevozchikov, I. V., Cheremetyeva, V. A., Volkova, T. V. and Bashlay, A. S. (1969) 'Concerning the Population Genetics of Native Peoples of the Siberian Eastern Sayans', *Voprosij Anthropologii*, 31: 3–32.

320. SAGU students (1955–6) in Oshanin, L. V. (1964) [231].

321. Sakiyama, C. (1956) 'Mishima Island, Yamaguchi Ken', *JK*, 3: 121.

322. Sanghvi, L. D. (1966) 'Genetic Adaptation in Man' in *The Biology*

of Human Adaptability, ed. Baker, P. T. and Weiner, J. S. (Oxford: Clarendon Press), pp. 305–28.

323. Sankalia, H. D. (1963) *Prehistory and Protohistory in India and Pakistan* (Bombay), p. 154.

324. Sansom, Sir George (1958) *A History of Japan* (Stanford University Press), vol. 3, p. 228.

325. Sarashina, Kenzo (1967) *The Ainu and the Japanese* (text in Japanese), NHK Books (Tokyo), 118, p. 51.

326. Sarkar, S. A., Ray, G., Bhattacharjee, P. and Banerjee, A. R. (1959) 'The Kadar of Kerala', *Man in India*, 39(3): 235–8.

327. Sarkar, S. S. (1935–6) 'Racial affinities of the inhabitants of Rajmahal Hills', *Transactions of the Bose Research Institute*, 2: 123–53.

328. Sarkar, S. S. (1954) *The Aboriginal Races of India* (Calcutta), p. 93, table 15.

329. Sartono, S. (1964) 'On a new find of another pithecanthropus skull: An announcement', *Bull. Geol. Survey Indonesia*, 1(1): 2–5.

330. Sauer, C. O. (1952) *Agricultural Origins and Dispersals* (New York: American Geographical Society).

331. Schanfield, M. S. (1971) 'Gm and Inverted Antigens in Asia and Oceania' (Ph.D dissertation, University of Michigan), p. 38.

332. Schurmann, H. F. (1962) *The Mongols of Afghanistan* (The Hague), p. 39.

333. Sebesta (Schebesta), Paul and Lebzelter, V. (1928) 'Anthropological measurements in Semangs and Sakais in Malaya (Malacca)', *Anthropologie* (*Praha*), 6(3–4): 183 (figures calculated).

334. Seligman, C. G. and Seligman, B. Z. (1911) *The Veddas* (Cambridge University Press).

335. Seltzer, C. C. (1936) 'The Racial Characteristics of Syrians and Armenians', *PMP*, 13(3).

336. Seltzer, C. C. (Huxley, H. M., data) (1940) 'Contributions to the Racial Anthropology of the Near East', *PMP*, 16(2).

337. Sen, D. K. (1962) 'The Racial Composition of the Bengalis' in *Indian Anthropology*, ed. Madan, T. N. and Sarana, Gopala (Bombay), pp. 203–20.

338. Sen, D. K. (1967) 'Ancient Races of India and Pakistan A Study of Methods', *Bull. 20–21, Arch. Surv. of India*, 1964–5, pp. 178–205.

339. Shanklin, W. M. (1935) 'The Anthropology of the Rwala Bedouins', *JRAI*, 65: 375–90.

340. Shanklin, W. M. (1936) 'Anthropology of the Akeydat and Maualy Bedouin', *AJPA*, 21(2): 217–52.

341. Shanklin, W. M. (1938) 'Anthropometry of Syrian Males', *JRAI*, 68: 379–414.

342. Shanklin, W. M. (1946) 'Anthropometry of Transjordan Bedouin with a discussion of their racial affinities' *AJPA*, n.s. 4(3): 323–76.
343. Sharma, J. C. (1957) 'Inheritance of secretor factor and the frequency distribution of the secretor gene among the Punjabis', *The Anthropologist* (Univ. of Delhi), 4: 44–9.
344. Sharma, J. C. (1968) 'Convergent Evolution in the Tribes of Bastar', *AJPA*, 28: 113–18.
345. Sheldon, W. H. (1940) *The Varieties of Human Physique* (New York: Harper & Bros.).
346. Simons, E. L. (1963) 'Some Fallacies in the Study of Hominid Phylogeny', *Science*, 141: 879–89.
347. Simons, E. L. (1964) 'On the Mandible of Ramapithecus', *Procs. Nat. Acad. Sciences*, 51: 528–35.
348. Simons, E. L. and D. R. Pilbeam (1965) 'Preliminary revision of the Dryopithecinae (Pongidae, Anthropoides)', *Folia Primat.*, 3: 81–152.
349. Simons, E. L. (1968) 'New Fossil Primates: A Review' in *Perspectives on Human Evolution*, ed. Washburn, S. L. and Jay, Phyllis (New York: Holt Rinehart & Winston), p. 57.
350. Simons, E. L. (1971) *Anthropology Today* (California: CRM Books), p. 165.
351. Singer, Milton (ed.) (1959) *Traditional India: Structure and Change* (Philadelphia: American Folklore Society), p. 152.
352. Simmons, R. T., Graydon, J. J., Semple, N. M. and Kodama, S. (1953) 'A Collaborative Genetical Survey in Ainu, Hidaka, Island of Hokkaido', *AJPA*, n.s. 11: 47–82.
353. Skeat, W. W. and Blagden, C. O. (1906) *Pagan Races of the Malay Peninsula* (London: Macmillan).
354. Smith, Vincent A. (1957) *The Early History of India*, 4th edn (Oxford University Press), pp. 406–29.
355. Smith, Vincent A. (1958) *The Oxford History of India*, 3rd edn (Oxford University Press), pp. 10–11.
356. Solheim, W. G. (1971) 'New Light on a Forgotten Past', *National Geographic Magazine*, (March) 139: 330–9.
356a. Solheim, W. G. (1972) 'An Agricultural Revolution', *Scientific American*, 226: 34–41.
357. Spate, O. H. K. and Learmanth, A. T. (1960) *India and Pakistan* (London: Methuen), p. 453.
358. Srinivas, M. N. (1962) *Caste in Modern India* (New York: Asia Publishing House), p. 14.
359. Staffe in Sarkar, S. S. (1954) *The Aboriginal Races of India* (Calcutta), p. 80.
360. Steinberg, A. G. and Matsumoto, Hideo (1964) 'Studies on the

Gm, Inv, Hp and Tf Serum Factors of Japanese Populations and Families', *Human Biology*, 36: 77.

361. Stevenson, P. H. (1938) 'Detailed Measurements of the Chinese of the North China Plain', *Anthropologica Sinica*, No. 2 (Ch'ang Sha, China).

362. Stoudt, H. W. (1961) 'The Physical Anthropology of Ceylon', Colombo (based in part on data collected by Lt-Comdr J. R. de la Haule Marett R.N., Asst. in Ethnology, Colombo Nat. Mus.) *Nat. Mus. Ethnog. Series Pub.* No. 2.

363. Subbarao, B. (1956) *The Personality of India* (Baroda), p. 6.

364. Suda, A. (1940) 'Anthropometry of the Ryukyu Islanders', *J. Anthrop. Soc.* (Tokyo), 55(628): 1–24 (in Japanese, with English summary).

365. Suda, Akiyoshi (1942) 'Anthropometry of the Oroks in Saghalin', *JZ*, 57(656): 217–33.

366. Sunderland, Eric and Smith, H. M. (1966) 'The Blood Groups of the Shi'a in Yazd, Central Iran', *Human Biology*, 38: 50–9.

367. Sutton, H. E. and Clark, P. J. (1955) 'A Bio-chemical Study of Chinese and Caucasians', *AJPA*, n.s. 13(1): 53–65.

368 Suzuki, H. (1969) 'Microevolutional Changes in the Japanese Population from the Prehistoric Age to the Present Day', *J.Fs.U.T.*, Sec. V, (4): 279–309.

369. Suzuki, J. (1936) 'On the secretor and non-secretor', *Juzenkai Zasshi*, 41: 903–20 (in Japanese).

370. Suzuki, Makoto and Sakai, T. (1966) 'Morphological Analysis of the Shovel-shaped Teeth', *JZ*, 74: 202–18.

371. Takashima, M. (1957) 'Somatological Studies of the Population of Keya-Mura, Fukuoka Ken', *JK*, 4: 345.

372. Takeuchi, H. S., Uyeda, S. and Kanamori, H. (1970) *Debate about the Earth*, rev. edn (San Francisco: Freeman, Cooper and Co.).

373. Tanaka, J. (1958) 'Mina City, Yamaguchi Ken', *JK*, 5: 43.

374. Tao, Y. K. in Woo, T. L. (1942) 'The Physical Characters of the Pa Miao People of Kweichow and other Peoples of South China', *JRAI*, 72: 45.

375. Taylor, Griffiths (1949) *Environment, Race and Migration* (University of Toronto Press).

376. Terakado, Y., Sasaoko, A. and Hashimura, T. (1960) 'An Anthropological Study of Miomote, A Small Isolated Mountain Village in Etigo, Japan', *JZ*, 68(727): 157.

377. Thomas, P. (*ca.* 1935) *Epics, Myths and Legends of India*, (Bombay, no publication date).

378. Thurston, Edgar (1896) 'Anthropology of the Todas and Koltas of the Nilgiri Hills', *Madras Govt. Mus. Bull.*, No. 4.

379. Tiwari, S. C. (1954) 'Anthropometric Studies of the Bhotias of Almora District (U.P.)', *The Anthropologist*, I(1): 22–32.
380. Tiwari, S. C. and Bhasin, M. K. (1975) 'Ethnic Composition of Some General Himalayan Populations' *Man in India*, 55: 128–35.
381. Trofimova, T. A. (1947) 'Tobolskie and Barabinski Tatars', *TIE*, 1, table 2, 194.
382. Turner, C. G. (1976) 'Dental Evidence on the Origins of the Ainu and Japanese', *Science*, 193: 911–13.
383. Vallois, H. V. (1959) 'Les Bedouins Taamre du desert de Judee Etude Anthropologique', *L'Anthropologie*, 63: 62.
384. Vallois, H. V. and Chambla, M. C. (1964) 'Recherches Anthropologiques sur les Alouites', *L'Anthropologie*, 68: 65–94, 317–62.
385. Vlcek, Emanuel (1965) 'Czechoslovak-Mongolian Archaeological Expedition, 1958', pt. III: 'Anthropology of Khalkha-Mongols', *Acta Facult. Rerum Naturae Univ. Comenianae*, (Slovenske Pedagodicke Nakladatelstvo, Bratislava), 9(6–7): 299–369.
386. Vogel, F. and Chakravartti, M. R. (1971) 'ABO Blood Groups and Smallpox in a Rural Population of West Bengal and Bihar (India)', in Bajema, C. J. (ed.), *Natural Selection in Human Populations*, (New York: John Wiley & Sons). Originally published (1966) in *Humangenetik*, 3: 166–80.
387. Vos, G. H., Kirk, R. L. and Steinberg, A. G. (1963) 'The Distribution of Gamma Globulin Types Gm(a), Gm(b), Gm(x) and Gm-like in South and Southeast Asia and Australia', *Am. J. Hum. Gen.*, 15: 44–52.
388. Vreeland, H. H. (1957) *Mongol Community and Kinship Systems* (New Haven, Connecticut: ARAF Press).
389. Vyas, G. N., Bhatra, H. M., Sukumaran, P. K., Balakrishnan, V. and Sanghvi, L. D. (1962) 'Abnormal Hemoglobins and other Genetical Characters in Some Tribes of Gujarat', *AJPA*, 20: 255–67.
390. Wallace, A. R. (1855) (Essay from Sarawak Borneo) 'On the Law Which Regulated the Introduction of New Species', *Ann. and Mag. Nat. Hist.*, 184.
391. Wallace, A. R. (1871) *Contribution to the Theory of Natural Selection* (Sarawak).
392. Walter, H. and Bajatzadeh, M. (1968) 'Studies in the Distribution of the Human Red Cell Acid Phosphatase Polymorphism in Iranians and Other Populations', *Acta Genet.*, 18: 421–8.
393. Walter, H. (1973) 'Uber die Anthropologische Bedeutung einiger neuer Serumprotein-Polymorphismen (Cerumplasmin B2-Glycoprotein I_1 (Pi))', *Anthropologische Anzeiger*, 34: 16–22.
394. Wang, C. L. (1957) 'Somatological Studies on the Tachen Islanders, China', *JK*, 4: 1–29.

395. Watson, William (1966) *Cultural Frontiers in Ancient East Asia* (Edinburgh University Press), pp. 8–10.
396. Weidenreich, Franz (1943) 'The Skull of Sinanthropus Pekinensis', *Palaeontologica Sinica*, n.s. 10, Geol. Survey of China (Pennsylvania: Lancaster Press).
397. Weidenreich, Franz (1946) *Apes, Giants and Man* (University of Chicago Press), p. 51.
397a. Weiner, J. S. (1971) *The Natural History of Man* (New York: Universe Books), pp. 53–75.
398. Wheeler, Sir Mortimer (1947) *Early India and Pakistan* (New York: Praeger).
399. Wiens, H. J. (1954) *China's March Toward the Tropics* (New Haven, Connecticut: The Shoestring Press), p. 35.
400. Wittfogel, K. A. (1957) *Oriental Despotism* (Yale University Press).
401. Won, C. D., Shin, H. S., Kim, S. W., Swanson, Jane and Matson, G. A. (1960) 'Distribution of Hereditary Blood Factors among Koreans Residing in Seoul, Korea', *AJPA*, 18: 115–24.
402. Woo, J. K. (1958) 'New Materials of Dryopithecus from Kweiyuan, Yunnan', *Vertebrata Palasiatica*, (Peking), 2: 31–43.
403. Woo, J. K. (1964) 'Preliminary report on a skull of Sinanthropus lantienensis of Lantian, Shensi', *Vertebrata Palasiatica*, 8: 1–12.
404. Woo, J. K. (1966) 'The Hominid Skull of Lantien, Shensi', *Vertebrata Palasiatica*, 10: 1–16.
405. Woodd-Walker, R. B., Smith, H. M. and Clarke, V. A. (1967) 'The Blood Groups of the Timuri and Related Tribes of Afghanistan', *AJPA*, 27: 195–204.
406. World Health Organization, Scientific Group (1964) 'Research in Population Genetics of Primitive Groups', *Tech. Reports Ser.*, no. 279.
407. Yamaguchi, Bin (1964) 'The Human Skeletal Remains from Bozuyama in Central Hokkaido', *JZ*, 71(737): 55–71.
408. Yamaguchi, Bin (1964) 'The Human Skeletal Remains from the Onkoromanai Shell-mound in Northern Hokkaido', *JZ*, 71(739): 131–48.
409. Yamaguchi, Bin (1967) 'A Comparative Osteological Study of the Ainu and the Australian Aborigines', Australian Institute of Aboriginal Studies, *Occas. Papers No. 10, Human Biological Series 2.*
410. Yamashita, S. (1954) 'An Anthropological Study of the Population of Shikanoshima', *JK*, 1: 220–72.
411. Yao, C. L. *et al.* (1973) 'New Discoveries of Peking Man at Choukoutien', *Vertebrata Palasiatica*, 2(2): 109–31.

412. Yarko, A. I. (1930) in Oshanin, L. V. and Zezenkova, V. Y. (1953) 'Voprosi Etnogenesa Narodov Srednei Asii' *Isdatelstvo Akad. Nauk* (Tashkent).

413. Yarko, A. I. (1931) 'Anthropological Composition of the Turkomans and Theory of the Scythian (Sacae) Origin of the Turkoman Nation' in Oshanin, L. V. [231].

414. Yoshimoto, K. (1956) 'Oshima Island, Yamaguchi Ken', *JK*, 3: 167.

415. Zezenkova, V. Y. (1948) in Oshanin, L. V. and Zezenkova, V. Y. (1953) 'Voprosi Etnogenesa Narodov Srednei Asii', *Isdatelstvo Akad. Nauk*, (Tashkent).

416. Zolotarev, I. (1962) 'Blood Group Distribution of the Peoples of North Siberia', *ICAES*, VII, 1: 502–8.

417. Zolotareva, I. M. (1968) 'The Khalkha Mongols and the Race Types of Northern Asia' *ICAES*, VIII (Tokyo-Kyoto), 1: 177–9.

Index